The American historical romance

Cambridge Studies in American Literature and Culture

Editor

Albert Gelpi, Stanford University

Advisory Board

Nina Baym, University of Illinois, Champaign-Urbana
Sacvan Bercovitch, Harvard University
Richard Bridgman, University of California, Berkeley
David Levin, University of Virginia
Joel Porte, Harvard University
Mike Weaver, Oxford University

The American historical romance

GEORGE DEKKER

Stanford University

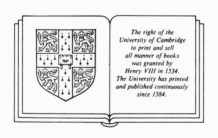

*The right of the
University of Cambridge
to print and sell
all manner of books
was granted by
Henry VIII in 1534.
The University has printed
and published continuously
since 1584.*

CAMBRIDGE UNIVERSITY PRESS

*CAMBRIDGE
NEW YORK   NEW ROCHELLE
MELBOURNE   SYDNEY*

Published by the Press Syndicate of the University of Cambridge
The Pitt Building, Trumpington Street, Cambridge CB2 1RP
32 East 57th Street, New York, NY 10022, USA
10 Stamford Road, Oakleigh, Melbourne 3166, Australia

© Cambridge University Press 1987

First published 1987

Printed in Great Britain at
the University Press, Cambridge

British Library cataloguing in publication data

Dekker, George
The American historical romance.–
(Cambridge studies in American literature
and culture).
1. Historical fiction, American–History
and criticism   2. American fiction–19th
century–History and criticism
I. Title
813'.081   PS374.H5

Library of Congress cataloguing in publication data

Dekker, George
The American historical romance.
(Cambridge studies in American literature and
culture)
Bibliography.
Includes index.
1. Historical fiction, American.   2. United States in
literature.   3. Romanticism–United States.   I. Title.
II. Series
PS374.H5D45   1987   813'.081'09   87–6400

ISBN 0 521 33282 6

SE

Contents

This book is dedicated to my colleagues and students
at the University of Essex
1964–72

nothing matters but the quality
of the affection –
in the end – that has carved the trace in the mind
dove sta memoria

Preface

The idea for an extended study of the American historical romance came to me in 1964 in the course of writing a critical survey of Cooper's fiction interlaced with biographical chapters analysing the connections between this fiction and the main issues in Jacksonian politics. I was able (so I believed) to see and explain how Cooper adapted Scott's narrative device of the "wavering hero" to American circumstances and his own very unwavering temperament. But I was also able to see that there was much more to the Scott–Cooper relationship than I could then explain or discover from extant scholarship, and that this "much more" involved other major American historical fictionalists as well. My work on Cooper's fiction and politics was followed by a study of the connections between Coleridge's poetry and the eighteenth-century European literature of Sensibility – a project seemingly unrelated to the question of Scott's American legacy but actually of close relevance inasmuch as it concerned contemporaries and predecessors of Coleridge and Scott who, with them, were the master spirits of Romanticism, including its American wing.[1]

I mention these earlier books because they help explain the genetic and "mid-Atlantic" character of the present one. A full explanation would involve more personal and professional history than seems appropriate in the preface to a work of literary scholarship, but I cannot fail to mention one part of that history. During the years 1964 to 1972, I had the good fortune to be among the first faculty members of the Department of Literature which Donald Davie founded within the School of Comparative Studies of the new University of Essex. The Essex approach to literature, cross-cultural and cross-disciplinary, was innovative and challenging: it placed canonical authors in a quizzical light and made others, e.g., Scott, seem vital and interesting again and central to the understanding of modern literary history.[2] Anybody familiar with the

Essex experiment will see that it has left a deep mark on this cross-cultural and cross-disciplinary study.

Many individuals have helped me make it a better book than it could have been through my efforts alone. Some have been helpful far beyond the call of friendship or collegiality, and to them I am especially grateful. But it seems best, in a public acknowledgement, simply to thank all who have taken a persistent interest in this project and contributed significantly to its improvement: Linda Jo Bartholomew, Morton Bloomfield, Jane Brooks, Gordon Brotherston, Andrew Brown, Simon Collier, Donald Davie, Howard Erskine-Hill, Don E. Fehrenbacher, Jay Fliegelman, Albert Gelpi, Joseph Harris, Wyn Kelley, David Levin, Robert Levine, Herbert Lindenberger, Peter Luther, John P. McWilliams, Jr., Warren Motley, Wilfred Stone, Charles Swann, and Ian Watt. Two friends I would but cannot thank for their counsel and encouragement are the late Claude Simpson and Brian Way.

Just as important, but different in kind, are my debts to scholars whose studies of Scott and his American successors have been the abiding stimulus and foundation of my own. The chief of these debts I have acknowledged in chapter 1 and in notes to subsequent chapters. However, with but few exceptions, I have not tried to make my argument take the form of a dialogue with other scholars, nor have I attempted more than to hint at the rich secondary literature associated with Scott and the major American historical romancers.

It is a pleasure to acknowledge the practical assistance I have received from various sources. The Faculty of English of Cambridge University enabled me to develop some of the organizing concepts of this book in a series of lectures during the autumn of 1976. The National Endowment for the Humanities furthered my progress with a research fellowship in 1977. The Institute for Advanced Studies of the University of Edinburgh provided a fellowship which allowed me to study Scott on his home ground in 1982. The Deans of Graduate Studies and of the School of Humanities and Sciences, Stanford University, responded promptly and generously to my requests for funds to cover research and preparation expenses.

I have already mentioned how much I owe to the university where I spent my most formative years as a scholar and teacher. What I owe to those who have been my colleagues and students since 1972 is more difficult for me to measure and express, but I may at least repeat what I tell anybody who asks me how I like Stanford. When I visited here for the first time nearly twenty years ago, I decided that in communal terms Stanford's was the best of English departments, and one of the best in any terms. I have not changed my mind – even after two tours of duty as chairman.

1

The American historical romance: a prospectus

For more than a century and a half, the biggest bestsellers, the favorite fictions of succeeding generations of American readers, have been historical romances. No other genre has even come close to the consistent popularity enjoyed by historical romances from *The Spy* in 1821 down to *Gone with the Wind* and *Roots* in recent times. Not to be provincial, we should have to push the date back to 1814 when the Waverley novels began to appear. For it was Sir Walter Scott who created both the genre as we know it and an immense international market for more books like *Rob Roy* and *Ivanhoe*: more books even than prolific successors like James Fenimore Cooper, Robert Louis Stevenson, Alexandre Dumas, or – sliding further down the aesthetic scale – Zane Grey and Frank Yerby could ever hope to supply. This was a market for "trash" but also for the work of serious popular writers like Victor Hugo and Willa Cather and, on momentous occasions, of highbrow artists like Nathaniel Hawthorne and Boris Pasternak. Writers of all levels of talent, all degrees of artistic and moral seriousness, could find models in the books that Scott and Cooper wrote at the outset of the tradition. For the earliest historical romances varied so widely in artistry and moral substance, in the times and places and peoples represented, that they sometimes appear to have anticipated all later developments of the genre.

Of course this appearance of containing all that followed is a mirage which not only distorts the truth but implies that the genre really has no history. In the course of being adapted to the interests and outlooks of diverse individuals, regions, and periods, the historical romance has inevitably undergone many changes that could not have been prefigured in the works of Scott and Cooper. Still, the history of historical romance as I have read it and wished to write it is long on continuity and short on foreseeable departures from family type. The departures are there and

1

crucial to this history, but I have made less of them than another critic, with other interests, might have considered essential. I have done so partly because the fictional genre under discussion itself makes more of continuities and reversions to type than is usual among the various forms of the "novel" but partly also because it is the nature of genre studies – their characteristic perceptiveness and obtuseness – to recognize family likenesses at the expense of individual differences. Had I wished to foreground, say, the qualities in *The Age of Innocence* that differentiate it from novels like *The Scarlet Letter* before and *A Lost Lady* after, I would have written an entirely different kind of study.

It may help to forestall misplaced expectations and unnecessary disappointments if I explain more fully what kind of study I have tried to write, and why. Explaining *what* entails defining terms and exposing methodological presuppositions as well as providing a straightforward inventory of "contents" and "coverage." Explaining *why* necessarily involves not only a preliminary look at the nature of the terrain to be explored but also some attention to the achievements of those who have been there before me. My procedure in the rest of this prospectus will be to comment, in three sections, on the premises and commitments implied in the three main words of my title, becoming progressively less "introductory" until, in my discussion of "Romance," I enter upon the main business of the book.

In calling this chapter a "prospectus," I am invoking the precedent of certain historical romancers who begin, interrupt, or close their literary–historical narratives with a "philosophical" overview, a "distant prospect," of their subject. Like the eighteenth–century poets and *philosophes* who are their models, they think of themselves as observers standing outside and above the contingencies of class self-interest, religious and racial bigotry, partial knowledge, and personal passion which blind the actors in history to its broad patterns and long-term trends. In practice, of course, these attempts to detach history-as-observed from history-as-experienced are never wholly successful and are sometimes profoundly self-deceived. But they are emblematic of an aspiration that deserves our respect. The word "prospectus" also has less recondite and elevated meanings which I cannot entirely disown. According to *Webster's New World Dictionary of the American Language*, it is "a statement outlining the main features of a new work or business enterprise, or the attractions of an established institution such as a college, hotel, etc." It is, in short, an evergreen American genre, as up-to-date as a tax shelter brochure and as venerable as Captain John Smith's glowing tract for potential settlers, *A Description of New England* (1616).

AMERICAN

The author whose theory, fictional strategies, and "background" I examine most fully in this study of the American historical romance is a Scotsman who never set foot in the New World. Indeed, I might have subtitled it "The Waverley Tradition in American Fiction." For Scott's example, as it variously affected our classic nineteenth-century historical fictionalists and their chief twentieth-century continuators, is the most obvious thread running through all the chapters and binding them together. Moreover, my interest in Scott's own writings goes deeper than might be expected or even desired from a book called *The American Historical Romance* and results in readings of particular Scott novels and, more importantly, in a general approach to the genre which I hope students of British fiction will find useful. However, the book is addressed chiefly to students of American fiction, and my excuse to them for devoting so much sympathetic attention to this foreign romancer is that Cooper, Hawthorne, Herman Melville, and millions of other nineteenth-century American readers did too. Without a quality of attention that matched theirs, I could not have written a study of Scott's impact on American historical fiction which came at all close to having the interpretive depth and historical range that the subject would seem to demand and deserve.

Tracing a generic tradition from its origins in eighteenth-century Europe through its domestication and early flowering in America down to its culmination in the masterpieces of Edith Wharton, Willa Cather, and William Faulkner – this is the kind of undertaking which if it is to be accomplished at all obliges one *not* to pursue other ventures, especially other people's ventures, along the way. Thus, although I pay close attention to the regional aspect of historical romance and devote an entire chapter to the fate of the genre in the American South, I may hope to supplement but not to match the richly informed account of Southern contexts in C. Hugh Holman's *The Immoderate Past: The Southern Writer and History*. Again, greatly though I admire David Levin's studies of the American romantic historians and of the interrelationships between the various subgenres of American historical literature, I can give these important subjects but a passing glance. For related reasons, I resist all temptations to repeat Harry Henderson's attempt to pin down (with, so it seems to me, inevitably procrustean results) that protean entity "The Historical Imagination in American Fiction," or to improve upon the half-dozen illuminating pages which Roy Harvey Pearce devotes to this subject in *Historicism Once More*. Neither do I seek to compete with the survey provided by Ernest Leisy's *The American Historical Novel* in which several hundreds of the tens of thousands of novels written by Americans about their national history are classified according to the period treated, deftly summarized, and judged with good-natured leniency.[1]

Nor, at the other extreme, have I tried to isolate for reverential scrutiny the dozen or so masterpieces of American historical fiction which form its great tradition. However, this book does have a critical agenda and a commitment to the proposition that some of the books like *Rob Roy* and *Ivanhoe* written by Americans repay the reading much more than others. The novels that I discuss in considerable detail are Cooper's *The Wept of Wish-ton-Wish* and *Satanstoe*; Hawthorne's *The Scarlet Letter*; Melville's *Benito Cereno* and *Billy Budd*; Mark Twain's *Pudd'nhead Wilson*; Cather's *My Ántonia*; Wharton's *The Age of Innocence*; Elizabeth Madox Roberts's *The Great Meadow*; Allen Tate's *The Fathers*; and Faulkner's *Go Down, Moses* and *Absalom, Absalom!* For reasons which will become clear later on, I also write about several books which, although by major authors, seem to me deficient on a number of counts: Cooper's *The Prairie*, Melville's *Israel Potter*, and Ellen Glasgow's *The Battle-Ground*. I would not argue with a reader who wished I had written about certain other books by these authors or had included a book by William Gilmore Simms or G. W. Cable or Esther Forbes or Ernest Gaines; but I would maintain that most of the books I do write about are among the best of their kind.

My decision to concentrate almost exclusively on the elite figures in the historical romance tradition was not taken lightly. For it involved sacrifices not only of "coverage" but also of the insights into greater writers to which readings of scores of their lesser contemporaries can often lead. Works of the stature of *Billy Budd* and *Absalom, Absalom!* are rare in any generic tradition and obviously must form but a tiny percentage of the total output of historical romances. An early product of and for the modern age of mass literacy and mass marketing, this genre has had more than its share of specimens deformed from birth by haste, ineptitude, silliness, ignorance, sentimentality, racism, sexism, nativism, chauvinism – the worst traits, that is, of the people who wrote and read them. Some of these traits also appear in a muted or disguised form in the masterpieces of the genre; their authors could not but be infected to some extent with the illusions and anxieties of the society in which they grew up and struggled to survive as artists, family providers, and citizens. Thus although Tate and Faulkner unquestionably operate on a far higher plane of moral and artistic intelligence than Thomas Dixon or Margaret Mitchell, the Southern myths and fetishes that control *The Clansman* and *Gone with the Wind* are not wholly exorcized from *The Fathers* and *Go Down, Moses*.

So it is impossible to draw an absolute line between high and low, clean and unclean, in the historical romance. *Shane* (a good "western") and *Forever Amber* (a bad "costume" romance) belong to the family as much as *The Scarlet Letter*. Fully to appreciate where a writer like Hawthorne came from and how far he surpassed all rival historical romancers of colonial New England, one must not only know his European literary antecedents but also follow Michael Davitt Bell's lead and sample many books like Lydia Maria Child's *Hobomok*, James Kirke Paulding's *The Puritan and His Daughter*, and Catharine Maria Sedgwick's more famous *Hope Leslie*.[2] Indeed, one must go much further than Bell and immerse oneself in Hawthorne's cultural context as completely as its surviving artifacts – not just printed ones – allow. Nothing that belonged to that context can be irrelevant and all things that did, including even things with which Hawthorne could not have come into contact, are grist for the mill of the scholar who knows how to use them.[3]

Yet it is possible as, for simple logistical reasons, it is necessary to make discriminations and practical choices. The premise of this study is that for writers of the highest caliber the single most important part of their cultural context is the work of their intellectual peers. Some things of the first consequence about writers like Hawthorne and Faulkner can be understood *only* by placing them in relation with other major figures in the historical romance tradition, with poets and dramatists they admired, and with social philosophers who directly or indirectly shaped their assumptions about the course of human history. For despite various moral blindspots and defects of taste, Hawthorne and Faulkner were capable – as, for instance, their elder contemporaries Child and Dixon never were – of making the insights of modern historiography their own and thus of appreciating finely how historical circumstances create situations ironic, comic, and tragic by curtailing or liberating the human actors' potential for understanding and action. They were also capable of recognizing and learning from the literary masterworks of their own and the preceding generation in a way that seems to have been beyond the comprehension or ambition of lesser writers. That which they had in common with other great minds may have been no more determinative of the cast or character of their historical fiction than what they shared with the author of *Hobomok* and the *Birth of a Nation* trilogy. But it has made the difference between survival and the oblivion that has overtaken alike the gentle reformer Child and the bellicose white-supremacist Dixon. (Nobody who has reflected seriously on the history of taste or the politics of canon formation can have much faith in the reliability of the survival test, but I believe that it usually works fairly well at the extremes of literary worth and worthlessness.)

Many of the books I have omitted may be considered present inasmuch as the books I do discuss represent their characteristic themes and values, strengths and weaknesses, and also inasmuch as the interpretive contexts I provide have a relevance that extends beyond the works I am able to treat. *The Battle-Ground*, an early imitative novel by an author clearly destined to do much better work, exemplifies the historical romance in a state of slick sentimental decadence – sabers and magnolias and all. *The Wept of Wish-ton-Wish*, a less polished but far greater book than Glasgow's, shares many characteristics with the dozen other romances of frontier settlement and Indian warfare that Cooper wrote and the many thousands that others have written since. *Israel Potter* illustrates a tendency in historical romance for "ideas" and "adventure" to crowd out character and credibility – and also illustrates the confusion of tone and tenor that can result when a writer of unruly genius tries to pander to the taste of a public with which he is radically out of sympathy.

Although I did not choose to write about any of these works principally because of their representative value, I did place my discussions of them in chapters organized around topics chosen because of their bearing on many or all historical romances. Chapter 2, "The *Waverley*-model and the rise of historical romance," examines the literary origins of the genre in the Romantic Revival of late eighteenth-century Europe and rehearses the reasons why Scott's American contemporaries regarded the earliest historical romances as modern versions of the epic. My example of an early American epic in the Waverley tradition is Cooper's sombre romance of frontier New England, *The Wept of Wish-ton-Wish*. In chapter 3, "Historical romance and the stadialist model of progress," I explain how the Scottish Enlightenment mentors both of Scott and his imitators around the globe supplied a theory of social development which in effect argued for the universality of the character-types and conflicts at the center of the Waverley novels. I demonstrate how this "Scottish" theory structures Cooper's conception of Leatherstocking, a quintessentially "American" hero if there ever was one. In chapter 4, "The regionalism of historical romance," I reverse the lens to show that historical romances in the tradition of Scott typically have a strong commitment to a particular "patria" and its people, and, as a rule, regionalize the "universal" conflicts characteristic of the genre in actions that pit Yankees against New York Dutch, or deracinated townsfolk against immigrant sodbusters who are paradoxically more Nebraskan (if perhaps not more "American") than themselves. Chapters 5 and 6, on Hawthorne and Melville, show how they brought in ambiguous verdicts on the two things in American history which were supposed to give Americans most patriotic satisfaction and which did attract the most attention from our nineteenth-century historical romancers – the pioneering of the New World wilderness and the War of Independence.

Chapters 7 and 8 bring the story down to recent times. In "The hero and heroine of historical romance" I trace the ways that historical romancers from Scott through Hawthorne to Cather have represented the relationship between fact and fiction in the performance of traditional gender roles. In the Scottish pastoral of American frontier societies depicted by Scott in *The Heart of Mid-Lothian*, by Hawthorne in *The Scarlet Letter*, and by Cather in *My Ántonia*, women play active and even heroic roles when their menfolk are unable to perform their traditional parts effectively. In Cather's frontier Nebraska the variety of creative roles available to women goes hand in hand with other kinds of variety – national, ethnic, linguistic – and contrasts boldly with the narrowly "exclusive" society of *The Age of Innocence* in which women revenge their confinements by turning their husbands into invalids. And finally, in "The historical romance of the South," I consider how some of the greatest modern Southern writers have employed the historical romance to assay the compound of heroism and folly, violence and suffering, that went into the pioneering of Kentucky and Mississippi, the materialization of the Cavalier/Plantation myth, the making of civil war, and the modernization of postbellum Southern society.

A last word about the resonance of "American" in my title. Although the most eminent historians of classic American literature have not wholly ignored the European Romantic Revival, they have tended to focus attention on those ideas, obsessions, genres, scenes, plots, and character-types which seem the more distinctively American because they can be traced back to colonial times.[4] Some of the best studies of American literature published since 1970 – notably those by Sacvan Bercovitch, Richard Slotkin, and, more recently, Robert Ferguson – have shown that there is still rich ore in that vein.[5] But since the first historical romance was published by a Scot in 1814 and American fiction and historiography manifestly took a new turn not long after that event, it would be fruitless to try to prove a pedigree extending back to the *Mayflower* or even to the ship that brought Moll Flanders to Virginia. Certainly some American historical romances are set in colonial times by writers whose own family histories may be covertly implicated in the fictional or historical actions, and so we can sometimes enhance our understanding of, say, *The Deerslayer* and *The Scarlet Letter* by rattling the skeletons in the Cooper and Hawthorne family closets. It is likewise true that the typological hermeneutic which Hawthorne and Melville inherited from New England Calvinism lent itself very serviceably in their fictions to an "explanation" of events perfectly normal in romance but unaccountable to modern historiography. One cannot afford to be ignorant of such matters in interpreting our early historical romances. In the main, however, the intellectual and literary-generic sources of the tradition are to be sought in the Old World or, as in an uncannily revealing mirror, in the writings of the eighteenth-century American who was most in touch with the ideas circulating in contemporary London, Paris, and Edinburgh: Thomas Jefferson. To achieve a precise critical and historical appreciation of Cooper's handling of the flight-captivity-and-pursuit plot in *The Last of the Mohicans*, it is important to know the Indian captivity narratives of early New England and New York, but it is even more important to know *The Mysteries of Udolpho*.

HISTORICAL

This study is concerned with both the history *of* historical romance and the history *in* historical romances. How did the genre rise, redomesticate itself in America, and retain an identity while also changing in response to the changing circumstances of American social, political, and intellectual life? What shape did our romancers see American history taking, and what settings did they favor for disclosing the emergence of this shape? Although my purpose here is less to address these questions than to explain how I try to deal with them later on, perhaps it will be helpful briefly to anticipate the tenor of my answers by supplying a second chapter-by-chapter overview, written this time to bring out the "Historical" rather than the "American" dimension.

In a passage to be examined in chapter 2, Coleridge maintained that the secret of Scott's success was his "subject" – the age-old contest between the forces of reaction and progress. Unfortunately, Coleridge pitched his analysis of this subject or major theme at a level of philosophical abstraction so elevated that he lost sight of the ways that the contest had revealed itself in recent history. It was, of course, precisely because of these recent manifestations – above all in the American and French Revolutions and in the worldwide imperialistic conquests by France and Britain – that Scott's subject had moral urgency and interest for the nineteenth-century reading public. In *Waverley* and its successors Scott created a readily adaptable model for the fictional or historiographical portrayal both of revolution (in this case an unsuccessful one by reactionary Catholic Jacobites) and imperialistic conquest (by the British Protestant armies of progress). My second chapter provides an abstract of this model and explains how Scott's understanding of the dynamics of history was influenced not only by the major socio-political events that occurred during his own lifetime but also by the earlier tremors of an international "Romantic" revolution (or revival) in literature. I conclude the chapter by showing how Cooper adapted the *Waverley*-model to American conditions in *The Wept of Wish-ton-Wish*, a frontier romance which counts the human costs of colonization with unusual honesty.

In chapter 3 I contend that the Scottish "philosophical historians," most notably Adam Smith and Adam Ferguson, led Scott and Cooper to regard history as a drama in which Providence was identified with and to a large extent replaced by Progress and in which the human actors were so culture-bound, so limited in outlook, that the course of history was inevitably characterized by blind conflicts and actions leading ironically to unintended consequences. This chapter pays special attention to *The Prairie* and the figure of Leatherstocking as the pathfinder and victim of progress. Chapter 4 explores historical romance's translation of the conflict between reaction and progressivism into a conflict between regional loyalties and the federalizing, colonizing drives of British and, later, American imperialism; it looks closely at Irving's and Cooper's portrayals of the Yankee "invasion" of New York. In chapter 5, I discuss Hawthorne's ambivalent view of the forces of progress as represented by the seventeenth-century Puritan colonists of New England and the eighteenth-century patriots who wrested independence from Britain. Chapter 6 shows how Melville's more radical critique of progress led him to see historical development assuming the shape not (as Jefferson would have it) of a line trajected toward perfectibility, nor (as Hawthorne would seem to have it) of an ascending spiral, but rather of an old-fashioned cyclic rise and fall.

My chapter on "The hero and heroine of historical romance" takes its departure from an analysis of how Scott's "wavering" heroes and "strong" heroines – especially in *The Heart of Mid-Lothian* – subvert traditional gender stereotypes and yet finally conform to the expectations of a society which rejects revolution but accepts gradual change. Scott's awareness of how gender roles are historically conditioned is further enlarged in the historical romances of Hawthorne, Wharton, and Cather. Finally, in "The historical romance of the South," I re-examine Mark Twain's famous argument:

> Then comes Sir Walter Scott with his enchantments, and by his single might checks this wave of progress, and even turns it back; sets the world in love with dreams and phantoms; with decayed and swinish forms of religion; with decayed and degraded systems of government; with the sillinesses and emptinesses, sham grandeurs, sham gauds, and sham chivalries of a brainless and worthless long-vanished society.[6]

And I go on to show what some of the greatest modern Southern historical romancers have made of the "sham chivalries" with which their region was allegedly infatuated and the "wave of progress" by which Mark Twain himself was, for a time, swept away.

To examine Scott's American legacy in any depth means paying close attention to matters which are of the first importance to Marxist criticism: social revolution, colonialism, and the relationship between literary-generic and socio-economic change. I make a point to do so, and like all students of historical fiction I am indebted to the greatest Marxist literary critic – Georg Lukács.[7] Most readers of this book will probably know that in *The Historical Novel* Lukács traces the rise of the historical novel from the rise of modern historical consciousness regarded as a product of (or at least as a process tremendously accelerated by) the dramatic social and political changes wrought throughout Europe by the French Revolution and Napoleonic wars. Beyond question, the promise or threat of these changes did have a transforming effect, which extended well beyond continental Europe and well after the Bourbon Restoration, on nearly everybody's sense of the security of the *status quo*. As Melville recalls in *Billy Budd*:

> That era appears measurably clear to us who look back at it, and but read of it. But to the grandfathers of us graybeards, the more thoughtful of them, the genius of it presented an aspect like that of Camoens' Spirit of the Cape, an eclipsing menace mysterious and prodigious. Not America was exempt from apprehension. At the height of Napoleon's unexampled conquests, there were Americans who had fought at Bunker Hill who looked forward to the possibility that the Atlantic might prove no barrier against the ultimate schemes of this French portentous upstart from revolutionary chaos.[8]

It was in this atmosphere that Scott (1771–1832) spent the twenty-five years of his adult life which preceded the publication of *Waverley*, and, as I substantiate in chapter 2, there can be no reasonable doubt that his account of modern Scottish history in the Waverley novels is (among other important things) an oblique commentary on the perils of internal revolution and foreign conquest through which Britain had recently passed.

However, warmly though I admire Lukács and some of his followers, I am a Marxist neither in politics nor scholarly methodology, and I believe that he assigns the French Revolution a more generative role in the development of historical consciousness in society and literature than even *that* epochmaking event could have had – at any rate outside continental Europe. He largely ignores the rise of historicist thought in pre-revolutionary Scotland and Germany and exaggerates the gap between the historical novel of Scott and the historical drama of Shakespeare and eighteenth-century Shakespearean imitators. Although these omissions in Lukács's version of the prehistory of the historical novel seem to have few adverse consequences for his study of the major French, Russian, and German practitioners, they limit the usefulness of *The Historical Novel* for anybody who wishes to understand where Scott came from and why he had such an awakening effect outside continental Europe. Indeed, Lukács's commentaries even on Scott are remote from the actual texts of the Waverley novels and occasionally inaccurate. To the reader who is not a Eurocentric Marxist, Lukács's opening chapter sometimes appears a misty mythic prelude to the wisdoms and chronicles of the chosen people.

Valuable correctives to Lukács are Donald Davie's *The Heyday of Sir Walter Scott*, Avrom Fleishman's *The English Historical Novel*, and Harry Shaw's *The Forms of Historical Fiction*.[9] Davie and Fleishman have a firmer sense of intellectual and literary traditions beyond the European continent, and Davie's work has the great British critical virtue of caring more for particular novels and poems than for "literature," "ideas," or critical system. Fleishman, by contrast, is richly informative about the social and intellectual contexts of British historical fiction but tends often to read it as a mere illustration or precipitate of those contexts. Like Davie, Shaw is a sensitive reader of some of the masterpieces of nineteenth-century British and continental historical fiction, and he has also introduced several useful categories for sorting out the ways that historical novelists employ history.[10] Yet much as I have learned from these three critics, I have not found that they do much more than Lukács to account for the semination and growth of a flourishing American tradition in historical fiction. Believing that "Lukács has provided what is likely to be the definitive *historical* study of historical fiction," Shaw treats his subject "in terms that are primarily synchronic" (pp. 10–11) and in any case, like Fleishman, takes scarcely any notice of American developments. Although Davie has a couple of perceptive chapters on the Leatherstocking novels, he does not undertake the kind of systematic study of the conditions of cultural transmission which is needed to explain why, once it was introduced to them, American fictionalists took to the historical romance like so many swifts to air.

In the course of trying to supply what I found wanting in these excellent books, I have become very conscious of the limits and biases of my own approach. Some of these I have already noticed in connection with my coverage of things "American," and I would like to say something further here about what I do and do not claim to offer in this study of a literary tradition which extends, prehistory and all, over a period of two centuries and cuts across several national literatures. Although I have tried to read widely among the novels and critical studies relevant to my topic, I have inevitably read more deeply in some authors and periods than in others – mainly because these seemed the most relevant, but partly too because to me they were the most consistently engaging. For the same reasons, I have devoted more space here to Scott, Cooper, Hawthorne, and Melville, and to British and American Romanticism generally, than I do to later developments. That I do does not mean that I have a lower opinion of the twentieth-century authors discussed in chapters 7 and 8 or, for that matter, that these chapters gave me less pleasure to research or trouble to write; quite the contrary. Neither does the amount of space accorded to individual novels necessarily reflect my sense of their worth: I write at greater length about *The Fathers* than I do about *The Age of Innocence* or *Absalom, Absalom!* not because I think it is the greater work but because it has been comparatively neglected by other commentators and because it lends itself especially well to interpretation in light of the Waverley tradition.

The most important *caveat* is also the most obvious: although this project calls for considerable familiarity with the intellectual and socio-political history of Europe and especially the United States since the early Enlightenment, it is primarily a literary study and I am primarily a literary scholar. To be sure, my findings should be of more than casual interest to students of American social and intellectual history. Although I do not discuss Bancroft, Prescott, or Parkman directly, my account of the beginnings of historical romance does, I believe, usefully supplement David Levin's landmark study of the shape and progress of American romantic history. Moreover, because of their immense popularity, the books I examine have undoubtedly had a profound effect, both individually and as a genre, on the way that Americans of all levels of education and intelligence have conceived of their past, present, and future. Therefore I believe that this book makes a contribution to the history of American ideas about history.

But I do not speak to students of American history as a social or political historian might. I have little or nothing to say, for instance, about the degree to which Cooper's representation of family life on the seventeenth-century New England frontier is or is not confirmed by recent demographic reconstructions. And although I happen to know a good deal about the documentary sources of *The Wept of Wish-ton-Wish* and might have described Cooper's treatment of them, I concentrate instead on the way that Cooper's own reconstructions of New England frontier family life were guided by the theories of certain Scottish Enlightenment philosophers and the way that this historical romance first published in 1829 is organized around clusters of opposed images, character-types, and values which likewise appear in Goethe's historical drama *Goetz von Berlichingen* a half century earlier and in Faulkner's *Go Down, Moses* a century later.[11]

In sum, this study belongs to a species of literary-intellectual history which, as I remarked at the beginning of this introduction, is long on continuity and conformity to type and *comparatively* short on the deviant particulars and contextual details which might be at the center of a different kind of historical study. I stress "comparatively" because, although I believe that histories of genres and ideas are important enough to justify the sacrifices necessary to write them, what I value above all as a scholar and teacher of literature are not "the" Waverley novels or "the" historical romance but rather the particular works – *The Great Meadow* and *Kidnapped* – that you and I actually read and care for because they move, delight, and instruct us. Accordingly, there is in this book some tension, I hope a fruitful one, between the impulse to generalize, to exemplify, to look before and after, and the contrary desire to linger over each novel, to approach and value it on its own terms rather than on terms imported from paradigms modern or ancient. I recognize that to try to do both is to run the risk of doing neither satisfactorily, of losing the thread of the main argument while also failing to give satisfyingly "full" readings of individual works; but that risk seems inherent in a project of this kind, and I can only hope that, for the most part, I have guarded against it sufficiently by signposting frequently and by avoiding the suggestion that mine is the last and all-sufficient word on any of the books I venture to discuss in detail.

Important in principle though I believe it is to keep the particular primary text at the center of attention, to keep its own terms constantly in view, and to respect the intentions of greater writers than ourselves, it is by no means always easy to know for sure what these terms and intentions were or whether they were even in consonance with each other. In practice, therefore, it is impossible not to have recourse (as wary as you like) to alien paradigms, and I have not scrupled to make use of the examples and insights of critics – Marxist, psychoanalytic, post-structuralist – whose principles differ from my own. However, real and substantial though my debts to other scholars are, they are not always what they appear to be: my discussion of gender roles in the historical romance, which may strike some readers as the chapter in which I try to break in on the critical dialogue of the 1980s, was the first conceived and written (in a shorter version dating back to 1964); while the simple but, for this study, absolutely crucial conception of the novel as an omnibus form capable of hosting, miming, and parodying other narrative genres I owe in the first instance not to Northrop Frye or Mikhail Bakhtin or Fredric Jameson but rather to W.P. Ker's scholarly classic *Epic and Romance* (1896).

Thus far I have concerned myself mostly with the history *of* historical romance or *of* my thinking about the problems involved in writing such a history, but what about the history *in* historical romances? Ever since Scott began publishing this new kind of novelistic fiction critics have worried about its mixture of "story" and "history," about how remote from the present the setting of a novel must be for it to qualify as "historical," and about whether a historical novel must have at least one character – George Washington, for instance, or Al Capone – who once actually lived and made a name for himself in history. The first of these topics is much too complex to be tackled here; to address it at all effectively would require a theory of the fictionality of history along the lines of (but perhaps less ambitious than) Hayden White's. But I believe I can dispose of the second and third in a couple of paragraphs.

In *The Forms of Historical Fiction* (p. 38), Harry Shaw follows Kathleen Tillotson in differentiating "historical novels" like *Henry Esmond* from "novels of the recent past" like *Vanity Fair*, but this distinction strikes me as little less arbitrary than those which prescribe that historical novels must deal with events at least a century old or which can be known about only as a result of reading other books. For a fiction to qualify as "historical," what more can be required than that the leading or (more to the point) determinative social and psychological traits it represents clearly belong to a period historically distinct from our own? I can readily conceive, for instance, of two novels about the Watergate case of 1973–4. The one focusses narrowly and intensely on its "timeless" moral and psychological features as an example of the way that power corrupts and corruption empowers. The other presents (and partially explains) Nixon's rise and fall in relation to the emergence of California as a major economic and political power, the tendency of most Americans during the final years of the Vietnam War to elevate real or supposed qualities of leadership above all other goods in a president, and the advent of a new communications technology capable both of generating powerful images of leadership and betraying its seamy private side. Although the second of these hypothetical novels deals with events which are only a little over a decade remote, it seems to me no less a historical novel than, say, a novel written today about Lincoln's Washington years; and it strikes me as much more a historical novel than a work like *The Red Badge of Courage* because Stephen Crane's powerful tale of combat initiation has virtually nothing to do with the American Civil War or any war in particular.

Likewise contrary to much received wisdom about what makes a novel "historical," I cannot see that any of the characters need to have been actual historical personages. If such characters do appear and are drawn as convincingly as Roberts's Daniel Boone or Pushkin's Pugachov, they may have greater authenticating force than any of the other time-and-place markers with which historical novelists compose their fictional worlds. They may have, but I am not sure that they are more effective in this role than the ebbing sea of shaggy red prairie grass in *My Ántonia* or the house at Pleasant Hill which is burned down by Union troops near the end of *The Fathers*.

ROMANCE

A curious aspect of many of the "real life" personages who appear as characters in historical fiction – Prince Charles Edward in *Waverley*, for instance, or Governor Bellingham in *The Scarlet Letter* – is that they are portrayed as anachronistic figures whose presence highlights historical change. Historical verisimilitude of course demands that the anachronistic attitudes and behavior of these characters or of fictitious ones like Leatherstocking be authentically of their particular place and time, and so, frequently, does the fictional or historical plot as well. For the action of historical romances often turns on the failure of a character or class to understand that attitudes and behavior recently appropriate and tenable are so no longer. *Waverley* is the great case in point. Because the Jacobite party and its chief are for perfectly comprehensible reasons out of touch with the political sentiments of the country as a whole and a full century out of date in their aims and methods, they are doomed to start and lose a gallant, a "chivalrous" rebellion.

Lest we get the message wrong, Scott begins *Waverley* with an elaborate and gently satiric history of young Waverley's self-education – which turns out to be very like that of Don Quixote. Thus Scott inaugurates the historical romance tradition with a Cervantesque guying of the old-fashioned romances of chivalry which seems to align him closely with Smollett, Fielding, and the author of *Northanger Abbey*. And although the Scottish scenes and actions which ensue modify this impression considerably, it is clear that, taken as a whole, Scott's kind of romance is a variant form of the novel rather than a romance resembling *Daphnis and Chloe* or *Amadis de Gaul* or the *Arcadia*. (For this reason I claim the liberty, where doing so should not cause any confusion, to refer to a historical romance as a "novel.") However, just as there is oddity and even paradox in the coupling of "historical" and "romance" – since the latter is normally associated with things archetypical and atemporal – so there is an apparent contradiction implicit in the novel's subsuming romance (any sort of romance), because each has so long been used as each other's foil and ideal opposite. Northrop Frye's theory of displacement can be adduced to resolve the contradiction quickly and neatly, but a theoretical resolution necessarily ignores the important developments in literary, intellectual, and social history which lie behind, and are implicated in, the uses to which the terms "romance" and "novel" have been put by some of our greatest fictionalists over the past three centuries.[12]

Although the word "novel" did not come consistently to mean what we now mean by it until well into the nineteenth century, the generic distinction between novel and romance has remained current and relatively stable in its starkly dichotomous terms for a little over two centuries, i.e., since the beginnings of a continuous tradition of novelistic fiction. So oversimple it appears as a scheme for discriminating between the major kinds of modern prose fiction that its survival seems something of a scandal. Even if it has some validity in theory, those who employ the distinction often press it so hard as to be very misleading about actual practice. For relatively few of the works so labelled by their authors or critics cluster near either the "novel" or "romance" pole. Hawthorne has more of Trollope's roast beef and ale while Trollope has more of Hawthorne's idealizing imagination than the latter somewhat enviously supposed. No wonder, then, that in "The Art of Fiction" (1884) Henry James dismisses this division as one of those "clumsy separations . . . made by critics and readers for their own convenience, and to help them out of some of their occasional queer predicaments, but . . . [having] little reality or interest for the producer."[13]

Yet a critical distinction which has survived so long and has been taken seriously by some of the greatest "producers" of fiction surely must point to something worth knowing about in their products or intentions. Despite his impatient disavowal of the "clumsy separation," James himself uses it regularly in his late as well as his early criticism (albeit mostly without linking the terms "novel" and "romance") and, in his 1907 preface to *The American*, validates it more brilliantly and persuasively than anybody else has ever done. Mainly following James or Hawthorne, that other American master practitioner/theorist of romance, academic critics have employed the distinction to get at the special character of the American novel or have hotly denied its "reality or interest."[14] Rather than rehearsing their arguments, I propose to come back to James by way of some earlier figures with the aim of saying only as much about the novel/romance debate as is necessary to explain what I mean by the oxymoron "historical romance."

So far as the history of literary apologetics is concerned, the novel/romance opposition is a legacy of Renaissance Humanism's hostility to artistic expressions of what it denounced as medieval monkish ignorance and superstition, especially the chivalric romances beloved of Don Quixote and a host of the Don's spiritual and literary descendants. Whether or not *Don Quixote* was the first "novel," it manifestly was a paradigmatic masterwork of world literature which popularized while in many ways it transcended the humanistic critique of romance as shapeless in form, fantastic in matter, and corruptive in influence, and it powerfully affected the theory and practice of fictional narrative (and of drama too, for that matter) down through the nineteenth century. Although at its best this critique was inspired by a desire, at once scholarly and creative, to revive and nurture classical literary forms – especially the Homeric or Virgilian epic – it also received some prompting from two parties which otherwise took slight interest in belletristic endeavors. The one, which we tend today to associate with "Puritanism" but which long antedated the Reformation, objected to the immoral influence of all of the more conspicuously mimetic forms of popular secular literature. The other, which reflected a new and increasingly dominant secular and scientific world view, materialist and sceptical in tendency, was suspicious of any representation of "reality" which stimulated the imagination excessively or which did not ring true to common experience and common sense. Although fundamentally opposed to each other, these great antagonists found a common enemy in romance and did not hesitate to use each other's and Humanism's arguments as well as their own.

Of course romance had its eloquent friends — the greatest of them (Sidney, Spenser, Milton) at the heart of the Protestant humanist camp — but so powerful and diverse were its enemies that we cannot wonder that writers as different and in some respects incompatible as Fielding and Richardson both joined the cry against romance and felt obliged to distinguish their own fictions from it as sharply as possible. In the preface to the second volume of *Pamela*, Richardson makes clear where he stands by venturing to hope "that the Letters which compose this Part will be found equally written to NATURE, avoiding all romantic flights, improbable surprises, and irrational machinery; and the passions are touched, where requisite; and rules, equally *new* and *practicable*, inculcated throughout the whole, for the *general conduct of life*."[15] Although Richardson's concern for the "practicable" and the "general conduct of life" identifies him with the Puritan tradition rather than that of Cervantesque Humanism with which Fielding associated himself, his emphasis on "nature" and "new" is also one which runs through Fielding's essays on what he called the "New Province" of writing. Today most of us would probably agree with Ian Watt that Richardson is a more distinctively "novel" fictionalist than Fielding.[16] But the point I wish to underscore here is that the need both writers felt to dissociate their books from the old romances helps to confirm the main historical thesis of Watt's *The Rise of the Novel* — namely, that there was during that period a *general* and permanent reorientation of the aims, procedures, and audience of fictional narrative such as could not have transpired without profound changes in the total culture in which Richardson and Fielding, and Defoe before them, worked. Without denying the novelistic quality of various isolated "harbingers" like *Troilus and Criseyde*, *Don Quixote*, and *The Princess of Clèves*, we may affirm that there was indeed a "New Province" in fictional narrative opened up by certain eighteenth-century English middle-class pioneers which, once the natives were slaughtered or subdued, proved wonderfully inclusive of diverse ranges of human experience and therefore also of other narrative genres — not excepting the despised aboriginal romances themselves.

Probably Fielding's best-known attack on romance is a Swiftian passage in *Joseph Andrews* where he ridicules "those Persons of surprizing

Genius, the Authors of immense Romances, or the modern Novel and
Atlantis Writers; who without any Assistance from Nature or History,
record persons who never were, or will be, and Facts which never did nor
possibly can happen: Whose Heroes are of their own Creation, and their
Brains the Chaos whence all their Materials are collected."[17]
Fielding's romancers are like the spider in "The Battel of the Books"
who is such a "great Genius; that he Spins and Spits wholly from himself,
and scorns to own any Obligation or Assistance from without."[18] Like
Swift's, Fielding's point is that the godlike "Genius" who arrogantly
depends on his own imagination for his characters and incidents is merely
recycling the stories of other romancers – spinning literature out of
literature rather than life. In common with all of the best "neoclassical"
critics of his era, Fielding believed that while the ancient Greeks and
Romans supplied the ideal models of literary form, the best way for a
modern writer to imitate the "matter" of Homer was to observe
contemporary manners and morals as closely and freshly as possible. As
might be expected, Fielding's apologias appeal more than once to the
authority of his century's favorite philosopher, John Locke, father of
British empiricism and no friend of the indistinct productions of the
imagination.

But in Britain, as in America, no artistic creed or school of philosophy
has ever had the field entirely to itself. Among Richardson's and
Fielding's contemporaries were forerunners of the Romantic Revival
who found their touchstones or models in *The Faerie Queene*, the *Arcadia*,
Shakespeare's romantic comedies, and Milton's early poems – and who
were champions too of Shaftesbury and neoplatonism, of the Sublime, of
the gothic strain in architecture, and of the old ballads lately unearthed by
Bishop Percy. The clusters of like-minded literary intellectuals who
shared these tastes constituted an unofficial, unorganized opposition to
the strengthening forces in science, philosophy, economics, and politics
of which the bourgeois novel is the supreme artistic expression. They
thereby anticipated many of the tastes, dilemmas, and strategies of
American Romantic writers – especially Hawthorne, Poe, and Melville –
a century later. Representative of their aesthetics is Thomas Warton's
defense of the old romances in his *Observations on the Faerie Queene*
(1754):

> For however monstrous and unnatural these compositions may appear to this
> age of reason and refinement, they merit more attention than the world is
> willing to bestow . . . They are the pictures of antient usages and customs; and
> represent the manners, genius, and character of our ancestors. Above all, such
> are their Terrible Graces of magic and enchantment, so magnificently
> marvellous are their fictions and fablings, that they contribute, in a wonderful

degree, to rouse and invigorate all the powers of imagination: to store the fancy with those sublime and alarming images, which true poetry best delights to display.[19]

Note that Warton lauds romance for precisely those effects which its critics deplore and ridicule. His book on Spenser is one of the earliest attempts to place a literary subject – any subject – in its historical context and judge it in terms of the values and resources of its age. And while the "pictures of antient usages and customs" which chivalric romances give are far less historistic than he supposed, Warton's defense of romance is important as a straw in the wind because it manifests both the new spirit of historicism and the age-old craving for out-of-the-ordinary "imaginative" experience. It points to the existence of a public for kinds of fictional narrative which the novel of contemporary middle-class manners and morals could not supply.

Ten years later, Horace Walpole engaged in quixotic combat with the bourgeois novel and the cultural values he associated with it by publishing a pseudo-chivalric romance, *The Castle of Otranto*. In the first preface he wrote to account for his remarkable experiment, he maintained defensively that he was but the translator of a late-medieval original in which there were departures from NATURE – ghostly and gigantic visitations such as Pamela Andrews never encountered – because the story belonged to "those dark ages" in which "every kind of prodigy" was credited.[20] With more truth than he can have intended, he speculated that the real author was no doubt "an artful priest" who wished "to confirm the populace in their ancient errors and superstitions" (p. 1). When his "Gothic Story" proved popular, he maintained in a second preface (1765) that his "new species of romance" blended the ancient romance, which was "all . . . imagination and improbability," with the modern: "Nature . . . copied" but "the great resources of fancy . . . dammed up, by a strict adherence to common life" (pp. lv–lvi). Despite this tribute to fancy, however, his apologia now glossed over the story's unnatural agents and events and made much of its novelistic fidelity to human nature. He wished, he said, "to conduct the mortal agents in his drama according to the rules of probability; in short, to make them think, speak and act, as it might be supposed mere men and women would do in extraordinary positions" (p. lvi). This commitment to psychological realism has been endorsed by virtually all subsequent apologists for the modern romance.

That Walpole thought he had conceded too much to the *Zeitgeist* in his second preface is shown by a letter he wrote shortly afterwards: "I have not written the book for the present age, which will endure nothing but *cold common sense* . . . I am even persuaded, that some time hereafter, when taste shall resume the place which philosophy [i.e., science] now occupies, my poor Castle will find admirers . . . I am not sorry that the translator has given the second preface; the first, however, accords best with the style of the fiction" (pp. xxxi–xxxii). Walpole's "Castle" did indeed find plenty of admirers in the following century, but the instinct which prompted him in the second preface to misrepresent his own practice by pretending to be more of the novelists' party than he actually was – presenting his experiment not as a counterrevolution in prose fiction but as a restoration of certain ancient *poetic* virtues within the thriving new order – proved prophetic. The "men of brighter talents" whom Walpole hoped would travel "the new route" he had pioneered generally steered clear of giants and ghosts. Yet they still caught many a glimpse of "those sublime and alarming images" (the Highlands, Niagara, white whales) which, according to Thomas Warton, "true poetry best delights to display."

Walpole was but one of the pioneers of novelistic fiction whose works Scott wrote about. However, although Scott was a shrewd analyst of the rhetorical strategies of individual writers, he did little to advance the theoretical understanding of modern prose fiction. In an article written for the *Encyclopedia Brittanica*, he defines romance (in *all* its forms) as "a fictitious narrative in prose or verse; the interest of which turns upon marvellous and uncommon incidents."[21] More striking and suggestive than this definition is his account of the parallels between "Temporal Romances" (chivalric romances) and "Spiritual Romances" (saints' legends):

> The distresses and dangers which the knight endured for the sake of obtaining earthly fame and his mistress's favour, the saint or martyr was exposed to for the purpose of securing his rank in heaven, and the favour of some beloved and peculiar patron saint. If the earthly champion is in peril from monsters, dragons, and enchantments, the spiritual hero is represented as liable to the constant assaults of the whole invisible world, headed by the ancient dragon himself. If the knight is succoured at need by some favouring fairy or protecting genius, the saint is under the protection not only of the whole heavenly host, but of some one divine patron or patroness who is his special auxiliary. Lastly, the conclusion of the Romance, which usually assigns to the champion a fair realm, an abundant succession, and a train of happy years, consigns to the martyr his fane and altar upon earth, and in heaven his seat among saints and angels, and his share in a blessed eternity.   (p. 142)

Scott's witty description of the easy interchangeability of the "monsters, dragons, and enchantments" of Temporal Romances and "the ancient dragon himself" of Spiritual Romances anticipates the method and main thesis of Northrop Frye. However, he never explicitly extends this principle of substitution or displacement to more recent forms of fiction, but merely reinforces the eighteenth-century novel/romance opposition with a definition of the novel as "a fictitious narrative, differing from the Romance, because the events are accommodated to the ordinary train of human events, and the modern state of society" (p. 129). As a tantalizing afterthought, which he does nothing to develop, he allows that "there may exist compositions which it is difficult to assign precisely or exclusively to the one class or the other; and which, in fact, partake of the nature of both."

Now Scott had plenty of evidence not only that such mixed or intermediate compositions do exist but also that modern romances and novels generally do, to varying degrees, "partake of the nature of both" classes of fiction. The "story" of *Mansfield Park* rather obviously contains many of the ancient ingredients of fairy tale and romance; the "mysteries" of Udolpho are all too plainly and completely "accommodated to the ordinary train of human events." The Waverley novels themselves perfectly illustrate how the "ordinary train" might be interrupted by "uncommon incidents" and how the manners of preceding centuries could be strikingly juxtaposed with those of "the modern state of society." Scott did himself and other writers a disservice by helping to perpetuate a simplistic generic dichotomy which made some sense when the "romances" measured against the new novelistic fiction were *Amadis de Gaul* or *Le Grand Cyrus* but could only lead to confusion when they were *Caleb Williams* or *The Bride of Lammermoor*. If he had done a better job of explaining himself and his contemporaries, perhaps Mark Twain's travesty of the Waverley novels as a revival of chivalric romance which undid all the good work of *Don Quixote* might have been recognized at once for the bizarre recrudescence of Renaissance Humanism that it was.

Inadequate though Scott may have been as a fictional theorist, his practice inspired others to take a fresh look at the modern prose romance. Heinrich Heine, for example, anticipated Mark Twain's critique by declaring that Scott's great achievement was to do for the modern age what Cervantes had done for the Renaissance:

> We do not find in Cervantes this one-sided tendency to portray the vulgar only; he intermingles the ideal and the common; one serves as light or shade to the other, and the aristocratic element is as prominent in it as the popular. But this noble, chivalrous, aristocratic element disappears entirely from the novels of the English . . . English novelists since Richardson's reign are prosaic natures; to the prudish spirit of their time even pithy descriptions of the common people are repugnant . . . [Scott] effected a revolution, or rather a restoration, in novel-writing . . . Scott restored the aristocratic element to romance when . . . only a prosaic *bourgeoisie* was to be found . . . the characteristic feature of the Historical Romance consists just in the harmony between the aristocratic and democratic elements.[22]

Whether Heine's analysis is altogether accurate or fair to other "English" novelists need not concern us here. Cutting across traditional generic boundaries, he recognizes the extraordinary range and heterogeneity of the elements which Scott brings into harmonious relation in a single work of fiction. The contest between the forces of progress and reaction which Coleridge defines as Scott's "subject" Heine elaborates into a formal principle of contrasts and tensions between opposites – the ideal and the common; the aristocratic and the popular; the poetic and the prosaic.

Lesser men of letters than Coleridge and Heine also remarked the composite character of Scott's fiction. Reviewing *Rob Roy* in *The North American Review* in 1818, Edward Channing pointed to Scott's frequent and effective contrasts between small and vast, ludicrous and awful, and especially to his description of "the Highland hovel, and . . . the contrast between its smoke and filth, its wretched furniture and vulgar brawls, and the fresh, tranquil, pastoral beauties which surround it."[23] Another early reviewer of the Waverley novels, Nassau Senior, observed that they "unite the most irreconcilable forms, and opposite materials. He exhibits, sometimes in succession and sometimes intermingled, tragedy and romance, comedy and novel."[24] According to Senior, these "irreconcilable forms" and "opposite materials" are brought together in a dynamic union of distinct elements; they are not averaged or homogenized out of existence. This combination of novel and romance, "history and fiction, mirth and pathos" opens "all the sources of literary excitement, mutually supplying the deficiencies and heightening the powers of each other" (p. 8). Behind this analysis lie the eighteenth-century defenses of Shakespearean tragicomedy which culminate in Dr. Johnson's great summation in the preface to Shakespeare, but Senior deserves credit for seeing the relevance of those defenses to Scott's historical romances.

He received but scant credit from one Henry James, Jr., whose first publication, in 1864, was a dismissive review of the book in which Senior exhumed the *Quarterly Review* articles he had written when the Waverley novels were first appearing. But James did share Senior's admiration for Scott and eventually, over forty years later in the preface to *The American*, wrote appreciatively of Scott in terms which seem to recall the older critic. "By what art or mystery," he asks, "what craft of selection, omission or commission, does a given picture of life appear to us to surround its theme, its figures and images, with the air of romance while another picture close beside it may affect us as steeping the whole matter in the element of reality?"[25] James does not answer this question immediately but goes on to assert that the interest of a novelist is greatest when he "commits himself" in the directions both of realism and romance not quite at the same time or to the same effect, of course, but by some need of performing his whole possible revolution, by the law of some rich passion in him for extremes.

Of the men of largest responding imagination before the human scene, of Scott, of Balzac, even of the coarse, comprehensive, prodigious Zola, we feel, I think, that the deflexion toward either quarter has never taken place; that neither the nature of the man's faculty nor the nature of his experience has ever quite determined it. His current remains therefore extraordinarily rich and mixed, washing us successively with the warm wave of the near and familiar and the tonic shock, as may be, of the far and strange.[26] (p. xv)

Following James, we may say that the "deflexion" *toward* romance definitely has taken place in *The Deerslayer* and *Heart of Darkness* and that the deflexion toward the other quarter has just as clearly taken place in *Emma* and *A Hazard of New Fortunes*. In fictions like *Rob Roy* and *Moby Dick* and *Germinal* the "current remains . . . rich and mixed."

Whether we call any of the works mentioned immediately above a "novel" or a "romance" is a matter of indifference so long as we are aware that the function of the generic tag we use is to direct attention to one set of attributes in it rather than another. If, by way of parallel, we call "Tintern Abbey" successively a "conversation poem," an "ode," a "greater romantic lyric," and an "extended epiphanic lyric," we are implicitly surveying the leading characteristics of that poem rather than revealing our own or Wordsworth's confusion about the kind of poem it is. For most literary works, and perhaps all modern ones, display a mixed, eclectic, or "sedimented" character. As Fredric Jameson explains in a brilliant though not always perspicuous essay on romance:

> The notion of the text as a synchronic unity of structurally contradictory or heterogeneous elements, generic patterns and discourses (what we may call, following Ernst Bloch, the *Ungleichzeitigkeit* or synchronic "uneven development" within a single textual structure) now suggests that even Frye's notion of displacement can be rewritten as a conflict between the older deep-structural form and the contemporary materials and generic systems in which it seeks to inscribe and to reassert itself. Beyond this, it would seem to follow that, properly used, genre theory must always in one way or another project a model of the coexistence or tension between several generic modes or strands; and with this methodological axiom the typologizing abuses of traditional genre criticism are definitely laid to rest.[27]

On this showing, all of the works James discusses in the preface to *The American*, and not just those of Scott, Balzac, and Zola, have a much more "rich and mixed" current than the novel/romance dichotomy allows for. In *Satanstoe* we may detect coexisting sequentially or (more often) simultaneously the *Bildungsroman*, the family chronicle, the romance, the historical novel, and the "western" or, speaking more broadly, the regional novel in the tradition of Maria Edgeworth – to mention but the most obvious and traditional "generic modes or strands." We may readily detect the same strands, in somewhat different proportions and with the important addition of the "mystery" genre, in *Absalom, Absalom!* To call *Satanstoe* or *Absalom, Absalom!* a historical romance is not to deny that several other strands are present in it as well, but rather to focus on important features it shares with *Billy Budd*, which, besides being a historical romance, is a "mystery" for sure and possibly a *Bildungsroman* but scarcely a "western" or family chronicle. The features in question are not ones we should expect to blend together as smoothly as oil and egg yolk but are, on the contrary, ones which would seem to resist combination because they are themselves the products of deep and abiding divisions within our culture. Some kinds of novelistic fiction, notably the historical romance, are "extraordinarily" rich and mixed.

I can clarify my meaning by returning to the question James asks in the preface to *The American*: "By what art or mystery, what craft of selection . . . does a given picture of life appear to us to surround its theme, its figures and images, with the air of romance while another picture close beside it may affect us as steeping the whole matter in the element of reality?" His metaphors ("air of romance," "steeping") and pun ("matter") imply that "reality" is a dense and perhaps limiting medium, and his subsequent description of the sort of *experience* with which romance – in all its subgenres – deals bears out this reading: "experience liberated, so to speak; experience disengaged, disembroiled, disencumbered, exempt from the conditions that we usually know to attach to it and, if we wish so to put the matter, drag upon it, and operating in a medium which relieves it of the inconvenience of a *related*, a measurable state, a state subject to all our vulgar communities" (p. xvii). Just how morally desirable it is to be thus "liberated" is a problem that cannot be entered into here, but it is at least clear that the "out of world" experience of romance is directly opposed to our experience of the world of all our vulgar communities, i.e., the world of the novel.[28]

The world of all our vulgar communities is likewise the world of historical relation in which characters are so engaged, embroiled, and encumbered that they think, feel, and act differently than they would in some other conjunction of time and space. Therefore all novels from *Moll Flanders* onwards are implicitly or potentially historical. From *Waverley* onwards, they become more fully and explicitly historical inasmuch as, whether a historical novel–romance like Balzac's *The Chouans* or a novel of contemporary manners like *Père Goriot*, they acknowledge and demonstrate the shaping power of the forces of historical causality over character, attitude, event. James himself makes this point repeatedly about Balzac's densely realistic and deterministic portraits of early nineteenth-century bourgeois society, but it applies even to novels like Jane Austen's or James's own, whose privileged fictional worlds appear blessedly free from the heavier burdens of the past and the most vulgar associations of the present. For once the forces of community and relation are admitted within a fictional world, it begins to stand in intelligible relation to the forces of historical causality – economic, religious, political – to which we are all subject.

Still we are not wrong to feel that there are important differences between the ways that "the historian's impulse to fix, preserve and explain" manifests itself in historical novels like those of Cather or Lampedusa and novels of contemporary manners and morals like those of Zola or Howells.[29] Most obviously, historical novels involve persons and events "known to history" – not just Napoleon but also the tens of thousands of anonymous French and Russian soldiers who perished at Borodino; not just the pistol shot at Ford's Theatre but also the slow silent passing of the Midwestern frontier. Therefore their authors add to the opportunities and constraints common to all novelists ones more like those which the matter of ancient myth and legend presented to Aeschylus and Sophocles. The "given" and comparatively intractable nature of the "history" in historical novels likewise affects the way we read them. When we read *Waverley*, we know at the outset that Culloden awaits Charles Edward, his followers, and his cause, and that neither he nor his adversaries nor Sir Walter Scott can avert that fate or stay the ensuing measures of "pacification" which will put a period to the feudal way of life in Scotland. The result is a kind of fiction in which persons and events appear not only to be shaped in the mass by various impersonal conditioning forces but also to be, in their historical individuality, unrepeatable and irrevocable, making us more poignantly aware than ever of the relentlessly serial nature of life in history.

So much the greater, then, is the contrast when the historical novelist turns romancer in the same work: exempting Waverley "from the conditions we usually know to attach" to a military deserter and Jacobite rebel; or, as happens in *The Last of the Mohicans*, recapitulating the battles of sunny Achaia in the dark forests of North America; or reincarnating the Gray Champion on the streets of Boston. No wonder that William Gilmore Simms claimed that "the poet and romancer are only strong where the historian is weak" and that the "privileges of the romancer only begin where those of the historian cease. It is on neutral ground alone, that . . . [the historical romancer's] greatest successes are to be achieved."[30] By a variety of means which I discuss later, the authors of historical romances are able to establish a "neutral ground" and so accommodate fleeting passages of romance "realistically" within the world of all our vulgar communities, making the historical romance an instance of what Tzvetan Todorov calls an "evanescent genre."[31] But to accommodate them is not to iron out the wrinkle they make in the novelistic fabric. Calling a novel a "historical romance" is therefore to direct attention to its extraordinarily rich, mixed, and even contradictory or oxymoronic character. Although Balzac may exhibit this character more than any other great fictionalist and *Moby Dick* more than any other great novel–romance, I believe that the historical romance exhibits it more than any other novelistic genre. It is indeed definitive of, although not exclusive to, the genre: a work of historical fiction which does not wash us "successively with the warm wave of the near and familiar and the tonic shock, as may be, of the far and strange" is not a historical romance.

Two aspects of my approach to this eclectic genre may occasion surprise. First, although Knickerbocker's *History* and Irving's and Hawthorne's historical tales are only near relations, I have found that they demand close attention because they introduce or expose themes, formal strategies, and characterizations which are developed later in Cooper's and Hawthorne's major historical romances. Then, too, it can be argued that Irving's and Hawthorne's historical tales of New York and New England add up to something more than the sum of their parts, collectively aspiring, like *Satanstoe* and *The Scarlet Letter*, to the status of regional epics. (Collections like *The Sketch Book* and *Legends of the Province-House* demonstrate that Irving and Hawthorne thought of some of their shorter, superficially unrelated works as composing larger wholes: so can we.) My discussions of these shorter works may serve to remind us once again of the protean nature of novelistic fiction and of the consequent need for a flexible and pragmatic approach to the question of generic identity.

Second, although much concerned with the efforts of "Romantic" writers to revive heroic forms of literature, I pay scant attention to the archetypal elements of romance which appear in the novels of Scott and his successors. As we have seen, Scott himself recognized that romance in its various forms has but a single master plot and cast of characters; and while his anatomy of the genre differs somewhat from Northrop Frye's or Joseph Campbell's, there can be no doubt that he understood the principle of displacement and also that he must have been at least intermittently aware of the romance *topoi* in his own novels. The quest journey, the hero's trial, and his eventual marriage to the king's daughter – these ancient romance elements are present most obviously and completely in the books that he, Cooper, and Mark Twain wrote for family consumption, and they survive in a recognizable (if often parodic) form in historical romances addressed to a more sophisticated audience. Therefore they should not be dismissed as mere vestiges which ingenious scrutiny might trace in almost any work of fiction.[32] But detecting and decontextualizing them is rather beside the point I seek to make in this book. For notwithstanding their authors' ambition to recover the primitive strength and truth of earlier forms of literature, historical romances are essentially a product of modern times: of the mixed feelings of pride and guilt experienced by the beneficiaries of bourgeois revolutions and European colonial conquests; of the English novel of manners and morals as developed by Fielding, Smollett, and Edgeworth; of Enlightenment social-historical theory; and, not least, of the literary theory and practice of the Romantic Revival.

This said, it should also be emphasized that nothing is more modern about the historical romance, more characteristic of the new ways of thinking and feeling that became widespread among educated people towards the end of the eighteenth century, than its authors' heightened awareness of the human need for myth in all ages and of their own need as historians of human behavior to know the myths by which their real or fictitious characters would have lived and, not infrequently, died. Allen Tate indicates the importance of this awareness in an analysis of the role of myth which takes its departure from a distinction drawn by T. S. Eliot between

> two kinds of mythology, a higher and a lower. The Roman *toga* of our early Republic was doubtless of a sort of lower mythology, inferior to the higher mythology of the Christian thirteenth century, and I suppose Mr. Eliot would prefer the higher vision, as I myself should were I allowed a preference. But we must remember that the rationalism of the eighteenth century had made myths of all ranks exceedingly scarce, as the romantic poets were beginning to testify; yet the Virginian did remarkably well with the minor myth that his age permitted him to cultivate. Mr. Custis'... blank-verse dramas, in which every hero is an alabaster Washington named Marcus Tullius Scipio Americanus, are unreadable today . . . but Mr Custis built Arlington, and Arlington is something to have built . . . Mr Jefferson could not have built Monticello had he not been dominated by the lower myth of the *toga virilis*.[33]

We shall see that Tate himself makes excellent use of these insights in his portrait of Major Lewis Buchan, the "Roman" hero of *The Fathers*. But Tate would have been the first to acknowledge that in focussing attention on the "lower mythology" by which his characters were guided or misguided in life, he was doing what historical romancers had been doing for over a century. Scott, Cooper, and Hawthorne all understood that the seventeenth-century Puritans would not and probably could not have done what they did, for good and ill, if they had not been "dominated by the lower myth" of the Old Testament Hebrews. The same could (and has been) said of their "Cavalier" opponents. In short, one of the powers of myth as defined by Tate is precisely to *liberate* experience "from the conditions that we usually know to attach to it" – self-interest, physical weakness, the decay of memory – and thereby to give a historical ground to the romance in historical romance. Myth thus defined is of the first importance to the genre and to the study that follows.

I conclude this prospectus by returning to a point made at the beginning. The history of historical romance would be astonishingly unlike that of any other genre if radical differences of authorial temperament and circumstance did not enforce a succession of modifications both minor and major. For Scott and most of his younger contemporaries, the historical romance was, above all, a modern version of the epic, hence a heroic and masculine genre preoccupied with the fate of entire societies and but little concerned with individualistic introspection or, reversing the mirror, cosmic questionings. That this form of historical romance was still viable for some greatly gifted writers long after "the Heyday of Sir Walter Scott" is proven by Stevenson's *Kidnapped* and Conrad's *The Duelists*. But the limitations of the classic form of historical romance were apparent even during Scott's own lifetime. Although not unmoved by the heroic clarions of epic literature, Hawthorne and Melville saw that the historical romance as written by Scott and Cooper would not meet their own needs unless its center of action and moral interest could be relocated inwards. Mark Twain and Edith Wharton, so dissimilar in most respects, were alike at least in their inability to commit themselves directly and explicitly to the high mimetic mode of romance. Modifications, accordingly, were made, and could be made because the model that Scott created was what today we would call a "flexible discourse." But modifications have been fewer and less drastic than might be supposed, presumably because the genre has a built-in resistance to change and because the historical conditions which gave it shape and currency in the first place are still with us under different guises and names. What astonishes, finally, is the extent to which the traits by which *Waverley* was first recognized as something new under the sun are still present and important a century and more later in *My Ántonia* and *Absalom, Absalom!*

2

The Waverley-model and the rise of historical romance

1. The contribution of Scott

The publication of *Waverley* in 1814 must be reckoned one of the major intellectual events of the nineteenth century. For in this tale of the 1745 Jacobite rebellion and in the half dozen novels of Scottish history with which he followed up its huge popular success, Scott developed a model of historical narrative that transformed the writing of fiction and history. Its influence was manifested in three principal ways. First and most important for the present discussion, *Waverley* and its early successors provided a flexible paradigm for historical romance, enabling other writers both to recognize and present a particular type of historical conflict in terms that seemed at once universal and authentically American or, as the case might be, Russian, Italian, Argentinian. Second, Scott's innovations in *Waverley* also enlarged the scope of the novel form generally by developing its historical consciousness (its conscience, too, for that matter) and by multiplying the variety of natural and social forces that impinged on its characters' behavior. Finally, his example inspired professional historians to reform their research methods and extend the range of interests and motives surveyed in their accounts of historical causation.

Scott's influence on the development of post-Enlightenment historiography can only be touched on here, but some notice must be taken of the basis of that influence. For the historiographical virtues of Scott's novels are also found in American novels like *Satanstoe* and *The Scarlet Letter*. Besides, historiographical and literary virtues are intimately related and sometimes even identical.

Scott was among the earliest writers, in the words of Hugh Trevor-Roper, "To see the past on its own terms . . . to respect its autonomy, to sympathise with its coherent assumptions, and at the same time not to surrender to mere nostalgia or lose . . . [his] own position in the present."[1] Yet important as his example of moderate and balanced historicism must have been at that time, younger contemporaries like Carlyle and Mill believed that Scott's most original contribution to historical narrative was to have expanded its scope and shifted its focus, so that the public acts of kings, bishops, and generals no longer engrossed all of the attention but were placed in a greatly enlarged human context subsuming the conflicting loyalties and cultural usages, the economic interests and technological means of all levels of society – of peasants and merchants as well as landed gentry and princes of the realm. Scott's novels, said Carlyle, first taught men that "the bygone ages of the world were actually filled by living men, not by protocols, state-papers, controversies and abstractions of men."[2] Clarendon and Hume, said Macaulay, wrote the history of English governments during the seventeenth century but left it to Scott to write the history of the English people of that period in historical romances like *Old Mortality* and *The Fortunes of Nigel*.[3]

This great extension of historiographical purview also involved a revolution in research methodology. Trevor-Roper points out that Scott departed from the normal practice of eighteenth-century historians by visiting the scenes of historical events, the better to understand and describe them with precision. Moreover, he drew not only from the standard sources of historians but also from those which especially interested poets of his generation – which is to say the generation of Coleridge and Wordsworth: "informal, private documents . . . legends, traditions, customary rites, ephemeral literature, popular poetry, portraits."[4] From such "humble" sources and first-hand observations Scott gleaned the vivid details that gave his narratives immediacy and verisimilitude. In Macaulay's and perhaps even more impressively in Parkman's masterpieces we can see how the great Romantic historians assimilated and disciplined Scott's historicism, his research methods, and his narrative techniques in works of history which are also major works of art.[5]

Neither by temperament nor design was Scott a "scientific historian" or systematic thinker about the means and ends of historiography. But to suppose that his historiographical achievements were inadvertent by-products of his fictionalizing is to misconstrue the nature of the relationship between literature and history as this was understood during and before his time. As it had been since antiquity, historiography was still classified as a branch of narrative literature and a rather loftier one than prose fiction. (Gibbon's status as a serious literary figure was secure in his own lifetime; that of Richardson or Smollett arguably was not.) To be a historian was supposed to require narrative skill and a penetrating judgment of men and affairs; it was not supposed to entail non-partisan professionalism or specialist training in the gathering, collating, and assessing of evidence. Not surprisingly, therefore, poets and philosophers considered historiography a fair field for exercising their talents. Hume and Voltaire are cases in point: both devoted many years to researching and writing histories which, in the eyes of their contemporaries, tended to overshadow the achievements for which they are now most remembered. Scott inherited this tradition and was able to move with comparative ease between what have since become distinct disciplines. Following the example of Poet Laureate Robert Southey, whose *Life of Nelson* (1813) was a great critical and popular success, Scott wrote a multi-volumed biography of Napoleon (1827) which, of necessity, recounted the political and military history of modern Europe as well. Other literary men followed the same pattern: for instance, Irving in his biography of Washington; Cooper in his history of the United States Navy; Simms in his history of South Carolina and biographies of Francis Marion and Nathanael Greene; and Hawthorne in *Liberty Tree*, a juvenile history of the American Revolution in New England. For their part, several of the great nineteenth-century historians not only created literary masterpieces in their histories but also wrote literary criticism, poetry, and fiction of note. The names of Macaulay and Carlyle come immediately to mind, but we should remember that, closer to home, Motley and Parkman and Henry Adams were novelists as well as historians.

The defensible position that narrative historiography and prose fiction had more in common than not could lead to confusion and blurring of generic boundaries. Carlyle sank not infrequently from history to melodrama in his version of the French Revolution; Dickens seems to have found the combined roles of novelist and historian in *A Tale of Two Cities* overstimulating and mutually destructive; Scott himself, as in chapters 19–20 of *Rob Roy*, occasionally gave disproportionate space to social history or failed to integrate it convincingly in his fictional narrative. Nor are American examples of misunion far to seek. Yet they are fewer than might be expected. After all, the grounds for distinguishing between the practice of "imaginative literature" as an art and of historiography as a social science or humanistic discipline were prepared well before the publication of *Waverley*. Eighteenth-century thinkers gave the word "imaginative" its modern meaning and currency, and, on the other hand, demonstrated in expository works of "philosophical history" (e.g., Montesquieu's *Spirit of the Laws*) that the narrative mode of presentation was not essential to historiography. Historical romancers and Romantic historians were aware of these developments, if not alert to all of their implications, and generally observed necessary generic distinctions while benefitting largely from a rich community of interests.

That community was more extensive (for the historical preoccupations of imaginative literature were more extensive) than I have so far indicated. Although Scott's impact on historiography was made chiefly through his novels, these were the products of middle age and by no means the first fruits of his historical studies. As a young man, he translated German historical drama and won early and merited fame as a collector and imitator of folk ballads. But wonderful, indeed of irreplaceable value, though his work as a ballad-finder and maker was, it was not the first of its kind. It was, rather, precisely the contribution that might have been expected from a son of the eighteenth-century Romantic Revival as this movement had been fostered and interpreted by late Enlightenment thinkers in Germany and Scotland. We shall see that the main themes and even many of the details of plot and character typology in the Waverley novels had already been formulated by the poets and philosophical historians Scott read in his youth. And these writers exerted an influence on the growth of historicism that, as it extended far beyond Scott, prepared the ground for the enthusiastic international recognition and influence of his novels.

As propagandists for, editors and adapters and historians of, the literature of "primitive" peoples – ranging from Hebrew psalms to Scottish Border ballads and American Indian speeches – they were instrumental in the formation of national historical consciousness and pride, especially in the countries of northern Europe. In their studies of the relationship between folk literature and the societies that made it, Enlightenment literary scholars and philosophical historians reinforced each other's work and often overlapped. But the latter tended to be interested in laws of social development and in the species "Savage Man" or "Barbarian Society" rather than in individual cultures. And so it was more often the literary scholars, preoccupied with a unique masterpiece in a particular social context, who were the pioneers in historical research methodology and first developed a truly historical perspective on the past.

One such pioneer, whom I shall have occasion to cite again, was the Homeric scholar Robert Wood. In his posthumous *Essay on the Original Genius and Writings of Homer* (1775), Wood described his aim to refer himself mentally

> back to the state of society and manners of that early period. I therefore examined the materials of the Iliad and Odyssey, not only where they were collected, but, as nearly as possible, in the same order, in the same light, and under the same point of view, in which I imagine they presented themselves to the Poet's choice.[6]

Especially when we bear in mind Wood's extensive on-the-spot fieldwork, these sentences may well seem to mark a major methodological advance in the history of historical research. Friedrich Meinecke comments on the enthusiasm with which Herder and Goethe responded to an earlier version of Wood's essay shortly before they produced work of the greatest importance to the development both of the historical romance and the German school of historiography.[7]

To call Wood a pioneer is to say that he was exceptional and that the Romantic Revival was more often characterized by enthusiasm for things ancient than by an informed inwardness with their historicity. Certainly this was true of its main prose-fictional offshoot, the Gothic novel, which tended to be as anachronistic in psychology as designedly remote from the normal experience of human beings in any century. Consequently, although the masterwork of the Revival provided Scott with nearly everything else he needed, it could not offer a ready-made model for novelistic fiction which was truly historical. I do not deny that Scott owed something to the Gothic novel, especially as practiced by Ann Radcliffe. But I do maintain that such inspiration and example as existing fiction could afford him in revealing the historical dimension of human experience he found, rather, in the regional novel of Maria Edgeworth and in the eighteenth-century English novel of contemporary manners and morals. In turn, Scott expanded the possibilities of these models for the successors of Edgeworth and Fielding.

In the previous chapter I explained how their authors' attention to circumstantial detail and causal relations in "a state subject to all our vulgar communities" made novels like *Moll Flanders* and *The Expedition of Humphery Clinker* implicitly or potentially historical: Defoe's Moll and Smollett's Matthew Bramble are not only *in* but very distinctively *of* their particular times and places. Scott could build on such novels and, in turn, deepen the historical consciousness of all kinds of novelistic fiction both by detailing past manners accurately and by demonstrating, as no previous novelist had, how the past exercised a powerful and sometimes destructive influence on the present. At the same time, he enlarged the scope of the novel form by bringing to it an epic or tragic poet's concern with the fates not just of individuals but of entire societies. Or, to view this enlargement from another perspective, Scott brought to the novel a philosophical historian's perception of the ways that such impersonal common factors as natural environment and technological progress shaped and linked in mutual dependence the public acts of statesmen and the behavior of obscure citizens. Robert Louis Stevenson explains this development by contrasting Scott's treatment of character and motivation with Fielding's:

> Fielding tells us as much as he thought necessary to account for the actions of his creatures; he thought that each of these actions could be decomposed on the spot into a few simple personal elements . . . [But in Scott's] work, the

individual characters begin to occupy a comparatively small proportion of that canvas on which armies manoeuvre, and great hills pile themselves upon each other's shoulders. Fielding's characters were always great to the full stature of a perfectly arbitrary will. Already in Scott we begin to have a sense of the subtle influences that moderate and qualify a man's personality; that personality is no longer thrown out in unnatural isolation, but is resumed into its place in the constitution of things.[8]

Stevenson is writing here about Scott's influence on the French historical romance, especially that of Victor Hugo, but his account of Scott's innovations can also be used to explain why the social–historical schema of the Waverley novels was so enfranchising for Balzac.

Readers used to viewing Scott through the satiric lenses of Mark Twain may be surprised at the coupling of his name with that of the founder of French literary realism, but the connection is close and direct. For, being himself very much "of" as well as "in" his age, Balzac began his novelistic career by writing a historical romance in the Waverley tradition. *The Chouans* (1829), while vigorous and original in its handling of French settings and the main love story, generally mimes Scott's characteristic historical themes, situations, and plot developments with enthusiastic fidelity. It was but one of many thousands of novel–romances in which the little and great writers of the period tested the adaptability of the *Waverley*-model to the historical experience of their own nations. The first to employ the *Waverley*-model successfully was the "American Scott," as James Fenimore Cooper hated to be called, in *The Spy* (1821) and *The Pioneers* (1823). Cooper was soon followed by Manzoni in *The Betrothed* (1827); by Pushkin in *The Captain's Daughter* (1831) and Adam Mickiewicz in the Polish epic *Pan Tadeuz* (1834); and much later by Tolstoy in *The Cossacks* (1852). These are but the greatest names among those who joined in extending Scott's achievement as a historical romancer into international tradition – something much more than a fad and less than a "movement" – of immense social as well as literary interest.

In the remaining sections of this chapter I shall discuss the abiding political relevance and meaning – the major theme – embodied in the *Waverley*-model; its origins in literary theory and practice before *Waverley*; its epic aspirations; and finally its embodiment in one of Cooper's major historical romances.

2. Historical romance and the Age of Revolution

"Scott's great merit," wrote Coleridge in 1820, "and at the same [time] his *felicity*, and the true solution of the long-sustained *interest* that Novel after novel excited, lie in the nature of the subject." And:

the essential wisdom and happiness of the Subject consists in this: that the contest between the Loyalists and their opponents can never be *obsolete*, for it is the contest between the two great moving Principles of social Humanity – religious adherence to the Past and the Ancient, the Desire and the admiration of Permanence, on the one hand; and the Passion for increase of Knowledge, for Truth as the offspring of Reason, in short, the mighty Instincts of Progression and Free-agency, on the other. In all subjects of deep and lasting interest, you will detect a struggle between two opposites, two polar forces, both of which are alike necessary to our human well-being, and necessary each to the continued existence of the other.[9]

This account of Scott's "subject" and its universal interest is a *locus classicus* applicable not just to the Waverley novels but to all historical romances in the Waverley tradition; it is as true of *My Ántonia* as of *Rob Roy*. That it is an accurate account, and not just a pattern which Coleridge imposes on Scott in order to illustrate a thesis of his own, can be confirmed only by reading more than a few of the Waverley novels with more than ordinary care. But there are summary passages scattered through Scott's writings which furnish *prima facie* evidence that Coleridge has indeed discovered and defined – with metaphysical generality but also with precision – Scott's abiding premises concerning the dynamics of social and political history. One such passage, from the *Life of Napoleon Buonaparte*, analyzes the polar structure of the British political system:

> From the nature of this grand national division, it follows, that the side which is most popular should be prompt in adopting theories, and eager in recommending measures of alteration and improvement. It is by such that the popular part of the constitution is maintained in its integrity. The other party is no less useful, by opposing to each successive attempt at innovation the delays of form, the doubts of experience, the prejudices of rank and condition, legal objections, and the weight of ancient and established practice . . . If there were no Whigs, our constitution would fall to pieces for want of repair; if there were no Tories, it would be broken in the course of rash and venturous experiments.[10]

Coming as it does from a committed Tory, this is an impressively detached and "philosophic" analysis of the way that, working within the established political framework, the parties of progress and reaction struggle with each other to achieve, all unintentionally, a dynamic and life-sustaining equilibrium. It is, if one likes, distinctly "Coleridgean."

Yet it is also sufficiently down to earth in its attention to "legal objections" and the ambitions of "men of talents" (like Scott himself) to alert us to profound differences between Scott and Coleridge as thinkers and artists. For Coleridge's analysis of the "subject" of the Waverley novels is anything but down to earth. It is deliberately pitched at a level of abstraction so elevated as to lose sight of the ways that the contest between the principles of progress and reaction had revealed itself in recent history. To be sure, Coleridge concedes parenthetically that the early Waverley novels are the more appealing "because the struggle between the Stuarts and the Presbyterians and Sectaries is still in lively memory . . . [and] because the language, manners, &c introduced are sufficiently different from our own for *poignancy* and yet sufficiently near and similar for sympathy" (v, 34). But in his effort to isolate what "can never be obsolete" in Scott's subject, what it shares with "all subjects of deep and lasting interest," he does not allow that the struggle between the Jacobites and their opponents in the Waverley novels might be regarded as representative of the age without thereby standing condemned as a subject of merely superficial and transient interest: that it might be reckoned to have immense enduring interest because it prefigures and epitomizes the revolutionary and imperialistic struggles which had been transforming the world during his own and Scott's lifetimes. Closer to the truth, or at any rate highly useful as a corrective to Coleridge's excessive universalism, is Lukács's Marxist contention that the historical novel as first written by Scott was, ultimately, the cultural product of the French Revolution. If neither of these great critics is quite right about the nature of Scott's achievement, the reason may well be that both seriously underestimate the extent to which Scott was a conscious and educated observer of the major literary, philosophical, and socio-political developments of the age.

Lawyer, novelist, and son of the Scottish Enlightenment, Scott was a far worldlier man than Coleridge. Although something of a philosophical historian in the tradition of Montesquieu and Adam Smith, Scott is unlikely ever to have contemplated his subject in terms so abstract and apolitical as those proposed by his metaphysical friend. To him it was of the first importance that he was living in the greatest period of revolutionary and imperialistic conflict which the world had yet known. So significant and urgent were the events of his own time, he argued around 1808, that they blotted out all interest in the past:

> the momentous revolutions which it has been our lot to witness have not only diminishd the value of history by annihilating as it were the states and kingdoms in whose service it has been employd . . . but by the grandeur and . . . [rapidity] of their operation they tend to darken and cast into shadow the . . . interest of those events and actions to which former ages attachd so much importance. – The battles both by land & sea which have occurd since the French Revolution . . . [are] upon a scale . . . which cannot be paralelld in the page of history and the reader may be permitted to . . . be weary of the detaild campaigns in which a single town was lost or relieved since he has seen the fate of empires decided in the conflict of one day. Situated then as we have been these twenty years past the time has been more fertile of events for future

historians than propitious to the labours of those who be now engaged in recording former events.[11]

These remarks, from an unfinished essay "On the Present State of Historical Composition" (c. 1807-8), may help explain why Scott lost interest in the novel "recording former events" which he began and abandoned in 1805 and did not conclude until (so it appeared) the Russian campaign had concluded Napoleon's career. They definitely do help us to understand why near the end of his life he again turned temporarily from historical fiction to research and write his monumental *Life of Napoleon Buonaparte*. Receding into the past, the greatest of all struggles between the forces of progress and reaction, so mighty that they temporarily destroyed interest in history, had become the greatest of all subjects for a historian. Although she does not refer to the *Life* of Napoleon, Marilyn Butler places Scott and his preoccupation with revolution in the right company when she observes that "The generation of nineteenth-century historians now growing up, Carlyle, Macaulay, De Tocqueville, were also to take the revolutions of their respective countries over the past two centuries as their prime historical subject. It has not been adequately noticed that Scott anticipated them, for revolution is more genuinely his subject than Scotland is."[12]

Scott devotes about 200,000 words to a preliminary "View of the French Revolution" which, besides narrating the central dramatic developments in Paris, reviews the consequences for England and France of the American War of Independence; describes the counterrevolutionary efforts throughout France – especially the guerrilla campaigns in La Vendée and Brittany which Balzac was shortly to write about in *The Chouans*; and details the early, pre-Napoleonic conquests of France's revolutionary armies. The *Life* proper allots nearly a million more words not just to the major campaigns and Napoleon's creation of a new Roman Empire but also to the wars of national liberation or resistance which preceded the Russian débâcle: notably, in Switzerland; in Calabria; in Spain; and, most ominously for Scott's Virginian or South Carolinian readers, on the black slave island of Santo Domingo.

The *Life* of Napoleon spells out, like a vast footnote, the political lessons embedded in the Waverley novels – firmly embedded, too, but not on that account any more accurately construed by Scott's readers than the direction of eighteenth-century events had been by British Jacobites before 1746 or French monarchists before 1793. Scott writes as a middle-aged Tory, and it is a safe inference that his résumé of the French Revolution was made long, detailed, and unsparingly realistic so that the young liberal intellectuals among his readers might be impressed by the fate of their French counterparts: a reminder that those who would not settle for King Log (Louis XVI heading a constitutional monarchy on

British lines) lived just long enough to behold the coming of King Stork (the Jacobins beheading all rivals). But Scott's "View of the French Revolution" is equally addressed to his own party as a warning of what would inevitably befall the hereditary governing classes of Great Britain if, like those of France, they ceased adapting intelligently and responsibly to social and economic change – e.g., by making timely concessions to the just ambitions of the rising middle classes. Perhaps the most memorable trope in the book (and one which later appears in *Benito Cereno*) is Scott's comparison of the French noblesse, once the formidable military caste of their nation, "to a court-sword, the hilt carved, ornamented, and gilded, such as might grace a day of parade, but the blade gone, or composed of the most worthless materials" (11, 10). Despite much preliminary parade, intrigue, and high hopes, Scott's Jacobites likewise always turn out to have too little true steel in their scabbards.

Yet it is misleading to speak simply of "Scott's Jacobites" as if either in historical fact or in Scott's historical fiction the Jacobites ever formed a monolithic party with identical interests and degrees of commitment to the Stuart cause. Taking *Waverley* as our exemplary text, we can draw a broad distinction between two major groups of Jacobite characters – both "reactionary" but each standing in its own relation to the party of progress.

First, there are the English and Scottish Lowland Jacobites represented by old-fashioned landed aristocrats Sir Everard Waverley, the Baron Bradwardine, and the novel's youthful hero Edward Waverley. These Stuart supporters share a common culture with each other and also, despite relatively deep party and philosophical differences, with the Whig adherents of a Hanoverian succession. They do so sufficiently for Edward to be the son of an English Whig politician and yet to serve in the Young Pretender's army and marry the Scottish Baron's daughter Rose. (Although traditionally emblematic of England, roses flourish no less well north of the Border.) Scott portrays these Jacobites as attractively quixotic characters who are misled by rural seclusion and a very bookish "religious adherence to the Past and the Ancient" to imagine that a Stuart counterrevolution could succeed and, if successful, would do the country as a whole a great service. Since they no longer pose a serious threat to the new political order, their conquerors can safely pardon them and score a second, moral victory by championing fraternal reconciliation.

These counterrevolutionary Jacobites provided American writers with a model for the fictional treatment of the losing sides in their own great fratricidal conflicts, the War of Independence and the Civil War. In *The Spy* (1821), the first of Cooper's tales of the painful division of loyalties occasioned by the Independence movement, the American

Tories are, unmistakably, the counterparts of Edward Waverley and his Jacobite relations. However, it should be said straightway that, despite the rich potential of the subject and some moving glimpses of what befell the American Tories (notably in Hawthorne's "My Kinsman, Major Molineux" and Cooper's *Wyandotté*), American historical romancers were generally unable to invest the American Loyalists with the dignity and pathos and intelligence which are to be found in many of Scott's Stuart Loyalists. Indeed, whether their poverty of interest be attributed to the prevalence of nationalist propaganda or some other cause, the revolutionary war novels with which I am familiar are mostly a poor lot, redeemed only by flashes of candor about the sordid motives and behavior of many partisans on both sides and by the gripping action sequences which American fictionalists from Cooper to Kenneth Roberts have always known how to bring off. Not until the conflict between the North and the South yielded fresh parallels with "the contest between the Loyalists and their opponents" did Scott's counter-revolutionary Jacobites find worthy heirs in the American historical romance.

A second group of Jacobites in *Waverley* confront the forces of progress across a cultural gulf so wide in so many ways – sectarian, ethnic, and socio-economic – as to appear unbridgeable in a single generation. Whereas Sir Everard and Baron Bradwardine are indulged in anachronistic attitudes and customs, "such as might grace a day of parade," by a society which can afford to regard them as picturesque vestiges of the island's ancient chivalry, Fergus Mac-Ivor's Highland clansmen are the real thing; their blades, though few and old-fashioned, are intact and of good metal. When they emerge from their wild glens, the contest between the principles of reaction and progress assumes the shape of an imperialistic conflict between Gaelic-speaking Roman-Catholic feudalists (or, less abstractly, primitively armed Highland clans rising on behalf of the royal house of Scotland) and an English-speaking Anglo-Saxon Protestant army, professionally trained and equipped to defend an advanced agrarian and mercantile state. These Jacobites are not fighting a modern war of national liberation; they are, rather, honoring hereditary clan loyalties. But it is clear that they, and Scott in writing about them, are also strongly moved by a feeling for things Scottish. Childlike in their adherence to a primitive code of loyalty and revenge, they are easily led to serve the ambitions of politicians like Fergus and Prince Charles Edward, Scottish chieftains by blood but sophisticated French courtiers by nurture.

At once more primitive and more decadent than their opponents, this second group of Jacobites established a pattern for the portrayal in both historical romance and romantic history of all the "backward" peoples who had lost or were losing their homelands and cultural integrity to the imperialistic nations of Western Europe. The first American writer to follow this pattern was, once again, Cooper. The ostensible main plot of his third novel, *The Pioneers* (1823), is concerned with the aftermath of the American Revolution and centers on a conflict between a dispossessed Tory family, the Effinghams, and a seemingly (but only seemingly) opportunistic partisan of Independence, Judge Temple, who now holds the Effinghams' sequestrated lands. In this conflict the aged figures of Leatherstocking and Indian John have the roles and social status only of humble allies of the Effinghams; they are the American equivalents of Baron Bradwardine's faithful family retainers. But the illiterate white hunter Leatherstocking has other affiliations and loyalties which make him a counterpart of Scott's Highlanders. In this role he is the principal spokesman for the old-fashioned Indian ways of relating to law and land and against the ways of Judge Temple in his role not of revolutionary partisan but of progressive land developer. With these changes of roles the contest between the forces of reaction and innovation shifts from the revolutionary to the imperialistic mode. Significantly for the future of the historical romance in America, what Cooper at first probably meant to be a subsidiary conflict, rather personal and local in interest, comes to life as the struggle between American Whig and Tory never does. The westering frontier was destined to provide successive generations of American historical romancers with their fairest fields (or bloodiest grounds) for conflicts akin to those in *Waverley*.

How closely kindred are Cooper's American representatives of the forces of progress and reaction with the British ones in *Waverley*? Like Scott's Highland clansmen in hard practice and the Waverleys in romantic principle, Leatherstocking, Indian John, and Major Effingham all are veteran warriors who cleave anachronistically to the old heroic disciplines and values. In *The Pioneers* Cooper imagines, somewhat sketchily, an adventurous past for them, and in subsequent Leatherstocking tales, dealing with an earlier phase of frontier conflict, he relates scenes and actions worthy of Waverley's beloved Froissart and not unlike some that are witnessed by Scott's hero in the Highlands. Despite these broad generic likenesses, however, Leatherstocking's Indian associates confront the forces of progress in America across a cultural gulf still wider, still less bridgeable, than that which lies between the Scottish clansmen and their opponents. For this reason Cooper's American frontier romances require an interpreter or mediator who is much more active and experienced than Waverley or Frank Osbaldistone in *Rob Roy*: a champion no less formidable than the

Highlanders themselves. Leatherstocking supplies this need and at the same time mediates between Old World and New World primitives, making an American translation of the *Waverley*-model imaginatively easier both for Cooper and his audience.

American counterparts of Scott's Hanoverian opponents of Jacobitism presented themselves in abundance to Cooper and his successors, and required comparatively little imaginative translation from the British originals. Judge Temple, bourgeois beneficiary of the American Revolution, has clear affinities with Scott's whiggish merchants and lawyers, themselves the heirs and beneficiaries of the Glorious Revolution of the preceding century. It is as easy and natural for him as it was for them to make the transition from progressive middle-class revolutionary to progressive *entrepreneur*, supplying the ambition, brains, and energy – albeit not the blood and derring-do – necessary for the imperialistic expansion of the modern nation-state. As for those American historical romances which are concerned with the seventeenth-century Puritans, their premise is that colonizing New England was essentially an alternative to fighting a civil war in old England; that imperialism and revolution were but different phases or expressions of the same progressive middle-class energy and continued to be so down to the time of the American Revolution. In fiction as in historical fact, the Puritan fathers who figure in Hawthorne's fiction are of basically the same stock and persuasion as the politic Cromwell of *Woodstock* or the fanatical Balfour of *Old Mortality*.

In his first novel, then, Scott created a flexible model for representing the kind of revolutionary or imperialistic conflict which issues in the overthrow of a heroic society by the modern post-feudal state. This is what, on a more sublunary view than Coleridge's, the "subject" or central theme of historical romances in the Waverley tradition turns out to be. In the present context "heroic" subsumes both "primitive" (Scott's Highlanders, Cooper's Mohicans) and "aristocratic" (the blood or spiritual survivors of an outmoded feudal order) and refers generally to the sort of traditional society which does, or in its full vigor did, memorialize its deeds in epic poems and sagas. Historical romancers tend to think of such societies as ideally whole and unfragmented, but they often detach individuals endowed with "heroic" qualities from their proper community and make them do lonely battle with a radically new and alien civilization. Although the defeats these individuals inevitably suffer normally have little of the sound and fury of Culloden or Gettysburg, they are invested with a broad cultural significance. However, even allowing that the defeats of, say, Hester Prynne and Leatherstocking have a synecdochic value and signal the loss of certain cultural possibilities in and for America, need it follow that the historical outlook of our historical romances is quite as gloomy as my formulation seems to imply?

Most of our major writers of historical romance have been cautiously progressivist in social philosophy, and on those occasions when they lend a rostrum to the expansive rhetoric of Manifest Destiny it appears that their theme might be better defined as the progress of civilization and the heroic founding of a new *patria* and a new national character. And indeed this would be a satisfactory formulation – except that the sombre note is rarely silent for long in this kind of fiction. It is of the essence of the genre that the author always slips in at least a hint concerning the appalling fate of the American cousins of Ossian's Gaels, Gray's Welsh Bard, Scott's Highlanders, and all the other doomed primitives of Romantic literature. The balance of sympathies varies considerably from work to work and from author to author, and therefore it is not possible to say that historical romances are mainly progressivist and optimistic in outlook or mainly primitivist and pessimistic. If my definition suggests that they tip the balance in favor of the defeated and dispossessed party, it does so because I believe that the masterpieces of the genre have tended to be more than commonly sceptical about the blessings of progress, more than averagely honest about the cost of epic colonizations and revolutions.

I began this section by quoting Coleridge's definition of "the subject" of the early Waverley novels, a definition perennially useful but nonetheless open to objection because it fails to register that these novels are, after all, about the causes and effects of revolution and imperialism in modern times. We cannot hope to understand their relevance and appeal to readers and writers outside of Britain unless we see them as products and reflections of the modern era. To be sure, the greatest of these novels are concerned with events which antedate the French Revolution by a half century or more, and it must be allowed that their abiding appeal also has much to do with the poignant sense Scott is able to create of human worlds once alive with present hopes and passionate loyalties but now irrecoverably past. No doubt, too, that he finds so much to warm to in the Jacobites of *Waverley* and *Rob Roy*, and to a lesser degree in the Covenanters of *Old Mortality*, precisely because their revolutionary fires are wholly extinct. But as Balzac was to demonstrate in *The Chouans*, there were many and close structural analogies between the civil conflicts imaged in the Waverley novels and the more recent wars described in the *Life* of Napoleon. As might be expected, the parallels are often at their closest in *Woodstock* (1826), the romance Scott wrote while he was still engaged on the great biography. Scott was too good a historian to turn the Cromwell of *Woodstock* into a Napoleon or the Napoleon of the *Life* into a Cromwell, but he used his knowledge of each to enhance his understanding of the other.

3. The Waverley-*model*

That *Waverley* had the potential to serve as a model for a new species of fiction was probably not obvious to Scott himself at first. But once he had gone on to *Guy Mannering* (1815) and *The Antiquary* (1816), and especially after he had published the great sequence of novels dealing with late seventeenth- and early eighteenth-century Scotland – *Old Mortality* (1816), *Rob Roy* (1817), *The Heart of Mid-Lothian* (1818), and *The Bride of Lammermoor* (1819) – it became clear that he was concerned not just with the struggles between the Jacobites and Hanoverians in eighteenth-century Scotland or the preceding ones between the Cavaliers and Roundheads, but with a class of conflicts of which there were numerous instances in the recent history of many countries. If not in *Waverley* by itself, then in this series of early novels Scott's younger contemporaries recognized a pattern which seemed to have universal relevance and adaptability.

To those writers it made available what a critic today might call a "flexible discourse." Or, to choose a structural analogy which would have made immediate sense to them as well as to us, the pattern in the Waverley novels must have struck Cooper and Pushkin as being very like the scientific paradigms embodied in Newton's *Principia* or Franklin's *Experiments and Observations on Electricity* which Thomas Kuhn has defined as "universally recognized scientific achievements that for a time provide model problems and solutions to a community of practitioners."[13] Nor are other functional parallels far to seek. Kuhn himself ventures a suggestive analogy between a scientific paradigm and an accepted judicial decision in Common Law: "an object for further articulation and specification under new or more stringent conditions" (p. 23). Given the strong and informed interest in the law which Cooper and Melville shared with Scott, it might seem more appropriate to turn to this field rather than to that of scientific research for an analogy to the *Waverley*-model. Another pertinent parallel might be drawn between this literary model and a "hereditary type." For Scott, Hawthorne, and Faulkner were all fascinated by the recurrence of family traits in individuals – of reversions to type sometimes more and sometimes less pronounced but always intriguing – and this interest, obsession almost, may well have affected their choice and treatment of historical subjects. Perhaps it also helped them resist the excessive demands for "originality" which, from the mid-eighteenth century onwards, Romantic literary theorists imposed on writers. Yet although the judicial decision and hereditary type are both analogues for the *Waverley*-model which should be borne in mind, I believe that the scientific paradigm offers a more instructive parallel. For one thing, the *Waverley*-model enjoyed an international currency comparable to that of a scientific paradigm; its influence reached far beyond the writ of English Common Law. For another, as will become clear in the next chapter, the *Waverley*-model had certain implicit claims to scientific validity.

This analogy with a scientific paradigm may help us to understand why the *Waverley*-model was seized upon by so many writers of powerful and independent genius. The "model problems" which Newton's or Franklin's achievements posed for other scientists did not invite duplications but rather showed these other practitioners where they might profitably carry out experiments of their own. Similarly, the *Waverley*-model taught writers like Cooper, Pushkin, and Balzac to search their own national histories for poignant transitional moments parallel to those in Scottish history. Romantic fictions which revolved around these important moments could satisfy nationalist cravings for American, Russian, or French epics while also claiming universal interest and importance as variations on the great theme discovered for fiction by Scott.

Almost exactly a century after *Waverley*'s potential as a model began to be recognized, T. S. Eliot described the potential of the "mythic method" of Joyce's *Ulysses* in terms very similar to those I have just employed:

> In using the myth, in manipulating a continuous parallel between contemporaneity and antiquity, Mr. Joyce is pursuing a method which others must pursue after him. They will not be imitators, any more than the scientist who uses the discoveries of Einstein in pursuing his own, independent, further investigations. It is simply a way of controlling, or ordering, of giving a shape and a significance to the immense panorama of futility and anarchy which is contemporary history.[14]

Eliot's reference to Einstein is striking and has a certain aptness, but a subsequent one to the great pioneers of modern anthropological research is still more to the point. For it was the work of Frazer and Frobenius that supplied Eliot and Pound not only with specific data and hints towards organizational devices for *The Waste Land* and *The Cantos*, but also with cogent evidence of a continuing community of interest and method between literature and science. The work of Enlightenment social scientists, itself much influenced by the examples of the *Principia* and *Opticks*, stood in a similar relation to the *Waverley*-model.

Despite real and important similarities, however, Eliot's explanation of the contemporary need for the mythic method reveals a world of difference between his attitude to his literary model and that of Scott's nineteenth-century successors to theirs. For the latter, recent or contemporary history was not an "immense panorama of futility and anarchy" on which shape and meaning had to be impressed. On the contrary, the faith at least of the early romancers was that it already had the shape and meaning of an inevitable progress from savagery to civilization which the *Waverley*-model could help them to reveal. A major reason why they had need of the "model solutions" suggested by Scott's early novels was that, in the nature of things, those who told the tale one or more generations later belonged to the winning side and therefore inherited the values of that side and only such partial information as it had filtered down to posterity. Historical romancers had much to reconstruct, especially concerning the motives, loves, and sufferings of the losing side.

This is not to minimize their efforts and successes in discovering documentary sources and creating pictures of the past which a professional historian might consider valuable. Scott's novels of seventeenth- and eighteenth-century Scotland earned the respect of great British social historians from Macaulay to G.M. Trevelyan – and not merely for their narrative verve. They still have value as introductions to the beliefs and manners of the period. Similar claims can be made for *Satanstoe* and *The Scarlet Letter*. However, their authors did not always find documentary sources abundantly available or, when they were, easy to interpret. Anybody who tries to track down the Indians of *The Wept of Wish-ton-Wish* to Cooper's sources and get at the truth about their relationships with the Puritan invaders by studying the documents that Cooper studied is likely to lose the trail. The records that survive are full of confusion about Indian names, full of contradictions about how their bearers died. The Puritan chronicles interpret King Philip's War as essentially one more historical episode in the timeless battle between Satan and Christ: nor is there any doubt about whose side represents the demonic, whose the messianic principle. As a conscientious historical writer, Cooper had to give that white Puritan viewpoint – or perhaps it would be better to say the Puritan myth – dramatic expression and at the same time transcend it. The *Waverley*-model enabled him to do just that. It helped him, as it helped other romancers, to interpret his historical data (such as they were) coherently, meaningfully, and even objectively. Of course the model had its own built-in biases and blinkers, and Cooper's resurrected Narragansetts are doubtless very romanticized versions of the actual people whom the Puritans demonized and destroyed. But the heroic society overthrown in *The Wept of Wish-ton-Wish* has credible human grievances and aspirations. Though tinged with primitivism, Cooper's portrait of that society and its enemies is comparatively complex and objective and altogether, as compared with those in previous accounts of King Philip's War, represents a substantial gain in human – and historical – understanding.

As Carlyle and Macaulay appreciated, Scott's primary concern in the Waverley novels was not with the great leaders nor with the high intrigues and mighty battles of modern political history, but rather with the ways that these affected and were affected by ordinary people and events – people and events hitherto "unknown to history" but increasingly the subjects of poetry and fiction in Britain and of drama in Germany. As a poet and amateur philosophical historian, Scott looked more deeply and widely into the popular causes of revolutions, and of their successes and failures, than a political historian would have dreamed of doing. What he saw and recorded in the Waverley novels came as a revelation to the fiction- and history-reading public. As a *"novelist,"* Scott has been equalled by few other writers. Yet just as the *Waverley*-model assisted later fictionalists, so the literary-philosophical education which taught him to look into matters beneath the notice of historians also suggested what shapes and relations these matters would have. Scott is both more and less innovative than is generally supposed.

Coleridge, we may recall, spoke not of Scott's subject but of "the" subject of Scott's novels. He did so, I believe, because he appreciated that although Scott was the first to bring the contest between the forces of reaction and progress to the center of the Western literary consciousness, he did not discover the subject for literature; that much of his achievement consisted in fleshing out and giving local habitations and names to sets of conflicting values which had been troubling the European literary imagination for several decades before the French Revolution gave many of them a cataclysmic expression; and therefore finally that, in Coleridge's own words, some "subtractions" from the credit given Scott must be made because of borrowings "from English and German sources" (v, 35). Who should understand these matters better than Coleridge?

Before proceeding to the next section, I wish to apologize for treating Scott rather reductively and especially for seeming to suggest that his romances were little more than clearinghouses for "influences." I believe, on the contrary, that what he did in *Waverley* was not much less astonishing than what Richardson did in *Clarissa*. But my main contention is that what was *not* original and astonishing in his romances was scarcely less important to his successors than what was. His influence could be so wide and enduring precisely because he was so open to influence himself.

4. *The literary origin of the* Waverley-*model*

What exactly was at stake, according to historical romancers, in the revolutionary or imperialistic conflicts they imaged in their fictions? Or to put the question in somewhat different terms: if the values associated with either side in historical romances were often ones which could not have been found, or could have survived only as ambiguous vestiges, in documentary sources or oral traditions, where did they come from? And what were they? I will address the second question first. Reduced to two brief lists of opposed cultural values, a historical romance in the Waverley tradition might be diagrammed as follows:

natural	artificial
spontaneous	labored
natural graces	studied graces
liberty/wildness	order/boundaries
poetry/mystery	prose/reason
individuality	mass
sublimity	correctness

On one side are the cultural values regularly associated (albeit not all of them all of the time) with declining aristocrats, e.g., Scott's Jacobite lairds or Faulkner's Confederate officers, and with such relatively primitive folk as Pushkin's Cossacks or the fierce Gauchos of Domingo Sarmiento's *Life in the Argentine Republic in the Days of the Tyrants*. On the other, are many of the values associated with the conquering legions of progress – usually Protestant middle-class and invariably of European origin. To these lists might be added a few of the physical features so frequently connected with either side of the conflict that merely to mention one of them was to evoke a cluster of related cultural values:

mountains	vales
paths	highways
excursions	marches
soaring	fettered

A point to be borne in mind here is that the deeply human habit of ordering reality in terms of one or more sets of binary oppositions was especially characteristic of the Romantic Revival. In the words of Claudio Guillén: "The tendency of the true Romantic was to polarize not only writers or writings but ideas and attitudes into opposite camps."[15] Often this tendency is not immediately obvious because Romantic authors generally eschewed the Augustan art of formal balance and antithesis in favor of literary surfaces contrived to appear unstudied, natural (Wordsworth's "the real language of nature"), or to mime the forms (songs, ballads, epics) created by peoples allegedly closer to nature and God. Below those surfaces, however, the polar principle which "true Romantics" believed to govern the life of nature likewise informed and ordered their literary imitations of nature – often down to quite small details of imagery and characterization. Examples of this tendency are Coleridge's analysis of "the subject" of the Waverley novels and Scott's analysis of the polar principle at the heart of the British political system. Despite profound differences of character and personality, Scott and Coleridge saw eye to eye on many subjects and understood each other very shrewdly because of their shared literary-intellectual background in the Romantic Revival.

Another result of this likemindedness is that the oppositions constellated in the *Waverley*-model can be found in many works of Romantic literature – including lyrics and descriptive essays as well as prose fictions – which cannot be plausibly categorized as historical romances. Yet although not peculiar to historical romance, these recurring polarities are definitive and even constitutive of the genre: for, in retrospect, they would seem to *demand* expression in a kind of fiction which yokes together novel and romance, romance and history. To demand is not always to receive, but in this instance two of the greatest literary talents of the age, Goethe and Scott, had the inclination as well as the opportunity to respond to the challenge: to create a generic vehicle that answered not just their own but their culture's need.

The polar constellation under discussion here was a characteristic product of the Romantic Revival in Britain and Germany. In those countries the Revival originated as a cultural movement in large measure animated by, and yet at the same time severely critical of, Protestant nationalism. Its hero and chosen exemplar was Shakespeare. Its most passionate shared interest was in national history, geography, and culture. Shakespeare and, later, Scott did not so much awaken this interest in other writers as show them where to look for appropriately heroic "matter" and how to objectify strong but mixed feelings about their *patriae* in enduring works of art. The contradictory spirit and major literary forms of the Romantic Revival were readily exported to countries which, like Russia and the United States, had recently waged wars both of national liberation and imperial expansion.

Rather than go directly back to Shakespeare, I begin my account of the prehistory of the *Waverley*-model *in medias res* with a literary theorist whose work I have already pillaged without acknowledgement. My lists of opposed cultural values and associated physical features in the historical romance derive from a work which antedates *Waverley* by half a century and which is in no direct way concerned with the social or political issues of a historical romance. They are taken *verbatim* from Edward Young's famous and influential treatise on literary aesthetics, *Conjectures on Original Composition* (1759). One might compile much the same lists from works by other Enlightenment aestheticians or philosophical historians, but a reference to this work is convenient as well as historically apt for a number of reasons. First of all, Young's treatise is addressed to one of the great originators of world literature – his friend Samuel Richardson – and its chief hero is an even greater English originator, Shakespeare. Young's is a familiar English and German Romantic Revival message not to imitate the classical models resurrected by the French and Italians, but to cultivate the national vernacular, revive native traditions, and develop new forms instead. His cultural nationalism has a specifically Protestant as well as English edge to it, and we are surely right to detect contemporary political and religious innuendo as well as literary precept in his warning that those who entrusted their protection to ancient Rome ended by being her slaves.

Slavery was what the Augustanism of Dryden, Swift, and Pope had come to mean to Young by 1759 and what it meant to many, perhaps most, readers of poetry for more than a century thereafter. On the great English Augustans were projected a host of constrictive attributes (those listed in the right-hand column above), and we have to remember that their continental contemporaries were much more constrained than they by classical precedent and neoclassical rules. Small wonder, then, that Young became a hero of young German writers: of Klopstock, Herder, and Goethe, whose struggle against French neoclassicism was animated both by artistic ideals and strong Protestant and nationalistic feelings as well. Goethe's first major work, the historical drama *Goetz von Berlichingen* (1772), was written under the influence of such feelings and also under the influence of the literary gospel preached by Edward Young and his German disciples. In turn, *Goetz* was translated by young Walter Scott in 1797; it certainly helped shape his conception of *Waverley* and thus the entire historical romance tradition. Indeed, the characteristic themes, situations, character-types, and ideological alignments of the historical romance are all clearly prefigured in Goethe's play.

Goethe's chief historical source for the play was a memoir written by the German baron, literally a robber baron, Goetz von Berlichingen, who was a free knight of the Holy Roman Empire at the time of the Peasants' War, at the very dawn of the Protestant Reformation. Goethe's source is therefore similar to Shakespeare's source for the History plays, and certainly *Goetz* is a very Shakespearean play, though its affinities are as much with *Antony and Cleopatra* as with the English history sequence or any of its parts.

The knight Goetz is a rough anachronistic figure out of the late Middle Ages. Half mercenary captain and half rustic robber baron, he is greatly attached to his independence, his castle, and the good old local customs.

His presence, and that of others like him, is intolerable to the new and wealthy alliance of worldly Renaissance bishops and town merchants who represent the new order in German society and politics. They look to the Emperor as a central authority to suppress Goetz and generally to establish the order and uniformity necessary for commerce and learning to flourish. As the play develops, the points of conflict become more pronounced and numerous; reconciliation proves impossible; and the action turns from high-spirited raids à la Robin Hood to the miseries of civil war and the inevitable defeat of Goetz. The larger social and cultural issues in the play may be abstracted as follows:

patriarchal authority	rule of law
local autonomy	central administration
feudalism	bourgeois society
country	town
Common Law	Justinian Code
vernacular	Latin
oral	literate
instinct	learning

No more than in *Waverley* subsequently are these conflicting characteristics presented as allegorical abstractions; rather, they emerge through the vigorous words and deeds of historically plausible characters.

The tendency of the opposed parties in *Goetz* is to draw further apart, increasingly to regard each other as inhuman or unnatural, and not to interact at all except with swords. Into this threatened dramatic and social vacuum Goethe thrusts a figure, the knight Weisingen, whose sympathies and loyalties are divided between the two sides. On closer inspection, indeed, it becomes evident that neither side is characterized by monolithic conformity of interests or values and that there is considerable potential for cross–cultural alliances. For instance, because Goetz's son has received a classical education, he has much in common with his father's enemies and, in a less polarized situation, would certainly have some kind of bridging relationship with their camp. In the end, the son is helpless and the wavering Weisingen, snared by the lures of wealth and sex, betrays his old companion Goetz. But temporarily their conciliatory presences offer a middle ground between the antagonists and humanize the conflict.

Young Goethe understood, what Scott and his greatest successors understood perhaps even better, that in a society undergoing rapid transformation economically, institutionally, and educationally, conflict between the old and the new was inevitable but that in historical actuality the warring sides could never be "pure" parties of reaction and progress. For the individuals who composed these groups were themselves deeply mixed and even likely to be members of subgroups with rival agendas.

To render this interplay of interests and values in its full complexity was beyond the scope of the historical drama or romance or, in fact, of any work of historical representation; but Goethe and Scott were able to hint at its nature while boldly delineating the main pattern of conflict. The more rounded characters in *Goetz* and *Waverley* rarely or never exhibit all of the traits generally ascribable to their respective parties, and, as we shall see, it is often their deviations from type, the relationships they form across party lines, that give their stories moral and psychological interest.

If the lists of opposed values in *Goetz* are conflated with the lists derived from Young's *Conjectures*, we have a fairly comprehensive abstract of what is culturally at issue in the historical romance. Of course it is with historical romances as it is with their chief characters: *no* historical romance conforms completely to this pattern; some vary fairly widely or repeat only a part of it. But the high degree of conformity that may be recognized in scores of minor and major works of historical fiction points to the shaping influence of the literary-historical paradigm I am describing. Scott made this paradigm available to the world by giving it a fresh and powerful re-embodiment in prose fiction at a time when the life of literature was flowing most strongly in the novel and lyric poem. At a time, too, when the aesthetic and socio-historical ideas of the late Enlightenment were internationally diffused and the Age of Revolution was sufficiently advanced for the shape of the post-feudal state to have emerged fairly clearly. But it was Goethe who first synthesized the paradigm in a work of literary art.

Although Goethe was one of the great originators of world literature, he might not have achieved what he did in *Goetz* had he not lived when and where he did. As a member of Herder's circle in the early 1770s, he was at once highly receptive to the new ideas about literature and history which were streaming in from Britain and yet far more sensitive than any English writer was then likely to be to the revolutionary pressures building up in Europe and her colonies. And so he became the first major literary artist to see that the truly great events in history were not changes in dynasty but shifts in economic, social, religious, and political structures. He saw, moreover, that these structures were closely related to, and dependent on, each other.

Goethe's Enlightenment understanding of historical development enabled him to accept that attractive Id-figures like Goetz were doomed to extinction and further that their disappearance would mean "progress" in the form of better roads and schools, more food, greater personal safety, and even more equal justice. To many later writers these positive benefits of "civilization" appeared still more valuable than they did to young Goethe. So they did to Scott and Pushkin, to Cooper and the American Romantic historians, and perhaps especially to Sarmiento when he wrote from exile about the bloodthirsty Gaucho governors of his country and summarized his theme curtly as the conflict between civilization and barbarism. However, as we shall see in the following chapter, for these heirs of Enlightenment social thought the term "barbarism" implied not merely ruthless or brutal behavior (the other face of "nature") but also and more precisely a distinct stage of social development with characteristic institutions, attitudes, virtues, and modes of subsistence. Subsequent stages might be more "advanced" in various palpable and impalpable ways, but even Sarmiento recognized a Dionysian principle in his barbarians which he, as a writer, was unwilling to reject entirely. By the same token, Goethe identified the free spirit of Goetz with the cultural nationalism of his own time and place. And so was a similar identification made by writers of historical romance, part of whose enterprise was to recover some of the ancient ground of fiction – the heroic, the mythic, the strange – which seemingly had been abandoned by novelists of contemporary morals and manners.

The *favorable* attributes they ascribed to their doomed barbarians were the very ones Young had ascribed many years previously to the genius of Shakespeare, who was enormously important not only for Goethe but also for the first generations of historical romancers. To them the English history plays must have seemed a glorious precedent for what they were trying to do in their own tales of Scotland, America, and Russia. And certainly they imitated Shakespeare in literally thousands of features, large and small. Scott and especially Cooper drew far more of their chapter verses from him than any other author. In *The Wept of Wish-ton-Wish*, some twenty-seven of Cooper's thirty-two epigraphs are from Shakespeare. In *The Bride of Lammermoor*, the work by Scott that most closely anticipates Cooper's great tragic romance, the proportion is only seven out of thirty-five, but no reader will fail to sense the shaping influence of Shakespearean tragedy and specifically of *Hamlet*, *Macbeth*, and *Romeo and Juliet*. In nearly all their romances, including those just mentioned, Scott and Cooper also combed the Shakespearean comedies both for apt quotations and hints on how to proceed. Indeed, to their life-long reading and rereading of the comedies may be traced some of their excessive reliance on such traditional plotting devices as captivity, disguise, and parental absence.

But what I want particularly to notice here is that one of Shakespeare's plays, *Antony and Cleopatra*, anticipates many of the themes, situations, and ideological conflicts which I have been discussing. In this, surely the most richly historical in conception of all Shakespearean tragedies, the bold and many-faceted contrast between the two worlds of ascendent Rome and declining Egypt is paralleled and intensified by a less striking but still immensely important contrast between two generations of

Romans – a binary pattern that is repeated, with variations, in many historical romances. When the "old ruffian" Antony challenges Octavius to single combat, he reveals not only his personal courage and desperation but also his failure to understand the new imperial ways of thinking and acting. Yet what alienates Antony from the coming generation of Romans gives him a kinship with the archaic non-Roman peoples he has helped to subjugate. Precisely because he belongs to the heroic age of Julius Caesar's conquests (Cleopatra among them) he is able, for a while, to bridge the gap between the alien worlds of Egypt and Rome. Thus Antony prefigures Goethe's Weisingen and a host of characters in historical romance whose wavering between two camps is as often due to their strengths as to their weaknesses. Seeking to mediate between the two, these characters are often torn apart in the process. Often, too, it is their very involvement with more than one camp that precipitates the catastrophe for themselves and others. Such is the case with Antony and with the tragic heroes of, for instance, *The Bride of Lammermoor* and *The Wept of Wish-ton-Wish*.

As for the principle that opposes Shakespeare's sympathetic but licentious hero, Octavius the Emperor of the West rules with the head rather than the heart; he is an astonishingly precocious politician rather than a leader of men. But he is something of a political visionary, too, already foreseeing the *pax Augusta*:

> The time of universal peace is nigh.
> Prove this a prosperous day, the three-nooked world
> Shall bear the olive freely.   (IV, vi, 5–7)

Under Augustus the undivided Empire will enjoy, as the fruits of peace, many of the advantages which later writers were to associate with "civilization." To be sure, the ideal of an Augustan golden age is not developed in this play, but Shakespeare's brief allusion recalls many earlier contexts from Virgil's Fourth Eclogue to Ben Jonson's *The Poetaster* (1601) where it was elaborated. As Howard Erskine-Hill has shown, the ideal was part of Shakespeare's intellectual inheritance as it has been of the European peoples generally at least until fairly recent times.[16] The modern (i.e., eighteenth-century) word "civilization," which derives ultimately from the Roman word for citizen, itself attests to the vigorous longevity of the ideal. But there have always been critics who pointed to a wide discrepancy between it and the reality of the Empire. *Antony and Cleopatra* does not do so directly but rather shows with incomparable richness of imagery and elegaic eloquence what qualities were sacrificed to make way for the Augustan order.

However, I believe that no Shakespearean play had, or could have had, the kind of impact on the historical romance that *Goetz* had on the

Waverley novels and that they had on the novels of the succeeding generation. Although the greatest hero of the Romantic Revival, Shakespeare himself was not a Romantic. Only at a level of generality that loses sight of numerous differences of emphasis and value can his Romans and Egyptians appear to move comfortably within the bounds of the *Waverley*-model. To be made available to the historical romancers, Shakespeare had to be Enlightened from a new angle, as eventually he was in *Goetz*. Perhaps the final judgment on the importance of *Goetz* and eighteenth-century Shakespeareanism to the shaping of the *Waverley*-model should be left to one who rarely underestimated Scott's originality. His son-in-law and first biographer John Gibson Lockhart described *Goetz* as a

> broad, bold, free, and most picturesque delineation of real characters, manners, and events; the first-fruits, in a word, of that passionate admiration for Shakespeare, to which all that is excellent in the recent imaginative literature of Germany must be traced. With what delight must Scott have found the scope and manner of our Elizabethan drama revived on a foreign stage at the call of a real master! . . . with what double delight must he have seen Goethe seizing for the noblest purposes of art, men and modes of life, scenes, incidents, and transactions, all claiming near kindred with those that had from boyhood formed the chosen theme of his own sympathy and reflection! . . . Scott had before him a vivid image of the life of his own and the rival Border clans, familiarized to him by a hundred nameless minstrels. If it be doubtful whether, but for Percy's Reliques, he would ever have thought of editing their Ballads, I think it not less so, whether, but for the Iron-handed Goetz, it would ever have flashed upon his mind, that in the wild traditions which these recorded, he had been unconsciously assembling materials for more works of high art than the longest life could serve him to elaborate.[17]

But Scott's artistic life was prolonged in the lives of his great foreign disciples who were quick to discover in the histories of their own nations "men and modes of life, scenes, incidents, and transactions, all claiming near kindred with those" which Goethe and Scott had portrayed.

5. Historical romance as epic

Closely connected though *Goetz* and the Scottish Waverley novels certainly were, Scott did not make the transition directly or at once. For between translating Goethe's historical drama and completing the first historical romance, Scott made his literary reputation with the *Border Minstrelsy* collection and a series of popular heroic narrative poems – notably *The Lay of the Last Minstrel* (1805), *Marmion* (1808), and *The Lady of the Lake* (1810) – based on "the wild traditions" of the Scottish clans. Later in life he drew on the same traditions to compose the historical drama *Halidon Hill* (1822), a "play" which like many others of the period was never meant to be performed on the stage and actually belongs more to the narrative than the dramatic mode. This generic ambiguity was characteristic of an age which loved and emulated Shakespeare above all other writers but read his plays a hundred times more often than it saw them performed. In the circumstances, how regard the tragedies and especially the Roman and English history plays except as heroic poems – differing in certain formal respects from the oral epics of ancient nations and from literary epics modeled on them but expressing the same epic impulse to tell the tale of the tribe? That this impulse might also be expressed in and through prose fiction was already well known to readers of James Macpherson's "translations" of Ossian – a weird Scottish masterpiece which enjoyed a great international vogue during the late eighteenth and early nineteenth centuries. However, the Ossian prose-poems were not at all historical or novelistic and had but little of the "rich and mixed" character of historical romance, the fictional genre which was Scott's and the Romantic Revival's most original and enduring contribution to epic literature.

It comes late in the history of such contributions. For to revive "the" epic in a form adapted to changed social and literary conditions has been one of the principal endeavors of writers in the West for more than two thousand years. Because the writers who have tried to bring this most prestigious narrative form back to life have been as different as Tasso and Steinbeck, Milton and Prescott, Fielding and Brecht, "epic" has inevitably meant many and often contradictory things – none of them perhaps very close to what the *Iliad* and *Odyssey* meant to Homeric Greece. In the present discussion, fortunately, we need be concerned only with what "epic" has meant to the authors of historical romances. I believe it is possible to distinguish four pertinent meanings of epic: (1) an Aristotelian model of narrative form and mimetic fidelity to nature; (2) the proper narrative (but sometimes dramatic) vehicle for treating "heroic" matter; (3) the product and portrait of a "whole" community; (4) the most inclusive narrative form, capable of containing romance. A caution to bear in mind as we examine these meanings is that traditional concepts of "epic," "romance," and "novel" are so linked that, when the meaning of one of the terms changes, those of the others do too, if only very slightly.

Surely the best-known argument that the epic could be reincarnated in modern prose fiction is Henry Fielding's in the preface to *Joseph Andrews* (1742). In this early manifesto Fielding maintains that, although belonging to a "Species of Writing . . . hitherto unattempted in our Language," *Joseph Andrews* may be fairly called an epic because it has all of "the constituent parts of an Epic Poem" enumerated by Aristotle except meter.[18] He calls his experimental fiction a "comic Epic-Poem in

Prose" to distinguish it from the "serious" or "grave Romance," a narrative kind which (like tragedy) deals with "solemn" actions and "high" personages. Nothing in Fielding's basic case precludes the possibility that a modern "grave Romance" might also qualify as an "Epic-Poem in Prose." However, his purpose is to contend for the dignity and respectability of *Joseph Andrews* rather than to make a disinterested contribution to critical theory; and so, as we have seen, he follows the polemical example of the Renaissance Humanists by dissociating his own "epic" fiction as completely as possible from the (allegedly) shapeless and improbable "voluminous Works commonly called *Romances*" (p. 251).

Fielding's dissociation helped to fix the novel/romance dichotomy as an enduring feature of subsequent critical discourse. However, in attempting to distinguish epic from non-epic by its formal qualities rather than by its matter, and in contending also that its matter could be comic as well as heroic, Fielding was swimming against the current of contemporary opinion. To readers of his own and the following century, his appeals to Aristotelian canons may have seemed somewhat pedantic and beside the point. Most of them were probably grateful for Lord Kames's assurance, in *Elements of Criticism* (1762), that it was "useless labor . . . to distinguish an epic poem by some peculiar mark."[19] In practice, he argued,

> Literary compositions run into each other, precisely like colors: in their strong tints they are easily distinguished; but are susceptible of so much variety, and of so many different forms, that we never can say where one species ends and another begins. As to the general taste, there is little reason to doubt, that a work where heroic actions are related in an elevated style, will, without farther requisite, be deemed an epic poem.   (p. 414)

Like Fielding's two decades earlier, Kames's construction of "epic" was liberal and inclusive on some counts, strict and exclusive on others. By rejecting the premise that an epic must be cast in verse, both Fielding and Kames opened up the field of contenders. But by adhering to Aristotelian (and post-Lockean) canons of formal unity and (empirically verifiable) fidelity to nature, Fielding deliberately shut the gate on most of the works which could meet Kames's criteria for entry. In turn, Kames's rules-of-thumb made a "comic Epic-Poem" a contradiction in terms, and it seems evident that he would have appealed to the authority of contemporary "general taste" and usage in answer to Fielding's appeal to ancient authority. Not that Kames was less old-fashioned than Fielding in all respects; for his definition of epic as "heroic actions . . . related in an elevated style" was no less a legacy of Renaissance Humanism than Fielding's invocation of Homeric precedent. But the blurring of generic boundaries in *Elements of Criticism* was a distinctly modern development

– and one which historical romancers, most of them, were bound to welcome.

Contrary to what we might expect, however, Scott himself never took advantage of this liberalization to claim epic status for the Waverley novels, singly or collectively. It is hard to say whether this seeming modesty was due more to conservatism in generic theory or – what was closely related – a guilty sense that his own historical romances were the hasty, imperfect productions of a commercial age and hence unworthy of the name of epic. At all events, he theorized in his essay on romance that the earliest romances supplied the crude heroic matter which epic poets later reformed in shapely and polished works of art. In effect, he accepted Kames's criteria for the matter (heroic) and tone and style (elevated) of epic, but he also accepted Fielding's contention that epic and romance differed from each other, radically, in form. I do not recall that Scott ever argues that verse is a necessary constituent of epic, but I suspect he would have felt that heroic narratives like his own *Lay of the Last Minstrel* or Southey's *Roderick the Last of the Goths* which observed the traditional measure and ceremony of verse were closer in form and spirit to Homeric or Virgilian epic than any work of novelistic prose fiction could possibly be.

Scott's American followers disagreed with him but had no wish to level the traditional generic hierarchy; rather, they aimed to preserve it while pressing the claims of their own popular fictions to incarnate epic form in the new age and new world of democracy. These are the claims implicit in a title like *The Last of the Mohicans* – a title certain to have had resonances for contemporaries of Scott, Southey, and Cooper which it can have for few twentieth-century readers. Campaigning for themselves, American historical romancers were bold to do for Scott what he would not do for himself: recognize him as the founder of a new "heroic school" of novelistic fiction. Placing the Waverley novels in relation to the eighteenth-century sentimental novel and the works of another, more realistic "school" of fictionalists, Cooper explains that

> Miss Edgeworth alone had supplanted the sentimentalists, before Scott was known, even as a poet. This whole school, which includes Mrs. Opie, Mrs. More, Miss Austin [*sic*], and Mrs. Brunton . . . was quite as free from sentimentalism as Scott, and, because less heroic, perhaps more true to every-day nature. Still he was vastly their superior, for he raised the novel, as near as might be, to the dignity of epic.[20]

The qualification "as near as might be" registers some uneasiness about the historical romance's pretensions to so much dignity, but there were other apologies for the new epic form which manifested a brisk confidence in the product.

Probably the most familiar of these to students of American fiction is

William Gilmore Simms's frequently cited "Advertisement" to *The Yemassee* (1835), which although insignificant as literary criticism has considerable importance as a straw in the wind:

> The modern Romance is the substitute which the people of the present day offer for the ancient epic. The form is changed; the matter is very much the same; at all events, it differs much more seriously from the English novel than it does from the epic and the drama, because the difference is one of material, even more than of fabrication. The reader who, reading *Ivanhoe*, keeps Richardson and Fielding beside him, will be at fault in every step of his progress . . . The Romance is of loftier origin than the Novel. It approximates the poem. It may be described as an amalgam of the two. It is only with those who are apt to insist upon poetry as verse, and to confound rhyme with poetry, that the resemblance is unapparent. The standards of the Romance . . . are very much those of the epic. It invests individuals with an absorbing interest – it hurries them rapidly through crowding and exacting events, in a narrow space of time – it requires the same unities of plan, of purpose, and harmony of parts, and it seeks for its adventures among the wild and wonderful.[21]

Simms contrives to answer all of the traditional objections to the form and matter of romance. In its "modern" avatar he discovers the formal excellences that Fielding and Scott claimed for epic. And while he distinguishes its matter – "the wild and wonderful" – from that of the English novel, and insists on the romancer's right to deal with "the possible" rather than with "what is known, or even what is probable," he affirms that the leading events of his *historical* romance are "strictly true to the region of country in which the scene is laid" (p. 6). Anticipating the criticism that his portraits of "the Indians, in their undegraded condition" are idealized, he protests that they are based on numerous authorities who wrote "from their own experience."

A less explicit but ultimately more cogent claim for historical romance's kinship with epic is Cooper's last word on the subject, his 1850 preface to the entire Leatherstocking sequence:

> It is the privilege of all writers of fiction, more particularly when their works aspire to the elevation of romances, to present the *beau-ideal* of their characters to the reader. This it is which constitutes poetry, and to suppose that the red man is to be represented only in the squalid misery or in the degraded moral state that certainly more or less belongs to his condition, is, we apprehend, taking a very narrow view of an author's privileges. Such criticism would have deprived the world of even Homer.[22]

Although Simms and other apologists for modern fiction may ridicule those who "insist upon poetry as verse, and . . . confound rhyme with poetry," they are not so prompt to say what actually "constitutes poetry." Always ready to stick his neck out, Cooper asserts that the epic and the romance are both poems, like each other and unlike the novel, because they "present the *beau-ideal* of their characters." Elsewhere in the preface, like Simms, he claims eye-witness authority of his portraits of Indians in their "undegraded condition"; but his reference to Homer points to far other sources for his "*beau-ideal*" of the red men. As Joel Porte has shown, the action in the second half of *The Last of the Mohicans* imitates – it is a tissue of allusions to – the action of the *Iliad*.[23] And not only the *Iliad*; for in the conflict between Uncas and Magua, Cooper also means us to discover epic parallels with the conflicts between David and Goliath and between Milton's Christ and Satan. Far removed from the historical world imaged in the first half of the romance, where the Indians are shown in a "degraded moral state" (drunkenness, the Fort Henry massacre), in the wilderness world of the second half, where "the *beau-ideal* of their characters" can be freely realized, Cooper's grave chiefs deliver speeches which echo Miltonic or Ossianic imagery and cadence, aspiring even to the form of epic verse.

From Virgil onwards literary epic has ritually asserted its kinship with the oral epics of Homer by means of imitations or parallels meant to recall the earlier works as summits of poetic achievement and to invoke a timeless heroic standard. So when Cooper reincarnates the heroes of Homer, Milton, and the Bible in the New York wilderness, when Hawthorne recalls the Gray Champion to life, or when Edith Wharton makes us see Helen of Troy in Ellen Olenska, they are doing what the authors of literary epic have always done. In their epic passages they may even appear so "poetic," so "literary" and, to boot, so ambitious in their choice of literary company as to lend some credibility to the novel/ romance opposition. For it is true that the pioneers of English novelistic fiction, concerned to render quotidian reality convincingly by means of what Ian Watt calls "formal realism," generally preferred to appropriate familiar or even "low" genres – letters, journals, rogue autobiographies – rather than conceive of their works as giving the ancient "high" literary forms a new lease on life. However, the novel quickly proved capable of assimilating high as well as low and in Fielding found a theorist and practitioner who in some important respects was nigher in spirit to Cervantes and Scott than to Defoe and Richardson. Indeed, because of its large inclusiveness and consciousness of (mock-) epic parallels, *Tom Jones* stands in nearly as close relation to the historical romance as to the bourgeois novel. Close but not kissing-close: the historical romance is an "Epic-Poem in Prose" so much concerned, at bottom, with the waning of the worlds which created traditional epic and romance that it could scarcely be labeled "Comic."

The classic scholarly account of those worlds and their characteristic narrative forms is W. P. Ker's *Epic and Romance*, a work which still holds its place as a basic study even though it first appeared in 1896. Ker contends that the medieval oral epic, like Homeric epic, was the product of a heroic society in which class divisions were not emphatically drawn; as such it sought to give a portrait of that society in its totality – to incorporate the whole business of life rather than a part. Although concerned but little with historical accuracy and not at all with imperial grandeur, the oral epic poet was expected to work within the bounds of national tradition, "to tell the stories of the great men of his own race."[24] By contrast, chivalric romance was an aristocratic ideal or fantasy picture of the refinement and marvellous adventures of but one social class. Therefore epic was much the more inclusive form: it could contain romance, but romance could not contain epic. Concluding his study, Ker ventures that "Chaucer's *Troilus and Criseyde* is the poem in which medieval romance passes out of itself into the form of the modern novel. What Cervantes and what Fielding did was done first by Chaucer" (p. 367). And the novel has "the substance of Epic" rather than the "phantasm" of its form.

Of course many great novels do not aspire to epic inclusiveness, but Ker's conception of the novel as an epic form able to incorporate a wide range of social and literary forms is highly pertinent to the present study. For Scott as for Ker, Fielding was the obvious exemplar: at least as compared with Richardson's or Austen's, his novels are positively Odyssean in their survey of many cities and many men's manners. No wonder that Byron eulogized "Fielding, the *prose* Homer of human nature" and that Scott praised Fielding's unparalleled "familiarity with the English character, in every rank and aspect, which made his name immortal as a painter of national manners."[25] But if panoramic painting of national manners is a defining characteristic of the epic novelist, Scott's claims are quite as strong as Fielding's. What he said about Fielding's familiarity with English character he said elsewhere, with equal justice, about his own familiarity with Scottish character.[26] With greater justice, indeed, since Scott knew and portrayed national manners as these had developed over a period of centuries; he showed how his countrymen were joined in community with each other not just across classes but also across the centuries.

Scott traces the origins of romance, and thus of epic (which in his scheme owes its heroic "matter" to romance), to an appreciation – conscious or unconscious – of the immense importance of the past to the present. In his conjectural account of those origins, he seems to be looking back to Exodus and the *Aeneid* and forward to the great regional–historical romances of America:

> The father of an isolated family, destined one day to rise into a tribe, and in farther progress of time to expand into a nation, may, indeed, narrate to his descendents the circumstances which detached him from the society of his

brethren, and drove him to form a solitary settlement in the wilderness, with no other deviation from truth, on the part of the narrator, than arises from the infidelity of memory, or the exaggerations of vanity. But when the tale of the patriarch is related by his children, and again by his descendants of the third and fourth generation, the facts it contains are apt to assume a very different aspect. The vanity of the tribe augments the simple annals from one cause – the love of the marvellous, so natural to the human mind, contributes its means of sophistication from another – while, sometimes, from a third cause, the king and the priest find their interest in casting a holy and sacred gloom and mystery over the early period in which their power arose.[27]

From *The Pioneers* through *Absalom, Absalom!* the American historical romance has often been a "tale of the patriarch" which recounts "the circumstances which detached him from the society of his brethren, and drove him to form a solitary settlement in the wilderness" and also, not infrequently, the circumstances which occasioned his decline and fall. This in general outline is the story Cooper tells in *The Wept of Wish-ton-Wish* – a historical romance which has the social and literary-generic inclusiveness of epic and a narrative design both complex and powerful. On all of the counts enumerated here, then, it qualifies as an epic fiction.

Of course the same cannot be said of all the novels which may be profitably regarded as historical romances. Some are so short on heroic matter that it seems perverse to call them "epic." What have the New York high-society intrigues and domestic power-struggles of *The Age of Innocence* in common with the mighty revolutionary and imperialistic conflicts waged in *Absalom, Absalom!* or *Satanstoe*? So little that it seems best to reserve the label "epic" for works in which heroic matter abounds: while allowing that because the heroic note is not altogether silent in *The Age of Innocence* and because its current washes us now and again with "the tonic shock . . . of the far and strange," it is something besides a great historical novel of manners and morals. Take another problematic case: if any book is, *The Scarlet Letter* is *the* American historical romance; and yet, to judge by most critical commentaries, it is so lacking in warwhoops and swordplay and so preoccupied with essentially personal and private concerns that it can have but little claim to epic status. But I will argue in chapter 5 that, after its own fashion and according to the standards of its time, *The Scarlet Letter* does deserve this status and that we do not do it justice unless we recognize its epic dimension.

6. *The Wept of Wish-ton-Wish*

Scott had many disciples in early nineteenth-century America besides Cooper, but only a couple, the southerners William Gilmore Simms

(1806–70) and John Pendleton Kennedy (1795–1870), wrote fiction of enduring literary interest. And even their finest works, respectively *The Yemassee* and *Horse-Shoe Robinson* (both 1835), fell short of the best novels that Cooper had written a decade or more previously. Still, some notice should be taken of the ways that his contemporaries followed or departed from his example in their adaptations of the *Waverley*-model to American conditions – if only because they discovered historical incidents or characters which he and later Hawthorne were able to develop in subsequent works. And, as may be gathered from my earlier citations, Simms in particular was an important representative figure: although not a powerful thinker and only occasionally a distinguished fictionalist, he was a serious, wide-ranging, and immensely productive man of letters of more than merely regional stature.[28]

If the historical romance aspires in one direction towards the universality of Enlightenment philosophical abstraction, in the other it is powerfully drawn to the concreteness and particularity of literary regionalism. Inspired by Scott's affectionate, indeed patriotic, evocations of the scenes and manners of old Scotland, American historical romancers turned to the histories of their own states and regions for the matter of their fictions. Nor did they lack encouragement. The first copies of *Waverley* had barely landed on Boston Wharf before reviewers and orators began instructing ladies and gentlemen with literary ambitions to pore over the colonial chronicles of their states or over such intermediary sources as Trumbull's *History of Connecticut*.[29] Whether Carolinians or New Englanders, Virginians or New Yorkers, they were especially attracted by two periods or phases of their respective state or regional histories: the Revolutionary War era and the times of frontier hardship, beginning with the earliest settlements by the patriarchs of the tribe.[30] These two great "matters" of the early American historical romance transcend but do not obliterate regional differences. As we have already seen, they correspond to the two principal types of conflict between the forces of progress and reaction which are present in *Waverley* – colonial conquest and civil war. (For later writers, the Civil War joined and surpassed the Revolution as the supreme American instance of fratricidal conflict.) Simms, for example, brought out his first Revolutionary War romance, *The Partisan*, the same year as his more famous frontier romance *The Yemassee*. Not surprisingly, his doomed Carolinian Tories and Yemassee Indians bear a very recognizable family likeness to Scott's counterrevolutionary Jacobites and Highlanders. No doubt they would have done so even if Cooper had never written *The Spy* or the early Leatherstocking tales.

Indeed, C. Hugh Holman argues persuasively that the "southern Cooper" actually turned not to Cooper but directly to Scott for his model of how to relate history to romance in a work of historical fiction.[31] In *most* of his romances, Cooper solved this problem by virtually dispensing with the kind of famous historical personages and events that figure so prominently in *most* of the Waverley novels. As a result, Cooper's casts of characters could be smaller, his plots simpler, and his natural settings could bulk larger than was usual in Scott's romances. For Simms, the potential gains of concentration which Cooper's practice offered did not outweigh the losses of panoramic effects and "real" historical interest; and so he crowded the plots of his romances with the notable figures and incidents that also appeared in his *History of South Carolina*. Too crowded, it might seem, for the purposes of fiction; but I believe that the history in Simms's romances fails to interest as much as it might principally because of his failings as a literary artist, and further that the one method of representing history in historical romances is neither better nor more truly historical than the other. Thus *Satanstoe* incorporates much documentable social, political, and military history, and it is one of the greatest American historical romances. But I would hesitate to claim that its depiction of history – if by "history" we mean historical process and the ways people thought, felt, and behaved in a particular historical context – is more true, vivid, or profound than the depictions of history in *The Bride of Lammermoor* and *The Wept of Wishton-Wish*, books in which recorded historical persons and happenings count for little.

New England had a history so rich in incident and issue, and had played so large a part in the formation of American national institutions and character, that it attracted the attentions even of romancers who were not natives of the region. Despite a New Yorker's prejudices against Yankees, Cooper himself wrote both the Connecticut frontier romance I am about to discuss and also a Revolutionary War romance, *Lionel Lincoln, or the Leaguer of Boston* (1825), notable for its superb descriptions of the Battles of Lexington and Bunker Hill and (until the disastrous Gothic finale) a representation of conflicting revolutionary loyalties and interests quite worthy of Scott. In *The Puritan and His Daughter* (1849) Cooper's fellow New Yorker James Kirke Paulding (1778–1860) followed him to the Connecticut frontier but went one better by adding the perils of a witchcraft trial to those of King Philip's War. But Paulding was striking out from Cooper merely in order to join a long train of historical romancers and dramatists from Longfellow's friend John Neal (1793–1876) to Arthur Miller who have found the New England witch trials fascinating as a problem in community psychology and perennially useful as a warning to their own times. At first sight the subject might seem a splendid one for historical romance since nothing could be easier than to present the victims as apostles of progress and their judges as reactionary powers of darkness. That is what, among others, John W. DeForest did in *Witching Times* (1856–7). However, as "Young Goodman Brown" reveals, a truly close student of the Salem Delusion would appreciate that this polarization misrepresents the beliefs, motives, and behavior of both parties in the trials. This may be *one* reason why Hawthorne made the persecuted heroine of his one full-length historical romance an adultress rather than a woman accused of witchcraft. The witchcraft trials were not well-suited to form the center of interest of a species of fiction concerned with a conflict between cultural *alternatives*. For such fiction New England provided abundant matter in a host of stories about the frontier and the Revolutionary War, but that matter was not essentially different from what could be found in the histories of other regions.

The Wept of Wish-ton-Wish comes early in the American historical romance tradition, but by the time he began writing it Cooper had already invented the frontier romance in *The Pioneers* (1823) and extended the genre in *The Last of the Mohicans* (1826) and *The Prairie* (1827). Already, too, other historical romancers had heeded the reviewers' exhortations to base their fictions on the "wild traditions" recorded in the chronicles of the seventeenth-century Puritans. In fact, they were all forestalled in this enterprise by Washington Irving, a New Yorker like Cooper and Paulding, whose sketches "Traits of Indian Character" and "Philip of Pokanoket" (1814) combined Ossianic melancholy with careful research into the motives and events of King Philip's War. As Irving perceived, the Wampanoag chief Metacom (*alias* Philip) and his Narragansett ally Conanchet were the very stuff out of which heroic narrative might be made: "Worthy of an age of poetry, and fit subjects for local story and romantic fiction, they have left scarcely any authentic traces on the page of history, but stalk, like gigantic shadows in the dim twilight of tradition."[32]

The success of *The Sketch Book* (1820), in which Irving republished his two Indian sketches, ensured the popularity and even international vogue of King Philip's War as a subject for historical literature. In 1820 Robert Southey began (but never finished) a narrative poem called *Oliver Newman* that was concerned with the war. And, much more important for the history of American literature, Scott included in *Peveril of the Peak* (1822) an episode in which Metacom's attack on a frontier village was thwarted by a sudden and mysterious visitant, actually one of the Puritan regicides then in hiding in New England. The episode was soon transferred, with sentimental additions, to the Philadelphia stage in James Nelson Barker's *Superstition* (1824), and eventually incorporated in *The Wept of Wish-ton-Wish*. Years later Hawthorne adapted it to form the central event of "The Gray Champion" (1835).

That Cooper knew Scott's *Peveril* and Irving's superb cameos is certain, and it is likely that he was familiar with Barker's play and at least one other work that seems to "anticipate" *The Wept of Wish-ton-Wish*: Lydia Maria Child's *Hobomok* (1824), a tale of seventeenth-century New England in which frontier hardship and interracial marriage and adoption are combined in a manner that is at once inept and highly suggestive. What do these debts, if such they be, amount to? The problem of Cooper's borrowings from Irving is a complicated one to which I shall return, but so far as the others are concerned a simple, traditional distinction needs to be made here. Every writer borrows details of plot and characterization as well as the favorite *topoi* and "matter" of the period from his contemporaries and recent predecessors. Even to a writer of great originality such borrowings are important, indeed indispensable; and yet, since they involve parts or aspects which must be recombined and reanimated in a new whole, they are individually replaceable by others of the same sort. However, the informing, organizing conception that Cooper and his contemporaries found in the *Waverley*-model was not of the sort that could be easily replaced: without it he would have been a very different writer and possibly (to judge from his ventures outside historical romance) a fairly minor one. To compare *The Wept of Wish-ton-Wish* with *Superstition*, *Hobomok*, or even a relatively inferior Scott novel like *Peveril* is to perceive that the "making" or remaking is nearly everything in literary art. To compare Cooper's novel with *Goetz* or a major Scott novel like *Old Mortality* is to understand that the remaking itself would not have been possible without the example and contagious power of masterwork within a coherent generic tradition.

Until fairly recently, commentaries on *The Wept of Wish-ton-Wish* have focussed on it less as a work of art than as a biographical document revealing "attitudes" to Puritanism and miscegenation. The emphasis has not been on Cooper's fictional design and intended meaning but on his unconscious or half-conscious prejudices. Consequently the latter have been misrepresented, and there is more than a little uncertainty as to what the book is really about. In a truly seminal study of the novel, John McWilliams has tried to clear up this uncertainty.[33] He insists that the central theme of this "frontier Indian romance" (as also of the last four Leatherstocking novels) is "not interracial warfare, nor racial contrast, but the difficulties white frontiersmen face in dispensing justice in the American wilderness" (p. 245). On this showing, neither miscegenation nor the heroism and suffering of the Indians is Cooper's principal concern, and neither is mentioned in McWilliams's introductory outline of the novel:

> Divided chronologically into two sections of equal length, the novel describes the life of a single settlement in the 1660s, and then again in 1676. Each of the two sections traces the rise and fall of the idyllic community established by

Mark Heathcote. In 1676 as in the 1660s, a fledgling community of pastoral civilization . . . is established. In both sections a fugitive regicide of the English Civil War, named Submission, arrives to warn and defend the dwellers of the valley against an attack of the Narragansetts. The civil authorities, officers of the crown or of the Connecticut Colony, appear in both sections to demand civil obligations of the Heathcote family, obligations which conflict with the biblical moral laws that govern their settlement. In the 1660s and again in 1676 the settlement is nearly destroyed by Indian attacks, but the Heathcote leaders survive to rebuild. In each section, a crucial decision between Christian forgiveness and heathen revenge is demanded of the head of the Heathcote family.   (pp. 247–8)

As McWilliams shows, in the first half of the novel Mark Heathcote exerts his patriarchal authority to enforce his view that the red men should be saved in the name of Christ rather than killed in the name of revenge. In the second half, Mark's son Content yields on two occasions to the commands or counsels of others to defend the colony by means of morally questionable – and in practice brutally murderous – pre-emptive strikes. Thus the contrast between the two generations of New England frontiersmen obliges us to read *The Wept of Wish-ton-Wish* as the story of "the fall of a humane patriarchy, with theocratic overtones, to a secular government in which power is subdivided among the vengeful" (p. 257).

The structural pattern of doubling, parallel, and contrast that McWilliams discovers in the novel does certainly control and signpost its meaning. Yet the binary pattern he describes is not quite the one that we might expect to find in a historical romance, since it does not include the most obvious primitive/civilized polarities ("natural"/"artificial" or "wildness"/"boundaries"). However, the more closely we compare the two settlements and two generations of settlers, the more of Young's, Goethe's, and Scott's favorite contrasts we discern. Mark Heathcote chooses liberty of conscience at the certain risk of privation and physical danger; his son Content, although basically a good and pious man, violates conscience to secure the order of civilization. At once father, military commander, and priest to his tiny hamlet, the patriarchal Mark is in touch with the central mysteries of his religion and often lifts his voice in spontaneous prayer: when he does so in chapter xvi, with his bereaved family and ruined homestead around him, he is one of the most sublime figures in all of Cooper's fiction. By this I mean not just that the scene is extremely powerful and moving but that Cooper's description of a great moral and spiritual victory in a setting of wildness and desolation fits the aesthetic category of the Sublime and was meant to do so. By contrast with his father, Content is devout but conformist, the first but not the leading citizen of a village which is ruled partly by the central administration in Hartford and partly by a local junta headed by the fanatical minister but including the conscientious though pedantic doctor and the intrepid, good-natured, but morally obtuse Indian-fighter Eben Dudley.

To call Mark Heathcote's original settlement "feudal" and its successor "bourgeois" would overemphasize conformity to the *Waverley*-model, and yet Cooper's descriptions of the two settlements do seem to invite comparison with the descriptions of feudal and bourgeois society in *Goetz* or perhaps *The Bride of Lammermoor*. The Enlightenment philosophical historians who shaped the social thought of Goethe, Scott, and Cooper believed that peoples with the same basic mode of subsistence were bound to have the same or at least very similar political institutions, military practices, and artistic forms. Thus the feudalistic Scottish highlander, described by Adam Smith as a "station-ary shepherd," had an underlying cultural kinship with the biblical Abraham. Mark Heathcote's kinship with the Old Testament partriarchs is one frequently claimed by Mark himself and given special emphasis by descriptions of the Heathcotes' flocks and herds. But although he had journeyed far to find his own Canaan in the North American wilderness, Mark is no wandering shepherd. The fortress he builds to protect his people and animals closely resembles that of a medieval castle and keep in its layout, while its site is very like that of the fortified abbey in *The Heidenmauer* – i.e., an "island-hill" rising abruptly in the middle of the river valley. And *The Heidenmauer* (1832), set in the same time and place as *Goetz*, is Cooper's study of the rise of Protestantism and the transition from feudal to modern social organization in Europe. He wrote it several years after *The Wept of Wish-ton-Wish*, and I know of no evidence that Cooper ever read Goethe's play. But the cluster of associations discussed here would have been available to Cooper in a variety of sources, including the historical romances of Scott.

In the panorama of the valley that opens the second half of the novel, the site once of Mark's blockhouse has become an apple orchard, and the Heathcotes' simple but extensive new residence stands below it. But the center of population has now shifted a half mile downstream to a small village, of which the most prominent buildings are the mill, the inn, the church, and the nearby stockaded fortress where, somewhat surpris-ingly, the minister has his home. Anybody familiar with the tableaux of the Waverley novels, which Scott modeled after the "packed" scenes in historical paintings, will recognize that Cooper too not only describes but invests pictorial details with emblematic meaning. Here the details point to important social changes in the community. Set apart by inherited wealth and prestige, the Heathcotes are also remote from the real base of economic and political power. The economy of this prosperous agrarian community is still too primitive to support much of a middle class, but the functions of the principal buildings in or near the village indicate the beginnings of regular commerce with the outside world as well as of the divisions of labor and authority associated with bourgeois society. In Cooper's colonial New England version of this historical transition, a heroic age of apostolic faith gives way to a secular age of material well-being and clerical despotism. Where once the old soldier-mystic practiced Christian forgiveness and prayed for the salvation of the red men, now the priest within the citadel exercises his learning and eloquence to work their destruction.

Thus far a reading of *The Wept of Wish-ton-Wish* that takes its bearings from the *Waverley*-model is in close agreement with the interpretation proposed by John McWilliams. Many of the by-now familiar features of that model reappear as integral parts of the binary pattern which he has shown to govern the meaning of the novel. However, as noted earlier, many features that we might expect to find in a historical romance are not mentioned by him, and we are bound to ask why. Apparently seeking to correct the over-emphasis on miscegenation of which Leslie Fiedler and others have been guilty,[34] McWilliams attends almost exclusively to Cooper's preoccupation with the moral contrast between the two generations of Puritan frontiersmen and the difficulties they encounter in "dispensing justice in the American wilderness." That preoccupation is central, to be sure, and his reading shows that *The Wept of Wish-ton-Wish* may be usefully approached as a family chronicle novel. But Cooper had other and complementary concerns which, generically speaking, belong especially to the historical romance, and these are left out of McWilliams's account of the novel. That their exclusion leads to yet another (though less serious) over-emphasis is suggested by his gloss on the title: "in four words, Cooper has suggested both the hopes of settlement and the eventual tragedy wrought by man's betrayal of a moral law" (p. 258). True enough, as a very generalized inference of the "larger" meaning of the title. But its specific and primary reference is to the words carved, in place of a name, on the grave of Mark Heathcote's granddaughter. The story of her miscegenetic alliance with the Narragansett chief Conanchet, the only one of its kind in Cooper's many novels, is an integral part of the action of the second half of the book as well as fulfillment of much that has been set in motion in the first half.

Taken captive as an orphaned youth, Conanchet is treated with kindness and trust by the Heathcotes and their secret guest, the regicide known only as "Submission." (The patriarchal Heathcote family is the very type of the "extended" family, taking not merely the Indian boy but several other orphans to its bosom.) Mark Heathcote's hope is that

Conanchet might be converted and made an instrument for saving his tribe, but the boy remains a prisoner only long enough to develop a deep affection for the Heathcote family and lose his belief in the rightness of racial revenge. In every other respect his loyalty to the Indian people and their culture is unshaken. Yet he appears a very compromised and wavering figure to his racist ally Metacom, and in the end he is captured by his worst enemies, the white colonists' Mohican auxilliaries, in an attempt to protect Submission from them.

Ruth Heathcote, or Narra-mattah as she is called by her adoptive tribe, is taken captive during the first Indian attack on Wish-ton-Wish and eventually marries Conanchet. Unlike his captivity, however, hers occurs at a very early age, and she grows up wholly converted (or so it appears) to "red" ways of feeling and perceiving. This ironic reversal – that Ruth, not Conanchet, becomes the "convert" – is given a further turn in the closing scenes of the novel. After experiencing a series of dislocating shocks that culminate in Conanchet's death, she suffers a momentary reversion to her long-buried white childhood and all of its terrors of the dark forest. Her reaction to her dead husband's countenance – "an evil spirit besets me" – recalls the "secret horror" of him that she felt as a child when her mother entrusted her to his protection:

> Flaxen locks, that half covered a forehead and face across which ran the most delicate tracery of veins, added lustre to a skin as spotlessly fair as if the warm breezes of that latitude had never fanned the countenance of the girl. Through this maze of ringlets, the child turned her full, clear, blue eyes, bending her looks, in wonder and in fear, on the dark visage of the captive Indian youth, who at that moment was to her a subject of secret horror.
>
> (p. 174)

Each an orphan, captive, and partial convert, fair Ruth-Narra-mattah and dark Conanchet are as intriguingly like and unlike as any lovers in American fiction. Whatever they might be supposed to reveal about his "secret horror" of miscegenation, Cooper's sensuous descriptions of the white woman and red man very deliberately draw attention to the extremes of unlikeness. These too find their place within a pattern of like and unlike in which love and fear are transformed into their opposites, and the "timid" Narra-mattah and "stern" Conanchet between them create a third, a child of both races who survives his parents and (so Cooper's dedication of the novel assures us) transfuses the Narragansett blood into the veins of future generations of "white" Americans. This dialectic extends well beyond the "love story" and includes several crucially important relationships in which the principals are of the same sex but of different ages, colors, and cultures.

For such relationships there are many precedents in the Waverley tradition. In *Waverley* and *Rob Roy*, for instance, Scott's youthful male protagonists are English by nurture but "romantic" by disposition, and they are therefore able, as their hard-headed Hanoverian fathers are not, to respond sympathetically to the moral and aesthetic excellences of the Scottish Jacobites. Edward Waverley and Frank Osbaldistone not only choose their wives from among the Jacobite families of the North but also find surrogate fathers in the Jacobitical Baron Bradwardine and Rob Roy McGregor. The surrogate-father *topos* is even more explicit in *The Captain's Daughter*, where Pushkin has young Pyotr dream that the Cossack Pugachov (later the pretender-Tsar Peter III, the "little father" of the Russian people) is found in his father's bed and demands the right to bestow a paternal blessing. Indeed, either because the hero is actually an ophan or because he is removed from his family sphere, adoptive relationships across cultures are nearly as characteristic of the historical romance as protagonists who waver between the rival claims of the cultures.

In American romances, where crossing from one culture to another frequently means crossing racial lines as well, such relationships are especially prominent and charged with emotion: for they are sometimes obliged to do double duty as substitutes for both blood relationships, fraternal as well as filial/paternal, and the heterosexual relationships across cultures that are usual in European romances.

The most famous adoptive relationship in Cooper's *oeuvre* is of course the fraternal friendship between Leatherstocking and the Mohican chief Chingachgook, but ones which cross generations as well as cultures are also common in his novels. As might be expected, they are important in *The Wept of Wish-ton-Wish*. McWilliams remarks that Mark Heathcote's true "spiritual son" is not Content but Conanchet. And if Mark has a second "son" in Conanchet, the latter finds a second white "father" in Mark's own worldly double, the soldier-regicide Submission. This relationship, like that between Conanchet and Ruth-Narra-mattah, brings like and unlike together in an extraordinary and perilous union. Red and white, young and old, heathen and Christian, the two men are nonetheless alike in so far as they are or have been warriors and exiles from their respective peoples and ways of life. For Conanchet the recognition of relation occurs when he discovers that Submission is obliged to live in hiding because "His hand took the scalp of the Great Sagamore of his people!" (p. 431). For Submission, the full recognition occurs when Conanchet's refusal to abandon him causes him to amend his earlier "My mind is ever with my people" (p. 396) to "I can almost say that my heart is Indian" (p. 437). The second statement transforms rather than contradicts the meaning of the first one, and this transformation is certainly one of the important moral events of *The Wept of Wish-ton-Wish*.

A more subtle instance of Cooper's moral dialectic, also involving Conanchet and Submission, occurs somewhat earlier in the novel in the antithetical descriptions of the two men's responses to exile. Cooper shows what, for each, "home" really means by "placing" them in relation to a landscape. As a captive in the valley, Conanchet often passes hours "gazing wistfully at those endless forests in which he first drew breath, and which probably contained all that was most prized in the estimation of his simple judgment" (pp. 115–16). Submission, driven to those endless forests and specifically to a mountain hideout overlooking the valley, passes his hours gazing down at the very spot where Conanchet had stood during his captivity. Yet although his heart is in the valley with the white intruders who are turning the wilderness into a garden, the old solitary is himself part of the sublime mountain forest landscape:

> The solitude of the place, the air of universal quiet which reigned above, the boundless leafy carpet over which the eye looked from that elevated point, and the breathing stillness of the bosom of the woods, united to give grandeur to the scene. The figure of the tenant of the ravine was as immovable as any other object of the view. It seemed, in all but color and expression, of stone.
>
> (p. 388)

This may remind us of Wordsworth's aged solitary in "Resolution and Independence," but Cooper's purpose in identifying man and landscape is rather different than Wordsworth's. It is to associate the stern heroic spirit of the English Puritan with the aboriginal landscape and people of North America. We shall find that in many later historical romances, by authors as different from Cooper as Hawthorne and Cather, the authentic Americans – spiritual kinfolk of the red men and personified American nature – are the recent-comers from Europe or Africa, often outcasts from society, who at first glance appear most alien and opposed. The *least* American, in this sense, are commonly the native-born white Anglo-Saxon Protestant owners of the land: they are the spiritual descendants of Content Heathcote and the other unheroic citizens of small town Wish-ton-Wish.

In execution *The Wept of Wish-ton-Wish* is fairly seriously deficient on several counts. Although extended passages have been singled out as among Cooper's best,[35] the staple of the prose is as poor as that of, say, Dreiser. If this fault is attributable to the haste with which the novel was evidently written, so are the several narrative inconsistencies which appear in its closing chapters. These and some other, more debatable, weaknesses make it a lesser novel than it might have been, and I believe that the more carefully written *Satanstoe* is a greater work. However, as McWilliams says, *The Wept of Wish-ton-Wish* has "the ethical depth, though not the literary finish, of tragedy" (p. 258). Because of that depth and the great strength and complexity of its narrative design, the novel survives its defects as the first major American historical romance. In its areas of strength, it probably surpasses its European model and anticipates the more perfectly achieved masterpieces of Hawthorne and Melville.

3

Historical romance and the stadialist model of progress

1

John Stuart Mill, looking back from 1843 to the appearance of Vico's *Scienza Nuova* (1725), observed that thinkers preoccupied with the laws of social change have "universally adopted the idea of a trajectory or progress, in lieu of an orbit or cycle."[1] Mill was careful to stress that in his own usage "progress" meant not necessarily social improvement but only "a course not returning into itself." Yet his astronomical metaphor is soaring, expansive, as well as austerely scientific in its associations; and he professed his personal conviction that "the general tendency is, and will continue to be . . . one of improvement; a tendency towards a better and happier state." Whether our own or any readily foreseeable state vindicates Mill's liberal optimism is often questioned (particularly by those for whom social change has meant a diminution of wealth, status, and power), but it is at least certain that the *idea* of progress has itself exercised an enormous influence over men's lives. For two centuries it has served both as the most widely accepted model of historical development and as the justifying secular faith of the North Atlantic peoples. As for its practical importance for American social development, according to de Tocqueville, "It can hardly be believed how many facts naturally flow from the philosophical theory of the indefinite perfectibility of men or how strong an influence it exercises even on those who, living entirely for the purposes of action and not of thought, seem to conform their actions to it without knowing anything about it."[2] An idea so potent to shape the aspirations and behavior of their ancestors and contemporaries could not but affect the lives and works of historical romancers – notably Melville, Mark Twain, and Cather – who wrote during the decades when progressivism was most strenuous and self-confident. Moreover, these writers inherited a concern with the meaning and price of progress which was, as it were, built into the genre by its earliest masters.

A detailed examination of the historical and structural relationships between this immensely influential linear model of historical development and the polar *Waverley*-model would be out of place in the present study, but perhaps I may venture a few generalizations about them by way of introduction.

The structural differences between the two models derive from differences of purpose and method more than from differing assumptions about the course of human history. In their most speculative moments, Mill and other philosophers of progress scanned the action of history as from a great height, looking for "the general tendency" and finding that it was unilinear and good. On the nearer view of historical romance, concerned as it was with particular characters and events, that action assumed the more ambivalent and troubling shape of, in Coleridge's words, a polar "contest between the two great moving Principles of social Humanity – religious adherence to the Past and the Ancient, the Desire and the admiration of Permanence, on the one hand; and the Passion for increase of Knowledge, for Truth as the offspring of Reason, in short, the mighty instincts of Progression and Free-agency, on the other." In historical romances the forces of progress (the future) are often invested with the oppressive characteristics associated with an expanding imperial state, while the retreating forces of reaction (the past) exhibit, along with some negative traits, such positive "heroic" ones as "nature," "freedom," "loyalty," etc. Yet the authors of these romances all shared the social philosophers' belief in some form of beneficent progress or abandoned it only after the most shattering personal or public disasters. And more was involved than just a broad consensus about the course of human history: there is evidence that Goethe, Scott, and Cooper built on specific theories and insights of Enlightenment "philosophical" exponents of progress just as later writers in other genres have built on those of (for instance) Marx, Frazer, and William James.

Although an enthusiastic faith in progress led later adherents like George Bancroft to a fixation on the future and a tendency to consider the past worth studying only so far as it could be regarded as the prehistory of the present, the French and Scottish philosophical historians who were the first to formulate the modern theory of progress were also among the earliest to develop a truly historistic understanding of their own and previous societies. Several of them – Adam Ferguson, William Robertson, and Dugald Stewart – were Scott's personal friends and teachers, and there can be no doubt that through their writings and direct tuition they taught him not only to think historically but to take a much more catholic interest in the past than would have been prompted by the available literary models. Through these same writings (plus those of other leading Enlightenment philosophical historians, especially Adam Smith) and also through the Scottish graduates who disseminated their ideas in schools and universities around the world, the ground was prepared for an international appreciation and imitation of Scott's historicism.[3] Almost as important, the "stadialist" theory of progress which they developed made Homer, the Old Testament, Shakespeare, and various other exemplary works of heroic literature available in a new way and, in effect, underwrote the universality of the *Waverley*-model. So attractive and widely applicable was this theory that its influence extended beyond written texts to the visual arts and in particular, as we shall see, to Thomas Cole's great series of paintings *The Course of Empire*.

2. Stadialism and the Waverley-model

According to these philosophical historians, there were four main stages of society resulting from four basic modes of subsistence: (1) a "savage" stage based on hunting and fishing; (2) a "barbarian" stage based on herding; (3) a stage considered "civilized" and based mainly on agriculture; (4) a stage based on commerce and manufacturing which was sometimes considered over-civilized.[4] Each stage had its characteristic social institutions and cultural forms, and in theory each followed the next in orderly progression from savagery to civilization irrespective of factors like race, place, or time. In the words of Robertson, "the human mind, whenever it is placed in the same situation, will, in ages the most distant, and in countries the most remote, assume the same form, and be distinguished by the same manners."[5] Thus, as hunters and fishers, the savage Germanic tribesmen described by Tacitus had much more in common with eighteenth-century American Indians or even the heroes of the *Iliad* than they had with their modern descendants in central Europe.

Although the progression was reckoned to be from lower to higher stages of civilization, philosophical historians observed that each stage could boast not merely the special skills (often very remarkable ones) necessary to its way of life but also certain qualities of mind or character which were deficient or atrophied at other stages. Heroic fortitude in the face of adversity was a stock example of savage virtue; spontaneous metaphorical expressiveness was a Rousseauesque power which American Indians allegedly shared with other savages (such as the ancient Gaels in Macpherson's counterfeit epic of Ossian) and with pastoral barbarians like the Old Testament Hebrews and contemporary Highlanders. Sometimes mere projections of primitivistic nostalgia and sometimes momentary glimpses of the essential otherness of foreign or ancient cultures, these acknowledgements of superior qualities in the first and second stages were often joined with apprehensions concerning the fourth. For the histories of Rome and other great empires argued that civilization contained the principle of its own corruption and decline, while observation of contemporary factory practices suggested that they might be more brutalizing than the working conditions of any previous stage. It was for reasons such as these that the younger Jefferson hoped America would never develop manufactures but remain perpetually agricultural – civilized yet hardy and independent.

The four-stage theory helped to counter the racism and extreme Eurocentrism then current in most other accounts of human society; and in capable hands it could be a powerful and subtle instrument of social inquiry. Here, however, we are concerned not with its strengths and weaknesses as history or anthropology but with its attractions to writers of imaginative literature. Duncan Forbes and more recently Avrom Fleishman have shown that the thought of the Scottish philosophical historians and especially of Ferguson pervaded that of Scott and profoundly influenced his conception of historical process in the Waverley novels.[6] As Fleishman says, "the appropriate context for Scott is neither Marx nor Burke but Scottish intellectual life – including the speculative historians, who were more concerned to define the form of historical progress than to insist upon a set of ends already achieved or to come."[7] Unexceptional in itself, this comment appears somewhat parochial from the standpoint of the present discussion. For the intellectual life of late eighteenth-century Scotland, affected though it doubtless was by local concerns, is ultimately inseparable from the contemporary intellectual life of Europe and the Americas. The stadial theory in particular was as much a product of French as of Scottish speculation, and its impact on the German Enlightenment cannot be irrelevant to discussion of the translator of *Goetz von Berlichingen*. In all likelihood, Goethe himself had encountered the theory through Herder or the Homeric scholar Robert Wood, and one way to read *Goetz* is as a dramatization of the tumultuous transition from the second to the third and fourth stages. However this may be, the international diffusion of the theory is a fact to be taken into account when one tries to explain the international vogue of the *Waverley*-model. It is from this perspective rather than the more narrowly focussed one of Forbes and Fleishman (invaluable though this has been for the study of Scott) that I should like to comment on two ways that the pioneers of social science provided guidance and reinforcement to the pioneers of historical fiction.

Works like Ferguson's *An Essay on the History of Civil Society* (1767) were informed by an enthusiastic interest in the "primitive" literature then being collected and imitated by contemporary poets and made extensive use of it as evidence for their pictures of the first and second stages. They therefore helped to moderate the effects of contemporary reports on savage life – mostly unflattering and mostly from the New World – on which they also necessarily depended for evidence. Ferguson's savages were neither the monstrous Devil's agents of the New England captivity narratives nor the equally fantastic prelapsarian Noble Savages projected by Europeans safely remote from the imperial frontiers:

> The fev'rish air fann'd by a cooling breeze,
> The fruitful vales set round with shady trees;
> And guiltless men, who danc'd away their time,
> Fresh as their groves, and happy as their clime.[8]

The so-called "barbarian" peoples were still greater beneficiaries of the philosophical historians' practice of collating all the available evidence concerning the manners and mores of all those who had the same mode of subsistence. Among the literary sources drawn upon for information about the earlier stages of society were two reverenced by Europeans as the fountainheads of their own civilization – the Hebrew scriptures and the epics of Homer. Under the scrutiny of Ferguson and Robert Wood, it became clear that the Hebrews and the heroes of Homer subscribed to the "rude" values of the second stage and were therefore to be classified with the northern tribes that had conquered the Empire of the West and brought classical civilization to an end.

As a result of such comparisons, Homer and the Hebrew patriarchs probably gained in humanity what they lost in elevation while their fellow barbarians – Huns and Highlanders, Cossacks and American frontiersmen – gained in both ways. To be sure, even sympathetic scholars like Wood and Ferguson, who had first-hand knowledge of pastoral life, did not abandon what they considered the superior values of their own stage of society when they assessed those of Homer. Yet they did try to grasp his world as a cultural totality and to see it from within as he would have seen it. To make this imaginative effort was, in effect, to humanize the barbarian world and to create a basis for historical fiction which, if inauthentic in many particulars, was nonetheless realistic and historistic in tendency.

A point closely related yet leading in a quite different direction is that the stadial theory would also have reassured Scott that he saw truly when he beheld "a vivid image of his own and the rival border clans" in Goethe's portrait of German feudal society.[9] The cultural likenesses observed were not accidental, not of the surface only, but were rather the outward signs of an inner identity of mind and spirit. This inference held as good in Russia and the Americas as in Scotland: it legitimized literary imitation as this was practiced by the historical romancers. It gave the *Waverley*-model a status and function analogous to those of the scientific paradigms described by Thomas Kuhn.

Of course this way of viewing the world was quite *un*historical in tendency, but it was sanctioned by the philosophical historians' belief in a suprahistorical "human mind" that had assumed no more than four basic "forms" in historical actuality. As novelists and cultural nationalists, writers like Cooper and Pushkin had their own ways of apprehending and registering the relationship between the timeless and the temporal, the universal and the local. They were historical–fictional chroniclers in the first instance, and both by necessity and inclination were more concerned with the individual and the species (Leatherstocking, frontiersmen) than with the class (barbarian). Yet the stadialist theory was the common point of departure for the social-historical thinking of these writers, and its influence was manifested not only in the ways I have so far indicated but also in their perception of the consequences of interaction between peoples at different stages of social development.

3. Stadialism in America

Like other theories of historical development, such as the Providential or Darwinian, the stadial was open equally to self-serving or generous inferences, demagogic vulgarizations or sophisticated adaptations to new circumstances. Moreover, although it will be convenient to go on discussing this theory as though it existed in one or at most two versions, we should remember that there were many. French and French-inspired variants doubtless tended to be more speculative and melioristic than Scottish ones. But broad national likenesses of intellectual temper were not sufficient to bring Scots or Frenchmen or, for that matter, Americans together in national "schools." Mirabeau and Condorcet were both stadialists and both influenced Thomas Jefferson, but their beliefs about the general pattern and eventual consummation of stadial progress were by no means the same. Scottish interpreters of the theory were perhaps more like-minded, thanks especially to the personal impact of Adam Smith on a much smaller intellectual circle, but they had their important differences as well.

For political and other reasons the French influence seems to have predominated in the United States, but it enjoyed no monopoly. Like their European forebears, Americans were eclectic in their intellectual appropriations and used them with varying degrees of understanding, honesty, and originality. What they chiefly shared with each other was a need for a common model of historical development, on the one hand firm enough to impose intelligible order on the strange and chaotic variety of American social experience, yet on the other hand flexible enough to accommodate many and sometimes contradictory points of view. Such a model might not lend itself to seeing, thinking, and communicating with uniform clarity, but it made these activities possible.

Because the European originators of the four-stage theory leaned heavily on descriptions of the North American Indian for contemporary evidence about the savage state, their ideas were bound to make some impression on the early literature and social thought of the United States. In the event, as has been demonstrated by many studies and pre-eminently those of Charles and Mary Beard, Henry Nash Smith, and Roy Harvey Pearce,[10] they had a decisive influence on the white American people's sense of national identity and historic mission, and thus, for good and ill, on their actual behavior towards the red American people. The arguments of Smith and Pearce are especially pertinent here, because they expose the "Mr. Hyde" aspect of the stadial thesis and take Cooper's fiction as their prime literary example. I shall summarize several of their main points while drawing my own distinctions between prejudices or limitations intrinsic to the original theory and American constructions on it which would certainly have horrified Ferguson or Turgot.

The idea that each stage was characterized by the distinctive social institutions appropriate to its mode of subsistence encouraged, up to a point, a historistic and sympathetic attitude towards "savage" or "barbarian" peoples. But the abstractive, universalizing methodology of philosophical history was designed to yield a composite "character" free of local peculiarities; and it therefore worked against rather than for the further inquiry and differentiation necessary to a fully historic under-standing of, say, Dakota as distinct from Pequod culture. Moreover, while the Scots generally tried to make these "characters" conform to the available evidence, the method of the *philosophes* was, in Ferguson's words, "too frequently . . . to rest the whole on conjecture."[11] In America, where the French influence more commonly prevailed,[12] the tendency was to convert the philosophers' character-types into popular stereotypes with a pronounced racist coloration.

The stadial thesis itself was not racist – quite the contrary. Adam Ferguson provided a social-scientific rationale for viewing "savage" or "barbarian" peoples of *all* races as standing in a relationship to "civilized" peoples which was both filial and paternal. According to Ferguson, "The Romans might have found an image of their own ancestors, in the representations they have given of ours" (p. 80). And it is in "the present condition" of such peoples as the "Arab clans" and "American tribes"

> that we are to behold, as in a mirrour, the features of our progenitors; and from
> thence we are to draw our conclusions with respect to the influence of
> situations in which, we have reason to believe, our fathers were placed.   (p. 80)

From another and more condescending viewpoint, these clans and tribes
are to be regarded as like our own people in its infancy:

> If, in advanced years, we would form a just notion of our progress from the
> cradle, we must have recourse to the nursery, and from the example of those
> who are still in the period of life we mean to describe, take our representation of
> past manners that cannot, in any other way, be recalled.   (p. 81)

However unacceptable to the modern student of anthropology, this
characterization of hunter and pastoral folk as a compound of father and
child is "colorblind," compassionate, and informed with a deep feeling
of natural piety. For Ferguson, who shared Wordsworth's primitivistic
belief that man in the "infancy" of mankind was a natural poet, the child
was indeed the father of the man and to be venerated as such. Because
Ferguson, in common with all the major Scottish stadialists, was well
aware of the "poison" administered to the American Indians "by our
traders of Europe" (p. 80), he may also have drawn the familial analogy
for rhetorical purposes: to arouse his readers' indignation against the
inhumanity of contemporary colonizing practices.

Unfortunately, those who wished to rationalize those practices could
build on the stadialists' conclusion – or hierarchical premise – that the
stage of society at which the European peoples had arrived was "higher,"
more "refined," than that of any hunter society. For aside from marginal
figures like Daniel Boone or the fictional Leatherstocking, the only
people in North America who depended on hunting for their subsistence
were red; and so, by way of an inference contrary both to elementary
logic and to the environmentalist thinking of stadialists, red men must be
hunters, i.e., savages and inferior, by nature. (That most Indians were
agriculturalists as well as hunters could be conveniently overlooked.)
Further, the stadialists' salutary emphasis on the otherness of savage
habits of perceiving and valuing could be construed to mean that Indians
were irreclaimably attached to their ways, hence ineducable, and that
any "mixing" of whites and reds would be injurious to both peoples. The
net result of these and other glosses on the four-stage theory was what
Roy Harvey Pearce has called "Savagism" – the belief that the Indian was
"the remnant of a savage past away from which civilized men had
struggled to grow."[13] A temporary impediment to national self-
realization, he was already conveniently doomed by the sentence of
History.

Although a necessary and even heroic transitional figure in this
scheme, the "barbaric" white frontiersman was condemned by the same

logic. At once the bloody agent and predestined victim of American progress, he was surrounded in fictional treatments with an aura of lawlessness and often with a suspicion of downright criminality. So he was rarely a friend to civilization by his own design, and, as Professor Smith has shown, even at his most eligible he lacked the refinement necessary to climb to the next stage of society and marry one of Cooper's "flowers" of civilized leisure. The anxiety that he might try to do so is a recurrent one in American "western" fiction but not in European stadialist theory. Like their American followers, European exponents of the theory generally accepted marked social inequalities during the third and fourth stages as the price that had to be paid for the cultural advantages of a leisure class and of institutions such as the university and civil bureaucracy. But they had no occasion to confuse a gulf between social classes with a gulf between stages of society, because in Western Europe the stages were separated from each other by long periods of time or by formidable topographical barriers like the Scottish Highlands which offered few inducements to peoples in search of *liebensraum*. In nineteenth-century America, however, where the stages were often thought of as being distributed across American space like colors across a spectrum, undesirable interactions might easily occur. "Thus it is," wrote Cooper in *The Wept of Wish-ton-Wish*, a work strongly marked by stadialist thought, "that high civilization, a state of infant existence, and positive barbarity, are often brought so near each other within the borders of this Republic" (p. 243). And thus, too, that the virile but unlettered frontiersman – modern counterpart of the Hun or Goth – might sometimes fail to understand his "place" in either the stadial or social-class scheme of things.

The last point brings us to Thomas Jefferson's classic formulation of the stadial thesis as applied to American experience. The passage is long and frequently quoted, but it deserves our close attention:

> Let a philosophic observer commence a journey from the savages of the Rocky Mountains, eastwardly towards our seacoast. These he would observe in the earliest stage of association living under no law but that of nature, subsisting and covering themselves with the flesh and skins of wild beasts. He would next find those on our frontiers in the pastoral state, raising domestic animals to supply the defects of hunting. Then succeed our own semi-barbarous citizens, the pioneers of the advance of civilization, and so in his progress he would meet the gradual shades of improving man until he would reach his, as yet, most improved state in our seaport towns. This, in fact, is equivalent to a survey, in time, of the progress of man from the infancy of creation to the present day. I am eighty-one years of age, born where I now live, in the first range of mountains in the interior of our country. And I have observed this march of civilization advancing from the sea-coast, passing over us like a cloud of light, increasing our knowledge and improving our condition, insomuch as that we

are at this time more advanced in civilization here than the seaports were when I was a boy. And where this progress will stop no one can say. Barbarism has, in the meantime, been receding before the steady step of amelioration; and will in time, I trust, disappear from the earth.[14]

From the standpoint of the present discussion the most striking feature of this prospect-piece (written in 1824 but distinctly eighteenth-century in its social theory and literary convention) is the way the military metaphor "march of civilization advancing" is at first transfigured into a gentle and creative "cloud of light" that passes, obligingly, "over us" and is then reintroduced in a less threatening guise as "the steady step of amelioration" before which barbarism has been "receding." As is usual in such moments of vision, Jefferson's westward gaze is too rapt, too elevated, to take in the grim details of "progress" in its American version. Perhaps the cost is implicit in the evasive metaphors and the ambivalent tone of "will in time, I trust, disappear from the earth." Optimism or resignation? Prayer or Ossianic elegy? But the ambivalence so essential to the *Waverley*-model and so often present in the writings of the Scottish stadialists is merely vestigial here. Jefferson is possessed by the dream of ultimate peace, plenty, and happiness for all promised by progressivists like Turgot and Condorcet, and no sacrifices contributing to its realization appear great or even regrettable. History, on this reading, has at last broken free of its cyclic pattern and is moving the human race on a comparatively straight short line to millennial bliss on earth.

Many a prospect-piece contemporary with Jefferson's might be cited to document de Tocqueville's contention that Americans of that period were obsessed with "the idea of progress and of the indefinite perfectibility of the human race."[15] One that appears in Cooper's *Notions of the Americans* (1828) is especially striking as evidence that even America's most poignant historical novelist could put aside nostalgia and guilt, and participate enthusiastically in the progressivist "excitement":

> We live in the excitement of a rapid and constantly progressive condition. The impetus of society is imparted to all its members, and we advance because we are not accustomed to stand still . . . men of all nations, hereditary habits and opinions, receive an onward impulse by the constant influence of such a communion. I have stood upon this identical hill, and seen nine tenths of its smiling prospect darkened by the shadows of the forest. You observe what it is today. He who comes a century hence, may hear the din of a city rising from that very plain, or find his faculties confused by the number and complexity of its works of art.[16]

Thus Cooper's mouthpiece Cadwallader, philosophic observer and New York gentleman. Like Jefferson's, his metaphors are of considerable interest. The national movement westward is an irresistible force of nature, a "living current"; it is also a religious "communion." The personified prospect, once "darkened by the shadows of the forest," is now "smiling" in the sunshine of civilization: for it, as for the savages covered with "skins of wild beasts" in Jefferson's image, the shearing is apparently pure again. No wonder de Tocqueville concluded in a famous passage that Americans "care but little for what has been, but they are haunted by visions of what will be; in this direction their unbounded imagination grows and dilates beyond all measure" (ɪɪ, 78).

Certainly the Scottish philosophical historians tended to be more cautious and pragmatic about the likely benefits of progress, more consistently aware of the cost that it exacted. They preferred the "civilized" state in which they lived, and believed that society was stepping forward further than it was falling backward. Yet they feared the withering effects on essential human charities and relations of a society divided, for the sake of material progress, into wholly separate and self-interested callings. Such a society, dominated by the mercenary interests of commerce and manufactures, was a society without a conscience. Ferguson commented acidulously on the "poison" administered to the American Indians by "our traders of Europe" (p. 80). And in some of the most prescient social criticism to come out of the Enlightenment, he noticed the dehumanizing influence of modern manufacturing processes: "Manufactures . . . prosper most, where the mind is least consulted, and where the workshop may . . . be considered as an engine, the parts of which are men" (p. 183). Where, an undistressed Alexander Hamilton was to observe later, the perfect "part" was a child. Perhaps, Ferguson speculated, the tendency of the progressive spirit was ultimately "to break the bands of society" (p. 218). By comparison, savage society and the savage individual appeared to have a certain wholeness and firmly grounded interdependence – evident, for instance, in the social function and diction of primitive poetry (pp. 172–4, 181).

Scott shared the outlook of the stadialists while responding even more warmly and inwardly than they did to the virtues, real and supposed, of primitive societies. Ambivalence in his case did not mean intellectual and emotional incoherence but, on the contrary, a unified perspective on past, present, and future that was notably free from sentimentality or fanaticism. However, in the case of his American successors, especially Cooper and Twain, ambivalence did sometimes mean incoherence or, at best, a drama of unresolved antinomies. For while as the literary heirs of the Romantic Revival they shared Scott's feeling for the savage and barbarian peoples doomed by progress, as American intellectuals they also (at least intermittently) dreamed the Jeffersonian dream. Sympathies that pulled thus powerfully against each other could not be easily contained in a single work of art or even within a single life. And so the idea of progress that in earlier and mainly Scottish stadialist formulations had helped shape the paradigm of historical romance, in later versions threatened to destroy it.

4. Stadialism in the Leatherstocking tales

Reviewing *The Spy* in 1822, W. H. Gardiner took the occasion to refute the already common view that America lacked the matter, the manners, and the romantic associations necessary for interesting fiction and especially for fiction like that of Scott. On the contrary, he argued, "the author of *The Spy*" had already revealed the rich potentialities of the American Revolution as a subject for historical romance, and there was equal promise in "the times just succeeding the first settlement" and "the aera of the Indian wars."[17] In sentences which echo the vocabulary and concepts of the stadialists, Gardiner anticipates some of the major themes, situations, and character-types of the Leatherstocking tales and *The Wept of Wish-ton-Wish*:

> Imagine some stern enthusiast, voluntarily flying the blandishments of more luxurious abodes . . . follow him through the perils and difficulties he surmounts, and witness the long struggle of civilization, encroaching on the dominion of barbarism; and you will then find that romantic associations may become attached even to this familiar spot. (p. 59)

> Is there no bold peculiarity in the white savage who roams over the remote hunting tracts of the West; and none in the red native of the wilderness that crosses him in his path? (p. 57)

> Gradually receding before the tread of civilization, and taking from it only the principle of destruction, they seem to be fast wasting to utter dissolution; and we shall one day look upon their history, with such emotions of curiosity and wonder, as those with which we now survey the immense mounds and heaps of ruin in the interior of our continent, so extensive that they have hardly yet been measured, so ancient that they lie buried in their own dust and covered with the growth of a thousand years, forcing upon the imagination the appalling thought of some great and flourishing, perhaps civilized people, who have been so utterly swept from the face of the earth, that they have not left even a traditionary name behind them . . . At any rate we are confident that the savage warrior, who was not less beautiful and bold in his figurative diction, than in his attitude of death . . . tracking his foe through the pathless forest, with instinctive sagacity, by the fallen leaf, the crushed moss, or the bent blade, patiently enduring cold, hunger, and watchfulness . . . is no mean instrument of the sublime and terrible of human agency. And if we may credit the flattering pictures of their best historian, the indefatigable Heckewelder. (p. 62)

Following Gardiner's suggestion, Cooper did give more credit to Heckewelder's flattering pictures than they deserved, but his more fundamental debt was to the Enlightenment stadialists whose theory of social development Gardiner here employs without acknowledgement because he assumed that none was necessary. We shall see later in the chapter that the stadialists provided Cooper with the main outlines and even many of the shadings for his own pictures of savage and barbarian life in America. But their most important contribution was a distinctive way of perceiving the causes and consequences of historical change. Not that Cooper merely saw them with other men's eyes – for he had very good ones of his own – but that the stadialists taught him where and how to look. To their influence, I believe, may be traced his heightened awareness of how narrowly the individual's conception of ends and command of means were limited by his natural and social environment – of how tightly culture-bound even the best and most observant person must be. In their pages he would have found as well a complementary awareness of the accelerating pace of social change in the New World. He would have found premonitory glimpses of his great theme: the tragic and comic consequences of an individual's or a people's failure to adapt to the changes brought about by progress. To be sure, Scott had shown a similar (but not identical) awareness and must have been, along with American stadialists like Benjamin Rush, an important intermediary. But whatever the provenance, *The Wept of Wish-ton-Wish*, *The Prairie*, and other works demonstrate Cooper's detailed familiarity with the ideas of the European originators of the four-stage theory, and in at least one respect his fiction was closer than Scott's to their essays in philosophical history. Like them, or as nearly like them as was well possible for a novelist, Cooper obeyed Dr. Johnson's injunction in *The Vanity of Human Wishes*: "Let Observation with extensive view / Survey mankind from China to Peru." For the sheer range of races and conditions that Cooper sometimes brought together in a single narrative (at whatever cost to realism) was unprecedented in serious fiction. Of course that range was also, if you like, distinctively American: being American gave Cooper the experience and the motive, which European historical fictionalists lacked, fully to exploit his intellectual kinship with the European philosophical historians.

Well before rapid social and economic growth became the patriotic boast of American writers ranging from Cooper and Jefferson to country newspaper editors, Adam Smith had explained both why such growth would occur here and, more fundamentally, why it proceeded at different rates in different societies. Smith's entire analysis of the "Causes of Prosperity of New Colonies" (*Wealth of Nations*, IV, vii, b) is of general relevance to the present discussion, but the key propositions are the following:

> The colony of a civilized nation which takes possession, either of a waste country, or of one so thinly inhabited, that the natives easily give place to the

new settlers, advances more rapidly to wealth and greatness than any other human society.

The colonists carry out with them a knowledge of agriculture and of other useful arts, superior to what can grow up of its own accord in the course of many centuries among savage and barbarous nations. They carry out with them too the habit of subordination, some notion of the regular government which takes place in their own country, of the system of laws which support it, and of a regular administration of justice; and they naturally establish something of the same kind in the new settlement. But among savage and barbarous nations, the natural progress of law and government is still slower than the natural progress of arts, after law and government have been so far established, as is necessary for their protection. Every colonist gets more land than he can possibly cultivate.[18]

Going to press in 1776, Smith had the history and present circumstances of Britain's North American colonies in view throughout his discussions of the savage state (e.g., v, i, a, 2) and colonial development. Even if the intrinsic importance and international reputation of his great work had not ensured him a large American audience, his sympathetic interest in America would have. And even if a keen interest in variable rates of historical change had not been characteristic of Americans of Cooper's and the preceding generations, it was certain to be one shared by historical novelists. Cooper would have found a brief Smithian essay on this topic in *Waverley* itself. In "A Postscript, Which Should Have Been a Preface," Scott commented on the changes that had taken place in Scotland since the Jacobite rebellion of 1745:

There is no European nation which, within the course of half a century, or little more, has undergone so complete a change as this kingdom of Scotland. The effects of the insurrection of 1745, – the destruction of the patriarchal power of the Highland chiefs . . . commenced this innovation. The gradual influx of wealth, and extension of commerce, have since united to render the present people of Scotland a class of beings as different from their grandfathers, as the existing English are from those of Queen Elizabeth's time.[19]

Like Americans contemplating their own swift progress, Scott was delighted to look forward to a time when his nation's social and economic development would catch up with England's, but change on the scale described in this passage also meant the very perceptible destruction of his childhood world. He and other novelists of the then-developing nations had a vantage point on the past and a motive to record it which English novelists generally lacked.

Putting first things first, Cooper opened *The Pioneers* (1823) by summing up the still more astonishing transformation that had occurred in New York during the forty-year period since the treaty of peace between Britain and the United States:

> Before the war of the revolution, the inhabited parts of the colony of New-York were limited to less than a tenth of its possessions . . . Within the short period we have mentioned, the population has spread itself over five degrees of latitude and seven of longitude, and has swelled to a million and a half of inhabitants, who are maintained in abundance, and can look forward to ages before the evil day must arrive, when their possessions shall become unequal to their wants.[20]

The Pioneers is a tale of the breathtakingly quick transition from the first to the third stage of society (the pastoral stage having been virtually bypassed in this case) as Cooper's family had known it in upstate New York. He understood from the start that the regional experience, rendered with such concreteness and fidelity in this novel, had a representative national significance, and it was not long before he extended the spatial and temporal boundaries of the Leatherstocking story to fit his conception of a truly national fiction. Thanks to the memory of the immensely aged Indian Tamenund in *The Last of the Mohicans* (1826), the action of the story is taken as far back as the coming of the whites to the Atlantic shore in the seventeenth century down to the early nineteenth century when the Louisiana Purchase first opened the Mississippi basin, and beyond, to white American settlement. As *The Prairie* makes clear, the settling of that vast territory was going forward vigorously at the time of writing and promised to continue into the remote future. However, important as these extensions before and after were to the development of the Leatherstocking sequence into a national epic, the temporal scale by which Cooper wished his readers principally to gauge the pace of social change in America was not one marked by state treaties or mass migration. It was, rather, the more humanly relevant one of a person's span of remembered experience from youth to age. Describing his purpose in *The Prairie* in words that might have been applied equally well to the sequence in its entirety, Cooper explained that he had seen something

> instructive and touching in the life of a veteran of the forest, who, having commenced his career near the Atlantic, had been driven by the increasing and unparalleled advance of population, to seek a final refuge from society, in the broad and tenantless plains of the West . . . That the changes, which might have driven a man so constituted to such an expedient, have actually occurred within a single life, is a matter of undeniable history.[21]

It is easy to see why Cooper eventually recognized the need to adapt his form to his theme by representing his hero as a young man, thus completing his fictional biography, in *The Pathfinder* (1840) and *The Deerslayer* (1841).

What Cooper described in *The Pioneers* as "that magical change in the power and condition of the state" meant of course that the hunting and fishing mode of subsistence was no longer viable or even lawful, and that figures like Leatherstocking were obliged to move on or remain stranded in obsolescence. Cooper's hero thus became the first memorable victim of socio-economic progress in world literature. Fictional adventurers before him, e.g., Don Quixote and Edward Waverley, had been characterized and motivated by anachronistic notions, but these derived more from literature than from any actual way of life, past or present. Although he shares certain family resemblances with these characters (in his privileged glimpses of moral truth as well as in his absurd misreadings of modern social "reality"), he is illiterate and therefore inaccessible to the influence of Froissart, *Amadis de Gaul*, or even John Filson's account of Daniel Boone. After making various allowances, as for the homilies of the Moravian missionaries he heard in his youth, we may affirm that Leatherstocking's notions are those belonging to the savage stage of society as this was described by the philosophical historians. He sees most things as his Indian companions do, not because he is a "white Indian" or even because he has been tutored by them, but because hunters see things that way. This being so, we should expect to find premonitions of Leatherstocking's social tragedy in the writings of the Enlightenment stadialists, and we are not disappointed:

> Addicted to their own pursuits, and considering their own condition as the standard of human felicity, all nations pretend to the preference, and in their practice give sufficient proof of sincerity. Even the savage still less than the citizen, can be made to quit that manner of life in which he is trained: he loves that freedom of mind which will not be bound to any task, and which owns no superior: however tempted to mix with polished nations, and to better his fortune, the first moment of liberty brings him back to the woods again; he droops and he pines in the streets of the populous city; he wanders dissatisfied over the open and the cultivated field; he seeks the frontier and the forest, where, with a constitution prepared to undergo the hardships . . . of the situation, he enjoys a delicious freedom from care.[22]

Cooper gave greater emphasis than Ferguson to the discipline that went with savage freedom, but the latter's picture of the displaced hunter wandering "dissatisfied over the open and cultivated field" closely anticipates many a scene in *The Pioneers*.[23]

Perhaps the central irony of the sequence is that Leatherstocking helps to bring about the end of his own cherished way of life, particularly by helping to remove the French barrier against English colonial expansion and more generally by deploying his "savage" skills in protection of those who are kin by color and religion but not by vocation or life style. Cooper calls attention to this irony in the last paragraph of *The Pioneers*:

> This was the last that they ever saw of the Leather-stocking, whose rapid movements preceded the pursuit which Judge Temple both ordered and

conducted. He had gone far towards the setting sun, – the foremost in that band of Pioneers, who are opening the way for the march of the nation across the continent.[24]

Leatherstocking's career thus illustrates what historians now call the "law of unintended consequences" (or the "law of the heterogeneity of ends") – a law of historical development variously formulated by Enlightenment philosophers but with special force and point by Ferguson:

> Mankind, in following the present sense of their minds, in striving to remove inconveniences, or to gain apparent and contiguous advantages, arrive at ends which even their imagination could not anticipate, and pass on, like other animals, in the track of their nature, without perceiving its end . . . Every step and every movement of the multitude, even in what are termed enlightened ages, are made with equal blindness to the future; and nations stumble upon establishments, which are indeed the result of human action, but not the execution of any human design. If Cromwell said, That a man never mounts higher, than when he knows not whither he is going; it may with more reason be affirmed of communities, that they admit of the greatest revolutions where no change is intended.[25]

Whether Cooper was familiar with this passage matters but little, since the basic idea was widely expressed by Ferguson's contemporaries, and, as Avrom Fleishman has argued, it permeated the historical thinking of the Waverley novels.[26] However, it was left to the "American Scott" to fully exploit the ironies implicit in it. For in no other country did the unintended consequences of one's actions follow so rapidly, visibly, and often painfully, as in the United States.

As might be expected of social thinkers working shortly after Locke, the eighteenth-century stadialists paid particular attention to the formation of attitudes and laws relating to property. Either directly or indirectly through Blackstone and his disciples their theories on this subject had broadcast influence throughout Europe and the Americas. Certainly they affected the dozen or so of Cooper's novels which are concerned with the acquisition or settlement of "new lands." In *The Pioneers* and *The Prairie*, the issue of land ownership is directly addressed, and with an appearance of speculative flexibility that has often surprised their readers. How was it that a social conservative like Cooper, who never doubted that property was "the base of all civilization,"[27] nonetheless represented alien and seemingly opposed points of view with such vigor and sympathy? Cooper's unruly Id has sometimes been invoked in answer. It may well have contributed psychic energy, but two other explanations seem more immediately helpful. First, Cooper had more of the novelist's or dramatist's negative capability than he is usually given credit for, and he was especially skilled in analysis and depiction of the cant and casuistry of those with whom he disagreed. In

the second place, however, he did not *simply* disagree with such views as
these of Leatherstocking and frontiersman Ishmael Bush:

> "He who ventures far into the prairie, must abide by the ways of its owners."
>
> "Owners!" echoed the squatter, "I am as rightful an owner of the land I
> stand on, as any governor of the States! Can you tell me, stranger, where the
> law or the reason is to be found, which says that one man shall have a section, or
> a town, or perhaps a county to his use, and another have to beg for earth to
> make his grave in? This is not nature, and I deny that it is law. That is, your legal
> law."
>
> "I cannot say that you are wrong," returned the trapper, whose opinions on
> this important topic, though drawn from very different premises, were in
> singular accordance with those of his companion . . . "But your beasts are
> stolen by them who claim to be masters of all they find in the deserts."[28]

Perhaps there is a populist taint in Ishmael's rhetoric, but the attitudes to
property in this exchange are those appropriate to the first two stages of
society and become inappropriate only when asserted outside these
contexts. The herdsman Ishmael can no more understand the hunter's
indifference to personal property rights in horses and cattle than he can an
agriculturalist's claim to hold land as personal property. As we shall see,
Cooper is at some pains later in *The Prairie* to establish Ishmael's dignity
and rectitude when he does act in context. But in nineteenth-century
America the contexts keep shifting, and borderers like Ishmael commonly find themselves at war on two fronts – outlawed as squatters by
"Civil Society" but unintentionally advancing its interests by violating
the treaty-guaranteed territorial rights of the natives.

The Old Testament associations that cling to Ishmael and his family
have a propriety in this connection that may not be self-evident.
According to Blackstone, the "ancient right of migration" or colonization is to be traced to the practices of the second stage of society when
herdsmen like Lot and Abraham felt free to move their tents and animals
onto any unoccupied lands. Colonization, says Blackstone,

> was practiced as well by Phoenicians and Greeks, as the Germans, Sythians, and
> other northern people. And, so long as it was confined to the stocking and
> cultivation of desert uninhabited countries, it kept strictly with the limits of the
> law of nature. But how far the seising on countries already peopled, and
> driving out or massacring the innocent and defenceless natives, merely because
> they differed from their invaders in language, in religion, in customs, in
> government, or in colour: how far such a conduct was consonant to nature, to
> reason, or to christianity, deserved well to be considered by those, who have
> rendered their names immortal by thus civilizing mankind.[29]

Blackstone's charge that in colonizing the New World the European
peoples violated the laws of nature, reason, and Christianity, is also the
charge of the Leatherstocking tales. To say so is not to deny that, just as
there may be a trace of equivocation in the complex Gibbonian ironies of

Blackstone's final clause, so there are inconsistencies and residues of "savagism" in Cooper's treatment. To take but one example: as *The Prairie* shows, America's "tenantless plains" were tenantless only in the eyes of the European invaders; but there appears not a hint of conscious irony when the phrase is used in the preface to that book. Few Europeans or white Americans could meet or bring the charge of colonial guilt with the manly frankness that Cooper sincerely admired and in fact used, often to his great cost, in most of his dealings with mankind. Consequently such guilt was usually dealt with through the oblique structures of irony, conscious or otherwise, and dramatic presentation. Cooper's Indians, not Cooper himself, deliver the most searching and powerful indictments of his ancestors and white contemporaries. Artistically speaking, this dramatic rendering is more effective than if he had made the same charge *in propria persona*, and there can be no doubt that the teachings of the Enlightenment stadialists helped him to understand and represent, with eloquence and consistency, the alien points of view of the victims of American progress.

5. *The Prairie*

A few trappers and explorers excepted, white Americans contemporary with Cooper had no firsthand knowledge of the western plains described in *The Prairie*. Cooper himself had none, but he combined bold imaginative conjecture with armchair research to construct a setting of peoples and landscapes as vivid as any in the Leatherstocking series. That he drew on the recent exploration narratives of Major Long and of Lewis and Clark as also on the schematizations of the stadialists has long been recognized, but the full extent of his debts to the latter has not been noticed.[30] These ranged from minor details of characterization to basic conceptions of literary form and purpose, and we need to know more about them if we are to understand – let alone judge – this most "philosophical" of the Leatherstocking novels.

There is no reason to suppose that Cooper was familiar with the following sentences, which Scott addressed to Southey in 1818, but every reason to believe that he would have sympathized with the spirit that informed them:

> The history of colonies has in it some points of peculiar interest as illustrating human nature. On such occasions the extremes of civilized and savage life are suddenly and strongly brought into contact with each other and the results are as interesting to the moral observer as those which take place on the mixture of chemical substances are to the physical investigator.[31]

Scott's terminology and analogies reveal that he had momentarily donned the *persona* of stadialist and philosophical historian. That is, just as

Adam Smith and Ferguson had done, he thought of himself as applying the "experimental method" of Boyle, Newton, and Franklin to the study of society. And although demonstrated by modern anthropologists to be factually unsound and oversimple, the theoretical model of the stadialists was "scientific" at least in so far as it ventured to explain social development in terms of natural (as distinct from supernatural) causes operating uniformly, hence with predictable effects, throughout time and space. No more than in Newton's model of the universe was provision made for unlawful interventions by Providence, and the human objects of study were likewise supposed to behave – because of the overwhelming influence of their total environment – in close conformity with ascertainable laws.

Nobody today is likely to suppose that the eighteenth-century philosophical historians, much less Sir Walter Scott, escaped the influence of *their* environment to achieve anything approaching scientific rigor in their gathering and evaluation of evidence. The danger is rather that their allusions to the laboratory will seem to convict them of a cool indifference to human suffering. In historical fact, however, Smith, Ferguson, Scott, Jefferson, and Cooper were notably humane men, and there is no evidence that the role of scientifically detached "observer" adopted by all of them when they thought in stadial terms was incompatible with strong moral feeling and practical humanitarian effort. It was characteristic of the age that its great men both of action and contemplation (often identical) felt the need to assume the role of "philosophic" (= scientific) observer from time to time and survey their handiwork – or that of God – without prejudice, as from a great height. Mill employed illustrative figures and terms from astronomy. Wordsworth could speak of the *Lyrical Ballads* as a "language experiment" and the American Founding Fathers could view their republic as a "political experiment." Such references bespoke no lack of personal investment in the success of these works, but constituted, rather, an appeal to a widely shared Enlightenment ideal of truth and openmindedness – an appeal directed quite as much at their readers as at themselves. To speak of "experiment" was to invoke, above all, the example of Newton and Newton's God.

Although more suspicious of scientific "presumption" than Scott and his forebears had been, Cooper was a keen lay student of scientific exploration and research, and this interest affected his fiction in many ways. A comparatively late example is *The Crater* (1847), a work in which he made copious use of Lyell's *Principles of Geology* and the pioneer sociologist Henry Carey's studies of social evolution.[32] Although usually classified as an "anti-utopia," *The Crater* can also be regarded as a work of science fiction. *The Prairie* is a more complicated, less obvious case of generic doubleness. We usually and rightly think of it as a historical romance, and its fairly close conformity to the *Waverley*-model is easily demonstrated. But unless we also see that its action takes the form of a social "experiment" such as could be launched only in a novel, we may judge its breaches of realism too severely.

As if following Scott's prescription, in *The Prairie* "the extremes of civilized and savage life are suddenly and strongly brought into contact with each other." Representatives of the intermediate stages are present as well, but they cannot function transitionally as they normally would in the stadial scheme (and in the typical historical romance). For social history is telescoped here, and the various stages are thrown into collision with each other in what, for most of them, is a foreign environment. Thus, with comic or tragic results, their characteristic behavior is constantly "out of place," and they are reduced to a condition of humbling dependence on the "in-place" wisdom of Leatherstocking. But although appreciative of the old trapper's help, they do not suffer their pride and obstinacy in their own ways to be much affected by the experience. This picture of human behavior accords with that of Enlightenment social science, and it draws attention to the special problems of a rapidly developing nation of nations. Not of course that it is supposed to be a mirror image of American society or indeed of any society ever seen on the face of the earth; its "realism" is closer to that of a time-travel romance like Mark Twain's *Connecticut Yankee* than it is to that of, say, *The Wept of Wish-ton-Wish*. But because Cooper shared the Jeffersonian idea that in contemporary America the progress of man was to be traced through space rather than time, commencing at the Rocky Mountains rather than the Stone Age, he was able to create an "experimental" mixture of peoples not unlike Twain's yet challenging the conventions of fictional realism less openly.[33]

Within the framework of the four stages, the representative of the "earliest" stage of social development is Leatherstocking himself. A trapper-gatherer now rather than the hunter he was in his prime, he is reduced to the most primitive form of subsistence, and he feels the degradation keenly. The Pawnee and Dakota Sioux, respectively the noble and ignoble savages of the novel, are full-fledged hunters; but as plains Indians who have learned to ride horses they have begun to acquire some of the property interests in domestic animals characteristic of the second stage of society. As we have seen, the Bush family are herdsmen whose criminality is due much less to personal wickedness or weakness of character (as is the case, however, with their kinsman Abirim White) than to a code that is radically out of phase with American social development. The bee-hunter Paul Hover shares some traits with the Bush family, some with Leatherstocking, but as a supplier of honey to others his mode of subsistence involves a division of labor characteristic of a more advanced stage of society. Thanks partly to the efforts of his more cultivated fiancée, Ellen, he is "raised" to the status of a yeoman farmer and fully assimilated into "civil" society. His benefactor, the gentleman officer Middleton, is a professional soldier in the service of an agricultural and commercial society that is "advanced" but still young and vigorous. On the other hand, Middleton's over-refined Spanish Creole wife Inez, whose abduction by Abirim White and Ishmael sets the narrative machine in motion, is a representative of civilization in decline. To describe her, as David Howard does, as "the decayed promise of the past and of the future" is to overstate a valid point: the fate of the Spanish Empire was the great modern confirmation of the cyclic theory of history, and no nineteenth-century American writer, whether Cooper in *The Prairie* or Melville in *Benito Cereno*, introduced Spanish Creole characters without a note of warning to his fellow countrymen.[34] Finally, a classifier and projector rather than the sort of empirical scientist that Cooper admired, Dr. Obed Batt is another, but grotesque, instance of over-refinement and over-specialization; his absurd researches serve as a satiric foil to those of Cooper himself.

A direct descendant of Swift's academicians of Lagado, Pope's "high Priori" *Dunciad* projectors, and also of Voltaire's Dr. Pangloss, Batt obviously does not exist as a realistic character in the same way that the other characters do. They may be "flat" or stereotyped, but they are distinctly of this world. Batt is not and that is Cooper's point about him and his doctrines. In one of his several debates with Leatherstocking (Ch. XXII), Batt emerges as a deistic proponent of man's perfectibility. Science, he believes, might eventually "eradicate the evil principle" and improve on the designs of nature. At the same time, he inadvertently supplies a good deal of the standard evidence (the ruins of Thebes, Balbec, etc.) for the cyclic theory of growth and inevitable decay here espoused by the illiterate but intuitively wise old trapper. The latter considers Batt's conjectures impious, but Cooper can afford to regard them with incredulous amusement because he has made their spokesman a figure of fun. Cooper himself appears to endorse a modified version of the cyclic theory. As Leatherstocking maintains, "It is the fate of all things to ripen, and then to decay." But American civilization (mainly white, Protestant, republican, and agrarian) is, or promises to be, as much superior to that of modern England as the latter in its turn was to that of France or Spain – and so on, although with some striking irregularities in the general pattern, back to the prehistory of human society. Thus, under Providence, there is both a prevailing progressive trend and a cyclic sequence in history. This compromise between a cyclic and unilinear theory, itself a recurrent one in intellectual history, is only implicit in *The*

Prairie, but it is spelled out in some of Cooper's later works.[35] It avoids the unacceptable extremes represented by the rival viewpoints of Leatherstocking and Batt: on the one hand, stoic resignation to history perceived as relentless natural process (history as seasonal change); on the other, overweening "humanistic" faith in the power of man to transcend nature and direct history towards a goal of his own choice.

Stadialists generally stressed the ascendent rather than the descendent phases of social change, the rise rather than the fall of empires. Some, like Jefferson and his followers, believed that there would be no more declines into savagery or barbarism. But stadialism itself was cyclic in tendency inasmuch as it argued for the recurrence of basic human character-types and institutions in a comparatively fixed sequence: in place of Leatherstocking's organic metaphor it offered a functional explanation for at least part of the cycle. Whatever the inadequacies of the explanation, the writer of either historical or science fiction was bound to be grateful for a theory of recurrence which supplied him with a scenario when other resources failed. As we have seen, Cooper had limited personal experience on which to draw when he conceived *The Prairie*, and the four-stage theory proved an invaluable aid to creation of one of the great group portraits in American fiction – the family of Ishmael Bush.

Some of their traits were doubtless derived from personal observation of backwoodsmen in New York state or, as Henry Nash Smith has suggested, from childhood memories of such men and women.[36] But more, and more crucial, traits were taken from a stadial prototype. Only a few examples out of many are Esther Bush's masculine leadership in battle, the barbarian ornamentation of Ishmael's dress, and the slothful demeanor of the entire clan except for moments when it is obliged to act in self-defense.[37] Certainly this American border family's finest hour occurs when, in Chapters xxxi-xxxii, their leader Ishmael momentarily re-embodies the stadial type of pastoral patriarch. He is less converted or transformed than awakened to his true self by a series of moral shocks, the chief of them being the murder of his eldest son. (Ishmael is consistently portrayed as a sleepwalking giant with a "dull eye" and "slumbering strength.") The circumstances, too, are right for such an awakening, since the absence of other judicial authority demands that he act and do so by extending the only authority he possesses – that of a head of family:

> He neither courted their assistance nor dreaded their enmity, and he now proceeded to the business of the hour with as much composure as if the species of patriarchal power he wielded was universally recognized.
>
> There is something elevating in the possession of authority, however it may be abused. The mind is apt to make some efforts to prove the fitness between its

qualities and the condition of its owner, though it may often fail, and render that ridiculous which was only hated before. But the effect on Ishmael Bush was not so disheartening. Grave in exterior, saturnine by temperament, formidable by his physical means, and dangerous from his lawless obstinacy, his self-constituted tribunal excited a degree of awe to which even the intelligent Middleton could not bring himself to be entirely insensible. Little time, however, was given to arrange his thoughts; for the squatter, though unaccustomed to haste, having previously made up his mind, was not disposed to waste the moments in delay.[38]

When Ishmael's tribunal concludes, Inez is restored to Middleton, Ellen is delivered into the arms of her beloved Hover, and the murderer is revealed and apprehended. I say "revealed" because the entire scene seems to be played out, like one from the Old Testament, under the superintending eye of a just and unforgetful God. Abirim White's hour is come, and although the discovery of his guilt is effected by human agency, it leaves Middleton "awe-struck by what he believed a manifest judgment of Heaven . . ." While the reader might be less impressed than Middleton (and a little annoyed by Cooper's insistence that he be impressed), the mythic grandeur of the scene is undeniable. In developing the parallel between the morally upright colonists of Wish-ton-Wish and the ancient Israelites in search of a homeland, Cooper did no more than the seventeenth-century Puritans and their historians and satirists had been doing for two centuries. To portray this people at all was to invoke (however sparingly) their special "lower mythology." But to discern the likeness of a Hebrew patriarch in the coarse and criminal features of an American frontiersman was an uncommon perception, as poetic as morally creditable to its author. Having said this, however, I must emphasize that the perception was enfranchised and probably suggested by Enlightenment social science.

6. The Course of Empire

One of the best known and studied of the many fruitful relationships between nineteenth-century American writers and painters is that between Cooper and Thomas Cole (1801–48).[39] Early in his career Cole painted two brooding Romantic landscapes (with human figures present but dwarfed by nature) based on scenes from the closing chapters of *The Last of the Mohicans*, and later returned the favor by completing two great sequences, *The Course of Empire* (1836) and *The Voyage of Life* (1840), which may have inspired, and certainly affected the shape of, *The Crater* (1847) and *The Sea Lions* (1849). Both sequences are based on cyclic schemes of organic growth, maturation, decay, and dissolution, exhibiting stages in the life of an individual who is representative of all empires, all persons, against a background of irresistible diurnal and seasonal change. The closing scenes of both sequences, marked as they are by violence and devastation of earthly hopes, must have spoken powerfully to Cooper at the close of his own life as he became increasingly religious and pessimistic about the course of American history.[40] In fact we know a great deal about Cooper's response to *The Course of Empire* because in 1849 he wrote an eight-page appreciation of the sequence in which he said: "Not only do I consider the Course of Empire the work of the highest genius this country has ever produced, but I esteem it one of the noblest works of art that has ever been wrought."[41]

To account for this enthusiastic praise, we need to consider not only Cooper's circumstances at the time of writing and his tastes in the pictorial arts, but also aspects of Cole's sequence which recall Cooper's own earlier historical romances. In his essay on *The Course of Empire*, he declares that "The series is a great epic poem, in which the idea far surpasses the execution, though the last is generally fine . . . It is quite a new thing to see landscape painting raised to a level with the heroic in historical composition: but it is constantly to be traced in the works of Cole" (p. 166). That these words could be applied to Cooper's greatest historical romances is immediately apparent, as it is likewise that his descriptions of the stages of society pictured in Cole's first and second canvases could find many parallels in his own frontier novels:

> the empire, in its spring and in its morning, is a spirited creature of the wilderness, just beginning to assert supremacy over land and sea, and exhibiting the simplest elements of society and the arts. Canoes ride the swells, scattered huts fling their smokes to the breeze, the rude inhabitants, clad in skins, send the arrow after the light-footed deer, or circle the crackling fire with dance and song.
>
> In the second picture . . . aboriginal canoe and hut are exchanged for the busy village by the water-side, and the bolder craft that can wing the seas. The savage is transformed into civilized man, rising from grosser superstitions into higher forms of natural religion, progressing in science and the arts, abandoning the chase for the sober toils of agriculture, and forgetting scenes of barbarous mirth in the gentler pastimes of the peasant. (p. 171)

Although Cooper's essay is, on the whole, about as good an introduction to *The Course of Empire* series as one could hope for, his account of the social progress shown in the second painting is not quite accurate. As might be expected of a scene which follows "The Savage State" and is called "The Arcadian or Pastoral," the inhabitants are not agriculturalists but shepherds with their flocks. It is not the pastoral but rather the agricultural stage that Cole omits as, in the third picture, entitled "The Consummation of Empire," he moves on to the fourth stage, commercial and urban, in which the canvas is crowded with people, monuments, and luxury. In omitting the agricultural stage, Cole was also bypassing the society which Jefferson and other stadialists believed most favorable to republican government. Since Cooper was versed in stadialist theory and shared Cole's belief that commercial empire would be the ruin both of the American republic and the American landscape, it is surprising that he overlooked a hiatus in the sequence which was very likely deliberate and pointed.[42]

Cooper also fails to take note of a feature of *The Course of Empire* which might almost have been put there expressly for his pleasure. Although the place represented remains the same throughout the series, the savages of the first scene look remarkably like Cooper's American Indians while the mighty temples, palaces, and monuments of the third and fourth bear an unmistakable resemblance to those of imperial Rome. A viewer unskilled in reading such works might wonder where on earth the developments pictured are supposed to be taking place. The answer, of course, is: anywhere and nowhere in particular. Cole is not being inconsistent or aimlessly eclectic; rather, he is creating a stadialist image of human community over time and space. "The Romans," wrote Adam Ferguson in a passage quoted earlier, "might have found an image of their own ancestors, in the representations they have given of ours"; and it is in "the present condition" of the American Indians "that we are to behold, as in a mirrour, the features of our progenitors" (p. 80).

Although probably most famous today for works which aspire to transcend particular times, places, and peoples, Cole first made his name as a painter of Irving's Catskill region and throughout his life was a devoted preservationist and lover of the local scene. In being thus pulled by the rival attractions of the near and familiar and the far and strange, he resembled the writers he most admired. It was while hard at work on *The Course of Empire* in 1835 that Cole recorded some reflections on several of those writers which can serve as a transition from the lofty abstractions of stadialism to the down-to-earth concerns of regionalism which are the subject of my next chapter:

> I have been reading Irving's Abbotsford . . . Irving was rather disappointed in the scenes in which Scott was so much delighted. After all, beauty is in the mind. A scene is rather an index to feelings and associations. History and poetry made the barren hills of Scotland glorious to Scott: Irving remembered the majestic forests and the rich luxuriance of his own country. What a beautiful exemplification of the power of poetry was that remark of the old carpenter who had been a companion of Burns: "and it seemed to him that the country had grown more beautiful since Burns had written his bonnie little sangs about it."   (p. 145)

4

The regionalism of historical romance

1

In Book III of *My Ántonia* Jim Burden's brilliant young classics teacher Gaston Cleric glosses the opening lines of Book III of the *Georgics*:

> '*Primus ego in patriam mecum . . . deducam Musas*'; 'for I shall be the first, if I live, to bring the Muse into my country.' Cleric had explained to us that '*patria*' here meant, not a nation or even a province, but the little rural neighbourhood on the Mincio where the poet was born. This was not a boast, but a hope, at once bold and devoutly humble, that he might bring the Muse (but lately come to Italy from her cloudy Grecian mountains), not to the capital, the *palatia Romana*, but to his own little 'country'; to his father's fields, 'sloping down to the river and to the old beech trees with broken tops.'[1]

A little later Jim wonders "whether that particular rocky strip of New England coast about which he had so often told me was Cleric's *patria*" (p. 265), and the reader is bound to wonder whether Willa Cather herself had in mind her friend Sara Orne Jewett and *The Country of the Pointed Firs* – Maine Theocritus to Cather's Nebraskan Virgil. For there can be no doubt that Cather felt a similar mission to bring the Muse to her own country: a region much larger than the "little rural neighbourhood on the Mincio" but also less abstract and heterogeneous than the entire state of Nebraska; a region with its own distinctive landscape, ethnic mixture, and way of life; in short, a region which is the American approximation of a Virgilian *patria*. And if "local" seems closer than "regional" to Virgil's word, that is just as well. We need a term flexible enough to suggest both – the Red Cloud vicinity as well as the prairie country generally, Hawthorne's Salem and Boston as well as New England – without invoking the idea of the nation-state. Of course there can be no exact modern equivalent, but thanks to her creative philology the Latin word has resonances that may help us to discover the ground of Cather's finest historical romances – and of many others as well.

That regionalism and historical romance tend to go together is suggested by the fate of most of our minor romancers. Such authors as Simms, Kennedy, James Lane Allen, Mary Johnston, Gertrude Atherton, and even Ellen Glasgow are remembered, if at all, principally as South Carolinian, Virginian, Kentuckian, or Californian novelists. But to be "regional" is not necessarily to be "minor." Most, though not all, of our obviously major writers of historical romance also share Cather's strong sense of "patriotic" mission. They do not merely give their stories a historically correct setting in time and place; in their greatest romances they are as much regional as historical novelists. Of Cooper, Hawthorne, Faulkner, and (with certain qualifications) Mark Twain this is certainly true. The important exception, Melville, is exceptional partly, I suspect, because he understood that Irving, Cooper, and Paulding had long since exhausted the novelty of New York regionalism and that he would have to strike a new vein. At any rate, *Benito Cereno* and *Billy Budd* remind us that the relationship between regionalism and historical romance is no necessary one. Why then has it been so constant, though not invariable, over the years?

2

In his introduction to *Castle Rackrent* (1800) George Watson explains that Maria Edgeworth's astonishing novella is "the first regional novel in English, and perhaps in all Europe; and, as Scott saw at once, the regional novel is the gateway to the ampler world of the historical novel, since it represents whole societies and conceives of individual characters as composing societies . . . *Rackrent* pictures a world identified in time and place; and *Waverley* (1814), the first historical novel, was begun in 1805 under its direct inspiration."[2] John Gibson Lockhart claimed that Scott was conscious "he should never in all likelihood have thought of a Scotch novel had he not read Maria Edgeworth's exquisite pieces of Irish character";[3] and the claim is borne out by generous acknowledgements in the 1814 postscript to *Waverley* and the 1829 General Preface to the collected edition of Waverley novels. Although Scott's two public expressions of indebtedness offer somewhat vague and inconsistent accounts of the nature of the debt, they are nonetheless highly suggestive and surely point in the right direction. For Scott, and for the historical romance tradition generally, Edgeworth's example may have been as decisive and her legacy as enduring as those of Goethe and the stadialists.

Castle Rackrent was not only the first regional novel, it was also possibly the earliest instance of a family chronicle novel and of a novel narrated throughout in a provincial lower-class dialect rather than in the cosmopolitan English of the middle and upper classes. So honest Thady's unintentionally ironic vernacular narrative of the decline of the Rackrent family must have furnished hints to many writers besides Scott. Is it coincidental, for example, that the faithless stewards of the Rackrent family and of Cooper's Littlepage family are named, respectively, Jason Quirk and Jason Newcome? Is it not likely, given Maria Edgeworth's popularity and high critical reputation in America, that Cooper was making a pointed allusion to her account of the pauperization of the Irish aristocracy by its own unscrupulous agents? At all events, Scott was less interested in the possibilities of the family chronicle (which were to be developed by John Galt and Cooper) and of the extended ironic vernacular narrative (perfected by Mark Twain) than in the new social range and authenticity of Edgeworth's fictional "world" and in the authorial stance she took up in relation to her "matter" (Ireland) and her audience (England).

Scott saw that Edgeworth's forte was not the management of plot, as plot was understood by Fielding or Austen; rather, as he explained in the "postscript" to *Waverley*, she excelled at the realization of various types of Irish character through an exact though spare description of "their habits, manners, and feelings" (p. 341). Eschewing the "caricatured and exaggerated use of the national dialect" by which other writers gained an easy external characterization, she rendered the idioms of Anglo-Irish with striking freshness and authenticity, not to label but to reveal national character. Yet to speak of "national character" may be misleading. In *Castle Rackrent* Edgeworth wrote almost exclusively of "remote" rural Ireland: to her aged but untravelled narrator the towns of London, Bath, and even Dublin appear strange, dangerous places where his masters squander or try to recoup the monies rackrented from the tenants of their estate; and his vernacular diction, intelligible yet outlandish, continuously calls attention to the provinciality of his point of view. But if Thady's field of vision does not reach very far on the horizontal plane, it takes in nearly everything on the vertical. Through him we become aware of all the people – squires, servants, tenant farmers, factors, merchants, and lawyers – living independently in a single neighborhood.

Thus the social world of *Castle Rackrent*, though narrow and primitive, had an inclusiveness and wholeness extraordinary, maybe unprecedented, in English fiction up to 1800. Scott was supremely equipped both by talent and experience to see how Edgeworth had extended the realism of the novel and how he might do the same on a larger and more truly national scale. (Describing his preparation for writing the Waverley novels, he spoke of his "having travelled through most parts of Scotland, both Highland and Lowland; having been familiar with the elder, as well as more modern race; and having had from my infancy free and unrestrained communication with all ranks of my countrymen, from the Scottish peer to the Scottish ploughman" [p. 353].) Later novels by Edgeworth, such as *The Absentee* (1812), may have suggested the usefulness for Scott's purposes of a less drastically limited narrator than Thady; but, as Watson maintains, the seminal book was certainly *Castle Rackrent*.

Edgeworth had a further exemplary importance for Scott, since her position with respect to the politics of literature was very similar to his own. As members of the Anglo-Irish and Anglo-Scottish upper classes, both writers were (in more senses than one) uniquely privileged interpreters, and both considered themselves duty-bound to assume a mediatory role between their countries and England. Reflecting on the origins of the Waverley novels, Scott recalled feeling that "something might be attempted for my own country, of the same kind with that which Miss Edgeworth so fortunately achieved for Ireland – something which might introduce her natives to those of the sister kingdom, in a more favourable light than they had been placed hitherto, and tend to procure sympathy for their virtues and indulgence for their foibles" (p. 353). Of course they wrote for the Irish and Scots too, but love of *patria* no less than authorial self-interest dictated that they address themselves especially to the capital of empire, the *palatia britannica*, in England. Living as they did through an era when the "sister kingdoms" seemed threatened variously by class revolution, violent national liberation movements, and Napoleonic conquest, they accepted that the general welfare demanded a strong United Kingdom with its base of government in London. Writing to Edgeworth in 1822, Scott commented on the "fierce and hasty resentments of the Irish, and the sullen, long-enduring, revengeful temper of my countrymen" and judged that "of the three kingdoms the English alone are qualified to mix in politics safely and without fatal results!" (iv, 22). Yet they saw likewise that a government so remote from its Celtic constituents must be educated and conciliated, lest it trample over their ancient customs and rights out of sheer ignorance or indifference.

If England was strong to defend her sister kingdoms against foreign enemies and themselves, she was equally strong to destroy their cultural identities without firing a shot. Edgeworth foresaw a time, not far distant, when Ireland would lose "her identity by a union with Great Britain" (p. 5), and by "identity" she clearly meant more than just Ireland's political existence as a sovereign state. Scott, as we have seen, concluded *Waverley* with a brief Smithian essay on the rapid transformation of Scottish society – in a word, its Anglicization. Neither writer considered this development altogether impoverishing. As Scott said, the change was "steadily and rapidly progressive" (p. 513), while Edgeworth, the Wolfe Tone rising of 1798 still fresh in her mind, implied that the disappearance of the old Irish identity was no cause for regret. Nonetheless, both writers took that great delight in human diversity which, as much as love of *patria*, is a hallmark of the best regional and historical fiction. Edgeworth might bid good riddance to the manners of "the drunken Sir Patrick, the litigious Sir Murtagh, the fighting Sir Kit, and the slovenly Sir Condy" (pp. 4–5) of her own social class, but her loving eye and ear for the quirky traits of the Irish peasantry are everywhere evident in *Castle Rackrent*. She knew that "Thady's idiom is incapable of translation" (p. 4) and cherished it the more for that reason. Scott's delight in "all trades, their gear and tackle and trim," in "All things counter, original, spare, strange," was greater even than hers, and it was intensified when the trades or things were Scottish. Indeed, a poignant consciousness that all manner of things Scottish – high and low, good and bad – were disappearing at an accelerating rate as Scotland grew yearly more Anglicized may have been the single most powerful motivating factor behind his creation of the first true historical novel.

Castle Rackrent was subtitled "An Hibernian Tale Taken from Facts, and from the Manners of the Irish Squires before 1782," but in spite of this and other strategic disclaimers Edgeworth's readers tended to suppose (not without reason) that her satiric portraits were of contemporary manners. Scott's *Waverley, or, 'Tis Sixty Years Since* was much more firmly placed in the past, partly because some of its leading characters and events had an actual historical existence, but also because ancient Border and Highland manners unfamiliar to an English reader were treated as being equally strange to a contemporary Scotsman. So Scott was as much a mediator between the Scottish past and present as he was between contemporary Scotland and England. Whether distanced by time or space, much that was "foreign" to his readers seemed to Scott worthy of remembrance and respect if not necessarily of emulation. And of course he did hope that many of his Scottish readers would be moved by his romances to become, in their generation, what "folks of the old leaven" had been, but without their Jacobite politics: "living examples of singular and disinterested attachment to the principles of loyalty which they received from their fathers, and of old Scottish faith, hospitality, worth, and honour" (p. 513).

In fact – to abandon a perhaps over-extended parallel – Scott was less "Anglo," less satirically inclined, and much more affected by the Romantic Revival than Edgeworth was. From her he undoubtedly learned much essential to the making of *Waverley* that he could not have learned from Goethe or Adam Ferguson, but they showed him how her regional world might be redrawn on an ampler scale and with historical depth. From Goethe in particular he already knew how to portray the decline of a provincial society in relation to the larger movements of economic, social, and military history. Indeed, an intense localism was already present in *Goetz* as a counter-current to the centralizing tendencies of the new socio-economic order. On the showing of *Goetz* and many historical romances, strong local or regional loyalties inevitably reinforced, and were in turn perpetuated by, the aristocratic view that the locus of historical value was not, as the democratic progressivists held, in a golden land of the future but in a heroic golden age of the *patria*.

3

No American novelist has been situated exactly as Scott or Edgeworth was, or nearly so close to either of them as they were to each other. Still, early authors like Irving and Cooper may be fairly described as "Anglo-American" in their social values as in their direct reliance on British literary models and on the British reading public. Another parallel, less obvious and less close but capable of further extension, may be drawn on the basis of our writers' dual national–regional or national–state identities. Especially during the nineteenth century and along the Atlantic seaboard where the federal union was less venerable than the Commonwealth of Virginia, say, or the New England confederation, American fictionalists witnessed and often felt within themselves conflicts of loyalty and interest similar to those experienced by Scott and Edgeworth. Commenting on John Adams's reaction to the British withdrawal from Boston in 1776, Hawthorne provides a very inward account of this national/regional conflict:

> "Fortify, fortify; and never let them get in again!" It is agreeable enough to perceive the filial affection with which John Adams, and the other delegates from the North, [then attending the Continental Congress in Philadelphia] regard New England, and especially the good old capital of the Puritans. Their love of country was hardly yet so diluted as to extend over the whole thirteen colonies, which were rather looked upon as allies than as composing one nation. In truth, the patriotism of a citizen of the United States is a sentiment by itself, of a peculiar nature, and requiring a life-time, or at least the custom of many years, to naturalize it among the other possessions of the heart.[4]

In 1774–6 the critical problem was whether regional differences might not be so strongly felt as to prevent the "Old Congress" delegates from forming even an effective military alliance. "Did one spirit harmonize them," asked Hawthorne,

> in spite of the dissimilitude of manners between the North and the South, which were now for the first time brought into political relations? Could the Virginian descendant of the Cavaliers, and the New-Englander with his

hereditary Puritanism – the aristocratic Southern planter, and the self-made
man from Massachusetts or Connecticut – at once feel that they were
countrymen and brothers? What did John Adams think of Jefferson? – and
Samuel Adams of Patrick Henry? (p. 360)

The immediate point of these contrasts is to suggest that the cultural
differences separating North from South during the early years of the
Revolution were not much less than, and not essentially unlike, the
differences separating "the New-Englander with his hereditary Puritanism" from the colonists' common enemy, the British "aristocrats." But
Hawthorne would not have been Hawthorne if he had not also had the
future consequences of these regional differences in mind. By 1844, when
he wrote these reflections on the patriotism of John Adams and his
contemporaries, the national/regional tensions were basically the same
but the tables were turned. At least from the perspective of a "Virginian
descendant of the Cavaliers," the problem now was how to preserve a
regional identity, how to defend a *patria*, against the dominant national
culture. In one form or another this problem has been a recurrent one
throughout the history of the United States, and even when it has not
erupted into xenophobic passions and civil war it has provided
inexhaustible motive and matter for historical romances in the tradition
of Scott.

Acting as interpreters of the past to the present, of provincial to
cosmopolitan society, the authors of such romances generally adopt the
current cosmopolitan idiom but not, not entirely anyway, the viewpoint
that idiom implies. Although they usually wish to reinforce regional
identity and pride, they acknowledge and condemn regional social evils
such as slavery in the South and theocratic repressiveness in the North,
but they solicit the compassion for Thomas Sutpen that he denied
Charles Bon, or for the Puritan elders that they denied Hester Prynne.
Above all, they champion cultural diversity and plenitude – Pinkster
celebrations in Dutch New York, Bohemian superstitions on the
Nebraskan prairie, a medley of dialects in Mississippi – in opposition to
uniformity of manners, language, and artifacts imposed by a white
Anglo-Saxon majority or by chainstore empires managed from the
palatia Americana in Chicago or New York.

Along with many other nineteenth-century observers, Hawthorne
and Cooper believed that the uniformity of democratic manners in
America was an insuperable obstacle to transplanting the English novel
of manners but that the provincial past offered the variety and romantic
associations necessary for historical romance. Hawthorne had more
interesting things to say on this topic than any considerable American
writer before James. For example, in the opening paragraphs of "Edward
Randolph's Portrait," the second of his four "Legends of the Province-

House," he draws a contrast between Boston architecture as it would have appeared before the Revolution and as it does today, i.e., 1838:

> The buildings stood insulated and independent, not, as now, merging their separate existences into connected ranges, with a front of tiresome identity, – but each possessing features of its own, as if the owner's individual taste had shaped it, – and the whole presenting a picturesque irregularity, the absence of which is hardly compensated by any beauties of our modern architecture.[5]

Whatever might be said for the social and economic utility of "our modern architecture" – and, on more strictly political occasions, Hawthorne was prepared to say a good deal in its favor – the expressive individuality and "picturesque irregularity" of the old buildings provide something for the romantic imagination itself to build on. Significantly, the pre-revolutionary building which Hawthorne has particularly in mind is the old Province-House, once the mansion of the royal governors of Massachusetts but now a rather shabby tavern hidden from the sun and public view by a giant modern "brick block" (p. 240). Despite this decline of fortunes, the Province-House still has a few features which associate it vividly with the provincial past: a grand ceremonial staircase; a chimney-piece "set round with Dutch tiles of blue-figured China, representing scenes from Scripture" (p. 240); and most striking of all, atop the house, "a gilded Indian . . . with his bow bent and his arrow on the string, as if aiming at the weathercock on the spire of the Old South" (p. 239). These features may remind us of more than one of Hawthorne's finest stories.

Many of Hawthorne and Cooper's contemporaries disagreed with the contention that the face of democratic America was featureless and devoid of literary interest. Literary nationalists argued that what the United States fortunately lacked, vertically, in multiple social-class gradations she more than made up for, horizontally, in variety of regional manners. "Do any of our readers look out of New-England and doubt it?" asked W.H. Gardiner in 1822.

> Did any one of them ever cross the Potomac, or even the Hudson, and not feel himself surrounded by a different race of men? Is there any assimilation of character between the highminded, vainglorious Virginian, living on his plantation in baronial state, an autocrat among his slaves, a nobleman among his peers, and the active, enterprizing, moneygetting merchant of the East, who spends his days in bustling activity among men and ships, and his nights in sober calculations over his ledger and day-book?[6]

Gardiner goes on to draw contrasts between other familiar regional character-types, but it is well to take note that the contrast which comes first and most forcibly to his mind is the politically significant one between Cavalier and Yankee. "It would be hard indeed out of such materials, so infinitely diversified," he concludes triumphantly, which "have in other countries been wrought successfully into every form of the popular and domestic tale, at once amusing and instructive, if nothing can be fabricated on this degenerate soil" (p. 57).

But Gardiner was a man of his age – which, so far as fiction was concerned, was the Age of Scott. He wanted something more heroic than "the popular and domestic tale" or Edgeworthian regional novel. He hoped to see the day when "that more commodious structure, the modern historical romance, shall be erected in all its native elegance and strength on American soil, and of materials exclusively our own" (p. 58).[7] Pregnant matter for such fiction might be found, he thought, in three "great epochs in American history": "the times just succeeding the first settlement – the aera of the Indian wars, which lie scattered along a considerable period – and the revolution" (pp. 59–60). He considered the first era promising because the diverse national/ethnic origins of the early settlers offered wonderful opportunities for exhibiting bold cultural contrasts like those in the Waverley novels. A historical romance which juxtaposed the early settlers of Virginia with those of Massachusetts would have "the additional value of developing the political history of the times, and the first beginnings, perhaps, of those conflicting sectional interests, which sometimes perplex us at the present day" (p. 61). Gardiner allowed that the distance between the two colonies might prove an impediment but thought that the difficulty might be surmounted with a little "poetical license, especially by the link of the New Netherlands" (p. 61). Cooper (e.g., in *The Prairie*) and Paulding (e.g., *The Puritan and His Daughter*) often made liberal claims to such license, but Gardiner himself inadvertently suggests why little license was actually needed in his thumbnail sketch of "the Connecticut pedlar, who travels over mountain and moor by the side of his little red wagon and half-starved pony, to the utmost bounds of civilization, vending his '*notions*' at the very ends of the earth" (p. 57). We come across this figure, or his cousins, again and again in the American historical romance. Nor was New England the only region of the United States to send its surplus children abroad in quest of personal freedom and economic betterment: we need only think of *The Bostonians* or *Absalom, Absalom!* to be reminded that Southerners too have been ready to migrate into alien territory when occasion demanded.

4

Regionalism in the American historical romance has been given its most powerful "patriotic" expressions in representations of two heroic phases of American social history. First, a homeland is founded in the wilderness; second, the cultural and/or territorial integrity of an established homeland is defended against foreign usurpation. The mainspring of the action during both phases is basically the same. It is a powerful migratory or colonizing impulse, "progressive" in tendency but not on that account always or in all respects morally superior to the reactionary repulse with which it is met. For the impelling force that is treated as creative and ennobling during the first phase is often made to appear destructive and degrading during the second (albeit perhaps acting unwittingly in the long-term interests of social progress).

This is the stuff out of which epics are made. Indeed, ancient and medieval European epic literature is rich in models for the representation of both phases. For the swarmings of the first phase, obvious models are to be found in Exodus, the *Aeneid*, and the Saga of Eirik the Red; for the heroic resistances of the second, in the last stands of Homer's Trojans, Roland, and the mighty protagonists of the old Celtic legends out of which James Macpherson, in the guise of Ossian, fabricated his mournful pseudo-epics shortly after the Jacobite defeat at Culloden. American historical romancers were mindful of such models and, as we saw in chapter 2, made extensive use of them as early as *The Last of the Mohicans*. A more recent example, and one more pertinent to the issue of historical romance as a regional epic, is mentioned by Allen Tate in an essay on Faulkner:

> The classical theocratic culture of New England merely declined; its decline could not be focused upon a great action in which the entire society was involved. But the Southern culture did not decline (so the myth goes); it was destroyed by outsiders in a Trojan war. The "older" culture of Troy-South was wiped out by the "upstart" culture of Greece-North. *Sunt lacrimae rerum.*[8]

Actually, neither Faulkner nor Tate fully subscribed to this "mythic" version of the fall of "Troy-South," but plenty of other Southern historical romancers did.

Tate's phrase "a great action in which the entire society was involved" may remind us both of W. P. Ker's claims for the totalizing character of epic and George Watson's comment that "the regional novel is the gateway to the ampler world of the historical novel, since it represents whole societies and conceives of individual characters as composing societies." The historical romance achieves the social inclusiveness which Ker attributes to epic by assimilating the regional novel. Or, to take a different but equally valid view of the relationship, in the historical romance regional fiction achieves the heroic and historical dimensions of epic, without any *necessary* loss of vernacular humor or poignancy, by retelling "the stories of the great men" of the region. A "Scotch Castle Rackrent . . . [in] a much higher strain" the *Quarterly Review* called

Waverley when it first appeared.[9] And so, with adjustments for regional or national differences, might we call *Satanstoe, My Ántonia,* or *Go Down, Moses.* To call *The Scarlet Letter* a "New England *Castle Rackrent* in a much higher strain" would no doubt assert a closer kinship than actually exists; but, as I try to show in chapter 5, Hawthorne's great historical romance and tales of the Puritans may be usefully regarded as regional epics – tales of the patriarchs of New England.

In the American historical romance, the tale of the patriarch is likely to recount not just "the circumstances which detached him from the society of his brethren, and drove him to form a solitary settlement in the wilderness" but also his eventual decline and fall. There appears to be a close causal relation between this pattern in fiction and the facts of social history. For the pace of modernization in America was so rapid, the economic base of land development so often speculative and insecure, that the phases of founding and losing a *patria* frequently either followed each other in swift succession or coexisted for a while, in the persons of past, present, and future owners of the land, in perilous proximity. Most American writers have had plenty of opportunity to observe these patterns in the careers of their neighbors and ancestors. As they were central to Cooper's early experience, it is not surprising that he was the one to give them paradigmatic expression. In some of his frontier novels – notably *The Wept of Wish-ton-Wish, Wyandotté,* and *The Crater* – little is left at the end save a tragic sense of waste; the foundations of the patriarch and his family lie in ruins or are possessed by people who have no earned or hereditary right to them. In his other frontier novels the tragic note is muted, but despite professions of faith in the future of American civilization, a poignant air of transience hovers over all the works of his pioneers as it does over the early scenes in Cole's *The Course of Empire.*

That later American historical romancers shared this sense of transience is neatly illustrated by a remarkable instance of epic imitation which is familiar to all students of American fiction. The passage imitated is the opening scene of *The Prairie* where the invading Bush family are astonished by the looming figure of Leatherstocking:

> In the centre of this flood of fiery light a human form appeared, drawn against the gilded background as distinctly, and seemingly as palpable, as though it would come within the grasp of any extended hand. The figure was colossal; the attitude musing and melancholy; and the situation directly in the route of the travellers.   (p. 8)

The imitation occurs in Book II of *My Ántonia*:

> There were no clouds, the sun was going down in a limpid, gold-washed sky. Just as the lower edge of the red disk rested on the high fields against the

horizon, a great black figure suddenly appeared on the face of the sun. We sprang to our feet, straining our eyes toward it. In a moment we realized what it was. On some upland farm, a plough had been left standing in the field. The sun was sinking just behind it. Magnified across the distance by the horizontal light, it stood out against the sun, was exactly contained within the circle of the disk; the handles, the tongue, the share – black against the molten red. There it was, heroic in size, a picture writing on the sun.   (p. 245)

Cather's heroic metonymy, emblem of agrarian triumph, is every bit as powerful as the Wordsworthian intimation of Leatherstocking's moral grandeur which is wrought by nature's rhetoric in *The Prairie*. But whereas it seems obviously right for Cooper to associate the decline of Leatherstocking and his hunter-gatherer way of life with the diurnal and seasonal decline of nature, it seems odd at first sight that Cather should gather the same associations of perishability around the works of her Nebrasken sodbusters. The very mechanism of celebrative enlargement – the setting sun – is a reminder of the transience of all glory and the disappointment that inevitably awaits, in Coleridge's words once more, "the Desire & the admiration of Permanence." Although My *Antonia* has perhaps the most convincing happy ending of any classic American novel, the book is haunted by the Virgilian sentiment which the narrator Jim Burden – or is it Cather herself? – chooses as an epigraph: *Optima dies . . . prima fugit*; "the best days are the first to flee."

Another unsettling implication of these apparitions is that whether the days are best or worst, the migrants heroes or villains, depends largely on the position of the observer and the time of day. From the perspective of its red American inhabitants, the "desert" claimed by white colonists was a beloved homeland and the "first" phase must have looked remarkably like the second. From the perspective of the tenant farmers on the great Hudson River estates owned by Cooper's friends, agrarian revolt against land monopoly had a pioneering, a founding aspect. Reducing the complexities of social history to the appealing epic simplicities of an early heroic phase of founding and a later heroic age of defending often hinged on adroit manipulation of odds and point of view. As Hawthorne remarked of one frontier encounter, "Imagination, by casting certain circumstances judiciously into the shade, may see much to admire in the heroism of a little band, who gave battle to twice their number in the heart of the enemy's country."[10] Hawthorne, himself a master at throwing various circumstances into the shade, rarely acknowledged the existence of an Indian viewpoint. Cooper did, but in such a way as ultimately to reinforce the claims of later, white "defenders."

A striking example of such manipulation is *The Wept of Wish-ton-Wish*. Cooper hints broadly enough that there is something perverse and egocentric as well as devout and heroic about Mark Heathcote's exodus from "the country of his fathers" (p. 354) to Massachusetts Bay and thence after many years to a place removed as far as possible from the contaminating influence of alien doctrines – and also from the protection of civil society. But whether we regard it as the work of a fanatic or a saint, the perilous isolation which Mark contrives for himself and his little flock ensures that we see their world as they see it, feel their dangers as they feel them. The mute presence of the captive Indian boy reminds us that there is another standpoint from which to judge Mark Heathcote's claim to the valley of Wish-ton-Wish as a new Canaan to which he has "been led by the flaming pillar of Truth" (p. 236). But that judgment is never fully articulated during the first half of the romance, and it is clear that while Cooper may not expect us to share Mark's sense of having a divine mission in the wilderness, he does wish us to conceive of the first Wish-ton-Wish settlement as a heroic synecdoche for the Puritan colonization of New England as a whole. (Cooper emphasizes Mark's representative significance by referring to him often simply as "the Puritan," as if he were, warts and all, the quintessence of what was best in the masculine Puritan character.)

During the second part of the narrative, Cooper not only gives the Indians a dissenting voice but also exposes the racism, hypocrisy, and vengefulness of the resurrected white settlement. Although still a temporary local threat, the Indians are now on the defensive. So both odds and point of view change, and with that change the current of our sympathies is redirected. To be sure, the founders do not regard the second wave of Puritan settlers as a hostile presence in the valley. But because they are no longer at the center of authority and because they and their ancient associate Submission have such strong personal ties with Conanchet, the Heathcotes appear to participate in the doom of the Narragansetts. Indeed, there is a direct causal link between the execution of Conanchet, ordered by the new colonial authority, and the deaths of Narra-mattah and her mother, Ruth Heathcote. Not that those responsible intend any such outcome or even desire the death of Conanchet; on the contrary, they are shown to be brave and well-intentioned. But by their self-righteousness and willingness to employ deceit they have already killed the moral spirit of Mark Heathcote's settlement, and it is therefore symbolically apt that they should bring about the deaths of the two purest and best-loved members of his family. In the Reverend Meek Wolfe and other second-generation settlers we behold a degeneration which, continued beyond the heroic founding era of New England history, will issue in the migrant Yankee, prototypical cuckoo and despoiler in the "New York" fiction of Washington Irving and the later Cooper.

5

Characteristically a man who put the past and his native region behind him, the Yankee was a serio-comic figure out of folklore, popular literature and drama who reflected the American people's very confused notions about the course and objectives of national development.[11] On an optimistic view, "the sagacious and enterprising New-Englandman" of Cooper's *Notions of the Americans* (1, 252) – or W. H. Gardiner's more plebeian "Connecticut pedlar, who travels over mountain and moor by the side of his little red wagon and half-starved pony, to the utmost bounds of civilization" – was the positive driving force behind such visible forms of national growth as westward expansion and commercial empire abroad; technological innovation and industrial production on the East Coast; and the spread of literacy throughout the land. Independent, intrepid, inventive, the Connecticut Yankee was the acknowledged errant champion of the Get-up-and-go faith long before Mark Twain entered him in the lists at Camelot.

From another perspective, however, this same son of the Puritans appeared to have inherited all of their leading traits in a sadly degraded condition. He was demagogic rather than truly republican; mercenary rather than frugal; a conforming canter rather than a nonconformist Saint; an Ishmaelite rather than a pilgrim. One of Cooper's New York Dutch characters in *Satanstoe*, speaking with neighborly fear and loathing, called the Yankees *en masse* "the locusts of the west."[12] Jefferson's army of progress – how strangely metamorphosed! Singly or in "hordes," the predatory Yankee appeared in many nineteenth-century fictions, seeking a new Canaan to appropriate whenever the migratory impulse took hold of him. Probably the most vigorous incarnations of the type are Jason Newcome in *Satanstoe* and *The Chainbearer* and Hank Morgan in *A Connecticut Yankee in King Arthur's Court*. A late one is "Wick" (short for Wycliffe and Wicked) Cutter, the hypocritical moneylender of *My Ántonia*.

But if Cooper and Twain created our greatest rival versions of Yankee character in Jason Newcome and Hank Morgan, the writer who set down the Yankee, or rather anti-Yankee, myth in definitive form was Irving. He never wrote a full-length historical romance; but with his shrewd if reactionary view of American progress and his genius for embellishing archetypal plots and characters, he contributed significantly to the domestication of the historical romance in this country. If not historical romance then historical tales and fictional historiography were his forte; his claim to be America's first artistically satisfying fictionalist is very firmly based on *A History of New York, from the Beginning of the World to the End of the Dutch Dynasty* (1809) and three further "Knickerbocker" legends of Dutch New York – "Rip Van Winkle" and "The Legend of Sleepy Hollow" from *The Sketch Book* (1820) and "Dolph Heyliger" from *Bracebridge Hall* (1822).[13] He was also a multi-volumed author of "serious" histories, and earned Prescott's gratitude by abandoning a projected history of the conquest of Mexico. But without denying the considerable interest of several of his nonfictional narratives (especially *Columbus* and *Astoria*), I think it is fair to say that his great enabling discovery was of the fictional "matter" of New York and specifically of the conflict between its first white settlers, the Dutch, and the usurping pedlars and squatters from New England. Not merely his fellow New Yorkers Cooper and Paulding but also the writers of other regions, such as Hawthorne and Simms, surely owed much to "Diedrich Knickerbocker" for revealing how rich was the literary potential of American regional history and legend.

Irving's influence seems to have complemented and reinforced that of his friend and patron Scott. His mock-heroic treatment of the eclipse of the Dutch by the combined forces of the British and their Calvinistic New England colonials strikes many of the same chords as do the romances in which Scott narrates the defeat of the heroic Jacobites by the English and their Calvinistic Scottish allies. Not surprisingly, either, since Scotland and British America had been deeply affected by many of the same social, religious, and intellectual forces, and since both Scott and Irving learned to gauge these forces by the standards of the late Enlightenment. Moreover, both writers inherited a venerable British tradition of anti-Puritan satire and polemic: a tradition which, from Shakespeare through Dryden and Swift to Burns, insisted on a Puritanical nature which was essentially mean, avaricious, intolerant, hypocritical, superstitious, disputatious, iconoclastic, fanatical, gloomy, and treasonable. Both Irving's Yankees and Scott's Border Presbyterians exhibit some of the marks of this tradition. But for a number of reasons – temperamental, patriotic, and even scholarly – Scott and Irving nearly always took an ambivalent view of the Puritan and his descendants and encouraged a similar ambivalence in Cooper, Hawthorne, and a host of minor writers. Indeed, Scott's magnificent achievement in *Old Mortality* and *The Heart of Mid-Lothian* was to recapture for the modern and decidedly non-Puritan reader that heroic dimension which the Puritans themselves never tired of praising in their ancient worthies and martyrs. Irving's achievement was less magnificent, but he showed how even a poor plotting Connecticut schoolmaster might, for a fleeting moment, be transfigured by the light of his own imagination into something that made the pulse beat faster.

But not in the aged arteries of Diedrich Knickerbocker. The ostensible author of Irving's parodic history of the Dutch empire in America is a narrative persona whose transparent biases relieve the real author of responsibility for libeling New England character. As a Dutch historian intent on memorializing the phlegmatic worthies of Manhattan, Knickerbocker does not see the Yankees as degenerate Puritans; rather, he views *all* New Englanders as a perverse and wayward race from the start – indeed, from before the time of their arrival in America. Against them he levels the usual charges of sharp trading, superstition, and intolerance, together with some others (the custom of bundling and clamorousness) peculiarly offensive to the sensibilities of the sedate New York burghers. Here we are concerned specifically with those traits which made the Yankees a progressive and therefore intrusive and unsettling force in the lives of other inhabitants of the North American continent:

> The most prominent of these was a certain rambling propensity, with which, like the sons of Ishmael, they seem to have been gifted by heaven, and which continually goads them on, to shift their residence from place to place, so that a Yankee farmer is in a constant state of migration; *tarrying* occasionally here and there; clearing lands for other people to enjoy, building houses for others to inhabit, and in a manner may be considered the wandering Arab of America.[14]

In line with the Puritans' own practice, Knickerbocker frequently draws parallels between them and the ancient Hebrews, but his parallels (as with the sons of Ishmael) are more often degrading than ennobling. Moreover, his reference to other pastoralists and his description of the New Englanders earlier as "a horde of strange barbarians, bordering upon the eastern frontier" (p. 117), remind us of the warlike and often rapacious nature of peoples at the second stage of social development – peoples such as the ancient Hebrews and Huns. Like Scott and Cooper, Irving was very much a son of the late Enlightenment: not only the stadialists (particularly Kames) but Goethe, Goldsmith, and Macpherson-Ossian were among the writers whose influence blended with that of his more obvious mock-heroic models.

In elegiac mood Knickerbocker laments that the Dutch colonists were simply no match for the shrewd and energetic Yankees:

> As their prototypes of yore went forth into the land of Canaan . . . so these chosen people of modern days would progress through the country in patriarchal style . . . resolutely bent upon "locating" themselves . . . and improving the country. These were the most dangerous kind of invaders. It is true they were guilty of no overt acts of hostility; but it was notorious that, wherever they got a footing, the honest Dutchmen gradually disappeared, retiring slowly as do the Indians before the white man; being in some way or other talked and chaffered, and bargained and swapped, and, in plain English, elbowed out of all those rich bottoms and fertile nooks in which our Dutch yeomanry are prone to nestle themselves.   (p. 257)

The most telling, though unobtrusive, detail in this passage is the phrase "in plain English": although a descendant of the Dutchmen who are his subject, this historian is obliged to write in the language of their conquerors. Thus complete is the ascendency of Yankee culture in "New York." Another and still more poignant picture of the immolation of the New World Dutch occurs when Knickerbocker regrets that the old aristocracy, "the real 'beavers of the Manhattoes,'" have been

> elbowed aside by foreign invaders, and more especially by those ingenious people, "the sons of the Pilgrims," who out-bargain them in the market, out-speculate them on the exchange, out-top them in fortune and run up mushroom palaces so high, that the tallest Dutch family mansion has not wind enough left for its weather-cock. (p. 249)

The image of the weathercock cut off from the wind has many associations – with loss of pride and sense of direction, with empty sails of commerce, and with failure of the breath of life itself. It is an affecting and truly poetic image, and yet the passage as a whole does not make us share Knickerbocker's unwillingness to accept the Dutch defeat. For we recognize, as Knickerbocker does not, that the mansions of the Dutch aristocracy were founded on the peltry of the *real* beavers of the Manhattoes, who were another industrious nation "elbowed aside by foreign invaders" and who are now memorialized only in the nickname of those who displaced them. Likewise the "rich bottoms and fertile nooks" of the earlier passage, which the "honest Dutchmen" lose to the crafty Yankees, once belonged to the Indians. Knickerbocker avoids saying that the *Dutch* drove out the native owners of the land; but by investing the Dutch decline with a borrowed pathos ("retiring slowly, as do the Indians before the white men") he inadvertently calls attention to a cyclic process in which the Dutch themselves were once "the most dangerous kind of invaders." To notice these ironic parallels is not to suggest that Irving regards the disappearance of the old Dutch folkways with indifference or that he fails to distinguish between various degrees and styles of acquisitiveness. But it is to say that he sharply qualifies Knickerbocker's threnody and implicitly rejects the latter's linear (degenerative rather than melioristic) model of history.

However, in the isolated rural settings of Irving's most famous tales of New York, the Dutch are able to hold their own against the force of historical change. Rip Van Winkle discovers after his generation-long sleep that the Kaatskill village inn has Yankee proprietor, "Jonathan Doolittle," and that, "instead of being a subject of his Majesty George the Third, he was now a free citizen of the United States."[15] But there are several hints that nothing essential has changed. The funniest one is that the rubicund countenance on the inn sign, formerly identified as that of George the Third, is the same except that it is now surrounded with

suitably republican appurtenances and labelled "GENERAL WASHING-
TON." Rip, we are told, "was no politician; the changes of states and
empires made but little impression on him" (p. 40); and Irving strongly
implies that so it is, and should be, with the majority of mankind. As for
the Yankees, in this story they are responsible for only one casualty –
Rip's termagant wife, who "broke a blood vessel in a fit of passion at a
New England pedlar" (p. 39).

The inhabitants of Sleepy Hollow are similarly shielded from Yankee
acquisitiveness, but in this case Irving's characterization of the two
peoples, while conforming strictly to type, shifts emphasis just enough to
make us adjust our moral perspective on the conflict. He describes the
"visionary propensity" both of the natives and those who visit the valley,
and explains that

> it is in such little retired Dutch valleys, found here and there embosomed in the
> great state of New York, that population, manners, and customs, remain fixed,
> while the great torrent of migration and improvement, which is making such
> incessant changes in other parts of this restless country, sweeps by them
> unobserved.   (p. 274)

The Connecticut schoolteacher Ichabod Crane, who descends on Sleepy
Hollow looking like "the genius of famine" (p. 274), is a stray rivulet
from that torrent of migration and improvement. Later in life, we are
told, after changing his quarters to a distant part of the country, he "had
kept school and studied law at the same time; had been admitted to the
bar, turned politician, electioneered, written for the newspapers, and
finally had been made a Justice of the Ten Pound Court" (pp. 295–6) – in
short, his was the typical success story of an enterprising Yankee ready to
turn his hand to anything "likely." Even while resident in Sleepy
Hollow, where trees and families alike quietly "vegetated," Ichabod was
never anything but restless. Daydreaming of food, wealth, and sex
commingled,

> as he rolled his great green eyes over the fat meadow lands, the rich fields of
> wheat, of rye, of buckwheat, and Indian corn, and the orchards burthened with
> ruddy fruit, which surrounded the warm tenement of Van Tassel, his heart
> yearned after the damsel who was to inherit these domains, and his imagination
> expanded with the idea, how they might be readily turned to cash, and the
> money invested in immense tracts of wild land, and shingle palaces in the
> wilderness. Nay, his busy fancy already realized his hopes, and presented to
> him the blooming Katrina, with a whole family of children, mounted on the
> top of a wagon loaded with household trumpery, with pots and kettles
> dangling beneath; and he beheld himself beside a pacing mare, with a colt at her
> heels, setting out for Kentucky, Tennessee, or the Lord knows where! (pp. 279–
> 80)

Irving's syntax expands in parallel with Ichabod's imagination, moving with ready fluency through "immense tracts" of space and time. "Our man of letters" (p. 276), it transpires, is a comic representative not only of Yankee get-aheadism but also of the democratic imagination. He is, in de Tocqueville's famous words, "haunted by visions of what will be; in this direction . . . [his] unbounded imagination grows and dilates beyond all measure" (ii, 78). As poet and pioneer of American empire, the rootless Yankee takes on, for a moment, a heroic dimension. We know from such later works as *Astoria* that Irving himself could be moved by the imperial vision and become its apologist. But the younger Irving, who was a great regional storyteller writing as Diedrich Knickerbocker rather than a grand old man of national letters, what did he think of the relationship between Yankee progress and the literary imagination?

He allowed that, as a rule, New Englanders had considerably more respect for learning, were less gross in their materialism, and certainly were no less imaginative than their neighbors. However, they and their descendants in upstate New York, "Kentucky, Tennessee, or the Lord knows where" had traits which made them enemies of the literary (as distinct from political or business) imagination – namely, their contentiousness, "rambling propensity," and mistrust of idleness. According to Knickerbocker's *History*, in a parable which is a minor comic analogue of "The May-Pole of Merry Mount," the Puritan arrival in the New World stilled all the voices of nature:

> And, in fact, no sooner did they land upon the shore of this free-spoken country, than they all lifted up their voices and made such a clamor of tongues, that we are told they frightened every bird and beast out of the neighborhood, and struck such mute terror into certain fish, that they have been called *dumb-fish* ever since. (p. 118)

The phrase "free-spoken country" means both a land of free speech and a land that was reserved or claimed ("spoken for") at no cost to the Puritans. In the course of time these shrewd bargainers acquired a rich regional history and folklore, but their migratory habits tended to detach them from this heritage. "Local tales and superstitions thrive best in these sheltered, long-settled retreats," the narrator of "The Legend of Sleepy Hollow" remarks, "but are trampled under foot, by the shifting throng that forms the population of most of our country places" (p. 289). How indeed should Ichabod's children, always in transit to the Lord knows where, have any familiarity with the local tales and superstitions which formed the stock-in-trade of a European romancer or a Diedrich Knickerbocker? (When Irving visited Abbotsford, shortly before writing "The Legend of Sleepy Hollow," he was struck by the number of scenes and incidents in Scott's work that had an immediately Tweedside origin and also by a few of Scott's fictions that were already repeated as local history. Although Irving's own Dutch-American tales relied heavily on German sources for their legendary matter, they nonetheless did for the Catskills what (so Thomas Cole believed) Burns's "bonnie little sangs" had done for Scotland: they made the country more beautiful. At once restless and highly disciplined in the pursuit of spiritual and material ends, Knickerbocker's typical Yankee was certain to be intolerant of Rip's wise passiveness or Dolph Heyliger's openness to impulse – Wordsworthian qualities subversive of the world of getting and spending, but winning access to the liberating world of imagination for both of these improvident heroes.

Admittedly, Ichabod is a complicated case. As a democratic visionary he values the past and present only as they promise to contribute to an orgiastic future. Equally "Yankee," however, are his learning and superstitiousness, which, especially under the influence of Sleepy Hollow, draw him back to his Puritan roots. We are told that "he had read several books quite through, and was a perfect master of Cotton Mather's History of New England Witchcraft, in which . . . he most firmly and potently believed" (p. 276). It is precisely because his imagination strays from visions of the future perfect into those of the haunted past that he is driven, empty-handed, from the spellbound land of the Dutch. To be made vulnerable by his rich responsiveness to the past might appear a hard and ambivalent fate for "Our man of letters," and it is indeed true that Irving never allows us to fall wholly out of sympathy with his pedagogue. Yet we are obliged to remember, too, Ichabod's impulse to convert Katrina's inheritance into cash, and to notice that he cultivates an anachronistic belief in witchcraft chiefly for the sake of cozy thrills by the evening fireside. In fact, his involvement with the past and other people is essentially parasitic and is heavily dependent on stimulus from the local legends of his Dutch hosts. The neighborhood

> was one of those highly favoured places which abound with chronicle and great men. The British and American line had run near it during the war; it had, therefore been the scene of marauding, and been infested with refugees, cowboys, and all kinds of border chivalry.   (p. 288)

Nearby is the very spot where one of the chief sentimental heroes of the war, the British spy Major André, was taken:

> To pass this bridge, was the severest trial. It was at this identical spot that the unfortunate André was captured, and under the covert of those chestnuts and vines were the sturdy yeomen concealed who surprised him. This has ever since been considered a haunted stream, and fearful are the feelings of the schoolboy who has to pass it alone after dark.   (p. 292)

Although no spy, Ichabod is a scheming foreigner among the Dutch, and it is easy to see why, traveling the solitary road after being rejected by

Katrina, he might feel a trembling sympathetic identification with "the unfortunate André" and fall an easy prey to his rival Brom Bones masquerading as the headless horseman.

6

Thus, with some help from such unlikely collaborators as Brom Bones and Cotton Mather, the *genii loci* of rural New York took their revenge on one of the rambling sons of Ishmael. But if the Dutch were comparatively safe from down-east incursions in Sleepy Hollow and the charmed vales of the Kaatskills, Irving knew well enough that elsewhere life could go hard with those who had neither the vigorous independence of the Netherlandish explorers and early settlers nor the means and business sense of the merchant classes. They "gradually disappeared," complained Knickerbocker in the *History*, "retiring slowly, as do the Indians before the white men." The irony noticed earlier qualifies but does not cancel the pathos of Dutch ethnic extinction. Especially in and near Manhattan were the Dutch inhabitants subject to an environment that had been growing increasingly English, competitive, and impersonal ever since New Amsterdam became New York. The nature of the problem is suggested, if not clearly defined, in "Dolph Heyliger," and a rather defiantly impractical "solution" is found.

"Dolph Heyliger" is the story of a scapegrace Manhattan lad who is reared in genteel poverty by his widowed mother. After an unsatisfactory apprenticeship to a doctor, the feckless but brave and resourceful Dolph stumbles into a series of adventures which lead him, as by a mysterious agency, up the Hudson River. There he is befriended by the famous Albany hunter and patroon Antony Vander Heyden, an anachronistic figure out of the earliest days of Dutch settlement in New Netherland. The Albany of which he is a leading citizen is a charming old-fashioned Dutch town, and its most charming inhabitant is Antony's daughter Marie. As one poor orphan-boy's wish after another is fulfilled, Dolph learns that Antony is a distant relative of his mother; successfully woos the beautiful Marie; and discovers a clue to ancestral treasure buried back in Manhattan. Eventually, after returning home, Dolph becomes the wealthy husband of Marie, the boon hunting-companion of her father, and at last a respected public figure and patron of all things that enhance the enjoyment of life. Such is the reward for his Candide-like faith that "things will all, some how or other, turn out for the best."[16] At one point, however, he asks with understandable impatience why he was sent "all the way to Albany, to hear a story that was to send me all the way back again" (p. 243). His answer, that he was meant to reunite both the family (by marrying Marie) and all of its wealth, may satisfy Dolph and the casual reader, but Irving is clearly inviting us to discover a rather more profound meaning in his improvident hero's journey.

The Manhattan of "Dolph Heyliger" is still, at the very beginning of the eighteenth century, a largely Dutch town, but it is obviously well on its way to becoming the city that Irving, Cooper, and Melville knew. Irving mentions that the most notorious of the British governors, Lord Cornbury, is actively suppressing the use of Dutch in schools and churches, and already there are signs that, outside the family, human relationships are understood in the contractual terms of urban capitalism. Because Dame Heyliger's husband had died in the service of the community, "it was universally agreed that 'something ought to be done for the widow'" (p. 251). But nothing ever is, and so, "living in a mercantile town," she catches something of the spirit and sets up as a very modest shopkeeper. Later, when help is urgently needed to save her little home and business from fire, "the populace" bends its efforts instead to saving the fine furniture of her wealthy neighbors. To be sure, this is not the alienating Manhattan of "Bartleby the Scrivener," but neither is it exactly hospitable to the strictly noncommercial virtues of Dame Heyliger's son. Dolph has "that daring, gamesome spirit, which is extolled in a rich man's child, but execrated in a poor man's" (p. 252); his is the spirit of Hendrick Hudson and the early settlers of New Netherland, and it is now sadly out of place in "the jolly, little old city of the Manhattoes."

The answer to Dolph's question, then, is that to "find himself" (for he *is* a "rich man's child") he must make a brave and generous passage back to his own Dutch pioneer roots – to Albany, the "stronghold of the patriarchs" (p. 284). The story of his journey from one of these sharply contrasted towns to the other is thus a fable both of initiation and ethnic survival. And we should notice in this connection that Dolph does not transplant himself permanently; for he is, unawares, a man with a public mission to fulfill. It is to restore to Manhattan some of the Dionysian spirit of fun and imaginative play that Irving regularly associates with seventeenth-century Dutch genius.

Although Dolph's adventures occur during the early eighteenth century, when British dominion is firmly established in New York, Irving opens a window on the expansive vistas of the previous century by interpolating the tale of a "storm-ship" which once haunted the Hudson. This Coleridgean phantom-ship, which first appeared during "the golden age of the province of the New Netherlands" (p. 280), was always seen "just after, or just before, or just in the midst of unruly weather" (p. 282); she continued "a matter of popular belief and marvellous anecdote through the whole time of the Dutch government," but since then "we have no authentic accounts of her" (p. 283). The tale is full of the wind and thunder that commonly betoken a visitation of the spirit of imagination in Romantic poetry and do also in "Rip Van Winkle." This spirit, a prankish one in Irving's comic tales, is no servant of the bourgeois virtues of thrift, sobriety, and good order; it is much more likely to advance the fortunes of a congenial soul like Dolph or Rip than to smooth the waters for the skipper of a merchant ship. Yet we must remember that this same wayward inspiring force that carries Dolph to Antony, Marie, and wealth, once filled the sails of Hendrick Hudson in his "quest of a northwest passage" to Cathay (p. 279) – a quest frustrated, it is true, but leading to far greater riches in the New World than the oriental trade could ever have yielded. The imagination, it seems, is not at odds with the pursuit of wealth, provided that the pursuers be not timid, humorless, or mean. Their boldness and ready largess make Irving's fictional Dutchmen forefathers of his capitalist friend John Jacob Astor and descendants of Goethe's romanticized Goetz of the Iron Hand.

The tale of the storm ship is related by Antony Vander Heyden, and we soon discover that this conservator of local traditions and spokesman for the folk imagination is himself the subject of many tales. For although he is firmly based in a town not "as yet . . . discovered and colonized by the restless people of New England," his own restlessness makes him appear "the Sinbad of Albany" (pp. 283, 290). However, in Antony's case restlessness leads to hunting expeditions which serve to maintain rather than obliterate the old heroic customs and relationships of the colony. At once a great hunter and patroon, the gray-haired Antony is a sort of composite of Leatherstocking and Judge Temple: a composite which neatly disposes of the problems of land ownership and use posed by these principal antagonists in *The Pioneers*. At all events, the wild thing in his heart that causes Antony to surround himself with Indian companions and artefacts also makes him an admirable surrogate father for Dolph, and Irving is as explicit as possible about this relationship: "The heart of the old bushwacker yearned toward the young man, who seemed thus growing up in his own likeness" (p. 283). So it turns out that for Dolph to discover his true ethnic paternity is likewise to establish a kinship with the aboriginal lords of the land. In the last sentence of the story, Irving tells us that "Dolph Heyliger was noted for being the ablest drawer of the long-bow in the whole province" (p. 300).

The opposed values which are embodied in the Yankee/Dutch conflict in Irving's fiction of New York are to be found not just in the *Waverley*-model but everywhere in Romantic literature. Besides, the *History of New York* antedates *Waverley* by five years. So what is principally involved in the Scott–Irving relationship is not influence but mutual appreciation and shared sympathies, although it is possible that Scott's advice and immense success with the matter of Scotland may have encouraged Irving to return from time to time to the matter of New

York. At all events, before Cooper published *The Spy* or *The Pioneers*, Irving had already domesticated some of the key themes, character types, and normative oppositions present or at least latent in the *Waverley*-model. Since the works in which he developed his great Dutch and Yankee antagonists were widely read and even achieved classic status during his lifetime, there can be little doubt that they helped to create both the model and the audience for the American historical romance. Knickerbocker's legends of New York may also have enforced some of the biases of the Cavalier myth of the South, where Irving shared some of Scott's huge popularity: perhaps we can discern literary descendants of Ichabod Crane and his confreres in the ravenous Snopeses of Yokna-patawpha County.

7

Cooper knew not only Irving's tales and Knickerbocker's *History* but also the same kinds of New Englanders and New York Dutch, in fact and folk fiction, that Irving knew. Therefore it might be maintained that resemblances between his fictional Yankees and those of Irving came about more because both writers had studied the same models than because they had read each other. Doubtless most of the parallels are best accounted for in this way. Yet so striking are they in the case of *Satanstoe* that it is hard to dismiss the possibility that "Dolph Heyliger" and "The Legend of Sleepy Hollow" in particular were sources of inspiration for this much later account of sectional and ethnic conflict in old York colony. This seems the more likely because Irving's tales of the 1820s and Cooper's great romance of 1845 were written under such radically different personal and social circumstances that it is somewhat surprising to find many points of correspondence in the works themselves. Cooper disapproved of Irving's Anglophilia and permissive temperament: is it possible that the parallels in question were deliberate and his deviations from them meant to be read as implicit criticisms of Irving's immensely popular and essentially sanguine treatments of the same subject?

Writing in Europe after a long absence from home, and writing partly for an English audience all too ready to believe the worst about their late ungrateful colonials, Irving was not inclined to vent dark forebodings or harsh criticisms regarding either his native land or "the paternal roof " of England. At that time, too – during the so-called "Era of Good Feeling" – many of the traditional sectional cleavages in America were not felt so strongly as they had been and would be again by the end of the 1820s. So Irving's portraits of the Yankee were less dehumanizing, his portraits of the Dutch less tinged with pathos, than they had been in 1809. Even Cooper, who inherited not only sectional but also social-class prejudices against the "Down-easterners" who had been the principal settlers on his father's lands around Cooperstown, New York, wrote eulogies of New England in *Lionel Lincoln* (1825) and *Notions of the Americans* (1828). But two decades later American society appeared to Cooper to be in a state of near disintegration, and he pinned much of the blame on the spirit of Yankeeism. In his home state the old Dutch buildings and customs were rapidly vanishing. In the towns especially, long-established families were being outnumbered and thrown on the defensive by immigrants from Europe and New England, while on the great landed estates of his friends and social peers the agricultural tenants were claiming as their own the lands that their families had rented for generations, maintaining (among other things) that a tenant-farming system was basically feudal and "un-American." Attempted evictions led to violence and the eventual breaking-up of the system, but before the end came Cooper published a trilogy of family chronicle novels, the first and much the best of them *Satanstoe*, written to show that the landed proprietors of his own time had a right to charge rents on lands which the prudence and practical sacrifices of their ancestors had earned for them.

As the trilogy develops and comes closer to the time of writing, the original Yankee settlers and their offspring come closer to the center of economic and political power, and Cooper's tone becomes increasingly strident. But thanks to the narrative convention of the trilogy he is able in *Satanstoe* to preserve some of Irving's detachment. For each book is ostensibly a memoir written by the heir in each of three generations of the affluent Anglo-Dutch Littlepage family, and in the mid-eighteenth century where the chronicle begins such a family could have afforded to regard a plebeian Yankee with amused condescension, little fearing the talents and ambition of such a peculiar being. Cooper was sufficiently interested in the technical problem of sustaining an eighteenth-century provincial point of view not to obtrude sentiments and wisdoms based on nineteenth-century experience. And he had two remaining books in which to unveil the full face of Yankeeism.

Jason Newcome, the patriarch of the Yankee clan that eventually seeks to dispossess the Littlepages, is a figure at once intriguingly like and unlike Ichabod Crane. An aspiring Connecticut schoolmaster who makes an unsuccessful bid for the hand of an Anglo-Dutch heiress, Jason is superstitious and shifts from pedagogue to pioneer in the course of the narrative. Although Jason is no coward and therefore cannot be sent scurrying out of the community, in broad outline his character and career are almost identical with those of Ichabod. As his name suggests, he is essentially a Yankee "type" with scarcely any capacity for moral growth. Still there is much more to Jason that this summary suggests. The fictional world of *Satanstoe* is drafted on an altogether larger and more realistic scale than that of Irving's tale, and Jason is correspondingly more particularized and complicated than Ichabod. However stunted his moral growth, he has the coolness, patience, and intellectual resources of a human adversary. In *Satanstoe* he is so situated that his breaches are mainly of social decorum rather than of morals, but his eye is constantly on the main chance; his time will come. So will Ichabod's, but his triumph will occur elsewhere at no cost to anybody we know – never, certainly, on the enchanted ground of Sleepy Hollow.

In *The Last of the Mohicans* the aged chief Tamenund, alluding to all the white invaders of his land, says: "I have often seen the locusts strip the leaves from the trees, but the season of blossoms has always come again!"[17] In *Satanstoe* the Dutch Colonel Follock more bluntly calls the Yankees "the locusts of the west" (p. 47). That Cooper recalled Tamenund's speech when he ascribed these words to Follock may perhaps be doubted, but it is no coincidence that these spokesmen for two beleaguered peoples should employ the same symbolism when referring to their enemies. As we have seen, Irving draws a similar parallel between the Dutch retreat before the Yankees and the Indian retreat before the whites. Parallels of this kind, heroic and tinged with Ossianic pathos but rich with satiric possibilities as well, were always on the minds of Irving and the historical romancers. In the typological terms of the *Waverley*-model, the Dutch were the Mohicans or Highlanders of the Littlepage trilogy. Cooper does not press the parallel hard and neither should we, since it is apparent that in historical actuality these peoples had little in common except a defensive posture before the armies of progress. As it often had been for Scott and Irving before him, however, this one crucial point of resemblance was sufficient for Cooper to evoke the characteristic polar oppositions of his model.

Jason's most important opposite number in *Satanstoe* is the daredevil Albany Dutchman Guert Ten Eyck. Guert is a still more richly individualized character than the Yankee and therefore even less justifiably reduced to his sources in American folklore and European Romantic Revival literature. All the same, if there is much more to Guert than to Dolph Heyliger or Antony Vander Heyden, his antecedents are the same as theirs – except, of course, in so far as *they* are his antecedents. In him reappears the roistering Dutch buck, of whom one obvious example is Ichabod's rival Brom Bones, and such products of the European literary imagination as Scott's Rob Roy, Pushkin's Pugachov, and the American Noble Savage. Toping, prank-loving Guert combines Dolph's youth and good looks with Antony's wealth and Albanian social connections, and with both of them he shares an instinctive respect and aptitude for Indian ways. Not invariably, to be sure, since certain Indian ways (such as scalping) always seem barbarous or incomprehensible to

Cooper's gentlefolk; but his deep affinity with the native creatures of America – birds, beasts, and men – is revealed in Cornelius (Corny) Littlepage's recollection that

> Guert, who was a capital mimic, had previously taught us several calls and rallying signals, all of which were good imitations of the cries of different tenants of the woods, principally birds. These signals had their origin with the red men. (p. 369)

Here we may usefully remember how, in Knickerbocker's *History*, the clamor of the Puritans silenced all the voices of nature in New England. But the contrast between Dutchman and Yankee in *Satanstoe* is most pointed in Littlepage's final tribute to Guert:

> Poor Guert! I passed a few minutes at his grave before we went south. It was all that was left of his fine person, his high spirit, his lion-hearted courage, his buoyant spirits, and his unextinguishable love of frolic. A finer physical man I never beheld, or one who better satisfied the eye, in all respects. That the noble tenement was not more intellectually occupied, was purely the consequence of a want of education. Notwithstanding, all the books in the world could not have converted Guert Ten Eyck into a Jason Newcome, or Jason Newcome into a Guert Ten Eyck. Each owed many of his peculiarities, doubtless, to the province in which he was bred and born, and to the training consequent upon these accidents; but nature had also drawn broad distinctions between them. All the wildness of Guert's impulses could not altogether destroy his feelings, tone, and tact as a gentleman; while all the soaring, extravagant pretentions of Jason never could have ended in elevating him to that character. (pp. 413–14)

In Guert Ten Eyck we may see how, in opposition to "the locusts of the west," a frontier Dutchman or an American savage might claim kinship with Cooper's civilized ideal, the American Gentleman. That ideal, which mattered greatly to Cooper, could be realized completely only when the advantages of inherited wealth and social station, as well as of good education, gave polish and shape to the essential diamond of gentlemanly character – what Cooper describes here as Guert's apparently innate "feelings, tone, and tact as a gentleman." On the showing of *Satanstoe*, neither rural New York nor rural New England society favored the realization of the ideal; but whereas the generous excess of the Albany buck was not at variance with the spirit of gentlemanliness, the meanness and avarice which Cooper associated with New England tradesmen and farmers were. To that extent, "Yankee" and New Englander were synonymous in Cooper's vocabulary. But ultimately, neither "Yankee" nor "Gentleman" was a regional, racial, or even a social-class denomination.

Ichabod Crane and the Heyliger-Vander Heyden pair stand in relation to Jason and Guert as miniature sketches or cartoons to full-length finished portraits. The relationship between Dolph and Cooper's youthful narrator-protagonist Corny is also close, but they resemble each other not so much in character as in career. Corny is very definitely an American Gentleman, which means that he is better educated, probably more intelligent, and certainly more "refined" than Dame Heyliger's wayward son. Moreover, as the scion of a prosperous Anglo-Dutch farming family, Corny has no need either to make his own fortune or to reclaim the traditional values of an oppressed people. But Corny too makes a journey to Albany and the surrounding wilderness, and the story of this journey can also be interpreted as a fable of initiation and ethnic survival. Corny journeys up-colony in order to locate a vast tract of land which his father has purchased dirt-cheap from the Mohawk Indians. Cooper is more direct than Irving about economic realities as he is about most other matters. We may feel that confronting those realities so painfully in his own life and the lives of his friends calloused his moral sensibilities. Or we may feel that Cooper is a bluff, honest Tory, while Irving is an evasive, ostrich-Tory. In either case, their fables of initiation and ethnic survival are substantially the same. For if we take the primeval wilderness and the old Dutch town of Albany to represent the past, it makes sense to say that both Dolph and Corny secure the future by traveling into the past. The problem is more complicated for Corny because his ancestry is both Dutch and English. Cooper solves the problem by having him travel still farther afield and undergo a baptism of gunfire with the 1759 British expeditionary forces against Montcalm and his Indian allies.

Having grappled successfully with the ancient enemies of his two peoples, Corny wins the hand of Anneke, the Anglo-Dutch heroine who chooses him in preference not merely to the unthinkable Jason Newcome but also to her attractive Dutch cousin Dirck Follock and her still more eligible English relation Harry Bulstrode. Corny at one point (p. 86) complains that everybody except himself appears to be related to Anneke, but what the two of them share as a result of the mingling of Dutch and English manners is far more important than blood relationship. The rejected Harry retires to England and, like Dirck, remains a bachelor. The ever-resourceful Jason, having acted on the "nothing ventured nothing gained" principle, simply looks around for another, more available helpmate. The meaning of Cooper's socio-political allegory is unmistakable: the foreseeable future of New York lies with those, the Anglo-Dutch, who have created something new out of the old stocks. Occupying a middle ground, like Scott's heroes, the new New Yorker can sympathize with and value both of the original colonizing peoples of the region; and, as they cannot, he can even tolerate and harbor a Yankee.

To say that Corny occupies a middle ground is not to suggest that he is a mere spectator or neutral party in the numerous conflicts which together create the pattern of antithesis and balance that unifies this diverse novel. Corny takes sides with the Dutch against the Yankees, the Anglicans against the Congregationalists, the British against the French, the whites against the reds, the colonies against "home." And taking sides involves making moral choices: of the heart rather than the head, the venerable rather than the innovative, Civilization rather than Savagery, *patria* rather than imperial province. Taking sides also involves forming a series of adoptive relationships – at least one of which is unwelcome. After rescuing Anneke from the clutches of a lion (a perfectly credible adventure, by the way), Corny is circumspectly adopted by her as a brother: "I beg of you," she says, "if you have a sister, to carry to her the proffered friendship of Anneke Mordaunt, and tell her that her own prayers in behalf of her brother will not be more sincere than mine" (p. 72). Already, of course, Corny has a quite different relationship in view and accepts the fraternal role only as a means to that end. But Corny is an only child and greatly cherishes his fraternal friendships with such varied male contemporaries as his black slave Jaap, Dirck, Harry Bulstrode, and Guert. No less important after he begins his travels is a series of filial relationships he forms with older men: his genial tutor the Rev. Thomas Worden, his future father-in-law Herman Mordaunt, his general Lord Howe (an officer very conscious of his paternal trust), and finally his Indian guide Susquesus. But for his astonishing prowess (and Corny's inexperience) as a woodsman and warrior, Susquesus might seem too young for a paternal role but as the action develops we discover that in many respects he is Corny's surest guide not only to the physical but also to the moral, social, and military wildernesses. And in adopting Corny, Susquesus also of course establishes the Littlepages' right relationship with the land: a relationship inherited as it were rather than merely purchased with a few trinkets. They will need every possible legal, moral, and sentimental claim because their ownership will be violently challenged in *The Chainbearer* (1845) by a New England squatting family closely modeled on that of Ishmael Bush, and in *The Redskins* (1846) by Jason Newcome's demagogic descendants.

Although I have stressed the features which *Satanstoe* shares with the fictions of Cooper's fellow New Yorker Irving, I might equally well have discussed those which relate it to Scott's "Scotch Castle Rackrent . . . [in] a much higher strain" earlier and Faulkner's family sagas later. Like those works, *Satanstoe* has the extraordinarily rich and mixed current, the ample social and generic inclusiveness of epic, bringing together an astonishingly wide range of narrative kinds, dialects, races, nationalities, and social levels. Ironically, it is precisely this strength of generosity in Cooper's finest historical romances that exposes the weakness in them which is most apparent to readers today, namely, their tendency to stereotype along racial, gender, and social-class lines.

It compounds the irony to know that Hawthorne, a writer equally socially prejudiced and more xenophobic than Cooper, has long appeared the more truly liberal spirit and friend to the disenfranchised not only because of the critique of Puritan exclusiveness in, but also because of the narrower purview of, *his* great regional-historical epic. To be sure, the differences of purview had much to do with their respective "matters." Like Scott's, Cooper's matter was intrinsically much richer in social manners than Hawthorne's. But these differences resulted likewise from dissimilarities of personality and artistic aim: Hawthorne narrowed his focus to achieve greater interiority, artistic refinement, and moral intensity. Those who have read and reread *The Scarlet Letter* and the best romances of Scott and Cooper over an extended period will gratefully acknowledge that Hawthorne was brilliantly successful in his venture and thus able to do things which his predecessors could not do, or at least not so well. But they will also appreciate that in sprawling epics like *Waverley* and *Satanstoe* Scott and Cooper were able to do things, no less valuable, which Hawthorne scarcely attempted.

5

Hawthorne and the ironies of New England history

1

In "The Custom-House" Hawthorne draws a wry, punning contrast between "the enervating magic of place" which enthralls the dismissed federal officer with mirages of Uncle Sam's future patronage and the "spell" of that very solid "native place," Salem, to which successive generations of his ancestors had clung with "oyster-like tenacity" and which pulls Hawthorne himself back as if it were "the inevitable centre of the universe."[1] Neither "place" offered him the security he needed in 1849, since the Whigs most responsible for despoiling him of office were Salem Whigs, his fellow townsmen. Nonetheless, the rival attractions of the two kinds of "place" continued to exert their power over him as they had done throughout his adult life, and they appealed to much besides material self-interest. To state the matter very simply and broadly, Hawthorne associated the future of society with American nationhood, its past with Europe and the ex-colonial regions of the Atlantic seaboard. He was drawn to both but perfectly at home with neither, and many – very many – of his maneuvers in life and art can be interpreted as attempts to effect a reconciliation or discover the one in the other. Obtaining the surveyor's post at the U.S. Custom House in Salem was but the most obvious and painfully unsuccessful one. More to the point here, in many of his greatest stories he joined his New England contemporaries in a filiopietistic reading of history which reconciled regional and national loyalties by highlighting those aspects of the New England past (e.g. Puritan love of "liberty") which could be construed to foreshadow or, like seeds, contain the future nation.

But a patriotic strategy which perfectly suited the historian George Bancroft, mystical progressivist and dispenser of Democratic party patronage, was fraught with historical, moral, and artistic problems for a writer too detached from any public "place," creed, or leader ever to commit himself unreservedly. More uncompromisingly than any Whig editor, Hawthorne could judge the jingoism and futuristic rhetoric of his own party's *United States Magazine and Democratic Review*; more devastatingly than the Tory victims, such as historians Thomas Hutchinson and Peter Oliver, he could expose the cruelty and rapacity of the "patriotic" mobs of the American Revolution; more evenhandedly than any historian before his time, he could weigh the good and evil, strength and weakness, of the founders of Bay Colony. This detachment, combined as it was with the most closely engaged study of the available sources, made Hawthorne a better historian than Bancroft; also, of course, it made him an ironist.[2] Or, rather, it made him more of an ironist than he surely would have been anyway as a follower of Scott. Later in this chapter, when there is more evidence in hand, we will see what relation the main forms of Hawthorne's historical irony bears to those of Scott. Meanwhile, we do well to remember that readers who try to fix an unwavering "position" for Hawthorne by the customary nineteenth-century political landmarks do so at their peril.

Still, the main tenor of his political beliefs and thus of his ideas about the political history of his region and nation is tolerably clear. We have no reason to doubt his claim in "The Custom-House" that, although "not a politician," he was "a faithful Democrat in principle" (p. 13). His association with the Democrats extended over a period of several decades, and we find repeated evidence in his private letters and published writings that it was the result not only of friendships, family connections, and prospects of patronage, but also of the deep appeal of that party's tradition of Jeffersonian-Jacksonian liberalism.

An adherent of this form of middle-class liberalism from college days onwards, he believed in American federal union as a future-oriented schema which promised not only enhanced individual liberty but democratic community as well. Although no American writer was more aware than he of how these ideals might be perverted in practice, and none more sceptical of reformers and perfectibilist visions, he never wavered in his adherence to the ideals themselves or to the belief that in *an* American union was their best chance for at least partial realization. With other New Englanders (such as Emerson) he seems to have thought of the democratic soul of the nation as residing in his own region, but when civil war came he argued neither for separate New England nationhood nor for the preservation of the old Union. He contended instead that the states of the deep South, ancient and inveterate in their commitment to slavery, should be permitted to secede while the border states and the entire "west bank of the Mississippi," land of the future, were retained as free soil within a free republic.[3] Whatever we may think of the humanity or practicability of this solution, it showed a characteristic balance between, on the one hand, resignation to the course of history already determined by sectional interests and character and, on the other, ever-hopeful yearning toward those future fields where humanity might sometimes find, and not merely pursue, happiness.

If I say that the solution was also distinctly Puritan insofar as its design was to reestablish a purified and like-minded community through a combination of ostracism (of the South) and exodus (to the West), I do not mean that its author was thereby a "Puritan" rather than a man of his own time. The "stern and black-browed" Salem ancestors he invoked in "The Custom-House" would have demanded *for what* was the community purified and made like-minded, and they would scarcely have been satisfied with any answer the "degenerate fellow" (p. 10) could have given. And if Hawthorne was very much a nineteenth-century man in his politics, he was no less so in his literary interests. Because his greatest fiction is concerned with the past or with the effects of the past on the present, we are apt to forget that only a small fraction of his total *oeuvre* deals with the early, Puritan period of New England history. Because Hawthorne's Quaker-whipping, witch-hanging ancestry is so well known to us, we tend not to recognize that it was as a "Romantic" in the tradition of Scott that his interest in the Puritan past of his native region was confirmed and deepened.

Scott was his boyhood favorite among novelists; Abbotsford and the Scottish Highlands were places of pilgrimage during his middle age; and reading the Waverley novels aloud to his family was one of the pleasures that lightened the gloom of the Civil War years at the close of his life. When Hawthorne began writing fiction in earnest, towards the end of the Bowdoin period (1821–5), Scott was at the height of his fame and success. Hawthorne's most prominent elder contemporaries, Irving and Cooper, were showing how Scott might be rivaled on the ground of New York history, and, as Michael Davitt Bell has revealed in *Hawthorne and the Historical Romance of New England*, dozens of New Englanders were busy developing the "Puritan" themes and character-types that Hawthorne was to subtilize in his finest tales and *The Scarlet Letter*. That his negligible first novel, *Fanshawe* (1828), was an imitation of Scott was therefore very much in the spirit and practice of the time, as likewise that his earliest promising literary project was an unpublished collection of stories called *Seven Tales of My Native Land*. A consciousness that his tales of early New England did not bear an obvious stamp of originality when read casually along with the other tales and sketches published in the magazines and gift books of the period may help explain why, in "The Custom-House," he made such a point of establishing that his was a very special "home-feeling with the past" (p. 9) of his native place.

Beyond question, then, Hawthorne was an active participant in the literary and political movements of his time, a follower of Scott and Jefferson rather than of Bradford or the Mathers, and it is especially with these kinships in mind that I shall approach him in the present chapter. Having said this, however, I must add a couple of important qualifications. Of course Hawthorne's home-feeling with the past *was* very special. Not only was his knowledge of New England history wide, detailed, and astonishingly accurate, but some of his characteristic forms of thought and feeling were perceptibly affected by those of the Puritans. Thus, as we have seen, he sometimes responded to the problems of contemporary society with solutions that bore a distinctively Puritan imprint, and although he could not accept the ideas of Original Sin and Providence in their Calvinistic formulations, he found them indispensable to his understanding of human history. Above all, perhaps, did his scrupulous moral and artistic conscience bear witness that, in his words, "strong traits of their nature have intertwined themselves with mine" (p. ɪo). In this he was unlike Scott, whose equally brilliant studies of Puritan character were the products of a Shakespearean "negative capability" rather than of any intense spiritual inwardness with the saints.

This difference points to others. As a budding prose fictionalist with strong regional and historical interests, Hawthorne could scarcely ignore the example of Scott or escape its influence. But his affinities of talent and temperament were in many respects closer to those of the English Romantic poets for whom Spenser and Milton were the great models. And so, in common with many nineteenth-century critics, he found Scott deficient in moral perception and purpose. "The world, nowadays," he wrote in 1845, "requires a more earnest purpose, a deeper moral, and a closer and homelier truth, than he was qualified to supply it with."[4] In spite of occasional flashes of former genius, the plots of Scott's later romances "become inextricably confused; the characters melt into one another; and the tale loses itself like the course of a stream flowing through muddy and marshy ground." Although there was nothing especially new or shrewd in these criticisms, they are interesting because Hawthorne wrote them at a time when he was thinking a good deal about the kind of historical romance he himself might attempt. A year later, reviewing *Views and Reviews*, he objected that Simms's ideas about American history as a subject for romance would bring out only "the lights and shades that lie upon the surface" and "produce nothing but historical novels, cast in the same worn out mould that has been in use these thirty years, and which it is time to break up and fling away."[5] In this brief manifesto, students of Hawthorne will recognize the democratic hyperbole with which, at times, he reacted to all sorts of Old

World forms – religious and political as well as artistic. The bent of his
genius even more than the reformed ("Victorian") taste of the world for
"a more earnest purpose" did indeed oblige him to recast the "worn out
mould" more radically than Cooper or Simms had found necessary. But
no more than they was he able simply to "break up and fling away" a
model that enshrined so many of the values, so many of the understand-
ings of human history, that they all held dear.

Especially in one respect, Hawthorne's charges that the South
Carolinian's theory of historical fiction lacked freshness, while true in
themselves, are misleading about his own practice. For in his stories of
colonial New England he too worked principally with the two great
"matters" which Cooper had opened up for American historical
romancers of all regions. One way to organize a discussion of
Hawthorne's historical fictions, therefore, would be around the matters
of the frontier and the Revolution. Another would be simply to follow
the sequence of their completion and publication, culminating with *The
Scarlet Letter*, his last and finest historical fiction. Each of these schemes
has advantages which make it attractive; but, for reasons which will
emerge more fully later, I have decided to devote the first, and by far the
largest, part of this chapter to Hawthorne's stories of seventeenth-
century Puritanism, and to foreground the relationship between his
portraits of the Puritans and Scott's. I conclude the chapter with a
comparatively brief account of the stories which deal with the
Independence movement in the eighteenth century.

2

Hawthorne's preparation to write *The Scarlet Letter* may be said to have
begun as early as William Hathorne's decision to emigrate to America
or, from the perspective of the present study, as early as Scott's
recognition of the rich potential that *Goetz von Berlichingen* had as a
model for prose fiction. On a shorter view, it began with his own
abortive *Seven Tales of My Native Land* and made astonishing progress
during the early 'thirties with a series of tales depicting the Puritan period
of New England history. All these tales show Hawthorne's extraordinary knowledge of Puritan psychology and the details of Puritan social
and political life. All, therefore, are truly historical fictions. However,
some of them, like "Roger Malvin's Burial" (1832) and "Young
Goodman Brown" (1835), are concerned principally or exclusively with
private – and of course fictitious – actions which, although historically
grounded in the doctrines, repressions, and anxieties of frontier New
England, do not purport to determine or "explain" the subsequent
course of regional or national history. On the contrary, their actions are

represented as essentially discrete events, bearing their historical contexts with them but so removed from the flow, the before and after, of historical development that we are invited to interpret them also as fables of universal human experience. As studies of the psychology of guilt, therefore, they anticipate the portrait of Arthur Dimmesdale, but they lack the concerns with long-term historical process and design that inform historical romances in the Waverley tradition, including *The Scarlet Letter*, and that are prominent in a number of Hawthorne's other early tales.

Such tales as "The Gray Champion" (1835), "The Gentle Boy" (1832), and "The May-Pole of Merry Mount" (1836) portray Puritan character not in its universal or "timeless" aspects but in those which mark it as special and historically determinative or prefigurative. In these stories, notable figures out of the pages of the Puritan chroniclers and Thomas Hutchinson reappear alongside ones of Hawthorne's own invention. And although only a small proportion of the characters and events are public and historical, as opposed to those "unknown to history," they gain, as the writer's professed *données*, a disproportionate prominence in his reader's mind. In this respect, then, these stories are (and are felt to be) less self-subsistent fictions than "Roger Malvin's Burial" or "Young Goodman Brown." The same may be said of their "plots." The simple *fictive* action of "The Gray Champion" is climaxed with Andros's retreat; that of "The Gentle Boy" with the Quaker child's death; and that of "The May-Pole of Merry Mount" with John Endicott's blessing of the Lord and Lady of the May. But the actors in these stories participate likewise in another and vastly more complex plot, that of American history, which is to have its *dénouement* a century or more later. The outcome of the implied "big plot," American nationhood and national character, makes the outcomes of the "little plots" momentous rather than merely apt and poignant. Of *The Scarlet Letter* this is true as well, although the fictional plot in this case is neither so simple nor so little.

"The Gray Champion," we may feel, is too simple to be taken seriously either as fiction or history; its place in literature is with Hawthorne's *Grandfather's Chair* or *A Wonder-Book for Girls and Boys* rather than with the fully adult tales with which it is given pride of place in his first collection, *Twice-Told Tales* (1837). And yet to describe the story in this condescending way is to do an injustice not so much to it as to the genre to which it belongs. Children's literature, whether fictional or historiographical, has its own proper seriousness and art; and "The Gray Champion," though truly simple and simplifying in its patriotic sentiments, is mature Hawthorne in its underlying aesthetic and theory of history. It provides an excellent introduction to Hawthorne's historical irony, and it is, besides, the clearest exemplification we have of the fact and nature of Hawthorne's debt to Scott.[6]

As noticed earlier, Scott's *Peveril of the Peak* (1822) supplied Cooper with hints for both the mysterious character Submission and the second Indian attack on the settlement of Wish-ton-Wish. Scott himself almost certainly had an American source for the legend of a Puritan regicide's sudden emergence from hiding to lead the defense of Hadley, Massachusetts, during King Philip's War, and it is certain that Cooper and most other writers who retold the story after Scott knew it in more than his version.[7] *Peveril* it must have been, however, that caused the rash of regicidal rescues in American fiction and drama during the second quarter of the century; for it was the "source" known to everybody. In any case, the internal evidence points conclusively to its direct inspiration of "The Gray Champion."

In *Peveril* the Puritan Major Bridgenorth recounts a personal experience to prove that "times of public danger . . . call into action many a brave and noble spirit, which would otherwise lie torpid, give no example to the living, and bequeath no name to future ages."[8] While visiting a remote village in New England, he witnessed an attack by Philip's warriors which surprised the Puritans at their worship. Confused and leaderless, the villagers were about to retreat when a "tall man of a reverend appearance, whom no one of us had ever seen before, suddenly was in the midst of us" (p. 226). With "the Unknown" at their head, they routed the attackers; after the victory, but not before Bridgenorth recognized him as the regicide Whalley, their deliverer disappeared as abruptly and mysteriously as he came. "The prevailing opinion was . . . that the stranger was really a supernatural being; others believed him an inspired champion, transported in the body from some distant climate, to show us the way to safety; others, again, concluded that he was a recluse, who . . . had become a dweller in the wilderness, and shunned the face of man" (p. 229). Bridgenorth himself believed the figure that of a living man but did not dispute "that it may please Heaven, on high occasions, even to raise one from the dead in defence of his country" (p. 229). Concluding his tale of the fugitive-rescuer, Bridgenorth ventures that perhaps "his voice may be heard in the field once more, should England need one of her noblest hearts" (p. 231).

To the by-then-traditional story, Scott made two major improvements which Hawthorne in his turn carried a step further. The first was to offer several possible "explanations" of the champion: "The prevailing opinion was . . . others believed . . . others, again, concluded. . . ." In "The Gray Champion," instead of speculating abstractly about the nature of their visitor, Hawthorne's Puritans dispute the nature of the evidence – what it was they actually *saw*. "Some reported, that when the troops had gone from King-street, and the people were thronging tumultuously in their rear, Bradstreet, the aged Governor, was seen to embrace a form more aged than his own. Others soberly affirmed, that while they marvelled at the venerable grandeur of his aspect, the old man had faded from their eyes [not 'from the *scene*' or 'from *before* their eyes'], melting slowly into the hues of twilight, till, where he stood, there was an empty space. But all agreed, that the hoary shape was gone."[9] This device, which Yvor Winters called "the formula of alternative possibilities," was one that Hawthorne used frequently in his later fiction and nowhere more brilliantly and ambiguously than in the concluding chapters of *The Scarlet Letter*.[10]

Besides providing Hawthorne with an example of the formula of alternative possibilities, Scott supplied the doctrine as well. In his "Life" of Ann Radcliffe (1824) he complains that modern romancers are expected to produce an explanation of any mysterious occurrences in their fictions; they are not "permitted to dismiss their spectres as they raise them, amidst the shadowy and indistinct light so favourable to the exhibition of phantasmagoria, without compelling them into broad daylight."[11] Unfortunately, writes Scott, explanations based like Radcliffe's on natural agency tend to trivialize the preceding action while supernatural explanations are met with disbelief. Confronted with this dilemma, "some modern authors" have tried

> to compound betwixt ancient faith and modern incredulity. They have exhibited phantoms, and narrated prophecies strangely accomplished, without giving a defined or absolute opinion, whether these are to be referred to supernatural agency, or whether the apparitions were produced (no uncommon case) by an overheated imagination, and the presages apparently verified by a casual, though singular coincidence of circumstances.

He then asks "Whether, as a painter of actual life, he [the novelist] is not entitled to leave something in shade, when the natural course of events conceals so many incidents in total darkness." These passages suggest that Scott's strategy for presenting and "explaining" supernatural visitations derived from his experience as a historical writer used not only to puzzle over all sorts of unreliable and fragmentary evidence but also "to compound betwixt ancient faith and modern incredulity." All of his successors have had to do much the same, but only a few – pre-eminently Hawthorne and Melville – have felt able, or even obliged by their priestly sense of the mystery at the heart of human experience both past and present, conspicuously "to leave something in the shade." In registering this mystery, in declining to resolve the state of uncertainty which Tzvetan Todorov calls "the fantastic" with a natural or supernatural explanation, Melville surpassed Hawthorne as much as Hawthorne surpassed Scott; but it may have been with Scott's "Life" of

Radcliffe in mind that Melville, pondering the "mystery of iniquity" in Claggart in Chapter 11 of *Billy Budd*, spoke to his incredulous readers of a "realism" as charged with the mysterious as anything the author of *The Mysteries of Udolpho* could devise.[12]

A second improvement of the fugitive regicide story that Scott introduced was the ancient *topos* of the national champion *redivivus*. (Charlemagne, Frederick Barbarossa, and especially King Arthur are probably the most famous examples.) For although Scott's most likely sources stress the villagers' initial belief that their deliverer was a supernatural being – "the Angel of Hadley" – they do not hint at his being a hero returned from the dead who might reappear in subsequent national crises. Nor does Scott himself develop the topic very far. It comes into the novel because, unknown to the reader, the fanatic who tells the story is plotting a mad insurrection against Charles II by a group of Roundhead veterans. Victim of "the insane enthusiasm of the time" (p. 729), Bridgenorth has in mind no visitation by a ghostly champion but a return to the field by the flesh-and-blood former associates of Whalley, Cromwell, and himself; but, lacking this information, the reader cannot dismiss the possibility raised by Bridgenorth's words, that a supernatural intervention has occurred and might occur again "should England need one of her noblest hearts." The stirring rhetoric is Bridgenorth's, not Scott's, and it is well to emphasize that the British Tory Scott would never have chosen one of the regicides of 1649 as a model of patriotic action. The American Democrat Hawthorne, on the other hand, could more readily sympathize with Bridgenorth's "insane" perspective on history.

Major Bridgenorth's story positively invited Hawthorne's sequel. For the "Revolution of 1689" in New England was inspired by much the same religious and political feelings that had brought Bridgenorth and his Civil War companions out of retirement ten years earlier in Old England. Hawthorne is careful to note that old "soldiers of the Parliament were here too, smiling grimly at the thought, that their aged arms might strike another blow against the house of Stuart" (p. 11). The presence of these veterans and of the ancient charter governor Simon Bradstreet ("a patriarch of nearly ninety") confers some chronological plausibility on the fiction of the regicide's reappearance nearly a half century after the sentencing of Charles I. But of course plausibility and "realism" in the presentation of the "angel" are not the concerns of "The Gray Champion" in the way that they so clearly are of *The Wept of Wish-ton-Wish*. There, in the spirit of Enlightenment historiography, Cooper insists on the regicide's stout corporeal presence and constructs an account which, although necessarily fictive, offers to clear up this and many other mysteries of a "superstitious" age. It formed no part of

Hawthorne's design to divest the incident of the regicide *redivivus* of its mystery either for the witnessses who were "there" in the dusk of an April afternoon in 1689 or for ourselves gazing backwards through the obscurity of time. Its ambiguous status as a "fantastic" happening not certainly natural or supernatural, not wholly historical or legendary, makes it the more effective as an ennobling trope that posits a single spirit animating a series of defiances of British monarchical "tyranny" from the Smithfield martyrdom of John Rogers down through the American War of Independence.

Like the first generation of historical romancers, Hawthorne sought to trace the recurrent in the flux, the species in the individual protagonists, of human history. But their stadialist scenario of historical development, with its universal typology of savage, barbarian, etc., was useless to him because his attention was so intently focussed on what may be termed the moral history of the European – and especially English-speaking – peoples since the Reformation. On a number of occasions from "The May-Pole of Merry Mount" to *The Scarlet Letter*, he even advanced his own half-playful, half-serious version of a depressing Enlightenment metascientific thesis which, in their day, the stadialists Jefferson and Cooper had rejected with all possible energy and indignation: the thesis that the good old European stock (ranging from roses to Salem gentlefolk) had suffered progressive decay as a result of being transplanted to the New World.[13] There is a hint of future decay (or, in the Puritans' own terms, moral declension) in "The Gray Champion":

> Though more than sixty years had elapsed, since the Pilgrims came, this crowd of their descendants still showed the strong and sombre features of their character, perhaps more strikingly in such a stern emergency than on happier occasions . . . Indeed, it was not yet time for the old spirit to be extinct; since there were men in the street, that day, who had worshipped there beneath the trees, before a house was reared to the God, for whom they had become exiles.   (pp. 10–11)

Contrary to what seems implied here, the tale as a whole strongly argues that, yes, the "features" of New England character might grow less "strong and sombre" because of environmental changes of the kind which Enlightenment thinkers always invoked to explain behavioral changes, but that, in defiance of such explanations, American history shows that the "time for the old spirit to be extinct" has never come – "yet." By reverting to type in times of emergency – the Gray Champion is "the type of New-England's hereditary spirit" (p. 18) – the people of New England have progressed, surely if not steadily, towards a democratic future secure against "domestic tyranny . . . or the invader's step." This seemingly paradoxical proposition, that linear progress is achieved by a cyclic movement, Hawthorne later resolved and expressed in the figure of an ascending spiral curve.[14] But in his earlier, and more truly historical, fiction he was concerned hardly at all with such theoretical resolutions; he tried, rather, to effect an implicit reconciliation between his own nineteenth-century progressivist understanding of colonial New England history and the typological readings of events which the Puritans themselves would have made.

The Puritan approach to history, based on an exegetical methodology which discovers in the Old Testament the "types" of personae and acts of the New, may be thought of as systematically anachronous. From the historicist's viewpoint the weakness of this approach is that it falsifies *both* the past and present by superimposing outdated analogies on experiences that, in spite of superficial likenesses, belong to a very different historical context. This criticism is implied by the narrator himself in "The Gray Champion" when, in response to cries of "a Smithfield fire in King-street!" and "a new St. Bartholomew!," he comments drily that "the wiser class believed the Governor's object somewhat less atrocious" (pp. 11–12). And the criticism seems well-taken: for – to return to an earlier topic – is there not something childlike in the Puritan crowd's expectation of a providential recapitulation of history for the benefit of "His" people in New England? So we might reasonably conclude when we learn that it "was actually fancied, at that period, that New-England might have a John Rogers of her own, to take the place of that worthy in the Primer" (p. 11). For "childlike" surely is the word for the crude block-print illustrations of Rogers's martyrdom in the early editions of *The New-England Primer* as likewise for the extraordinary *Primer* distich which propounds the time-collapsing doctrine underlying Puritan typology: "In *Adam's* Fall/We Sinned all." And children, presumably even Hawthorne's "intolerant brood" of Puritan children, delight in Rip Van Winkle-ish dislocations of time quite as much as they do in Gulliverish telescopings of space. But to the adult, or at least worldly, perspective of Andros's Cavalier party, such dislocations are merely ridiculously unfashionable and therefore fit subjects for a joke: "See you not, he is some old round-headed dignitary, who hath lain asleep these thirty years, and knows nothing of the change of times? Doubtless, he thinks to put us down with a proclamation in Old Noll's name!" (p. 16). The joke contains, of course, an unintended (because anachronistic) allusion to Irving's childlike hero.

According to Hawthorne's Romantic morphology of growth and decay, individuals and societies tended to suffer a loss of instinctive wisdom and imaginative power during the busiest years of their prime, and so it was no insult for him to associate Puritan ways of interpreting experience with those of children. In "The Gray Champion" the joke turns out, after all, to be on the Cavaliers, because it is *they* who know "nothing of the change of times." The joke is also, if you like, on adults and historicists, because the action of the tale not only defies time and common sense; it affirms the active, creative power of faith and myths in human history. " 'Oh! Lord of Hosts,' cried a voice among the crowd, 'provide a Champion for thy people!' " And at once he appears, as if in instant response to the prayer. The prayer contains, not unintentionally, an allusion to one of the supreme types of deliverance in the Judeo-Christian tradition – David's intervention against Goliath in 1 Samuel, 17. ("Then said David to the Philistine, Thou comest to me with a sword, and with a spear, and with a shield: but I come to thee in the name of the Lord of hosts, the God of the armies of Israel, whom thou hast defied.") Puritan against Cavalier: Jew against Philistine: extreme youth or age against mature "tyrannical" strength. Hawthorne invites us to view these oppositions as distinct and yet, in this context, interchangeable. That the potent champion is not a seemingly feeble stripling like David but a seemingly feeble old man is itself a childlike joke, albeit a joke based on a favorite Romantic paradox and thoroughly appropriate in view of the point that Hawthorne is making about New England's perpetually rejuvenating "hereditary spirit."

That spirit, British in origin, was at once liberating and determinative for American politics. The same may be said of the spirit that animated American writers of historical fiction as they developed models and materials borrowed from each other and Scott. When Scott interpolated the "Angel of Hadley" incident as a tale within the tale of *Peveril of the Peak*, he did so partly because it was an irresistibly good story and partly because it so aptly illustrated the astonishing resilience and intrepidity of British Puritanism. For American writers, however, the incident belonged to the history of American Puritanism and the American independence movement; Scott's annexation of it was, however intended, an open challenge to them. Inspired by hints in *Peveril* and perhaps also by the series of reshapings of the same regicidal rescue, Hawthorne extended the champion's career by inventing another and later incident brilliantly calculated to articulate the *topos* of the national champion *redivivus*.

Not the least interesting aspect of this development is the way Hawthorne's fiction transforms (or returns) a quasi-historical anecdote into pure legend; in the process, it exchanges a dubious historicity for the representative truth of a symbolic action which epitomizes many actions over many centuries. When I speak of this action as "symbolic," I have in mind Coleridge's description of the symbolic nature of sacred history which gives "both Facts and Persons . . . a two-fold significance, a past and a future, a temporary and a perpetual, a particular and a universal application. They must be at once Portraits and Ideals."[15] He goes on to define a symbol as "characterized by a translucence of the Special in the Individual or of the General in the Especial or of the Universal in the General. Above all by the translucence of the Eternal through and in the Temporal. It always partakes of the Reality which it renders intelligible; and while it enunciates the whole, abides itself as a living part of that Unity, of which it is the representative." Doubtless all serious historical fiction aspires to a similar relationship to chronicled event, but usually it does so less nakedly than "The Gray Champion" and with fewer hints that history may only be another form of fiction.

By removing the action of "The Gray Champion" to Boston in 1689, Hawthorne was able to concentrate on Puritan *vs.* Cavalier and American *vs.* British oppositions to the exclusion or subordination of other oppositions present or potential in the Angel of Hadley story. He could allude delicately to the white colonist *vs.* native American and patriarchal Puritan *vs.* degenerate Puritan oppositions which Cooper had developed so fully and powerfully in *The Wept of Wish-ton-Wish*, but to have done more than that would have been supererogatory and even disruptive in "The Gray Champion." He was more than content to leave Indian warfare and, for that matter, all other forms of physical adventure to Scott and Cooper: unlike Submission or Cooper's more famous gray champion Leatherstocking, Hawthorne's champion achieved his victory without a shot, by sheer moral force of character. That was the quality in his ancestors that Hawthorne wished to have venerated and emulated by Americans of all ages, and in "The Gray Champion" he found a way of isolating the pure essence from the contaminants with which, in the brazen world of historical actuality, it was nearly always melded. However, he was not always so Platonistically inclined, and in his stories of earlier seventeenth-century New England he portrayed a very mixed Puritan character – paternalistic rather than childlike, more oppressive than oppressed, as severely tried by the New World wilderness as by Old World enemies. What persisted through all the stories discussed here was his admiration for the moral force of the Puritan character, however misdirected at times, and his insistence on their essential role in what I have called the "big plot" of American national history.

3

Although this is not the place for a complete anatomy of Hawthorne's irony, I should not proceed further without a brief review of the ways that irony shapes his reading and rendering of New England history. For interpretation and evaluation of Hawthorne's historical fictions often hinge on our sense equally of the presence and the proportion of irony in them. If he is the thorough-going ironist that proponents of a "subversive" Hawthorne take him to be, the method and meaning of stories like "The Gray Champion" are not what most readers have always "naively" and "complacently" supposed.[16] That such dismissive terms enter the debate suggests that it is as much about critical temper and ego as about literary texts and contexts, and therefore that consensus is probably unattainable. But in a book about the Waverley tradition in American fiction, it behooves me to find common ground if I can. Indeed, since Scott too was both an ironist and a student of Puritanism, I will keep his example constantly in view, and confine my survey chiefly to those kinds of irony which clearly affect the presentation and understanding of history in Scott's and Hawthorne's tales of the Puritans.

In spite of a rivalry which was national and temperamental as well as professional, Hawthorne shared many of Scott's convictions about Puritanism and history. No less than Scott and Cooper was he a believer in the "law of unintended consequences" discussed in chapter 3. "The Gray Champion" illustrates the operation of this law on a small scale when Governor Andros's parade of military force provokes the spirited opposition it was intended to forestall: "The role of the drum, at that unquiet crisis, seemed to go through the streets, less as the martial music of the soldiers, than as a muster-call to the inhabitants themselves" (p. 10). In "The Gentle Boy," the attempts of the Puritan colonists to escape from the sectarian conflicts of the Old World and later "to purge the land of heresy" ironically make New England, as "the place of greatest uneasiness and peril" for their Quaker pursuers, also the place "most eligible."[17] These are relatively minor instances of a kind of irony which pervades Hawthorne's rendering of New England history and is most familiar to us in the contrasts between somnolent modern Salem in "The Custom-House" and vigorous mid seventeenth-century Boston in *The Scarlet Letter*. These contrasts are complex and by no means clearly favorable to either place or age, but there can be no doubt that neither the secularized democratic America represented by contemporary Salem nor "the degenerate fellow" (p. 10), Hawthorne himself, is anything like the result that the Puritan planters had in view when they established their Israel in the New England wilderness.

To observe this irony of unintended consequences in *The Scarlet Letter* is not to deny Hawthorne's awareness that his America could have evolved only from those beginnings, nor is it to dispute his contention that "strong traits of their nature have intertwined themselves with mine" (p. 10). He might concede the justice of many of Scott's criticisms of the Puritans, but ultimately, as a son of New England, he could not share Scott's view of them as dangerous fanatics whose iconoclastic principles were opposed to the true welfare of mankind. From the vantage of nineteenth-century Concord or Boston, the Puritans were builders rather than destroyers of the fabric of civilization. This difference of vantage may remind us of the way, touched upon in the previous section, that Hawthorne shifts Scott's perspective on the Puritans so as to view their "insane enthusiasm" with what can be called patriotic irony.

It is easy to see why Scott questioned the sanity of some of the leaders of the late seventeenth-century Puritan rebellions depicted in *Peveril* and *Old Mortality*. Given that the Puritans' military resources were exhausted and that the odds against them were immense, their last desperate risings against the Stuarts had no realistic prospects of success. Because it is historical fact that they did not win in the end, and because we are persuaded that their winning was impossible from the start, we read about their schemes and strivings, their faith in final victory, with that luxury of Olympian ironic foreknowledge which educated readers of historical fiction always enjoy to some degree. However, this luxury is not without the hazard of self-recognition. As suggested at the end of chapter 1, there is a kinship between historical fiction and classical tragedy. The matters of both genres are "given," the outcomes of their stories known to the audience in advance, and their ironies generate the further ironic reflection that, after all, we are not gods and in our own time may be little wiser about the course of future events than the legendary or historical protagonists were in theirs.

The Olympian foreknowledge we bring to Hawthorne's historical tales is quite different, and so are its effects. What we know in advance is an essentially comic plot in which Major Bridgenorth's spirit lives on in New England and eventually wins the long war against British monarchical "tyranny." And so the principal irony in these stories is very pointedly at the expense of the worldly King's officers and prelates who are certain that, backed by the big battalions, they have history on their side. Stories like "The Gray Champion" and "Lady Eleanore's Mantle" are structured to throw this patriotic irony into unsubtle high relief. Since he wrote at a time when the clamor for American historical fiction was at its height and when the potential audience for his stories was thoroughly familiar with Scott's views on democracy as well as his portrayals of the Puritans, Hawthorne must have hoped that his readers would appreciate how deftly he had stood Scott's irony on its head and thus won yet another victory over British Toryism.

The varieties of historical irony discussed thus far are fairly straightforward, and are the more accessible to us because they are related to the ironies present in ancient literary genres. Others are more elusive and can be appreciated only if we are sensitive to a comparatively modern subtextual debate about the nature of history and historiography. Horace Walpole, it will be remembered, complained that his own age would

endure nothing but "philosophy" and "*cold common sense.*" He exaggerated, of course, but it is true that the greatest narrative historians of the
age – Voltaire, Hume, and Gibbon – made it their business to expose, as
superstitions and pious frauds, precisely the sort of happenings which
Walpole himself wished to revive in fiction. True, too, that the new
breed of philosophical historians sought to apply Newton's experimental
method to social history on the assumption that men in the mass were the
products of their material circumstances (climate, mode of subsistence)
and generally behaved in obedience to laws as universal and discoverable
as the law of gravity. These "Enlightenment" innovations made modern
historiography and social science possible, and virtually all "Romantic"
historical writers recognized their importance and value. Still, these later
writers shared Walpole's defensive feeling that scepticism and empiricism, allied as they increasingly were with powerful new fictional and
political forms, threatened to dry up "the great resources of fancy" and,
in historiographical and fictional practice, failed to deal at all adequately
with those ranges of "extraordinary" experience – heroic, supernatural,
and imaginative – which elevate human beings above brutes and
vouchsafe a glimpse of worlds less brazen than our own. Historical
romances, while utilizing the methods and insights of eighteenth-
century historiography, typically incorporate some of those ranges and
exhibit the power that myth has to change the odds and thus the future
shape of history.

By nobody was that power more strikingly illustrated than the
Puritans. Scott points to the source of their "incredible" capacity to
endure and revive, although not in this case to triumph, when Julian
Peveril overhears a preacher exhort an armed company of Cromwell's
veterans "to be strong, to be up and doing; and promised those miracles
which, in the campaigns of Joshua, and his successors the valiant judges of
Israel, supplied all odds against the Amorites, Midianites, and Philistines"
(p. 726). Hawthorne does the same in "The Gray Champion" when, in
answer to a prayer, a new David appears to lead his people against the
Philistines. Informed by the myth of the Old Testament Hebrews, the
Puritans' rhetoric has a contagious elevating power which enables us
briefly to share their suprahistorical view of themselves as God's chosen
people participating in a cosmic struggle between the forces of good and
evil.

In *Peveril* and *Old Mortality*, however, it elevates only to let down; the
myth has enough power left to inspire the believing remnant to try to
repeat the past, but no longer enough to supply "all odds" against
history. (The same can be said of Scott's Jacobites and their Cavalier
myth. In reading Scott, we are very conscious of "history" as a living
force or stream which, passing by the Puritan and later the Jacobite

extremists, represents the changing collective interests and loyalties of the British people.) It is a different story in Hawthorne's New England, a place, in the seventeenth century, not unlike that "neutral territory, somewhere between the real world and fairy-land," described in "The Custom-House" (p. 36). In "The Gray Champion," "Endicott and the Red Cross," and "The May-Pole of Merry Mount," Hawthorne ironically demonstrates that here, in a New World alleged by Old World philosophers to cause European stock to degenerate, the Puritan myth retains and actually redoubles its ancient potency. So far from dwindling, it becomes stronger than other myths and stronger than history too – if history is what the British rulers suppose it to be and what the historians Voltaire, Hume, and Smith say it is.

Myth is stronger than history in another sense as well. Scott's and Hawthorne's Puritans are able to persevere in spite of repeated defeats and sacrifices because their myth is so powerful that it can make an ally of history by assimilating and converting it into myth. Whether the history they enact goes for or against them, the history they write invests its heroes and events with a typological significance like those of the Bible, and so makes secular history sacred and reconfirms the faith of following generations. The tale of the regicide *redivivus* perfectly illustrates the relationship between Puritan historiography and revolutionary action.

Another memorable illustration, which must also have struck Hawthorne forcibly, is Scott's account of "Old Mortality," the eighteenth-century Puritan stone mason who traveled through Scotland restoring the gravestones of the slaughtered saints of the previous century. As a consequence of his efforts, upon those weathered stones "may still be read in rude prose, and ruder rhyme, the history of those who sleep beneath them . . . persecuted Presbyterians who afforded a melancholy subject for history in the times of Charles II. and his successor . . . The peasantry . . . when they point them out to their sons, and narrate the fate of the sufferers, usually conclude by exhorting them to be ready, should times call for it, to resist to the death in the cause of civil and religious liberty, like their brave forefathers."[18] Here, for a change, Scott manifestly writes about the Puritans with fellow feeling. Like his countryman John Galt, whose *Ringan Gilhaize* (1823) may well be the masterpiece of fictionalized Puritan autobiography, Scott saw kindred spirits in the old Puritan chroniclers who, like Old Mortality, retrace the inscriptions on the saints' headstones.[19] Perhaps there is something grotesque as well as ironic about the stubborn persistence of such remembrancers of a lost cause as Bridgenorth and David Deans, the hairsplitting but good-hearted Covenanter of *The Heart of Mid-Lothian*. But there is also something heroic. As for his own battles against moss and weather, Scott was prepared to take the ironic view that they too were quixotic and yet the more morally worthwhile because ultimately unavailing.

Puritan historians, fictitious or historical, figure only very marginally in Hawthorne's pages, and their marginality makes us wonder whether he felt the same kinship with these predecessors that Scott obviously did with his. If not, one of the reasons might be that he did not consider their efforts unavailing, and could not easily identify with their success. At any rate, it is certain that a long memory is a defining characteristic of Hawthorne's Puritans, and that they are a race of historians inasmuch as they keep the past always in mind to interpret the present and future: "a new St. Bartholomew! . . . We are to be massacred, man and male child." These hysterical "explanations" of Governor Andros's purpose conflate (1) the present situation with (2) a famous event in secular history, the massacre of the French Protestants on St. Bartholomew's Day, 1572, and both of these with (3) an episode from scripture, Herod's order to slay the innocents (Matthew 2, 16). Doubtless this is questionable history, not only by our standards but also, the narrator assures us, by those of "the wiser class" of Bostonians in 1689. Yet it is potent revivalism, and if revivalism is by no means all that Puritan historiography is about, it is the part that Hawthorne chooses to highlight in "The Gray Champion," the Endicott stories, "Howe's Masquerade," and "Edward Randolph's Portrait." The last, published in 1838, is clearly a kind of sequel to "The Gray Champion," and one of Hawthorne's most searching statements about Puritan historiography and the ironies of New England history.[20]

The chief protagonist of "Edward Randolph's Portrait," Thomas Hutchinson, combines the roles of Tory governor and Enlightenment historian and so is doubly doomed by Puritan "history." He also makes the adult's error, usually fatal in Hawthorne's fiction, of ignoring the warning that God "hast hid these things from the wise and prudent, and hast revealed them unto babes" (Matthew 11, 25). And so *hubris*-laden Hutchinson dismisses, as the "girlish fantasies" of a "silly child," Alice Vane's admonitions to heed ominous parallels out of the New England past.[21] Shortly before sharing Governor Andros's fate, he remarks smugly that Cotton Mather, historian of the "Revolution of 1689" and Alice Vane's source, "has filled our early history with old women's tales, as fanciful and extravagant as those of Greece or Rome" (p. 262). The sensation of *déjà vu* that we experience, as readers already familiar with "The Gray Champion," is one that Hutchinson, as the author of *The History of the Colony of Massachusetts Bay* (1764), should also experience: for this book gives the earliest printed account of the Angel of Hadley story.[22] The meaning of New England history is there on his own page if he could but read it aright, as Scott and Hawthorne were later to do. He knows everything about his fellow New Englanders except the one needful thing known by Alice Vane, "silly child" and voice of Puritan historiography.

Hawthorne combines Alice Vane's knowledge with Thomas Hutchinson's and is therefore a wiser as well as a very different kind of historian. But exactly what kind of historian is he? Or, as turns out to be the same question in a different guise, what kind of historical ironist is he? Broadly speaking, our choice lies somewhere between two extremes. (1) With a few prominent exceptions like "My Kinsman, Major Molineux" and "The Gentle Boy," Hawthorne's historical fiction represents a belletristic cloning of Bancroft and bicentennial Plymouth Rock oratory. (2) On the contrary, as Michael Colacurcio argues, this fiction slyly deconstructs Bancroft, simultaneously exposing the inadequacies and dangers of both Puritan historiography and its descendant, Bancroftian historiography. The second position, or something close to it, has many attractions. For the "exceptions" which the first position must admit confirm our doubts that *any* of Hawthorne's tales is as simply and wholeheartedly patriotic as most of his nineteenth- and early twentieth-century readers evidently supposed them to be. And even if Colacurcio's deconstructionist reading exceeds the mark, by making Hawthorne's hidden "subversive" agenda too programmatic and cunning by half, there are still compelling reasons for wishing to find irony in works like "The Gray Champion," "Endicott and the Red Cross," and even *The Scarlet Letter.* For they contain passages of patriotic uplift which, frankly, are embarrassing if they are not ironic.

As we shall see, one passage of this kind which has attracted numerous ironic readings is the report of Dimmesdale's Election Sermon. Another, which matters less to us but is more blatantly in need of the absolution of irony, is the opening of "The Gray Champion":

> There was once a time, when New-England groaned under the actual pressure of heavier wrongs, than those threatened ones which brought on the Revolution. James II., the bigoted successor of Charles the Voluptuous, had annulled the charters of all the colonies, and sent a harsh and unprincipled soldier to take away our liberties and endanger our religion. (p. 9)

Colacurcio comments that the "rhetoric is extravagant and the political style – here, and in everything that follows – is 'paranoid,' in just the sense that Perry Miller has taught us to recognize. The *narrator* of 'The Gray Champion' . . . has been reading too much Cotton Mather" (p. 209, my emphasis). Perhaps; but there is also the unwelcome possibility that *Hawthorne* has been reading too much Mather or too much Bancroft and that he, rather than a radically subverted narrator, has been carried away. Or, a third possibility which is more true to my own sense of the man and the artist, Hawthorne has been reading just enough Cotton Mather to be able momentarily to fuse the narrative viewpoint of 1835 with that of 1689 ("our liberties . . . our religion"), while hinting through "There was once a time" that what follows will be "gospel true" rather than "history true."

The third reading differs from the first and second chiefly in that it does not identify Hawthorne's viewpoint with Perry Miller's *or* Cotton Mather's *or* George Bancroft's, but insists instead on a Hawthorne who, in 1835, was an ambitious young American historical fictionalist reaching out for community with both the America of Andrew Jackson and the America of Cotton Mather. He was, in other words, primarily a writer of stories whose best hope for both short- and long-term success was to make the great American myths his own, to plug into their power as it were, by revealing vivid embodiments of those myths in the dusty corners of New England history – all of this to the full extent that his temperament and historical conscience allowed. To the extent that they required dissent or psychic relief, he could slip in ironic hints that the heroes of one tale might well figure as villains in another. In "The Gray Champion," for example, he quietly records the presence of "veterans of King Philip's war, who had burnt villages and slaughtered young and old, with pious fierceness, while the godly souls throughout the land were helping them with prayer" (p. 11). His aim in this and other "patriotic" tales is to have it both ways: to apotheosize the Puritans as founders and liberators while interjecting ironic notes, sometimes obvious and sometimes not, that remind us of their acts of destruction and confinement.

Seeking thus to have it both ways, because what is true at one level of discourse may not be true at another, is characteristic of what we call "Romantic" irony. Friedrich Schlegel, the seminal theorist of Romantic irony, described it as permanent parabasis, referring to interruptions in the action of Greek comedy where imitation is suspended, and authorial commentary briefly holds the stage. Anne Mellor describes the Romantic adaptation of parabasis as a process requiring the artist to play a dual role: "He must create, or represent, like God, a finite, ordered world to which he can enthusiastically commit himself; and *at the same time* he must acknowledge his own limitations as a finite human being and the inevitable resultant limitations of his merely fictional creations. The artistic process, then, must be one of simultaneous creation and de-creation: a fictional world must be both sincerely presented and sincerely undermined, either by showing its falsities or limitations or, at the very least, by suggesting ways of responding to it with other than whole-hearted assent."[23] In Hawthorne's case, the "ordered world" is partly his own mythic creation and partly that of Bancroft and the commemorative orators. The undermining, equally "sincere," is entirely Hawthorne's own ironic response as a historian.

I do not expect to convert proponents of a "subversive" Hawthorne to my belief that he is both enthusiastically committed to and quietly critical of the patriotic myths which figure so prominently in his historical fiction. Their sense of the man and the artist differs fairly widely from mine, and the difference probably has as much to do with the subject as with the object of perception. However, it also has to do with divergent assumptions about the proper role and limits of scholarly commentary. Because Michael Colacurcio takes a forthright stand and defends it with formidable learning and ingenuity, it is with him that I quarrel. But I have no doubt that he speaks for many when he remarks that there is "no perfect litmus test for detecting irony on the tongue of the speaker; it always exists (or not) pretty much in the ear of the listener. But in the end most of us will think better of Hawthorne's intelligence if he doesn't quite mean *all* that his 'narrator' says . . . This is how we always decide the question of irony: how plausible – and how admirable – is the literary result?" (p. 209). To my mind, these axioms give the irony game pretty completely away. I am not sure exactly what checks on scholarly inference are implied by "plausible," but some are urgently needed if the highly subjective business of "detecting" irony is governed otherwise only by the detective's sense of what is most "admirable." Whether the "literary result" is admirable or not is surely beside the point: our answer to the question of irony in each case should be controlled by our historical understanding of Hawthorne's aims, passions, knowledge, and normal practices – and least of all by our judgment that a passage or entire work must be ironic because otherwise it is aesthetically or morally unworthy of Hawthorne and so makes us think worse of his intelligence (not to mention our own, for having invested so much time in studying him).

Precisely because detecting irony is such a subjective business, we should be wary of readings in which elaborate structures of irony are built on authorial silences and on knowledge which the author may or may not have had. In his discussion of "The Gray Champion," Colacurcio makes much of Hawthorne's and his audience's likely familiarity with other treatments of the Angel of Hadley legend, and also of "intriguing omissions" from the tale which, he claims, "may count for as much as his insistent inclusions" (p. 214). Let us take up the problem of assumed knowledge first: "If he could rely on readers to 'have heard' of his Champion in Scott's *Peveril of the Peak* (1822), could he not count on at least some of them to have read of his further exploits in James McHenry's *Specter of the Forest* (1823) or James Nelson Barker's *Superstition* (1824)? Certainly we must suppose his own familiarity with these notable uses of American materials" (p. 214). Hawthorne, I would reply, had every reason to rely on his readers' familiarity with *Peveril* and to hope that the more thoughtful among them would appreciate how his own innovative and distinctively American treatment of the Angel of Hadley legend differed from Scott's. On the other hand, although it is quite possible, it is far from certain that Hawthorne knew McHenry's romance and Barker's play, and hardly likely that he would have entrusted any meanings that he cared about to the uncertain chances of "some" of his readers being acquainted with two works of modest fame and circulation.[24] But why, according to Colacurcio, does it matter whether Hawthorne knew *Superstition* and *The Specter of the Forest* and assumed that some of his readers did too? Principally because Scott's regicide-deliverer reappears in both of these works to oppose the persecution of alleged witches. If readers saw that "The Gray Champion" was "haunted by the hostile specters of McHenry and Barker" (p. 216), they would be alerted to its chief "omission": any direct reference to the witchcraft trials which followed hard upon the 1689 rebellion. This omission reverberates with irony for Colacurcio because, he says, the Salem Delusion of 1692 is the unmentionable "one Puritanic event which Democratic myth never *could* subsume" (p. 215); "tribal mythographers would not touch it with a ten-foot totem" (p. 217).

Now silences sometimes are pregnant with ironic import, and Hawthorne's silence about the witchcraft trials is one which any thoughtful reader might remark without prompting from the specters of Barker and McHenry. By way of parallel and antecedent, we may suppose that Hawthorne himself sometimes wryly remarked what was left out or played down in orations commemorating the founding of New England. Searching historian of New England that he was, he could scarcely have done otherwise. Yet it is unlikely that these silences deafened Hawthorne or any other auditor with unintended irony; for every adult who participated in these rituals, in whatever role, would have understood that the speakers were observing the decorum of commemorative oratory rather than trying to deceive anybody. All of them had also met the ugly other face of Puritanism in a host of historical sketches and romances, e.g., those of Scott, Irving, and Cooper. Thus accustomed to blocking out, while also being well acquainted with, the sinister features of Puritanism, many of Hawthorne's contemporaries may well have brought the same generic expectations to his "patriotic" tales that they brought to commemorative oratory. If they did, as reviews and letters of the time suggest was often the case, they were most seriously mistaken. For Hawthorne's decorum allows for carefully regulated bursts of static in the system to remind us (but not too loudly) of the Puritans' imperfections and to indicate what and how much we should hear in his silences: neither a gentleman's agreement to ignore the unpleasantness, nor yet a critique of Puritanism and its legacy more damning than Scott ever delivered in his most high-Tory moods, but rather an echo of the seasoned scepticism with which "the wiser class" in "The Gray Champion" responds to rumors of devilish conspiracies and impending martyrdoms.

Colacurcio's Hawthorne is himself a conspiratorial figure, a kind of good wizard engaged in subverting "that idolatrous civil religion which Jacksonian ideologues were rearing on the foundations of the New England Covenant" (pp. 214–15). Since detection would cost this Hawthorne both readers and party patronage, he is careful to cover his tracks: "Once again, the operative literary effects exist at the level of latent irony and inhere in certain undeveloped suggestions which run counter to the import of the most obviously 'interpretive' rhetoric which the tale supplies. At this level the discerning reader sees that Esther Dudley has performed certain 'offices' . . . which the editorial mentality of the *Democratic Review* [where 'Old Esther Dudley' was first published in 1839] would utterly reject if it could recognize" (p. 460). This risky procedure counts heavily on the obtuseness of Hawthorne's paymasters, and, just as venturously, it leaves so much to the learning, ingenuity, and discretion of "the discerning reader" that this important personage comes to enjoy a power over Hawthorne's text remarkably like that once exercised by the New Critics. For although opposed in principle to the historicism which Colacurcio eloquently advocates and the intentionalism he usually assumes, they too were connoisseurs of irony and ambiguity who contended that the texts under scrutiny had never really been read before, and found more and sometimes more interesting things to say about a few lines or pages than anybody had ever supposed possible.

One of the ironies of history that Hawthorne himself most savored, and the last that I will discuss here, can be represented by the rhetorical figure of chiasmus, or crossover, where traits traditionally associated with one party are ironically transferred to its opponent. The most familiar example of this kind of irony in Hawthorne's fiction is probably that of the persecuted Puritan turned persecutor. Another, which takes us back to the references to "place," "attachment," and historical prefiguration in "The Custom-House," can be found in his self-deprecating mock-heroic picture of himself as a supposed party "place-man" suffering decapitation by the political "guillotine" and thereby winning the "crown of martyrdom" even though "his inactivity in political affairs, – his tendency to roam, at will, in that broad and quiet field where all mankind may meet, rather than confine himself to those narrow paths where brethren of the same household must diverge from one another, – had sometimes made it questionable with his brother Democrats whether he was a friend" (pp. 41–3). The guillotine obviously belongs to the French Revolutionary Jacobins; the crown of martyrdom, however, probably belongs not to their victims but rather, given Hawthorne's historical purview, to Charles I. As for the roamer of the common or neutral ground, for writers and readers of Hawthorne's generation he could only be a hero in the mold of Scott's Waverley – in this case, however, a Waverley who shares the fate of his defeated friends. To cap these parallels, Hawthorne goes on to liken his "figurative self" (p. 43) to Irving's Headless Horseman, supposed ghost of a Hessian trooper killed by American Revolutionary partisans. All of these "foreshadowings" of the Whig "revolution" of 1848 align the Whigs (the gentleman's party, so they flattered themselves) with the sanguinary levelers of history and the Democratic Hawthorne with the "noble" victims.

This ironic transposition plainly invites us to revise our ideas about political identities and their shifting relationship to the past. In terms of contemporary politics, it hints that the Whigs have debased themselves by enthusiastically adapting the worst aspects of Jacksonian politics (the spoils system, running a military hero for president), and that in these changed circumstances the Democrats are the true conservatives because they are the party that has kept faith with the ancient high principles of democracy. Hawthorne himself was a conservative in this sense, and went on being one through thick and thin. Much as we might wish that later in life he had seen the ultimate wisdom and humanity of Lincoln's policies, he supported the "Peace" platform of Franklin Pierce, keeping faith with the compromising spirit of the party of Jefferson and Jackson to the end, a bitter end for Democrats of his generation and persuasion.

4

In a passage later excised from "The Gentle Boy," Hawthorne explains why the "extenuating circumstances" of the Puritans' treatment of the Quakers "are more numerous than can generally be pleaded by persecutors":

> The inhabitants of New England were a people, whose original bond of union was their peculiar religious principles. For the peaceful exercise of their own mode of worship, an object, the very reverse of universal liberty of conscience, they had hewn themselves a home in the wilderness; they had made vast sacrifices of whatever is dear to man; they had exposed themselves to the peril of death, and to a life which rendered the accomplishment of that peril almost a blessing. They had found no city of refuge prepared for them, but with Heaven's assistance, they had created one; and it would be hard to say whether justice did not authorize their determination, to guard its gate against all who were destitute of the prescribed title to admittance. The principle of their foundation was such, that to destroy the unity of religion, might have been to subvert the government, and break up the colony, especially at a period when the state of affairs in England had stopped the tide of emigration, and drawn back many of the pilgrims to their native homes.   (p. 614)

Now whether Hawthorne eliminated this apologia because he decided that it was mistaken in principle, socially dangerous for his own times, or rhetorically premature, need not concern us here. For what was best omitted from "The Gentle Boy" can still hold a place in the Hawthorne canon as an unusually explicit, albeit partial, statement of the main issues in his historical fiction of frontier New England, including *The Scarlet Letter*.

As the passage indicates, *the* issue in that fiction, submerged for brief or extended periods but always resurfacing, is national survival and its human cost. What price the *patria* – to the Puritans and others?[25] For Hawthorne's Puritans, survival means, in the first place, preservation of sheer physical existence in the face of a formidably harsh New World environment. But it also means preservation of their "original bond of union" as a community purified of Old World contaminants, such as Quakers and Cavaliers, who still refuse to leave them alone. Waging war on two fronts, against the American wilderness on one side and their European religious–political adversaries on the other, the Puritans necessarily guard their "city of refuge" with high walls and strong gates. Hawthorne, I believe, does not seriously question that his (and our) ancestors acted as they sincerely believed necessary or that their epic struggle for survival as a people standing at once together and apart was, in the end, historically justified. The passage is full of premonitions of coming events – above all the War of Independence and the new "bond of union" enshrined in the Constitution – and the clear implication is that, if the tree is indeed known by its fruits, no patriotic reader could wish it to be essentially otherwise.

I say "essentially otherwise" because I do not wish to suggest that Hawthorne was complacent about either the present or the past. A much closer student of the psychologies of victims and persecutors, he was less inclined than Cooper to see longterm good issuing from temporary evil or to minimize the losses exacted by America's special form of historical development. Whether the New World is quite as inhospitable or the Old World enemies quite as intrusive and provocative as the Puritans believe is forcibly questioned in most of Hawthorne's seventeenth-century tales, and the central irony of "The Gentle Boy" is that in their determination to exclude heresy the Puritans reenact the ancient crime of excluding and at last murdering the Son of God. At the conclusion of the tale, although the Quaker boy's suffering and death teach "his parent a true religion" by softening "her fierce and vindictive nature," the changed conduct of "her once bitter persecutors" signifies no change of heart but only an indulgence in "that degree of pity which it is pleasant to experience" (pp. 104–5). The child Ilbrahim has suffered to some purpose, no doubt, but Hawthorne does not suggest that the boy's martyrdom has redeemed New England or that there is any adequate compensation for the loss of his "airy gaiety" and "heavenly nature" (pp. 89, 93). Survival has been achieved, but at a cultural and spiritual cost to posterity nearly as great as the practical, moral, and political benefits of the Puritan legacy.

Hawthorne does not reverse this judgment in his subsequent fiction of seventeenth-century New England. Indeed, nearly all of the elements of that fiction – its major symbols, character-types, situations, and moral dilemmas – are already present in "The Gentle Boy." Development here is not a matter of abrupt new departures but of ripening sympathies and rhetorical means; the result of this development within a few years is a fiction in which the Puritans' worst traits are admitted but their better ones given prominence. One of the finest fruits of this maturation, and one that from our vantage point promises still finer to come, is "The May-Pole of Merry Mount."

The prefatory note to "The May-Pole of Merry Mount" stands in relation to the tale much as "The Custom-House" does to *The Scarlet Letter*:

> There is an admirable foundation for a philosophic romance, in the curious history of the early settlement of Mount Wollaston, or Merry Mount. In the slight sketch here attempted, the facts, recorded on the grave pages of our New England annalists, have wrought themselves, almost spontaneously, into a sort of allegory. The masques, mummeries, and festive customs, described in the text, are in accordance with the manners of the age. Authority on these points may be found in Strutt's Book of English Sports and Pastimes.[26]

Like the fiction of the discovery of the veritable Scarlet Letter and Mr. Surveyor Pue's MS, the references here to Strutt and "the facts" are calculated to persuade the reader of a much greater concern with, and adherence to, the historical record than actually exists. The truth is not that "the facts . . . have wrought themselves, almost spontaneously, into a sort of allegory" but that Hawthorne has telescoped, rearranged, omitted, and invented such "facts" as he needed to make a "philosophic romance" in miniature – one in which the binary oppositions are basically those of the *Waverley*-model, enriched and modified by ones drawn from Spenser, Milton, and their Romantic imitators. Of course the rhetorical fiction of historicity misleads to good purpose and may even be said *not* to mislead inasmuch as Hawthorne's account of the Puritan destruction of Thomas Morton's rival plantation at "Ma-re Mount" is the first to deal sensitively or even-handedly with the pyschological meaning of the episode and with its consequences for regional character.[27] But if Hawthorne arrives at a deeper historical understanding than his predecessors, he does so because of the insights to which he was led by his fictional models rather than because of any new or more accurate historical data.

Yet in "The May-Pole of Merry Mount" Hawthorne differs from Scott and resembles the Puritan allegorists or the eighteenth-century philosophical historians in his concern to abstract the true "characters" of the rival factions rather than to embody them in the comparatively fuller and more factual contexts of narrative history or historical romance. There is not so much even as the idealized portrait, drawn years later in "Main Street" (1849), of Thomas Morton as "the very model of a Cavalier, with the curling lovelock, the fantastically trimmed beard, the embroidery, the ornamented rapier, the gilded dagger, and all other foppishnesses that distinguished the wild gallants who rode headlong to their overthrow in the cause of King Charles."[28] Instead, he presents us almost at once with a pair of allegorized abstractions:

> Bright were the days at Merry Mount, when the May-Pole was the banner-staff of that gay colony! They who reared it, should their banner be triumphant, were to pour sunshine over New England's rugged hills, and scatter flower-seeds throughout the soil. Jollity and gloom were contending for an empire.   (p. 54)

The allegorical mode does not encourage us to reflect that, while jollity and gloom were contending for an empire in New England, the Cavalier and Puritan factions in Old England were warming to a much greater contention for the entire empire of Great Britain. It achieves universality by ignoring most – though not all – of the specific theological, political, and economic issues that excited seventeenth-century Englishmen's fanatical hatreds and loyalties in both hemispheres. There is no hint in the tale, for instance, that Morton's shrewd and opportunistic fur-trading activities were a practical threat to the safety and prosperity of the infant Puritan settlements which, until 1630, a year *after* the maypole incident, lacked the force and authority finally to crush Merry Mount. These activities seemed important to Governor Bradford when he wrote his account of the Merry Mount episode, and close scrutiny of Hawthorne's tale can still trace faint references to other incidents and controversies recorded in the *History of Plymouth Plantation*. Such "omissions" or vestigial references can be usefully footnoted, but we should be wary lest a heavy-handed scholarly gloss undo all of Hawthorne's delicate labor of selection and subordination, of leaving some things in the shade and maneuvering others into prominence. To complain that Hawthorne fails to particularize the issues and *dramatis personae* of the Puritan/Cavalier conflict as fully and explicitly as Scott does is to fail to appreciate the subtle, epitomizing nature of the former's art. Encroaching on Scott's territory – or so it must have seemed in 1836 – Hawthorne creates a historical fiction so economical and austere as to be what Ezra Pound calls "Criticism in new composition."[29]

Having thus underscored Hawthorne's self-conscious independence as an American artist, I repeat my suggestion that insofar as "The May-Pole of Merry Mount" is a "philosophic romance" concerned with the meaning of an incident in the story of the long struggle between the Puritans and Cavaliers, it surely owes something to Scott besides the negative example of a "worn out mould." As the tale develops, the values and images associated with either side assume the following pattern of oppositions:

jollity	gloom
light/rainbow	shadow/drabness
masques	sermons
glees	psalms
maypole	whipping post
silk/flowers/native vine	iron
spontaneity/adaptability	swords/horseload of armor
evergreen	withering
play	toil
pagan/catholic	Puritan of Puritans
Arcadia	Israel

These lists of opposed values and symbols are not precisely identical to those given in chapter 2, but the overlap is sufficient to warrant our calling this tale a historical romance in epitome. Hawthorne has his own emphases, of course, but the recurrent theme of his historical fiction – American national survival and its human cost – is a recognizable variation on Scott's and Cooper's major themes. Hawthorne's Merry Mounters are Stuart Cavaliers in aspect, and when thrown into collision with the progress-bearing Puritans, they exhibit many of the qualities that doomed peoples ritually do in historical romances. As in *Waverley*, our sympathies are at first enlisted warmly on their side.

Confronted with a choice between two utopian communities, the one seeking to recreate Arcadia and the other Pentateuchal Israel in the North American wilderness, how many post-Enlightenment readers could be expected to knock at the bolted gates of the Puritans' city of refuge? At the open air festival of Merry Mount, Old World culture is accommo-dated to New World nature; the maypole is a New England pine tree; the English Priest wears a chaplet of the native vine leaves; and the wedding wreath unites wild American roses with roses "of still richer blush, which the colonists had reared from English seed" (p. 55). If the accommodation is at the cost of some "stooping," of rejecting nearly everything from European Christian culture except its pagan vestiges, the Merry Mounters' approach to life has at least enabled them to find those authentic "blossoms of the wilderness" and "sunniest spots of the forest" where the Puritans can see only a "black wilderness" (pp. 55, 56). If the lengthening shadows and frequent mention of "sunset" are ominous reminders that night will inevitably come, the brave rainbow banner is not thereby reduced to an emblem merely of the illusory nature of Merry Mount's "systematic gaiety" (p. 66). For, associated as it is with light, air, and the union of heaven and earth, the rainbow banner is, and remains, a compelling Romantic figure for those qualities of spirit and imagination which Ilbrahim represented in "The Gentle Boy" and Pearl will also, though more complexly, in *The Scarlet Letter.* Such qualities, like sunshine itself, may not be the whole of life itself, but any creed that ignores their existence must be partial and inadequate.

We discover as early as the first paragraph that there is something unreal or unnatural about the jollity of Merry Mount:

> Midsummer eve had come, bringing deep verdure to the forest, and roses in her lap, of a more vivid hue than the tender buds of Spring. But May, or her mirthful spirit, dwelt all the year round at Merry Mount, sporting with the Summer months, and revelling with Autumn, and basking in the glow of Winter's fireside. Through a world of toil and care, she flitted with a dreamlike smile, and came hither to find a home among the lightsome hearts of Merry Mount. (p. 54)

The spirit of May, with her "dreamlike smile," is made perpetual in a region subject to extreme seasonal variations. The narrator's enthusiastic praise is undercut from the start, because the Merry Mounters' utopian scenario simply does not suit New England conditions. "Oh, people of the Golden Age," he exclaims, "the chief of your husbandry, was to raise flowers!" (p. 55). So it may have been, but the setting here is a fallen "world of toil and care" and more particularly a tiny clearing surrounded by the vast American wilderness. Nature anywhere is double – cheerful and melancholy, light and dark – and therefore not to be comprehended truly by the single-minded, simplifying vision either of Puritan or Cavalier; but here, where the winters are long and the forests endless, the Puritan vision is *more* adequate to the facts.

Later in the tale, the sandy economic foundations of the Merry Mount experiment are hinted at in references to poor harvests and extravagant misuse of the colony's timber resources for all-night bonfires. Moreover, as the tale develops, moral reservations that at first were only implicit are openly urged, and our sympathies are brought round to the other side. To the key oppositions already abstracted from the tale, I must add:

worldliness	otherworldliness
systematic gaiety	moral gloom
subhuman innocence	fallen human nature
pleasures	passion/love
illusion	truth

Hawthorne's sober, half-regretful judgment on Merry Mount is in basic agreement with Scott's on the Stuart monarchy: that it failed, and deserved to fail, because of its leaders' hedonistic cynicism and improvidence.

As in *Peveril* and *Old Mortality*, so in "The May-Pole of Merry Mount" are the rival creeds of Puritans and Cavaliers shown to be distorting and dehumanizing. As in Scott's romances, so in Hawthorne's tale the essential humanity of the two sides is tested by their respective responses to the plight of two young lovers. The device is an ancient one but especially effective in historical fiction in the tradition of Scott both because they are practical examples to their elders of what is most centrally human – examples of which the fierce old controversialists always have need.

In "The May-Pole of Merry Mount" there are two poignant moments of recognition when, this test being applied, the gay masquers fail and "the men of iron" pass. The first occurs when, their hearts glowing with "real passion" for the first time, the Lord and Lady of the May suddenly feel that "they had subjected themselves to earth's doom of care, sorrow, and troubled joy, and had no more home at Merry Mount" (p. 58). The second happens when grim John Endicott, "the Puritan of Puritans," is touched by "the fair spectacle of early love" and foreknowledge of "the inevitable blight of early hopes" (p. 66). Placing the wreath of roses over the heads of the couple, Endicott not only joins them in wedlock but also symbolically insulates them in their mutual love from the dehumanizing polemics and paranoias of their adoptive community. I do not mean that the hard old iconoclast would have interpreted his gesture this way; but he clearly sees that the lovers have the future in their keeping, and so his extraordinary and maybe unpremeditated act is a saving gesture not merely for them but for himself and all the Puritan people in New England as well.

The rhetorical strategy of "The May-Pole of Merry Mount" is to expose first the Puritans' ugly aspects and their opponents' comely ones but then gradually to reveal the former's massive human strengths and the latter's incapacitating weaknesses. The portrait of the two sides is "balanced" and yet the Puritans have the last word. This pattern is followed in "Endicott and the Red Cross" (1838) and again, though with a host of complications and enrichments, in *The Scarlet Letter*. No more than in "The Gentle Boy" does Hawthorne withdraw his charge that Puritan intolerance had evil consequences in the seventeenth century and afterwards, but in the later works his emphasis falls on those traits of his ancestors which joined them in imperishable community with each other and ourselves. Most important, he moves us to a positive view of the Puritans' role in American historical development by emphasizing their cliff-like stability and powerful homing instinct. As for the individuals whom Hawthorne's Puritans persecute and ostracize, from

"The Gentle Boy" onwards they are nearly always disrupters of familial order, betrayers of the "home." This picture of the Puritans and their enemies is in striking contrast to the one developed by the New Yorkers Irving and Cooper, which stressed the "Yankee" – separatist and migratory – side of Puritanism in opposition to Dutch or Anglican traditionalism. That side too could be viewed positively and patriotically inasmuch as it gave an "onward impulse" to the Westward Movement and other forms of American progress, but Salem-born-and-bred Nathaniel Hawthorne had far other legacies in mind when, near the end of *The Scarlet Letter*, he chanted the epic role-call of New England's "primitive statesmen": "Bradstreet, Endicott, Dudley, Bellingham, and their compeers" (p. 238).

5

In chapter 7 I shall discuss the close relationship that subsists between *The Scarlet Letter* and one of Scott's romances, *The Heart of Mid-Lothian*. The question I am concerned with here is one of generic continuity rather than of specific influence. To what extent does this famous historical fiction conform to or depart from the *Waverley*-model? Certainly Hawthorne did in practice reject a number of the all-too-well-proven narrative ingredients of the historical romance. But for him to have rejected Scott's example altogether or even in large part would have been to fling away much of their common inheritance from the Romantic Revival, and it would have been likewise to make himself over into a writer quite unlike the one who in his early historical tales formulated the Puritan/Cavalier (and American/British) conflict in terms distinctly reminiscent of *Old Mortality* and *Peveril*. No such transformation occurred. For Hawthorne's problem was less that the old mold for historical novels was worn out than that he had nearly exhausted his ideas for, and his interest in, the history of early New England as a matter for fiction. And so his first full-length historical romance was also his last, and in respect of theme, imagery, and rhetorical design it was a consummation rather than a new departure.

In the penultimate chapter of *The Scarlet Letter* Arthur Dimmesdale follows the triumph of his Election Sermon with a sharply contrasting yet, if anything, more dazzling performance on the public scaffold. The former, delivered from the high place of honor within the church, is musical and masterful, inspired, prophetic of a glorious national destiny; the latter, delivered from the high place of ignominy outside, is "fierce" with the supreme last effort of individual will it entails, retrospective, revelatory of the speaker's own secret sin. With these twin revelations of communal success ahead and personal failure behind, Dimmesdale's earthly mission is fulfilled and the *éclaircissement* of Hawthorne's dark plot achieved. No doubt the apotheosis of the Election Sermon is a rhetorical foil – Dimmesdale's as well as Hawthorne's – for the abasement of the confession from the scaffold, but it is not merely that. For the action of *The Scarlet Letter* has, if not precisely two plots, then two main aspects which the sermon and confession are meant to bring into a final sharp focus in relation to each other. On the one hand, the story of Dimmesdale, Hester, Chillingworth, and Pearl has the characteristics which I attributed earlier to such historical tales as "Roger Malvin's Burial" and "Young Goodman Brown": private, fictitious, universal and yet firmly anchored in the social context of seventeenth-century New England. On the other, their story is inseparable from the public history of the Puritan people in America as Hawthorne interpreted it in tales like "The Gray Champion" and "The May-Pole of Merry Mount" – tales in which the fictional characters interact with historical personages such as Endicott and Bradstreet, and participate in a story of emerging nationhood which has its ending, not within the lifetime of Hester or even of Pearl, but a full century later. That story cannot be contained within the narrative framework of Hawthorne's romance except by means of the ancient epic device of a prophetic vision, in this instance Dimmesdale's Election Sermon.

At first sight Dimmesdale appears one of the least "heroic" male protagonists, Hawthorne one of the least "epic" writers, of the Romantic period of our literature. And certainly we listen in vain for any clash of swords in Hawthorne's stories of early New England. "Roger Malvin's Burial" begins with references to the "open bravery," "valor," and "chivalry" displayed by both white and red men in the battle known as "Lovell's Fight" – "One of the few incidents of Indian warfare, naturally susceptible of the moonlight of romance."[30] But after these glancing allusions to Scott and especially Cooper, Hawthorne tells a tale of private suffering, of retreat, failure of nerve, and the withering effects of unconfessed guilt that reminds us irresistibly of the *un*heroic aspect of *The Scarlet Letter*. Even in those tales centrally concerned with public confrontations between the Puritans and their Quaker or Cavalier adversaries, the triumphs are primarily of moral rather than physical courage, of will or humanity rather than arms. Indeed, Hawthorne's loathing of physical force is to be observed throughout his writings; we feel that he could not have written a violent Romantic national epic like "Taras Bulba," *Martín Fierro*, or the Leatherstocking sequence.

Yet Hawthorne was a man of his time, and the works under discussion in this chapter constitute a Romantic regionalist *epos* as surely as do the bloodier contemporary sagas of Gogol, Hernández, and Cooper. Like Cooper before and Cather and Faulkner after, he was captivated by the heroic image of a Virgilian/Mosaic migration and founding in the North American wilderness. If the fathers of his *patria* never lop off arms or let blood in his stories of early New England, the reason is that he chose to take up the action where others left off, to show the sequel to heady moments of violence and passion, and not because his characters fail to experience them. Thus, in chapter VII of *The Scarlet Letter*, Governor Bellingham's armor is suspended peacefully in his hall, but Hawthorne insists that it is not there for mere show, that its owner had worn it not so long before

> at the head of a regiment in the Pequod war. For, though bred a lawyer, and accustomed to speak of Bacon, Coke, Noye, and Finch, as his professional associates, the exigencies of this new country had transformed Governor Bellingham into a soldier, as well as a statesman and ruler.   (p. 106)

Here, it should be noted, Hawthorne is employing Scott's (and later Cooper's) "antiquarian" strategy of picturing an object or scene, making a tableau, and then expounding or leaving the reader to expound its historical significance. But Hawthorne typically invests his antiquarian objects with rather more resonance than do either Scott or Cooper.

The description of Bellingham's armor is followed by a more famous transformation, as the distorting mirror of the breastplate so magnifies the scarlet letter that Hester seems "absolutely hidden behind it." Yet so powerful is this complex double metonymy's indictment of the Puritan fathers' failure to see Hester as a human being that *we* are apt to lose sight of Hawthorne's admiration for Bellingham's practical capabilities and resourcefulness when confronting "the exigencies of this new country." Clearly, the Governor is a man ready to confront them again if necessary – an ever-present possibility at the time of the romance's action (1642–9), when the Puritan beachhead was well-established only in the vicinity of Boston and Boston itself was only "a little town, on the edge of the Western wilderness" (p. 57). Hawthorne does not make much of the frontier circumstances in which his characters move and live and have their moral being, but he clearly expects us to bear them in mind.

On the several occasions when Hawthorne epitomizes their leading traits of mind and character, he tells us plainly enough that the very qualities which made the Puritan fathers successful in founding a home in the wilderness precluded their sympathizing with, much less approving of, the qualities that Hester brought from the Old World. Bellingham, writes Hawthorne, was

> a gentleman advanced in years, and with a hard experience written in his wrinkles. He was not ill fitted to be the head and representative of a community, which owed its origin and progress, and its present state of development, not to the impulses of youth, but to the stern and tempered

> energies of manhood, and the sombre sagacity of age; accomplishing so much, precisely because it imagined and hoped so little.   (p. 64)

Just the opposite of Hester Prynne. The same unstated opposition appears in a later passage written in frank admiration for the early New England public leaders:

> These primitive statesmen, therefore, – Bradstreet, Endicott, Dudley, Bellingham, and their compeers, – who were elevated to power by the early choice of the people, seem to have been not often brilliant, but distinguished by a ponderous sobriety, rather than activity of intellect. They had fortitude and self-reliance, and, in time of difficulty or peril, stood up for the welfare of the state like a line of cliffs against a tempestuous tide.   (p. 238)

Hawthorne's writing here is at its most Johnsonian and may be said in its weightiness and balance to mime its subject – just as the Puritan leaders, for their part, necessarily grow more and more like their hard land of adoption. What place could there be in this world of toil and hardship for the "rich, voluptuous Oriental" nature and tempestuous passions of Hester? What place, either, for the extraordinary spiritual or intellectual capacities of Dimmesdale and Chillingworth? In the end, except for Pearl's, their lives are twisted and thwarted, partly because the natural bent of each is at variance with English Puritanism but likewise because the New World itself is inhospitable to them.

In Governor Bellingham's garden is a

> garden-walk, carpeted with closely shaven grass, and bordered with some rude and immature attempt at shrubbery. But the proprietor appeared already to have relinquished, as hopeless, the effort to perpetuate on this side of the Atlantic, in a hard soil and amid the close struggle for subsistence, the native English taste for ornamental gardening. Cabbages grew in plain sight; and a pumpkin vine, rooted at some distance, had run across the intervening space, and deposited one of its gigantic products directly beneath the hall window; as if to warn the Governor that this great lump of vegetable gold was as rich an ornament as New England earth would offer him.   (pp. 106–7)

Hawthorne makes a careful distinction, often overlooked by his readers, between the "Papist" or "pagan" things which all English Puritans rejected and the innocent sensory and aesthetic pleasures such as ornamental gardening, which many of them enjoyed as lawful. When Dimmesdale scourges his own flesh, he does so "more in accordance with the old, corrupted faith of Rome, than with the better light of the church in which he has been born and bred" (p. 144). Dimmesdale's venerable colleague Mr. Wilson, on the other hand, suggests by his appearance and demeanor that

> pears and peaches might yet be naturalized in the New England climate, and that purple grapes might possibly be compelled to flourish, against the sunny

gardenwall. The old clergyman, nurtured at the rich bosom of the English Church, had a long established taste for all good and comfortable things.

(pp. 108–9)

Hence there is a very *un*ascetic note in his response to the gorgeously attired Pearl:

> "What little bird of scarlet plumage may this be? Methinks I have seen just such figures, when the sun has been shining through a richly painted window, and tracing out the golden and crimson images across the floor. But that was in the old land." (pp. 109–10)

A little later in the same chapter, Hawthorne himself picks up one of Wilson's metaphors and describes Pearl standing in a window "looking like a wild, tropical bird, of rich plumage, ready to take flight into the upper air" (p. 111). In the end, of course, she does take her flight from New England – like the child Ilbrahim and the rainbow banners of Merry Mount.

To those who would tame New England nature, then, she is hard and unkind; making a home in her bosom requires the heroic "fortitude and self-reliance" of the Puritan founders, a spirit "naturally stern" (p. 110) that answers her own. Yet there are many suggestions that Pearl and Hester (and even Roger Chillingworth) are closer to the wild heart of New *and* Old World nature than any true English Puritan ever could be. Both are associated with the "delicate gems" of the native rose that grows by the prison door and with the imported red rose in the governor's garden (pp. 48, 112). "Pearl? – Ruby, rather! – or Coral! – or Red Rose, at the very least, judging from thy hue!" exclaims Mr. Wilson (p. 110). At other times, as when she gathers flowers and twigs in the forest, Pearl's metamorphoses are explicitly identified as pagan: "With these she decorated her hair, and her young waist, and became a nymph-child, or an infant dryad, or whatever else was in closest sympathy with the antique wood" (p. 205). Seeing her thus arrayed, Hester remarks that "It is as if one of the fairies, whom we left in our dear old England, had decked her out to meet us" (p. 206). And Hester is but echoing an identification made earlier, though less approvingly, by Mr. Wilson: "Or art thou one of those naughty elfs or fairies, whom we thought to have left behind us, with other relics of Papistry, in merry old England?" (p. 110). Pearl's appearance reminds Bellingham of his

> days of vanity, in old King James's time, when I was wont to esteem it a high favor to be admitted to a court mask! There used to be a swarm of these small apparitions, in holiday-time; and we called them children of the Lord of Misrule. But how gat such a guest into my hall? (p. 109)

How, indeed? European pagan, Catholic, and Cavalier associations cluster around Pearl and Hester as they do around the people of Merry

Mount. Not merely the party of heterodox pleasure, of Acrasia's Bowre or Comus's crew, they bring the New World a gift of imaginative sympathy that could discover, in the doubleness even of New England nature, flowers among the rocks and roots which, John Endicott complains, "break our ploughshares, when we would till the earth."[31]

This analysis suggests that there were qualities in both English Puritanism and New England nature that might have made them more hospitable to Hester, Pearl, and even Dimmesdale and Chillingworth if the time had been ripe. Like Scott and most of his followers, Hawthorne was keenly interested in the problems caused by faulty historical timing, i.e., anachronistic ways of feeling and behaving. The Gray Champion and Donatello in *The Marble Faun*, for instance, are characters whose successes and failures stem like Edward Waverley's from their being "throwbacks" to another age. The same may be said of Thomas Morton's Gothic monsters who are as much out of time as out of place in frontier America. So too are Dimmesdale and Hester in so far as their sins of the spirit and flesh are linked with "the old, corrupted faith of Rome" and, paradoxically, the "sacred image of sinless motherhood, whose infant was to redeem the world" (p. 56). Indeed, Hawthorne appears to have understood Puritanism as a historical movement which superseded the matriarchal cult of Catholicism by regressing to the patriarchalism of the Old Testament: the progress-through-regress pattern of "The Gray Champion." However, Hester and Dimmesdale are not merely throwbacks: they are also thrown forward. Hester, clearly enough, has some of the traits of a nineteenth-century feminist like Margaret Fuller or Hawthorne's sister-in-law, Elizabeth Peabody; Dimmesdale, those of the inspired but mortally sick *poète maudit* of Romantic legend and actuality. Twice, in chapter XIII and in the penultimate paragraph of the novel, Hester envisages a millennial society enlightened by "a new truth" (p. 263) where the masculine and feminine principles would be brought into enduring harmony; twice Hawthorne suggests that Hester's utopia is only a mirage. Dimmesdale, however, standing on the threshold of eternity, is lifted by inspiration out of his own time to a true vision of the American future, and himself contributes to its realization by inspiring his auditors to glimpse it as well. Poet-priest of his people, he adds something – by imagining and hoping greatly – that the colony now needs as, with the death of Governor Winthrop in 1649, it moves beyond the first phase of settlement.

6

My reading of *The Scarlet Letter* takes the reports given of the style, substance, and effect of the Election Sermon at their face value. "According to their united testimony" (p. 248), those who heard the sermon regarded it as a triumph at once of rhetorical power and prophetic truth – Dimmesdale's shining patriotic Book of Revelation to set against the dark old myth of personal guilt and suffering which he is shortly to retell outside the marketplace. Taken on these straightforward unironic terms, the sermon contrasts the more sharply with its antithesis and pair, Dimmesdale's confession from the scaffold. For the testimony supplied by the narrator does not permit us to decide whether Dimmesdale at last succeeds in publicly confessing his sins of adultery and hypocrisy, much less whether he achieves personal salvation. We may believe that the best-informed judge of the matter is Chillingworth, who repeatedly cries, "Thou hast escaped me!" But the evidence of other witnesses suggests a different conclusion, and one of the alternative possibilities must be that the minister's supposed moment of truth is actually his greatest lie.

I believe that Hawthorne wishes us to conclude not that Dimmesdale succeeds or fails, is saved or damned, but rather that the evidence available to human beings in such cases is never sufficient to draw firm conclusions: God alone can be certain. Yet the "greatest lie" construction cannot be disproven, and its proponents are not likely to stop there. If the confession on the scaffold is a final act of hypocrisy, why credit the Election Sermon either? For it is possible that here too Hawthorne is being subversively ironic in his portrait of Dimmesdale and his gullible parishioners. It can even be maintained that Hawthorne had *better* be ironic, for otherwise the gush about the Election Sermon is a moral and aesthetic embarrassment.[32] Although I do not agree with these contentions and have argued against similar ones in connection with Hawthorne's earlier historical fictions, I believe that the case for an ironic reading of the Election Sermon episode should be given a hearing. After all, the episode in question is one of the most important moments in our most important, or at least our most celebrated and widely read, American historical romance.

Earlier in the novel, Dimmesdale tells Hester that any good which he, "a ruined . . . a polluted soul," might do "must needs be a delusion" (p. 191). While composing the Election Sermon, he wonders "that Heaven should see fit to transmit the grand and solemn music of its oracles through so foul an organ-pipe as he" (p. 225). However, he is so carried away by the "impulsive flow of thought and emotion" that, more like Nathaniel Hawthorne than his own self-tormenting over-scrupulous self, he leaves "that mystery to solve itself, or go unsolved forever." Clearly, the mystery is beyond human solution, but it is somewhat surprising that Arthur Dimmesdale does not pause to reflect that, as a "valued advisor" once vainly warned Emerson, "these impulses may be from below, not from above."[33]

If the source of the sermon is suspect, its tenor and rhetoric may appear to be still more so. I say "appear" because it is impossible to know what the sermon says. Rather than report any of Dimmesdale's words, Hawthorne gives detailed descriptions of the minister's feelings of inspiration while composing, his physical appearance before and after delivery, the musical quality of the performance, and especially the ecstatic response of his auditors. Even the subject of the sermon is only reported indirectly and after the event:

> His subject, it appeared, had been the relation between the Deity and the communities of mankind, with a special reference to the New England which they were here planting in the wilderness. And, as he drew towards the close, a spirit as of prophesy had come upon him, constraining him to its purpose as mightily as the old prophets of Israel were constrained; only with this difference, that, whereas the Jewish seers had denounced judgements and ruin on their country, it was his mission to foretell a high and glorious destiny for the newly gathered people of the Lord.   (p. 249)

By being so vague about Dimmesdale's message and so definite about everything surrounding it, Hawthorne risks suggesting that the sermon was rather like one of the windy Fourth-of-July orations which the recent war with Mexico had inspired. Is Hawthorne guilty here, at one of the climactic moments of his historical romance, of both crude jingoism and clumsy anachronism? Rather than admit such charges, might it not be best to settle for an ironic reading of the Election Sermon episode – the irony being aimed not only at Dimmesdale and his parishioners but also at Hawthorne's own naive nationalist contemporaries?

It must be allowed that the sermon and its auditors' rapturous response are anachronistic. The sermons delivered by seventeenth-century Calvinist ministers were not concerti for displaying the "rich endowment" of the minister's "vocal organ" (p. 243) but rigorous works of scholastic analysis and exposition. Although not necessarily devoid of powerful feeling, they offered little scope for the free play of inspiration. Dimmesdale's audience, had it been responding in true historical character, might well have been alarmed by signs that the minister was being thus carried away. It could of course be said, in mitigation of the historical inaccuracy, that religious enthusiasm and prophetic impulse were also strong forces in the Puritan character even if they normally found vent elsewhere than in sermons.[34] But there is no need for partial excuses: the anachronism is as real as it is also, I believe, deliberate and daring. Although we may decide that he miscalculated when he left Dimmesdale's words entirely to our imagination, there is every indication that Hawthorne's rhetorical strategy throughout the closing chapters of *The Scarlet Letter* was meticulously planned and executed. Irony, irony aplenty, is doubtless present – but not in the form of a nihilistic and untimely satire which would undermine the seriousness and dignity not alone of the Puritans and their great enterprise but of Hawthorne and his.

That Dimmesdale and his Election Sermon audience are "carried away" is very much in keeping with the images of involuntary motion, of "transport," which grow in frequency and importance from chapter xvi ("A Forest Walk") onwards. In these last chapters, after years of comparative stasis and stagnation within the narrow bounds of Boston, the characters suddenly begin to march, to take journeys, to be lifted out of themselves. After intercepting Dimmesdale on his return from visiting the Apostle Eliot, Hester speaks at length of the narrow "forest-track" and "broad pathway of the sea" (p. 197) which lead to freedom; and although the shattered minister protests that "thou tellest of running a race to a man whose knees are tottering beneath him" (p. 198), Hester takes "upon herself to secure the passage of two individuals and a child" (p. 215) on a ship shortly to weigh anchor for Europe. As Hester grows in confidence and activity, Dimmesdale, "poor pilgrim, on his dreary and desert path" (p. 200), dwindles into an almost purely passive being – not immobile, however, but possessed by unnatural energies and purposes. Now he does not hurry but is "hurried . . . townward at a rapid pace" (p. 216), and at the beginning of this period of hyperactivity and presumed afflatus he seems to be possessed by fiends rather than by any divine spirit. "At every step he was incited to do some strange, wild, wicked thing or other, with a sense that it would be at once involuntary and intentional; in spite of himself, yet growing out of a profounder self than that which opposed the impulse" (p. 217).

This strange new state of libidinal unrest seems to be the result of his having reenacted not just Eve's sin of passion but Adam's sin of deliberate rebellion: "Tempted by a dream of happiness, he had yielded himself with deliberate choice, as he had never done before, to what he knew was deadly sin . . . And his encounter with old Mistress Hibbins, if it were a real incident, did but show his sympathy and fellowship with wicked mortals and the world of perverted spirits" (p. 222). His will is thereby impaired, but in Hawthorne's version of the *felix culpa* this second fall humanizes Dimmesdale and opens him more fully to *both* malign influence and unmerited Grace. Although enigmatic, his final private interview with Chillingworth suggests that in his hour of greatest need Grace comes to his aid. Here, in marked contrast with what precedes and follows, the syntactical constructions are active in mood and the minister is master of the situation, firmly meeting his adversary's ironic challenges with sombre wit and courtesy. Of course when Chillingworth exits we cannot be sure whether Dimmesdale has just saved himself by rejecting the Devil or mired himself more deeply by rebuffing (what he later recognizes this particular devil to be) God's scourging agent. Neither can we be sure, when he tells Chillingworth that he expects to be "gone" before long "to another world," whether he has decided against flight with Hester and Pearl or whether he is merely trying to dupe his pursuer. Despite this baffling ambiguity, however, it is at least possible that when Dimmesdale turns from confronting Chillingworth to writing the Election Sermon and surrenders himself to "inspiration," the impulses are from "above." And it is possible, likewise, that when his feeble frame is "carried . . . along" in the procession by a strength that "seemed not of the body" (p. 239), that strength may have the same divine source.

After the sermon, the "energy – or say, rather, the inspiration which had held him up" is "withdrawn" and Dimmesdale is left stranded "by the retiring wave of intellect and sensibility" (p. 251). But rather than collapse as might be expected, he "yet tottered, and did not fall!" He calls for Hester's support, but their roles are now reversed: "Hester Prynne – slowly, as if impelled by inevitable fate, and against her strongest will" (p. 252) joins Dimmesdale, who with resinewed will ends his life's pilgrimage on the "one place" where he could escape Chillingworth's pursuit. He is too pious and orthodox to suppose that he has done so unaided: "Thanks be to Him who hath led me hither!" (p. 253). The paradox that he has at last struggled to the scaffold of his own volition and yet by God's predestination is not one likely to daunt a Calvinist minister. The struggle is the more convincing and moving because of the stark contrast with Dimmesdale's recent passive "transports," while our sense of foredoomed destination is reinforced, not only by the many foreshadowings, but by a correlative sense of Hawthorne's narrative design circling to completion.

The contention that Dimmesdale is too corrupt to be the source or conduit of "golden truths" is in line with his earlier despairing view of himself as a polluted priest but receives scant support from Christian doctrine. Moreover, it ignores the long tradition, extending from the *Ion* to Peter Shaffer's *Amadeus*, of poets, musicians, and priests who are personally unworthy of the great gifts bestowed upon them by God. Romantic literary theorists and practitioners were fascinated by the supposedly high incidence of nervous disability, loose living, alcoholism, despondency, madness, and suicide among great artists. They often hypothesized that such disorders were the usual accompaniments of genius; for the finer and more complex the spiritual organization, they reasoned, the more readily and severely it must be deranged by the shocks of everyday living. They invoked the legendary cases of Chatterton, Burns, Mozart, and Coleridge to support the Wertherian view that, in modern times at least, men with artistic sensibility were almost inevitably estranged from the prosaic world of health and common sense.

Dimmesdale clearly belongs to this company of morbid geniuses, greatly gifted at a great price. He himself laments that, had he been "a wretch with coarse and brutal instincts," he would have "found peace, long ere now"; instead, "whatever of good capacity there originally was in me, all of God's gifts that were the choicest have become the ministers of spiritual torment" (p. 191). Hawthorne virtually plagiarizes the creative theory of the Age of Sensibility (compactly exemplified and criticized in Wordsworth's "Resolution and Independence") in his description of Dimmesdale's alternating bouts of lassitude and superhuman achievement: "Men of uncommon intellect, who have grown morbid, possess this occasional power of mighty effort, into which they throw the life of many days, and then are lifeless for as many more" (p. 239). To the same tradition belong Hawthorne's favorite metaphors of "temperament" and "sympathy" which, in *The Scarlet Letter* if not in all his works, he uses with an informed sense of their origin in musical theory and their function in Romantic poetics. Not only is Dimmesdale richly endowed with a splendid "vocal organ"; the man himself is a highly sensitive instrument played upon by Chillingworth with diabolical skill but available also to be the "organ-pipe" for "Heaven . . . to transmit the grand and solemn music of its oracles" (p. 225). When Hawthorne speaks of Dimmesdale's "earnest haste and ecstasy" while composing the sermon, he has in mind an "ecstasy" far different from that which Chillingworth experiences when he uncovers the minister's guilty secret. He is thinking, as a good Romantic inevitably would, of these lines from *Il Penseroso*:

> There let the pealing organ blow,
> To the full-voiced choir below,
> In service high, and anthems clear,
> As may with sweetness, through mine ear,
> Dissolve me into ecstasies,
> And bring all heaven before mine eyes.[35]

In a state of musical ecstasy, according to the "World Music" lore in which Milton was schooled and with which Hawthorne and other Romantics were at least acquainted, the rapt soul was "beside itself" and could enjoy supernatural visions. As we learn from Milton's "At a Solemn Music," an inspired musical performance could uplift an audience and allow it to share the performer's ecstasy. If the Election Sermon is unlike a Puritan sermon, perhaps it is like a Puritan "solemn music."

What is the answer, then, to the question which Hester puts to Dimmesdale in the forest: "And what hast thou to do with all these iron men, and their opinions?" (p. 197). Inasmuch as he is so patently unlike them in many crucial respects – is as out of place among them as, say, the albatross among the coarse sailors which Baudelaire uses as an emblem of the fettered poetic spirit – the answer must be, "Very little." Yet as my discussion of the musical analogies in *The Scarlet Letter* might suggest, Hawthorne is very cunning at adapting his Romantic psychology and iconography to historical exigencies. Thus the instrument which in a Romantic poem would be an aeolian harp is here a church organ. And if Dimmesdale suffers agonies and exaltations similar to those attributed to Chatterton and Burns, he does so precisely because, despite his differences from the Puritan "iron men" he shares all too many of their "opinions." Unlike heretical Hester, he has a powerful sense of his Christian pastoral identity and mission, and is therefore subject both to the most depressed sense of debasement and the most elevated sense of prophetic powers. It may be that in his own way he is as much of an apostle to New England as his unworldly friend the missionary John Eliot.

If so, the good news he brings to his audience may well be called "The Revelation of the Scarlet Letter." For although the ambiguous words of the title of chapter XXIII most obviously refer to Dimmesdale's public revealing of the mark he bears in secret correspondence to Hester's scarlet *A*, so elaborate is Hawthorne's design of doubling and antithesis that they also suggest that the minister's oracles are the product of his private suffering. Read in this way, the chapter title recalls the Puritans' belief that they could "interpret all meteoric appearances . . . as so many revelations from a divine source" and also Hawthorne's comment that "It was, indeed, a majestic idea, that the destiny of nations should be revealed, in these awful hieroglyphics, on the cope of heaven" (pp. 154, 155). Hawthorne distinguishes sharply between this idea, "majestic" even if scientifically untenable, and Dimmesdale's egoistical illusion of an immense letter *A* in the night sky – "a revelation, addressed to himself alone, on the same vast sheet of record!" By the time of the Election Sermon, the scarlet letter, agent as well as object, has done its work so well that Dimmesdale transcends morbid self-preoccupation to become the prophet of his people. Although not constituted to bear the Puritan regimen or to share in the practical work of building a new England, he is thus enabled to make his contribution to the communal effort through a bracing vision of the nation's "high and glorious destiny."

Nor should we be misled by the deflated mood of "The Custom-House" to suppose that Hawthorne would have regarded this vision as a pious illusion or presage of spread-eagle nationalism. In other moods Hawthorne could argue earnestly that the sadly imperfect liberal democracy nurtured in the United States, and especially in New England, was the best hope of mankind. A shy and private person like

Dimmesdale, and one still more incongruously employed in the public service, he seems to have yearned at times not only to be heard and "honored by his mortal brethren" as the minister was but also to participate in "the universal impulse which makes . . . one vast heart out of the many" (p. 250). Nathaniel Hawthorne was neither Arthur Dimmesdale nor yet – still another protagonist of American fiction – the democratic seer Walt Whitman. But aspects of both belonged to him, too, and I think we will not go far wrong if we say that Dimmesdale's patriotic message to the people of New England is also, and simultaneously, Hawthorne's.

For, as those who detect anachronism in chapters xxii and xxiii allege, it is perfectly true that the shimmering prophecies and the excited behavior of the audience belong more to the nineteenth than to the seventeenth century. Hawthorne's lack of detailed specification allows us, if we will, to associate this scene with Daniel Webster and a Fourth-of-July crowd. But we surely come very much closer to Hawthorne's tone and intention if we imagine Dimmesdale and his listeners transformed for a moment into their own best heritage – Emerson, say, and a rapt lyceum audience – or borne into the future and united in spirit with their descendants, the readers of Hawthorne's romance. For it is at this point in the narrative that the imagery of "transport" reaches an Emersonian climax, the style as deftly adapted to the substance as it was earlier in Hawthorne's Johnsonian descriptions of the Puritan fathers:

> The eloquent voice, on which the souls of the listening audience had been borne aloft, as on the swelling waves of the sea, at length came to a pause. There was a momentary silence, profound as what should follow the utterance of oracles. Then ensued a murmur and half-hushed tumult; as if the auditors, released from the high spell that had transported them into the region of another's mind, were returning into themselves, with all their awe and wonder still heavy on them. In a moment more, the crowd began to gush forth from the doors of the church. Now that there was an end, they needed other breath, more fit to support the gross and earthly life into which they relapsed, than that atmosphere which the preacher had converted into words of flame, and had burdened with the rich fragrance of his thought. (p. 248)

So the temporal dislocations and breaches of historicity in the concluding chapters of *The Scarlet Letter* are not lapses resulting from ignorance or oversight. Nor, in my judgment, are they ironic deconstructions of Bancroft and the nationalistic orators of Hawthorne's own times. Rather, as in "The Gray Champion," they are designed, first, to reveal an underlying long-range pattern in American history and, second, to enforce a sense of community between the Puritans and ourselves. Indeed, although the constraints of realistic convention oblige Hawthorne to be more circumspect than Whitman, the Election Sermon scene is a stroke as bold in its way as the time-collapsing, time-traversing lines from "Crossing Brooklyn Ferry":

> And you that shall cross from shore to shore years hence are more to me, and more in my meditations, than you might suppose.[36]

7

If we seek to explain why *The Scarlet Letter* and Hawthorne's best tales of early New England are generally more exquisitely crafted, more psychologically inward, and more morally searching than the rest of his fiction, we cannot ignore his profound sense of personal involvement in the good and evil deeds of his Puritan forefathers. But a sense of ancestral sin is unlikely to have been the sole or overriding determinant of his choice of colonial New England as a subject. As we have seen, for writers of Hawthorne's generation the two great matters of American historical romance – matters corresponding to the civil and imperialistic conflicts in *Waverley* – were to be found in the Revolutionary War era and the times of frontier hardship, beginning with the earliest plantations. It would have been odd if an ambitious fictionalist of his place and time had not written about the seventeenth-century Puritans, and the wonder is that the stories which concern them form such a small, albeit superior, part of his *oeuvre* and no part at all after *The Scarlet Letter*.

That part of his fiction which treats the second great matter of American historical romance is likewise comparatively small and early. But it is extremely uneven in quality and most of it appears to have been written under the combined pressures of literary fashion, patriotic duty, and financial necessity rather than out of any deep personal interest. Why this should be so is something of a puzzle. Although the Hawthorne family played a less conspicuous role in winning the Revolution than it had in founding Massachusetts, Nathaniel's eighteenth-century ancestors (especially his sailor grandfather) were active on the "patriot" side. Hawthorne himself was undoubtedly a close student of the Revolution, or at any rate of its early stages in New England, and he seems to have been ideally distanced from it for the purpose of historical fiction. Just as Scott was in relation to the '45 or Cooper to the colonizing and military ventures of eighteenth-century New York, he was close enough to have had some personal contact with eyewitnesses yet remote enough to take a view at once clear and compassionate.

This ideal distance is maintained fairly consistently in *Liberty Tree*, the excellent juvenile history of the commencement of the Revolution which he published in 1841 – partly as a potential money-spinner, no doubt, but partly also as a proud memorial to the important role which his native state had played in the American Independence movement. In fact, *Liberty Tree* is in some respects less "juvenile," in the pejorative sense of being weakened by stock characters and sentiments, than most of the Revolutionary War fictions he wrote for adults. Given Hawthorne's talent, however, the detailed and intimate familiarity with the (Massachusetts) matter of the Revolution which *Liberty Tree* demonstrates was bound to yield some historical fiction of enduring interest. Certainly it yielded one early putative masterpiece in "My Kinsman, Major Molineux" (1832) and Hawthorne's closest approach, in the framed narrative quartet "Legends of the Province-House" (1838–9), to a full-length historical romance before *The Scarlet Letter*.

Hawthorne's Revolutionary War stories and sketches fall into two main groups. A few, like "Howe's Masquerade" and "Old Esther Dudley," deal with the Revolutionary period itself and include historical personages, such as General Howe and John Hancock, who were leaders in the conflict. Better known and generally superior are the stories which deal with earlier characters and events interpreted as anticipating or "typifying" those of the Revolution. Anthology favorites "The Gray Champion" and "Endicott and the Red Cross" belong to this group, and so of course does "My Kinsman, Major Molineux." Evidently the Fourth-of-July bonfires and torchlight processions smoked and glared so fiercely during the 1830s and 1840s that Hawthorne could see the Revolution steadily and penetratingly only when he viewed it indirectly.

The indirection practiced in "My Kinsman, Major Molineux" is so elaborate as to leave Hawthorne's "real" subject somewhat in doubt. But since the tale is remarkably vivid and powerful, this uncertainty has prompted a huge volume of commentary on its meaning(s) and sources. To review this commentary here or add to it might well seem supererogatory, but perhaps something useful can be said here about the relationship this elusive tale bears to the historical romance tradition.

Robin Molineux, whose frustrated search for his kinsman and potential patron, Major Molineux, supplies the explicit main action and motivation of the tale, is usually identified as an American hero in the Ben Franklin mold inasmuch as he is a resolute "shrewd youth" of humble origin seeking his fortune in a strange city.[37] However, he differs from the protagonists of Puritan biography (including Franklin and such fictional representatives as Defoe's Crusoe and Moll) and resembles such heroes of historical romance as Edward Waverley and Corny Littlepage inasmuch as he has a blood connection with the privileged classes and intends to exploit it. Like theirs, his initiatory journey to adult independence is not supposed to lead to a violent rejection of patriarchal authority but rather to a proof that the son is worthy of his fathers. But things do not fare with Robin according to plan, and he is carried along by emotions and events too powerful and inscrutable for him to govern. When he joins spontaneously in the mob's mockery of the "tar-and-feathery dignity" of "his kinsman, Major Molineux" (p. 228), his participation in the rebellion is not a temporary aberration like Waverley's but seemingly an unpardonable and irreparable act. Robin himself does not at first realize that in mocking the surrogate father he has rejected the entire system of reverence for patriarchal authority and patronage by which he has hitherto lived; he supposes that it is still possible for him to return home. But the Boston gentleman who has befriended Robin knows better, and there is doubtless prophecy as well as much meaning packed in his concluding speculation that "if you prefer to remain with us, perhaps, as you are a shrewd youth, you may rise in the world without the help of your kinsman, Major Molineux" (p. 231).

Read as a political fable, "My Kinsman, Major Molineux" delivers a very ambivalent judgment on the Revolution. On the one hand, the gentleman's speculation concerning Robin's future seems to imply approval of the American colonies' bid for independence. And if, as appears to be the case, Hawthorne is here resurrecting the allegorical language of filial/paternal relation which Jay Fliegelman has shown to dominate much eighteenth-century revolutionary and counterrevolutionary polemic, Robin (the colonies) really has no natural or self-respecting alternative to independence since as a second son he is denied a share in the patrimony (full political and economic rights) enjoyed by his elder brother (England).[38] But even if Hawthorne's political allegory is less intricate and historically sensitive than I suppose it to be, the action of the story supports much the same judgment. For although Robin's involuntary shout of laughter – "the loudest there" – in response to the public humiliation of the patriarchal figure does no honor to its perpetrator or to human nature, it does argue that a prolonged state of filial (colonial) dependence and reverence inevitably breeds resentment and rebellion. Independence is therefore both natural and necessary. On the other hand, Hawthorne characteristically suggests that doing what comes naturally and necessarily may well, in our present fallen state, ally us with the Devil's party. Certainly his description of the mob which humiliates Major Molineux is meant to remind us of Milton's description of Pandemonium, and the most startling and disturbing moment in the story occurs when the narrator abruptly abandons his tone of amused ironic detachment and in ringing sentences identifies the "patriotic" mob with Satan's crew:

> On they went, like fiends that throng in mockery round some dead potentate, mighty no more, but majestic still in his agony. On they went, in counterfeited pomp, in senseless uproar, in frenzied merriment, trampling all on an old man's heart. On swept the tumult, and left a silent street behind.   (p. 230)

Not Scott himself in the *Life of Napoleon Buonaparte* ever denounced revolutionary mob violence or affirmed his sympathy for its victims with greater passion or rhetorical effect than Hawthorne does here.

It is ambiguous whether the nightmarish ordeal of Major Molineux is an "actual" event which Robin witnesses or, as seems more likely, a dream which projects his unconscious desires. In either case, the happenings imaged in the closing pages of "My Kinsman, Major Molineux" call to mind various historical acts of the early 1770s, notably the Boston Tea Party and the sacking of Governor Hutchinson's house, which have commonly been celebrated, or at least excused, on the grounds that they awakened the spirit of American resistance to tyranny and presaged the Revolution.[39] Here, as later in "The Gray Champion" and "Endicott and the Red Cross," Hawthorne freely adapts historical incidents so that they become symbolic pre-enactments of the Revolution – illustrations, as it were, of the truth of John Adams's remark that "The revolution was in the minds and hearts of the people . . . before hostilities commenced."[40]

In this story, however, the Revolutionary party can boast no stern heroic profiles like those of the Gray Champion or Endicott. The leader who rallies the people is a diabolical figure who "by his fierce and variegated countenance, appeared like war personified; the red of one cheek was the emblem of fire and sword; the blackness of the other betokened the mourning which attends them" (p. 227). And what is less surprising than that this "horseman, clad in a military dress," bears no resemblance whatever to the hagiographical portraits of Revolutionary leaders which were still current in Hawthorne's day, is that the Tory victim is described in terms regularly applied to George Washington: "an elderly man, of large and majestic person, and strong square features, betokening a sturdy soul" (p. 228). The effect of this description is to ally the greatest hero and leader of the Revolution with the very class of Americans who most loyally opposed it. Here, and with a vengeance, is historical irony in the form of chiasmus. The point of this irony, that a "Whig" leader like Washington had more in common with a "Tory" leader like Thomas Hutchinson than with the revolutionary mobs, is of course historically well taken. The irony sharply qualifies, but does not finally undercut, the implicit argument of the tale in favor of independence as natural and necessary: for we know that, when the revolutionary fires have died out, the newly enfranchised Robin Molineux will cast his vote not for a *sans culotte* but for a patriarchal leader who has proven himself worthy of his sons and who will oppose Jacobin incendiarism with all possible firmness and vigor.

Perhaps it was because the story presented a relatively unflattering picture of the Revolution that Hawthorne chose not to republish it in any of his collections until 1852, some twenty years after its first appearance, by which time *The Scarlet Letter* had established his literary reputation, and stories like "The Gray Champion" and "Lady Eleanore's Mantle" had demonstrated his political orthodoxy. Yet it would be misleading to suggest that Hawthorne simply did an expedient about-face on the subject of the Revolution, abandoning the sympathies of a "modern Tory" for the more marketable ones of a "thoroughgoing Democrat."[41] Although he never again exposed the dark underside of the Revolution so starkly as he did in "My Kinsman, Major Molineux," he developed a fuller range of revolutionary and counterrevolutionary character-types. This extended range allowed him to represent the main factions of the Revolution more fairly and comprehensively – especially in the "Legends of the Province-House" sequence, where at least four major character-types are juxtaposed and the judgments of one story are balanced and qualified by those of a neighboring story. These character-types represent the following principal factions: British officers and aristocrats, Revolutionary demagogues and their followers, American Tories, and American Patriots.

The British officers and aristocrats who appear in "Legends of the Province-House" are the literary as well as national and social-class descendants of the villain of "The Gray Champion," Sir Edmund Andros, the Royal Governor whose "tyranny" was successfully resisted in the "Revolution of 1689." That this is so is made clear by Hawthorne in the first of the "Legends," the ambiguously titled "Howe's Masquerade," when General Howe's masqued ball, designed to mock his Revolutionary opponents, is inexplicably supplanted by a spectral procession of all the past governors of Massachusetts "summoned to form the funeral procession of royal authority in New England."[42] Howe significantly mistakes a group of Puritan figures representing the earliest governors of the Commonwealth for a "a procession of the regicide judges of King Charles, the martyr" (p. 247). He is set straight by a Gray Champion figure, the aged Whig Colonel Joliffe, who, although he denies having seen the living faces of the seventeenth-century Governors, is said to be "the best sustained character in the masquerade, because so well representing the antique spirit of his native land" (p. 244). Howe's ignorance of New England history and thus of the warnings it contains for men in his position is symptomatic of what ails the imperial government and makes it unfit to rule. Because both foreign- and high-born, its representatives have slight respect for provincial pieties and no ability to enter into the American view of correct political and economic relations. As we have seen, these are the staple and mostly well-founded complaints of Romantic regional literature generally, of *The Heart of Mid-Lothian* quite as much as of *Satanstoe*. In "Legends of the Province-House" they are raised to a revolutionary pitch.

A stereotypical soldier rather than a stereotypical aristocrat, Howe is not portrayed as a cruel or corrupt governor like Andros. As is shown by the fourth of the Legends, "Old Esther Dudley," his ignorance and pride are due to defects of education, to his backgound as a soldier and foreigner, rather than to a radical incapacity to suffer or sympathize. In this respect he contrasts sharply with Lady Eleanore Rochcliffe, who, as her family name implies, is removed from sympathy with humankind because of a "harsh unyielding pride, a haughty consciousness of her hereditary and personal advantages, which made her almost incapable of control" (pp. 273–4). When a crazed, rejected (American) suitor offers his body as a footstool, she accepts, commenting that "When men seek only to be trampled upon, it were a pity to deny them a favor so easily granted – and so well deserved!" (p. 276). Hawthorne, perhaps supposing nothing too crudely explicit or warmly fraternal for the readers of the *United States Magazine and Democratic Review* where the legends were first published, moralizes that "never, surely, was there an apter emblem of aristocracy and hereditary pride, trampling on human sympathies and the kindred of nature, than these two figures presented at that moment" (p. 276). (An instructive parallel may be drawn between this simplistic emblem of oppression and the similar, but incomparably more complex and suggestive, emblem of the two satyrs in *Benito Cereno*.)

Lady Eleanore's pride is humbled and her kinship with the most poor and provincial subjects demonstrated when she falls, with them, the victim of a smallpox epidemic – justifiably likened by Hawthorne to that most terrifying agent of Death the Leveler, the plague. Like the British administration in America, she brings about her own destruction; for it transpires that she has herself brought the disease to America in a gorgeous mantle, emblem of her pride and apartness, whose "fantastic splendor had been conceived in the delirious brain of a woman on her deathbed, and was the last toil of her stiffening fingers" (p. 284). This image of class exploitation may strike us as melodramatic and "Victorian," but it has some of the strengths that characteristically accompany the weaknesses of similar passages in Dickens. In particular, its political symbolism is capable of vivid and surprising extension, as we see when Hawthorne turns the plague carried by the mantle into a harbinger of the Revolution:

> That night, a procession passed, by torch light, through the streets, bearing in the midst, the figure of a woman, enveloped with a richly embroidered mantle; while in advance stalked Jervase Helwyse, waving the red flag of the pestilence. Arriving opposite the Province-House, the mob burned the effigy, and a strong wind came and swept away the ashes. It was said, that, from that very hour, the pestilence abated. (p. 288)

Led not by the sinister parti-colored demon of "My Kinsman, Major Molineux" but instead by Lady Eleanore's rejected suitor, this mob acts destructively, but not vengefully or sadistically, for the sake of a necessary purification.

This radical-Romantic view of the Revolution and its mobs is not one shared by the British administration or by its American Tory supporters. In "Edward Randolph's Portrait" a British officer exclaims, "The demagogues of this Province have raised the devil, and cannot lay him again. We will exorcise him, in God's name and the King's" (p. 265). Patrician Lieutenant Governor Hutchinson, whose private mansion was sacked by the mob, reads the early outrages of the Independence movement in over-simple class-conflict terms:

> When there shall be a sentinel at every corner, and a court of guard before the town-house, a loyal gentleman may venture to walk abroad. What to me is the outcry of a mob, in this remote province of the realm? The King is my master, and England is my country! Upheld by their armed strength, I set my foot upon the rabble, and defy them!   (p. 266)

When Hutchinson says that "I set my foot upon the rabble," he is behaving more like an English aristocrat than an American gentleman. For his figure differs but slightly from the "emblem of aristocracy and hereditary pride, trampling on human sympathies and the kindred of nature" in "Lady Eleanore's Mantle." When the conflict is polarized in these terms, Hawthorne counters with a Jeffersonian–Jacksonian rhetoric which transforms the "mob," the "rabble," the "misguided multitude" of Hutchinson's political vocabulary into "the People." Hutchinson's Whiggish niece Alice Vane (obviously a descendant of Puritan regicide Henry Vane) warns her uncle that "When the rulers feel themselves irresponsible, it were well that they should be reminded of the awful weight of a People's curse" (p. 262). And at the end of the story, when Hutchinson lies dying in England and complaining that he is "choking with the blood of the Boston Massacre," Hawthorne's narrator recalls Alice Vane's words and asks, "Did his broken spirit feel, at that dread hour, the tremendous burthen of a People's curse?" (p. 269).

Historian of Massachusetts and descendant of one of its most distinguished old families, Thomas Hutchinson has none of General Howe's excuses for misjudging the temper and motives of the natives. Hutchinson's historical insight is revealed, in one of the best scenes in the "Legends of the Province-House," when he calls a meeting of the Province Council and Boston Selectmen to witness his signing an order for the landing of British troops in Boston. Responding to the British officer's boast that his troops would soon exorcise the Devil from Massachusetts, an American-born officer present at the meeting warns:

"If you meddle with the devil, take care of his claws!" answered the Captain of Castle William, stirred by the taunt against his countrymen.

"Craving your pardon, young sir," said the venerable Selectman, "let not an evil spirit enter into your words. We will strive against the oppressor with prayer and fasting, as our forefathers would have done. Like them, moreover, we will submit to whatever lot a wise Providence may send us, – always, after our own best exertions to amend it."

"And there peep forth the devil's claws!" muttered Hutchinson, who well understood the nature of Puritan submission. (pp. 265–6)

Nonetheless, and also despite the ominous example of his predecessor Edward Randolph who was cursed by "The People" for betraying their liberties, Hutchinson proceeds to order the British military occupation of Boston. His reasons for doing so are intelligible and, up to a point, perfectly creditable. A committed Loyalist, he believes that he and his fellow colonials are Englishmen first and Massachusetts-men second, and therefore that their clear duty is to obey the English King and, if necessary, to use English troops to restore law and order. As we have already seen, he dismisses the popular account of the misdeeds and marvellous suffering of Randolph, "styled the arch enemy of New England," remarking that "too implicit credence has been given to Dr. Cotton Mather, who . . . has filled our early history with old women's tales, as fanciful and extravagant as those of Greece or Rome" (p. 262). Blinded by his rationalism no less than by his class and loyalist prejudices, he is incapable of drawing the correct lessons from the history he knows so well. Ignoring the involvement of civic leaders in earlier outbreaks of rebellion in New England, he is convinced that the recent disturbances are the work of a "wild, misguided multitude" and that the more respectable members of the community are only "infected" by a "merely temporary spirit of mischief" (p. 265). Just as seriously, he fails to understand that the "old women's tales" of the Puritans are dangerous precisely because they are mythic.

Hutchinson is much the most complex and rounded character in "Legends of the Province-House" and may well be the most successful of a series of attempts by Hawthorne and his contemporaries to create a critical yet not unsympathetic portrait of American Tory character comparable to Scott's Jacobites. Like many other Tories in American Romantic fiction, Hawthorne's Hutchinson is middle-aged, a man of reflection rather than of action, ruled quite as much by a fear of anarchic violence as by principles of loyalty, and troubled by political divisions within his own household. But he departs from type and hence from predictability because, unlike Old Esther Dudley and most other fictional Tories, his political conservatism is the product of his rationalism rather than of his latent superstition. Indeed, he conforms to an earlier typology in that he inherits some of the scepticism of Andros's Cavaliers along with a smaller yet still active portion of the Puritan's superstitious faith in miraculous reenactments. Thus he is torn painfully "betwixt ancient faith and modern incredulity" when he witnesses the seemingly miraculous reappearance of Randolph's visage in a blackened painting hanging in the Province-House:

> Within the antique frame, which so recently had enclosed a sable waste of canvas, now appeared a visible picture, still dark, indeed, in its hues and shadings, but thrown forward in strong relief . . . The expression of the face . . . was that of a wretch detected in some hideous guilt, and exposed to the bitter hatred, and laughter, and withering scorn, of a vast surrounding multitude.   (p. 267)

An act of Providence to warn Hutchinson? A clever trick of restoration by Alice Vane? Hawthorne of course does not opt for either of these alternative possibilities, but the Lieutenant Governor, his life's faith as a Tory politician and Enlightened historian in jeopardy, violently rejects the supernaturalist explanation and scrawls on the fatal order, "in characters that betokened it a deed of desperation, the name of Thomas Hutchinson" (p. 268).

Biographically faithful or not, Hawthorne's Hutchinson seems drawn from life whereas Hawthorne's portrait of the aged Tory gentlewoman Esther Dudley, who lingers on in Province-House after Howe's evacuation of Boston, is a literary caricature based on Scott's most extreme type of lovable fossilized Jacobite. The daughter of "an ancient and once eminent family, which had fallen into poverty and decay," she maintains the old customs and adorns "herself with an antique magnificence of attire" (p. 292). Howe, leaving the key of Province-House with her, "deemed her well-fitted for such a charge, as being so perfect a representative of the decayed past – of an age gone by, with its manners, opinions, faith, and feelings, all fallen into oblivion or scorn – of what had once been a reality, but was now merely a vision of faded magnificence" (p. 294). Howe's judgment (which comes somewhat oddly from a British general and military governor) is echoed years later by John Hancock, "the people's chosen Governor of Massachusetts" when he meets a dying Esther on the steps of Province-House. Hancock's bald contrast between the parties of reaction and progress has a cartoonlike simplicity about it:

> "Your life has been prolonged until the world has changed around you. You have treasured up all that time has rendered worthless – the principles, feelings, manners, modes of being and acting, which another generation has flung aside – and you are a symbol of the past. And I, and these around me – we represent a new race of men, living no longer in the past, scarcely in the present – but projecting our lives forward into the future. Ceasing to model ourselves on

ancestral superstitions, it is our faith and principle to press onward,
onward!" (p. 301)

When Hancock claims the key to Province-House from Esther, he is
described as "this New England merchant" whose "foot now trod upon
humbled Royalty" (p. 301). So, as the recurrent emblem manifests, the
American Revolution ends in triumph for the middle classes and not for.
either "aristocracy and hereditary pride" or, as Hutchinson feared, the
urban "rabble." In Hancock's case, moreover, middleness means not
mediocrity but a variousness capable of reconciling all factions save the
most die-hard royalists or fanatical levelers. As the "monarch's most
dreaded and hated foe" he is a legitimate successor to the Puritan
Governors of Massachusetts, while as a spokesman for the forward-
looking spirit of the age he is a leader with great contemporary popular
appeal. Although a merchant with the driving "onward" energies of
modern capitalism, his dress and manners betoken "gentle blood, high
rank, and long accustomed authority" (p. 300). Esther recalls confusedly
that she had known him long ago "among the gentry of the Province"
(p. 301), and, as she sinks towards death, he lends "her his support with all
the reverence that a courtier would have shown to a queen." In this
portrait, Hancock combines the best of the past and the present, or rather
the future, and of the Tory and Revolutionary parties. Hawthorne's
fictional rhetoric seems to have a design analogous to that of the
oratorical rhetoric of Jefferson's First Inaugural Address: i.e., to effect a
sense of closure to an era of conflict by presenting a dynamic new leader
who has neither wish nor need to settle old scores, neither time nor leisure
to linger over past differences, but who only seeks – as much through his
own many-sided personality as through his policies – to bring the rival
factions together in creative union.

Yet just as the new president's triumphant deduction that "we are all
republicans – we are all federalists" must have prompted sceptical
auditors from both parties to inquire where, if he existed at all, the real
Mr. Jefferson stood, so the conclusion of "Legends of the Province-
House" might lead us to ask the same question about Hawthorne's
Hancock and about Hawthorne himself. For although the "Legends"
appear to be a straightforward paean to the Revolution and the
victorious middle-class heirs of the Puritans, the hero who ushers in the
new era is a brilliant but equivocal figure; and in the narrative frame there
are several hints that the old era was perhaps not so bad after all. Once
again we must consider the possibility of sly ironic subversion – and this
at the very moment when Hawthorne seems to be most affirmatively
nationalistic.

Certainly the actual stories of eighteenth-century Boston which are
told in "Legends of the Province-House" never present the Revolution

in the unfavorable light of "My Kinsman, Major Molineux." Obviously prejudiced characters like Hutchinson and Esther Dudley denounce their opponents, but their Tory animadversions are always eloquently countered by attractively frank and humane spokesmen for "the People" like Colonel Joliffe in "Howe's Masquerade," the old Selectman in "Edward Randolph's Portrait," and Doctor Clarke in "Lady Eleanore's Mantle." And although Old Esther, Hutchinson, and even General Howe are treated with considerable sympathy and respect, there is never any doubt that they are the deluded adherents of an obsolete socio-political system which, at its worst, fosters and takes pride in moral monsters like Lady Eleanore. Especially in the first two stories of the sequence are we encouraged to embrace the view propounded in "The Gray Champion" that the Revolution is the predestined culmination of the centuries-old Puritan struggle for "Liberty" and republican government. Since this is likewise the message of *Liberty Tree*, written only two years after the "Legends," Hawthorne must have been a very great and persistent hypocrite if he did not believe it.

To believe, however, is not necessarily to be free from all adult doubts, reservations, and ironic awareness of discrepancies between aspiration and performance. In "Legends of the Province-House" Hawthorne generally excludes these from the narratives of times past, which record and celebrate a heroic era and the sustaining, creative power of a simple and sincere political faith. The misgivings creep in around the edges. They do so most obviously and explicitly through his descriptions in the narrative frame of the Province-House and its surroundings in modern times. By the period of the frame narrative (i.e., 1838–9), the Province-House has been reduced to a tavern where the narrator hears the tales which he then proceeds to relate for our benefit.

Although a narrative frame in which stories are recounted over drinks in a tavern is a device of ancient provenance which Chaucer used to excellent effect in the *Canterbury Tales*, it is likely that Hawthorne had a more recent example in mind. Scott's early Waverley novels, called "Tales of My Landlord," were supplied with a humorous frame involving multiple comic alter egos, including the landlord of the "Wallace Inn," a tippling schoolteacher, and usually a visitor who in some way occasions the ensuing narrative. The relationship between frame and main narrative varies in minor ways from book to book, but the basic contrast is between a heroic national past and a genial but diminished local present where deeds are replaced with words, passions with potations, and *éclaircissements* of historical motive and identity with mystificatory authorial self-displays. Scott's "Tales of My Landlord" thus exemplify one of the principal varieties of Romantic irony or parabasis.[43] Given Hawthorne's predilection for this kind of irony, it is scarcely surprising that he developed a frame of his own for the "Legends of the Province-House" and subsequently used "The Custom-House" sketch for much the same purpose in *The Scarlet Letter*.

In "Legends of the Province-House," the grand but sadly decayed old mansion supplies not only historical settings for the pre-revolutionary tales but also occasions for the narrator to draw nostalgic contrasts between the aristocratic past and the materialistic democratic present. On their showing, American colonial society was more spacious, individualistic, festive, and tasteful than the society which the Revolution produced. Yet these criticisms of the Revolution, or rather of its outcome, are undercut by the prevailingly whimsical tone of the narrative frame; and what they allege in favor of the old order does not begin to balance what the tales urge against it. Hawthorne's most damaging criticisms are implied rather than directly stated and might go unnoticed altogether but for the extraordinary closing portrait of Hancock.

The "people's chosen Governor of Massachusetts" – with his "my fellow-citizens, onward – onward! We are no longer children of the Past!" (p. 302) – is doubtless, for reasons already stated, the political leader that the times require. Yet it might appear that the political leader that Hawthorne's historical schema requires is not the ambivalent Hancock but a Gray Champion like Hancock's successor, the stern old patriot Samuel Adams whose "character was such," Hawthorne was to write in *Liberty Tree*, "that it seemed as if one of the ancient Puritans had been sent back to earth, to animate the people's hearts with the same abhorrence of tyranny, that had distinguished the earliest settlers."[44] Had he wished to do so, Hawthorne could have found a way to close the "Legends" sequence with Adams, who incarnated not only the Puritan character and "abhorrence of tyranny" but also its historical-mindedness. He chose instead to close it with a much more modern figure in whom Puritan iconoclasm has degenerated into the radically antihistorical spirit of nineteenth-century Progressivism. This spokesman for the "onward" philosophy is quite as grotesque in his way as his obverse, old Esther, was in hers. As the leader of "a new race of men, living no longer in the past, scarcely in the present" he promises to have all of the weaknesses which de Tocqueville and others have criticized in American Progressivists. Surely Hawthorne did intend his more thoughtful readers to reflect ironically that because of "our faith and principle to press onward, onward!," the stately and picturesque old Province-House would be abandoned to become a fusty tavern hidden behind the modern brick block of shops "with a front of tiresome identity" (p. 256) facing Washington Street. To reflect, too, that Hancock and other American leaders impatient of the past were bound to repeat Howe's and Hutchinson's arrogant and fatal mistake of ignoring the warnings of history. And to note that the heirs of Homer, historical romancers like Hawthorne himself, would come to seem no better than frivolous antiquarians who "babbled about dreams of the past" (pp. 302–3), stupefying themselves as much with the historical as with the alcoholic concoctions of the Province-House Tavern.

These disillusioned reflections on the effects of the innovative spirit set loose by the Revolution need not be considered inconsistent with, or ironically subversive of, a veneration for the Revolution itself. For right up to the arrival of Hancock, the Revolutionary party is presented as (in the best sense) backward-looking, engaged in a heroic and successful struggle to restore ancient liberties and at last complete the task which the Puritan fathers set themselves when they came to New England in the early seventeenth century. The conclusion of the "Legends" acknowledges that the Revolutionary movement was also impelled by a forward-looking principle and that, as conservative republicans would learn to their dismay, the triumph of Sam Adams inevitably meant the triumph of John Hancock as well. On this reading, the conclusion of the sequence is indeed ironic but in a way that does not undercut or confuse; the advent of Hancock can be regarded as yet another illustration of the historical law of unintended consequences.

If this reading does not entirely persuade, I believe the reason may be that Hawthorne himself is something of an ambivalent Hancock figure. At his greatest and wisest he exhibits the middle-class strengths of balance and varied responsiveness which characterize the masters of historical romance from Scott onwards. He is then supremely able to "hold the Present at its worth without being inappreciative of the Past," as Melville describes the ideal humane historian.[45] In *The Scarlet Letter* he achieves not only an unprecedented inwardness with Puritan psychology but also an appreciation of the strengths and weaknesses of Puritan character, as contrasted with those of mid-nineteenth-century American character, which does justice to both. In *The Scarlet Letter* too he takes a sad but not despairing measure both of the need which individuals and nations have to free themselves from the past and of the very limited scope they have to gain that freedom. So he makes us share – share with the liveliest creaturely sympathy – Hester's forest dream that she had at last "flung" the scarlet letter, symbol of the past, "into infinite space" (p. 211). But our sense of release and expansion is brief because Hawthorne soon brings home to us through the person of Pearl how delusive and even irresponsible must be a finite creature's hope to "undo" the past and "make it as it had never been" (p. 202). His own most radical strategy for dealing with the constrictions of the past in *The Scarlet Letter* is the eminently practicable (and "Puritan") one of "frequent transplantation" (p. 9).

Elsewhere in his writings, however, the middle-class responsiveness remains but the balance is sometimes lost, and then the expressions of a Jeffersonian longing to undo, burn, or fling aside the past are not dampened or checked by a cautionary remark or untoward event. Such is the case when, *in propria persona*, he judges that "it is time to break up and fling away" the "worn out mould" of historical romance "that has been in use these thirty years." The phrasing and intonation of this comment sound disconcertingly like an echo of Hancock's charge against Esther Dudley that she had "treasured up all . . . which another generation has flung aside." Isn't this what the historical fictionalist does? To be sure, we have to distinguish between more and less critical and historically sensitive ways of treasuring up the past; but it is clear that Hancock, leader and representative of "a new race of men," would not be interested in the distinction. Hawthorne of course would be, and was. But no other great author of historical romance so frequently suggests that for him personally the past is less a magnificent resource than a frustrating burden and that the genre itself is inferior to the novel of contemporary manners. Had he felt otherwise, or rather felt otherwise more consistently, we might have less cause to speculate why our most brilliantly equipped nineteenth-century historical romancer did so little with the matter of the Revolution and did not do even more with the matter of the New England frontier.

6

Melville: The red comets return

1

Melville it was who found a truly new mold for historical romance, but he did not do so until his career as a fictionalist was nearly over. He began writing fiction during the '40s, the decade when Scott was suffering a sea change from live literary model to Victorian classic. Although the historical romance continued to be a popular literary genre with the reading public, it no longer presented the fresh challenge and opportunity it had to the preceding generation of American writers. This is not to suggest that young Melville owed nothing to Scott, much less that he was indifferent to the example of Scott's greatest American disciples.[1] The works of Cooper, wrote Melville in 1852, "are among the earliest I can remember, as in my boyhood producing a vivid and awakening power upon my mind . . . [Cooper] possessed not the slightest weaknesses but those which are only noticeable as the almost infallible indices of pervading greatness."[2] Thomas Philbrick's study of the thematic and imagistic relationships between *Moby Dick* and *The Sea Lions* shows that the "awakening power" of Cooper's example extended well beyond Melville's boyhood imagination.[3] However, it was not Cooper's greatest historical romances that mattered to him as the youthful author of *Redburn*, *White Jacket*, and *Moby Dick*, but rather Cooper's sea romances – fictions whose actions were set in the past but effectively left history behind just as soon as anchors were weighed and the characters freed to experience high physical, moral, and spiritual adventure on the immemorial, unremembering sea. As for Hawthorne's attractions as a model, the quality that Melville prized was his "power of blackness" rather than the strengths Hawthorne had as a great *historical* romancer.[4] Nor was literary fashion the only or, I suppose, the main

186

reason why young Melville simply ignored the *Waverley*-model and did not turn his hand to historical romance until his career as a fictionalist was nearly over.

Nor was literary fashion the only or, I suppose, the main reason why young Melville did not turn his hand to historical fiction until after the commercial failures of *Moby Dick* and *Pierre*. He had the extraordinary fortune actually to witness the immolation of primitive peoples by modern European civilization which Cooper and Hawthorne knew about only through the romances of Scott, family traditions, and historical records. In the South Seas he saw not merely the meridian of the American whaling industry but the commercial exploitation of the islanders and the introduction of prostitution and sexual shame. Out of this experience he wrote *Moby Dick* (1851) and two earlier books about the Polynesians and the destruction of their culture, *Typee* (1846) and *Omoo* (1847), and the allegorical voyage-romance *Mardi* (1849) which has a "South Seas" setting though little authentic connection with Polynesia. To the end of his days Melville remembered the lost world of Typee as an earthly Paradise, as these stanzas from "To Ned" (1888) reveal:

Where is the world we roved, Ned Bun?
Hollows thereof lay rich in shade
By voyagers old inviolate thrown
   Ere Paul Pry cruised with Pelf and Trade.
To us old lads some thoughts come home
Who roamed a world young lads no more shall roam.

But, tell, shall he, the tourist, find
   Our isles the same in violet-glow
Enamoring us what years and years –
   Ah, Ned, what years and years ago!
Well, Adam advances, smart in pace,
But scarce by violets that advance you trace.

But we, in anchor-watches calm,
   The Indian Psyche's languor won,
And, musing, breathed primeval balm
   From Edens ere yet overrun;
Marvelling mild if mortal twice,
Here and hereafter, touch a Paradise.[5]

The nostalgia of old age casts a golden haze over Melville's image of Typee. There is no hint of the dark side of nature – cannibalism in *Typee*, the shark devouring its own innards in *Moby Dick*, or the skeleton figurehead, image of savage revenge, in *Benito Cereno*. Nor is there anything in the rest of the poem to tincture the "violet-glow" of the

"Edens ere yet overrun." Melville characteristically apprehended reality in terms of bold polarities and rendered them dramatically, i.e., through one or more personae none of which (so far as we can tell) ever fully expresses its author's views. Thus for Melville the dark and the light side of nature (including human nature) were both "true" or at any rate true to experiences of nature so contradictory, though distinct and luminous, as usually to defy synthesis or summary judgment. The lyric persona of "To Ned" recalls not the whole nor yet a false paradise like Merry Mount, but a part, the paradisal aspect, of Polynesian reality.

For young Melville, then, paradise was part of contemporary reality albeit one which both observation and literary tradition taught him was fast withering at the touch of the European trader and missionary. So he wrote not about dead Indians or Quakers but about live Polynesians threatened with cultural blight. When he wrote about social evils in America, he wrote about contemporary ones: chattel slavery in chapter 162 of *Mardi*; New England wage slavery in "The Tartarus of Maids"; flogging aboard U.S. naval ships in *White Jacket*; and urban social alienation in "Bartleby the Scrivener." Indeed, although his social conscience was, his historical consciousness was not quite fully developed before his trip of 1856–7 to England, Greece, Constantinople, Egypt, Palestine, and Italy. It was not, that is, if our comparison is with Hawthorne's or Cooper's, or with what his own was to become from *Battle-Pieces* (1866) onwards. Still, by any ordinary standards the historical consciousness at work in *Israel Potter* (1854–5) and *Benito Cereno* (1855), his earliest historical fictions, is profound and searching.

There are, moreover, a few passages in the still-earlier *Mardi* on the past and future of the United States which today seem as penetrating as disturbing. Among the precepts uttered with laconic authority by a "Voice from the Gods" in chapter 161 is that "the Past is an apostle."[6] Nations, the voice tells us, are like human beings, generous and idealistic in their early manhood; but eventually the "bold boy is transformed . . . He yields not a groat; and seeking no more acquisitions, is only bent on preserving his hoard. The maxims once trampled under foot, are now printed on his front; and he who hated oppressors, is now become an oppressor himself." The mysterious voice traces the evolution of "Romara" from monarchy to republic to empire. "In nations . . . there is a transmigration of souls; in you [Americans], is a marvelous destiny. The eagle of Romara revives in your own mountain bird, and once more is plumed for her flight" (p. 527). Is the voice Melville's? Its source is never identified, and I believe it is best to regard it as expressing a viewpoint, pessimistic and conservative in its political values and cyclic theory of history, with which Melville could sympathize but not altogether identify. *Mardi*, we should recall, was written during the portentous and troubled years 1847–8 – when for humane Americans like Melville guilt and anger over the rape of Mexico were followed by renewed anxiety over the westward expansion of the slave power, and yet when it was not possible simply to rejoice over the daily news of bloody revolutions in Europe or the prospect of fratricidal war at home. "Long absent, at last the red comets have returned. And return they must, though their periods be ages" (p. 529). The figure of the ominous comet was itself to return in Melville's writings as the century wore on.

2

Why did he turn in 1854–5 not just to historical fiction but to a variety of it which, as it committed him to retelling the factual narratives of unreflective men of action, imposed a much tighter rein on the Romantic Imagination than he had submitted to in *Moby Dick* or *Pierre*? One obvious explanation is that he sought this discipline because he half-accepted the charges of excessive subjectivity and self-indulgent meta-physicality to which he had been opened by bookish protagonists like Ishmael, Ahab, and Pierre. To present the world through the eyes or over the shoulder of simple souls like Private Israel Potter and Captain Amasa Delano, and yet to present it without a sacrifice of moral and historical vision, was both a technical challenge and a wholesome corrective. But it was also a strategy for dealing with a reading public on whose patronage Melville depended but whose intellectual capacities had turned out to be as limited as those of his new historical-fictional heroes. In Delano, if not in poor hapless Israel, Melville holds up the mirror to his fatuous American readers and in Delano's story appears to bow to their superior wisdom by showing how a Yankee sea captain was made safe and wealthy by the combined forces of Providence and his own generous good nature – how, too, Spaniards were moody and decadent and blacks were by turns doggedly faithful and impulsively savage, improvidently carefree and smolderingly vengeful. At the same time in the same story, but invisible to the eyes of Delano-like readers, Melville poses a cautionary fable of the course of American empire which flatters none of the leading parties of the day.

The meaning or "tendency" of *Benito Cereno* has been much debated by twentieth-century literary and social critics, and it must be allowed that the drift of every detail in the story isn't invariably clear. But the novella as a whole exhibits so much verifiable evidence of the *author's* powers as a reader (i.e., of his "source," the historical Delano's memoir), and likewise of a thoroughly executed formal design, that I do not see how there can be much informed doubt about Melville's basic intentions in *Benito Cereno*. A more puzzling case, although at first sight a more open book, is his Revolutionary War romance *Israel Potter; His Fifty Years of Exile*.

The concluding chapters of *Israel Potter* open up bleak and empty prospects which are no more flattering to national or party vanity than those we view in *Benito Cereno*. For Melville it was too late in the day, his own and the nation's, to recapitulate the conventional oppositions of reactionary aristocratic Tories and progressive republican Patriots which had been employed with varying degrees of political and literary sophistication by his predecessors, including Hawthorne in "Legends of the Province-House." Neither did the true life story of Israel Potter lend itself finally to fireworks and nationalistic preening, since it was the actual fate of this obscure veteran of the Battle of Bunker Hill to be captured by the British, then to skid from a life of military adventure to a harder battle for survival among London's poor, and at last in extreme old age to return to New England and be received more like an unwelcome immigrant than a war hero or prodigal son.

Yet it is clear that Melville did not feel obliged to stick very closely to the record given in the *Life and Remarkable Adventures of Israel Potter*. It would have been consistent with his practice elsewhere in the novel to aim at "general fidelity to the main drift of the original narrative," but to invent, omit, or telescope whatever the fictional occasion required – or whatever his audience required.[7] To mollify his readers, he could have softened and sentimentalized Israel's exit: perhaps even provided the old soldier with a final moment as spirited and upbeat as that which Cooper devised for Natty Bumppo in *The Prairie*. Something of the sort was probably Melville's intention when he began publishing *Israel Potter* as "A Fourth of July Story" (for so it was subtitled) in *Putnam's Monthly Magazine*. In magazines like *Putnam's* and the *Democratic Review*, where "Legends of the Province-House" first appeared, there was a ready if not especially lucrative market for fiction which exploited the matter of the Revolution, and scores of what might be classified as "Fourth of July Stories" were published in them during the first half of the century. In its first installment *Israel Potter* does seem to belong to this genre. In fact, Melville assured the editor of *Putnam's* that there would be nothing in the romance "to shock the fastidious. There will be very little reflective writing in it; nothing weighty. It is adventure."[8] He very likely meant to honor this promise.

Despite frequent tongue-in-cheek satiric protrusions, Melville's account of his Yankee hero's early career as a frontiersman and soldier is as genial as it is eventful, and his portrait of Israel as the quintessential Minute Man, humble but intrepid in defense of the *patria*, I take to be essentially respectful and affectionate. What is more, Melville opens Israel's life story with an incident which is patently meant to be construed as a patriotic allegory. Prevented by his father from marrying the girl of his own choice, Israel heads west and gains both manly independence and a modest fortune; he returns home only to be thwarted a second time by "the tyranny of his father" (p. 8) and leaves home for good, ready at a minute's notice to take up arms against the tyrant George III.[9] In this little private tale of filial forbearance and reluctant rebellion may be read the great public legend of the Puritan exodus to New England and of the growth of the American Independence movement. Melville then proceeds to serve up a generous ration of the war heroes and founding fathers, the battle scenes and good old-fashioned disguise-flight-pursuit adventures which Cooper and other writers of Revolutionary War romances had led readers to expect. He introduces Israel to Benjamin Franklin and Ethan Allen and makes him a sea-going squire to John Paul Jones. His rendering of the famous contest between the *Serapis* and the *Bon Homme Richard* is an astonishing concrescence of elegant mock-heroic and Cooperesque nautical derring-do. Indeed, the entire sequence involving Jones must have been meant to recall Cooper's *The Pilot* (1824), the first and best known of Revolutionary War romances which have a maritime setting.

Unfortunately for any hopes which Melville had of emulating Cooper's and his own early popular success by recombining the customary ingredients of "A Fourth of July Story," the matter of the Revolution had a way of turning refractory in the hands of serious and gifted writers. In "Legends of the Province-House," as we have seen, Hawthorne's contradictory feelings about the Revolution surface confusingly and perhaps disruptively when John Hancock arrives to usher in the new democratic era. In the closing chapters of *Lionel Lincoln* (1825), Cooper's contradictory feelings render a potentially great Revolutionary War romance incoherent and nugatory when one of the leading Patriots, a sage old advocate of Liberty who seems to anticipate the Gray Champion, turns out to be a madman escaped from an asylum. In *Israel Potter* the problems occasioned by Melville's contradictory feelings emerge earlier and more gradually, but the damage they do to the unity of the work is nearly as serious. Contrary to his promises to George Putnam, from chapter 7 through 21 his romance of pure "adventure" becomes increasingly "reflective" and "weighty" as his attention turns from Potter and the actual events of Potter's life to larger subjects: American national destiny and American national character. What Melville had unexpectedly to get off his chest on these subjects was unlikely to commend his serial to the "fastidious" readers of *Putnam's*. Moreover, as the action sequences grew ever more frenzied and improbable, some of these readers must have scented parody and, not unjustifiably, resented being defrauded of the type of pleasure which the author had engaged to supply.

Their loss is our gain. Although seriously botched by his changes of mind and mode, *Israel Potter* is unquestionably a far richer and more interesting book because Melville was unable to stick to his original commitment. Yet the book is redeemed and raised briefly to the level of Melville's greatest art not so much by the satiric middle chapters, where he loses interest in Potter's story, as by the concluding chapters (22–7) which focus on Israel's grim experiences in London and eventual return to America. These chapters, which together form the final magazine installment, may be considered apart from the rest of the novel as an astonishing fragment which develops and inverts many of the main themes and situations of the American historical romance.

Although Melville's London is oppressively, overwhelmingly material, it is not merely a place but also, as these chapter headings suggest, a mythic projection of the literary imagination: "Israel's Flight towards the Wilderness," "Israel in Egypt," "In the City of Dis." At once Dantesque Hell, Wilderness, and City of Bondage, London is the infernal antitype of paradisal Typee:

> Whichever way the eye turned, no tree, no speck of any green thing was seen – no more than in smithies. All laborers, of whatsoever sort, were hued like the men in foundries. The black vistas of streets were as the galleries in coal mines; the flagging, as flat tomb-stones, minus the consecration of moss, and worn heavily down, by sorrowful tramping, as the vitreous rocks in the cursed Gallipagos, over which the convict tortoises crawl.
>
> As in eclipses, the sun was hidden; the air darkened; the whole dull, dismayed aspect of things, as if some neighboring volcano, belching its premonitory smoke, were about to whelm the great town, as Herculaneum and Pompeii, or the Cities of the Plain. And as they had been upturned in terror towards the mountain, all faces were more or less snowed or spotted with soot. Nor marble, nor flesh, nor the sad spirit of man, may in this cindry City of Dis abide white. (p. 227)

This vision of London was not fueled by contemporary accounts, Potter's or others', of the late-eighteenth-century city which the historical Israel Potter entered towards the end of the American War of Independence. It was prompted by the early Victorian city which Melville himself visited in 1849 and by this passage from Benjamin Haydon's *Life*:

> So far from the smoke of London being offensive to me, it has always been to my imagination the sublime canopy that shrouds the City of the World. Drifted by the wind or hanging in gloomy grandeur over the vastness of our Babylon, the sight of it always filled my mind with feelings of energy such as no other spectacle could inspire.
>
> "Be Gode," said Fuseli to me one day, "it's like de smoke of de Israelites making bricks." "It is grander," said I, "for it is the smoke of a people who would have made the Egyptians make bricks for them." "Well done, John Bull," replied Fuseli.[10]

The mythic parallels with which Industrial Revolution London filled the minds of Fuseli, Haydon, and Melville excluded an over-fastidious concern to get every historical detail right. They inspired instead a grand cyclic vision of London as the successor, arrogant but doomed, to the Cities of the Plain, Babylon, Egypt, and the pleasure resorts of imperial Rome.

We may conjecture that Haydon's words would not have been so suggestive, leading Melville even to invent an episode in which Israel becomes a brickmaker (chs. 23–4), had the hero of the story been named Billy, say, or Pierre. Further, that this story of captivity and exile might have been much less appealing to Melville in the first place had its author–protagonist not had the extraordinarily suggestive Yankee name of Israel Potter. For given the outline of its bearer's career, the name invites not only the mythopoeic elaborations already noticed but also some grim reflections on the course of "Anglo-Saxon" empire. Israel's name reminds us that he is a descendant of those heroic English Puritans who, taking the ancient Israelites as their model, set forth to found a new Canaan in the western wilderness. Perhaps but for his capture by the British, this Israel too might have joined in the great migration; for when at the end of his life he at last returns to his native New England in search of relatives and familiar scenes, he finds only change, emptiness, and the ambiguous explanation, "gone West." But if the movement into the wilderness is still in progress, Melville's descriptions of Franklin, Allen, and Potter himself suggest that the Puritan character has altered drastically since the seventeenth-century plantations and that the meaning of the migration has likewise.

Melville's Franklin, although much too polished and cosmopolitan to be confused with such rural Yankees as Ichabod Crane and Jason Newcome, is also a man on the make whose interests appear to be entirely worldly. Indeed, so far has the Puritan character degenerated in this version of Franklin that Melville draws a startling analogy between Poor Richard and the materialist philosopher Hobbes (arch-enemy of the seventeenth-century Puritans), describing them both as "labyrinth-minded, but plain-spoken Broadbrims, at once politicians and philosophers; keen observers of the main chance; prudent courtiers; practical Magians in linsey-woolsey" (p. 64). His portrait of Ethan Allen is much more positive, but it nonetheless implies the disappearance of the original New England character: "Though born in New England, he exhibited no trace of her character. He was frank, bluff, companionable as a Pagan, convivial, a Roman, hearty as a harvest. His spirit was essentially Western; and herein is his peculiar Americanism; for the Western spirit is, or will yet be (for no other is, or can be), the true American one" (p. 212). Although the tone of this description appears wholly affirmative, the coupling of "Western" and "Roman" should give us pause.

For in this context "Western" must mean not only the rapidly expanding American West, the arena once of Andrew Jackson and more recently of Sam Houston and "Pathfinder" John Charles Frémont, but also ancient Rome, capital of the Empire of the West and matrix of Roman expansionism. In other words, Melville is alluding to the historical parallel drawn by the "Voice from the Gods" in *Mardi*. That he should return to the idea that "The eagle of Romara revives in your own mountain bird" in *Israel Potter* and again in *Benito Cereno* (through a reference to the Holy Roman Emperor Charles V of Spain) is not at all surprising. Both of these historical romances are concerned with the fate of great empires; and, as already noticed in chapters 2 and 3, Rome has always been the empire of empires for the "Western" imagination. Positively, it has been the supreme image of enduring order, peace, and "civilization" – hence the inevitable model (or at any rate the source of imperial trappings) for the states ruled by order-restoring Caesar-figures (Czars, Kaisers) from Charlemagne through the seventeenth- and eighteenth-century English "Augustan" kings (*both* Stuart and Hanoverian),[11] through Napoleon, down to Mussolini and Hitler in recent times. Negatively, it has served moralists from Tacitus onwards as a principal example of the over-extended, over-centralized state which, despite its investment in both brick and marble, was doomed to disintegration by the remoteness, vice, and duplicity of its rulers. Like Thomas Cole in *The Course of Empire* or Joseph Conrad in the London sections of *Heart of Darkness*, Melville is of a mind with Tacitus.

Yet it is important to recognize that the chief historical parallels drawn in *Israel Potter* are not between Rome and the United States but between Britain and the United States. In emphasizing the unflattering likenesses rather than the flattering differences between the child and parent country, Melville reverses the normal procedure of a Revolutionary War romance. Speculating on the meaning of the engagement between the *Serapis* and the *Bon Homme Richard* – usually construed as a democratic victory over British pride and power – he upsets expectations by suggesting that the true American spirit is at least as graspingly imperialistic as the British:

> It may involve at once a type, a parallel, and a prophecy. Sharing the same blood with England, and yet her proved foe in two wars – not wholly inclined at bottom to forget an old grudge – intrepid, unprincipled, reckless, predatory, with boundless ambition, civilized in externals but a savage at heart, America is, or may yet be, the Paul Jones of nations. (p. 170)

It is inconceivable that Melville did not have this passage in mind when he wrote the later one defining the American spirit as "Western." Here, however, his emphasis is on the blood traits shared with Britain – Jones was a Scot by birth, an American only (and temporarily) by adoption – and the character that emerges is that of a pirate or slavemaster. On this showing, the Americans are the true-blue swaggering rivals and descendants of, in Haydon's words, "a people who would have made the Egyptians make bricks for them."

Where does this leave the "American" Israel Potter? He is a rural Yankee like Cranse or Newcome but without their education and ambition to get ahead by cunning. Industrious and intrepid, yet patient, mild, and guileless, Israel at first appears destined for great things as a frontiersman or soldier in the mold of Boone or Israel Putnam. But his long career turns out to be a series of dispiriting mishaps and failures. Instead of leading the way west, he flees east to the "wilderness" of London: "Nor did ever the German forest, nor Tasso's enchanted one, contain in its depth more things of horror than eventually were revealed in the secret clefts, gulfs, caves and dens of London" (p. 218). With the end of the War of Independence, Israel's need to hide in the urban wilderness also ends, but by this time he has become, like Bartleby in New York, a spiritual prisoner of his environment and incapable of self-liberation. By this time, too, he feels allegiance much less to his fellow Americans than to his fellow wretches of London, many of them discarded British veterans of the American War, who scavenge the great city's streets and sewers or tend her dark Satanic mills. When Israel's longings for home are at last awakened, the cause is not any residual nationalism but a stray glimpse of nature trapped like himself. In St. James's Park is

> a little oval, fenced in with iron pailings, between whose bars the imprisoned verdure peered forth, as some wild captive creature of the woods from its cage. And alien Israel there – at times staring dreamily about him – seemed like some amazed runaway steer, or trespassing Pequod Indian, impounded on the shores of Narraganset Bay, long ago; and back to New England our exile was called in his soul. (p. 233)

The analogies with the steer and particularly the impounded "trespassing" Pequod Indian are telling in more ways than one. In the first place, of course, Israel, the steer, and the Indian are alike as imprisoned wild American creatures. But the poignancy of the analogy is deepened and made ironic when we reflect further that, maimed as well in will as in body, Israel is a descendant of those acquisitive British Puritans who exploited the native Americans quite as ruthlessly as ever the modern British upper and middle classes do the urban proletariat. Perhaps Israel's hard fate in London is to be read as "at once a type, a parallel, and a prophecy" for other Americans – the ones, that is, who are not strong and predatory like John Paul Jones, Ethan Allen, or the old Puritan governors who concluded the Pequod War by selling large numbers of the tribe into slavery in the West Indies. For we know from contemporary works like "Bartleby" and "The Tartarus of Maids" ("Tartarus," the abyss *below* Hades, i.e., the Lowell mills) that Melville saw New York City and industrial New England heading in the same direction as industrial old England.[12] For the present, because of her vast extent and advanced stage of industrialization, London was unique; but the evil was not peculiar to her and was in fact but a late phase of the same imperialistic activity that elsewhere in the world – in the South Seas, for instance, or the American South and West – was caging and emasculating all humankind.

In a mock-obsequious dedication "To His Highness The Bunker Hill Monument," Melville draws a wry contrast between the summer sun shining warmly on the brow of the monument and the winter snow resting on Israel's grave. This image anticipates the chilly reception Israel experiences when he returns to America. Disembarking on the anniversary of the Battle of Bunker Hill,

> the old man narrowly escaped being run over by a patriotic triumphal car in the procession, flying a broidered banner, inscribed with gilt letters:

"BUNKER-HILL

1775

Glory to the Heroes that Fought!"   (p. 238)

Although one of "the Heroes that Fought," Israel is eventually "repulsed in efforts after a pension"; his scars prove to be "his only medals" (p. 241). And according to the dedication (p. vi) he is but one of "the anonymous privates of June 17, 1775, who may never have received other requital than the solid reward" of the granite monument. The gap thus exposed between American public show and private performance, platform glorification of heroes and behind-the-scenes indifference to their sufferings suggests that, as foretold in *Mardi*, the young nation's revolutionary idealism is being rapidly transformed into granite conservatism. The austere young republic is fast becoming the imperial democracy. Indeed, the monument, the triumphal car, and the rhetoric of "Glory to the Heroes that Fought" all have a distinctly Augustan stamp.

Still more Augustan is another monumental column which appears later in Israel's story. "Augustan" is a word we associate not only with the period of Octavius Caesar's rule in ancient Rome but also with the literary age of Dryden, Rochester, Swift, Gay, Pope, Fielding, and young Samuel Johnson. The English Augustan Age, we should recall, was a time both of great demolitionary satire and, especially after the Fire of London in 1666, great works of public and private building – works which sometimes, for political and/or aesthetic reasons, became conspicuous targets for satirists. One that drew Pope's wrath, because of an inscription on it accusing the Roman Catholics of being the incendiaries, was the triumphal column built to commemorate the Fire.[13] The same monument appears in *Israel Potter* in a passage which recalls both the imagery of Melville's dedication to the Bunker Hill monument and the mock-heroic biblical parallels of Dryden's *Absalom and Achitophel*:[14]

> In that London fog, went before him the ever-present cloud by day, but no pillar of fire by the night, except the cold column of the monument, two hundred feet beneath the mocking gilt flames on whose top, at the stone base, the shiverer, of midnight, often laid him down.   (p. 229)

This scene is ironic not only in that the gilt flames atop the monument mock the shiverer rather than warm him but also, more generally, in that the commemorative emblem of London's phoenix-like triumph of rebuilding after the Fire now seems a mockery of the houseless condition of London's poor. Ironic too is the implied contrast between Israel's abandoned existence in the wilderness of London and the heroic mission of God's chosen people. This irony we may define as "mock-heroic" – provided we recognize that the mock-heroic mode in *Israel Potter* never ridicules or belittles Israel himself but, on the contrary, insists on his amazing power to endure amidst the most dispiriting and degrading circumstances and confers a gloomy infernal grandeur even on them. The mock-heroic mode was available to Melville, as it was earlier to the great British Tory satirists, precisely because he was capable of being stirred by heroic ideals and believing that they were sometimes actually embodied in flesh and blood. Notwithstanding the hard things he has to say about Franklin, Jones, and Allen, they and the Revolutionary era still have a titanic quality that is not diminished but rather enlarged by Melville's epic parallels and by his contrasts with post-revolutionary Britain and America. Thus despite its uncertainty of tone and direction, likewise despite its moments of mockery and parody, *Israel Potter* definitely belongs to the historical romance tradition. And lest we suppose that it is too satirical, too disrespectful, for a historical romance, we should recall how severe Scott is in his judgments on Charles Edward Stuart and other "great" historical figures – and also how often the action in Scott's historical romances verges on the (quixotic) mock-heroic.

3

In his next experiment with historical fiction, Melville again turned for his basic "story" to a humble personal chronicle, Captain Amasa Delano's *A Narrative of Voyages and Travels in the Southern Hemisphere* (1817). This time, however, Melville based his fiction on a single complex incident which lent itself, as Israel Potter's life story did not, to compact and unified presentation. Concerned as it was with both Yankee enterprise abroad and a slave insurrection staged in a remote South American coastal setting in the year 1799,[15] the incident belonged to the era of the French Revolution (and of the associated black slave rebellion on Santo Domingo) and was wonderfully rich in the two principal matters of historical romance: imperialistic confrontation between "savagery" and "civilization," and revolutionary confrontation between feudalism and modern bourgeois society. It is therefore not surprising, although it may be quite coincidental, that in *Benito Cereno* Melville used the same trope of an empty sword scabbard to figure the enfeebled decadence of the Spanish American slaveholding class which Scott had used in the *Life of Napoleon Buonaparte* to represent the weakness of the pre-revolutionary French nobility. Doubtless Scott would have been surprised to discover a historical romance in which the forces of reaction and progress were so outlandishly represented; in which there was no conventional love story; and in which so much was said in such a brief compass. But I am sure he would have recognized that *Benito Cereno* belonged to the legitimate progeny of *Waverley* and also that it was Melville, not Hawthorne, who in this great novella at last succeeded in forging a new mold for the historical romance. Some readers, from his earliest editors down to his most distinguished recent biographer, have thought that he botched the conclusion by "putting . . . dreary documents at the end" rather than transforming them into a "connected tale,"[16] but we shall see that this criticism is founded on a misunderstanding of Melville's design.

What Melville found in chapter 18 of Delano's *Narrative* was the straightforward account of an extraordinary deception practiced by a band of insurgent black slaves, first on their trusting owner and Captain Cereno, and thereafter on Delano himself when, unaware of the mutiny, he boarded Cereno's ship, the *Tryal*, off the Pacific coast of South America one foggy February morning in 1805. In all likelihood Delano would have been murdered, as the slaves' owner had been, if Cereno had not collaborated with them by pretending still to be in command of his ship and if Delano had not been predisposed to place a very benevolent construction on numerous telltale violations of shipboard discipline:

> as I was deceived in them, I did them every possible kindness. Had it been otherwise there is no doubt I should have fallen a victim to their power. It was to my great advantage, that, on this occasion, the temperament of my mind was unusually pleasant. The apparent sufferings of those about me had softened my feelings into sympathy; or, doubtless my interference with some of their transactions would have cost me my life.[17]

Delano goes on to describe how Cereno unmasked the mutiny by jumping overboard as soon as Delano disembarked from the *Tyral*, how the ship and slaves were recaptured, and finally how the ring-leaders were tried and executed and the ungrateful Cereno avoided paying his Yankee rescuers the salvage money he had promised. So far as Delano was concerned, the sour moral pointed by this tale was:

> When I take a retrospective view of my life, I cannot find in my soul, that I ever have done any thing to deserve such misery and ingratitude as I have suffered at different periods, and in general, from the very persons to whom I have rendered the greatest services.   (p. 86)

Never mind that "the greatest services" in this case were rendered with the expectation of a cool $50,000 profit (p. 83) or that earlier, when his behavior *was* actuated by charitable rather than mercenary motives, he was rewarded with his life!

It is easy to see why Delano's story of duplicity and reversed roles aboard the *Tyral* should have appealed immediately to the author who was shortly to write *The Confidence Man* (1857), and many of the changes and additions that Melville introduced in his version of the *Tyral* incident do seem to anticipate the cosmic scepticism of that novel. Among the more obvious and insistent ones are the ironic references to "confidence" and "fidelity" and the change of the name of Delano's ship from *Perseverance* to *The Bachelor's Delight*. These reinforce the irony, shrewdly noticed by the historical Delano himself, that he was saved by his own good-natured impercipience, and the same can be said of the only major alteration that Melville made to the main outline of Delano's story. For Melville wholly revised the character and fate of the Spanish captain Cereno, making him an honorable though broken man, and thus saved the fictional Delano from the unkind awakening which the historical Delano had suffered. So far from turning out to be an ungrateful scoundrel, Melville's Cereno heaps praises on the "generous" and "noble" American captain and attributes Delano's survival while visiting the Spanish ship to "the Prince of heaven's safe-conduct through all ambuscades" (p. 73). Whether the dying Spaniard also recompenses his rescuer with the ducats denied him in real life, Melville never reveals.

But to read *Benito Cereno* as a mere sketch for *The Confidence Man* is to diminish its actual significance and stature. A closer look at Melville's alterations and additions to the *Narrative* account of the *Tyral* incident reveals that, besides augmenting Delano's Panglossian faith, they give the story an important extra dimension as a cautionary fable of imperial decline. The revised character and fate of Cereno are at the heart of this fable. Melville's Cereno is a proud, pious man, "courteous even to the point of religion" (p. 73), who at the end of the novella retires from the evil of the world to die in a monastery. He is much less of a realistic slave-ship captain, and much more of an ideal melancholy hidalgo, than the Cereno of the *Narrative*. And this major change in turn affects the way we perceive the other characters. Delano inevitably seems much more Protestant, sense-bound, and cheerfully ingenuous; the blacks more heathen, cunning, and savage. In other words, the *Tyral* incident is transformed into a world-historical encounter between "Anglo-Saxon" types, "primitive" black slaves, and "decadent" Spaniards; and both historical romance tradition and Melville's understanding of imperial history dictated that the survivor and winner of such an encounter should be the Yankee. As Hawthorne does in "The Gray Champion" and "The May-Pole of Merry Mount," so in *Benito Cereno* does Melville exchange factuality for the representative truth of a symbolic action, reshaping historical anecdote into predictive synecdoche.

Melville enlivens his typology with a host of allusions and suggestive details not present in his source. Of these the most striking, certainly the most "gothic," is the figurehead made of the slavemaster Aranda's skeleton ("prepared . . . in a way the negroes afterwards told the deponent, but which he, so long as reason is left him, can never divulge" p. 70). But the most important, without doubt, are those with which Melville makes Cereno and his ship incarnate the late Spanish American Empire – and all empires in their decadence.

Just as Melville's Cereno is no ordinary slave-ship captain, so the ship itself is like none that ever sailed from Valparaiso in the early nineteenth century. The ship's "general model and rig," we are told, "appeared to have undergone no material change from their original warlike and Froissart pattern" (p. 3). (Froissart, Edward Waverley's favorite reading, also of course provided the pattern of chivalric sentiment and behavior for the feudal aristocracy of Europe – a sadly decayed, indeed grotesquely anachronistic, representative of which is Cereno himself.) This drifting relic of late-medieval grandeur Melville ironically rechristens *San Dominick*, alluding both to the founder of the militant order of inquisitors, suppressors of heresy and rebellion, and to the site of the first successful major slave insurrection in the New World. This link between monasticism and slavery is maintained in the description of the *San Dominick* as at first appearing "like a white-washed monastery": "Peering over the bulwarks were what really seemed, in the hazy distance, throngs of dark cowls; while, fitfully revealed through the open port-holes, other dark moving figures were dimly descried, as of Black Friars pacing the cloisters" (p. 3). At first glance the yoking together of black slaves and Dominican Black Friars seems merely fanciful, but we have to bear in mind that, although the conjunction of the two institutions may have been unusual, it was a commonplace of Melville's era that slavery and monasticism both debilitated any body politic that tolerated them; that they both undermined the character and will of secular authority. This is the burden of, for instance, Cooper's Jeffersonian critique of American slavery in *The American Democrat* (1838), and there can be no doubt that Melville wrote about the anachronistic aristocrat Cereno and the slaves' mutiny aboard the *San Dominick* with American parallels very much in mind. This is the burden likewise of William Stirling's popular *The Cloister Life of the Emperor Charles the Fifth* (1852) which H. Bruce Franklin has identified as "a source in many ways more important" than Delano's *Narrative*.[18] Whether or not he is right about Stirling's influence, Franklin is certainly right to stress the crucial importance of Melville's allusions to monasticism, the Santo Domingo rebellion, and Charles V, Spanish King and Holy Roman Emperor who, abandoning much of his power to the Church and eventually retiring to a monastery, permitted the Spanish Empire to fall into decrepitude.

Yet it may be unwise to look for very close or extended parallels between what happens aboard the *San Dominick* and specific events in nineteenth-century Virginia or sixteenth-century Spain. The parallels exist, to be sure, but to focus principally on them is to fail to take the long perspective on human history which other references in the story suggest we should take. The most "universal" of these is Melville's description of a "shield-like stern-piece, intricately carved with the arms of Castile and Leon, medallioned about by groups of mythological or symbolical devices; uppermost and central of which was a dark satyr in a mask, holding his foot on the prostrate neck of a writhing figure, likewise masked" (p. 4). By calling the masterful satyr "dark" rather than "black" Melville creates a crucial ambiguity; for "dusky," "saturnine," and "dark" are words associated with Cereno – and with Spaniards generally in nineteenth-century Anglo-American fiction; and so the identities of the master and slave in the mythological device are by no means certain. This uncertainty as to who is playing which role has an obvious relevance to the shipboard drama staged for Delano, but it may also lead us to reflect that the master classes have not always been light complexioned. The slave leader Babo remarks that in Africa, before becoming a white man's, he was a black man's slave. Before being united under the arms of Castile and Leon, Spain herself was a province of the Moorish Empire. Outside historic place and time, a "dark" masked figure, half beast and half human, gains ascendance over another masked figure of undisclosed color, maybe white but also maybe black, in what seems an emblem of the eternal, revolving struggle for dominance or freedom in human relations – irrespective of race.

However, the struggle for dominance or freedom aboard the *San*

Dominick occurs at a particular place and time, and the actors are not mythological projections but characters who are presented as very much the products of their respective peoples' histories. The action occurs in the wake of the French and American revolutions and just before the wars of national liberation that swept the Spanish viceroys forever from Latin America. The overall shape and scope of the historical action, of which the action in *Benito Cereno* is a tiny and fictive but immensely significant part, can be inferred from the analogies Melville draws between Cereno's ship and "superannuated Italian palaces . . . under a decline of masters" (p. 3) and "tenantless balconies hung over the sea as if it were the grand Venetian canal" (p. 4). The decline of the Venetian Empire coincides with the rise of Spain, the decline of the Spanish Empire with the rise of Britain, and so on. As in *Mardi*, Melville still subscribes to a cyclic theory of history involving a "transmigration of souls" from one great nation to another. The progression hinted at here is less flattering, more ominous, for the young country of which Captain Delano is the representative than when the spiritual ancestor was Rome.

It must be admitted that interpretations of *Benito Cereno* based principally on the allusions implanted in Melville's over-Delano's-shoulder descriptions of Cereno and the *San Dominick* are not easily validated and often seem to assume a great deal not only about Melville's reading (astonishingly wide though this was) but also about his method of meaning. A careful reading of the ship's hieroglyphical stern-piece and shrouded figurehead is, I believe, necessary but far from sufficient. More than once Melville suggests that there is no "key," no single act or speech or cluster of symbols, that all at once reveals the meaning of his novella. After reproducing the (carefully edited) deposition in which Cereno gave his version of his ship's disastrous voyage, the narrator remarks, subjunctively, "If the Deposition have served as the key to fit into the lock of the complications which precede it, then, as a vault whose door has been flung back, the San Dominick's hull lies open today" (p. 73). Melville leaves the reader to form his own conclusion as to whether *Benito Cereno* is a tale of mystery which, like one of Mrs. Radcliffe's romances, can be simply "unlocked" by one of the characters disclosing information not previously available. But supplied with so much evidence of both Delano and Cereno's inadequacy as witnesses and judges, the alert reader is likely to reach a more sceptical conclusion and also to recall the earlier scene in which an aged Spanish sailor presents Delano with a rope intricately knotted:

> "What are you knotting there, my man?"
> "The knot," was the brief reply, without looking up.
> "So it seems; but what is it for?"
> "For someone else to undo," muttered back the old man.

Pragmatic Delano, needless to say, does not "undo" the knot, nor does the hermeneutical old black who retrieves the knot and, "turning his back, ferreted into it like a detective custom-house officer after smuggled laces" (p. 33). Yet the one is right to ask, "what is it for?" and the other to search for a message. The principal beauty and meaning of the knot, regarded as a work of art rather than a mere device for fastening or encipherment, resides in the way the several strands are tied. The surest guide to the intended meaning of *Benito Cereno* is to be found in its narrative structure.

The first two-thirds of *Benito Cereno* present, over the shoulders and through the eyes of Captain Delano, the events of a single momentous day in the lives of the three principal characters and a host of subordinate characters. During this part of the narrative, neither Delano nor the reader really penetrates behind the masks prepared for Delano by Cereno and, with brilliant improvisational skill, by the black leader Babo. It is wholly appropriate that this, the part of the tale presented through scene rather than summary, should be given from the point of view of Delano, who is very much a creature of the senses and the immediate moment. Even at the end, after learning of the savagery aboard the *San Dominick*, he is able to say, "But the past is passed; why moralize upon it? Forget it. See, yon bright sun has forgotten it all, and the blue sea, and the blue sky; these have turned over new leaves" (p. 74). Although he has none of her excuses or inside knowledge of suffering, Delano sounds like Hester Prynne when she cries to the shattered Dimmesdale, "Let us not look back . . . The past is gone!"

But the no-less-shattered Cereno is wiser, or at least more his own man, than Dimmesdale, and his reply to Delano's admonition to forget is to observe that the sun, sea, and sky "have no memory . . . they are not human." Most of the remaining third of the narrative is given from Cereno's point of view in the form of a historical summary of the events which took place during more than two months. As for understanding what has happened, Cereno is not much better off than Delano, who is unable to learn from experience because his facile optimism is founded on the easy certainties of the white captain of a New England ship. These certainties are so strong and high, like walls against unpleasant truths, that he, and the civilization he represents, appear to be indestructible – for the time being. Cereno's will to live is destroyed because the different certainties of his world as a Spanish gentleman have been pulled down and caricatured with ferocious irony. Unable either to forget or to confront his traumatic memories, he is unwilling, even as a legal witness, to describe some of the things that befell him or look at Babo long enough to identify him as ringleader of the mutiny. This brings me to the third, but missing, narrative: that of Babo, who, after being captured, could not be forced to utter another word.

Beyond question, Babo is in important ways a diabolical figure – dark in spirit as in body, a nineteenth-century critic might have said. His vengefulness and also his cunning as a deceiver remind us, however, of such devilish white folk as Chillingworth, or Iago – the inscrutable confidence trickster who also refused to say a word after he was caught. Is Melville here, contrary to everything he wrote before and after this tale, associating himself with the racialist implications of Cereno's answer to Delano?

> "You are saved," cried Captain Delano, more and more astonished and pained; "you are saved: what has cast such a shadow upon you?"
> "The negro."   (p. 74)

Assuredly, like Kurtz in Conrad's *Heart of Darkness*, Cereno has had a glimpse, if not of pure evil, then at least of an atavism so sinister, intelligent and profound, as to shatter forever his sense of what it is to be human. But there is more to be said of Babo, who, like Ahab and many other satanic figures in nineteenth-century fiction, has as great a potential for good as for evil. In the end he is defeated partly by chance though chiefly by the ignorance inseparable from his condition as a slave. But his ambition to return his people to Senegal is worthy of a Moses, while the words he has chalked on the bow of the *San Dominick* – "Follow your leader" – echo some of Christ's last words after the Resurrection (according to John). Depending on whom "leader" refers to at different moments in the narrative – the slave master Aranda, Babo, the mate who leads the boarding party, or Christ himself – these words are used with different, ironic shades of meaning. In Babo's case, the leader is both a practical revolutionary and a kind of black messiah. At the end of the novella, though it is Cereno who dies on Mount Agonia, it is Babo, with "his slight frame, inadequate to that which it held," who is publicly executed and exhibited like Christ:

> Some months after, dragged to the gibbet at the tail of a mule, the black met his voiceless end. The body was burned to ashes; but for many days, the head, that hive of subtlety, fixed on a pole in the Plaza, met, unabashed, the gaze of the whites; and across the Plaza looked towards St. Bartholomew's church, in whose vaults slept then, as now, the recovered bones of Aranda: and across the Rimac bridge looked towards the monastery, on Mount Agonia without; where, three months after being dismissed by the court, Benito Cereno, borne on the bier, did, indeed, follow his leader.   (p. 75)

We have followed the action of the story through Delano's eyes and then through Cereno's but never through those of the man who made it all happen: no revelatory soliloquies, like those of Iago or Milton's Satan or Ahab, for the little black rebel. Only when he is dead are we permitted to see things from his perspective. As Delano's is of the present and Cereno's of the past, so – who can doubt? – Babo's vision is of the future. What that future holds neither he nor Melville can say; but as the eyes come to rest on Mt. Agonia whence Cereno followed his leader, we may assume that Babo's vision is of further black martyrdoms, of servile rebellions, and perhaps of the return of his people to their homeland. As Melville says at the start of the story, "Shadows present, foreshadowing deeper shadows to come" (p. 1). What Melville feared – bloody slave insurrection or bloody civil war – soon came to pass:

> Hidden in the cap
>   Is the anguish none can draw;
> So your future veils its face,
>   Shenandoah!
> But the streaming beard is shown
> (Weird John Brown),
> The meteor of the war.[19]

These lines come from the prefatory poem to *Battle-Pieces and Aspects of the War*, the collection of poems which Melville published in 1866 as a record of his reflections on the course of the Civil War. Complicated and shifting though his attitude was to the conflict between North and South, his basic position can be fixed accurately enough from these lines in "Misgivings" describing the war as

> The tempest bursting from the waste of Time
> On the world's fairest hope linked with man's foulest crime.　　(p. 13)

Although neither an abolitionist nor, later, an advocate of punitive reconstruction, Melville was a much firmer Unionist than the regionally inclined Hawthorne: the enormous national tragedy of the war had the salutary effect of drawing him out of himself and at least temporarily rekindling his faith in the value and possible success of the American political experiment. His antagonism to slavery and racialism had always been consistent and frank. The attack on Calhoun ("Nulli") and the peculiar institution in *Mardi* is not delivered *in propria persona*, to be sure, but it goes unanswered and is of a piece with Melville's description of slavery in the "Supplement" to *Battle-Pieces* as an "atheistical iniquity" (p. 268).

As for Melville's attitudes to race, the first thing that should be said is that in common with most other great historical romancers he relished the diversity of mankind and took more delight in identifying and juxtaposing a variety of class, racial, and regional character-types than in exploring a few individual characters in depth. Thus Amasa Delano is not a character as Dorothea Brooke or Rodion Raskolnikov so magnificently are but is rather a brilliantly observed regional character-type whose typicality is constituted, in large part, by the obfuscating racial stereotypes he harbors. Delano survives because he cannot conceive of the little black man being capable of strategy, leadership, or evil – in other words, being fully human – but Melville can. More often, of course, the dark-skinned characters in his fiction are noble primitives as yet unmarked, for better or worse, by the manacles of civilization. But we must remember that Melville sincerely admired such primitives – at any rate as he recalled them from his sea-going days – and assigned them a high place in his Romantic hierarchy of human types.

His most famous primitive is not black, as a matter of fact, but rather the fair-haired angelic "Handsome Sailor," Billy Budd. But as if to anticipate and confute any charge of racial favoritism, Melville presents as his first instance of the "Handsome Sailor"

> a common sailor, so intensely black that he must needs have been a native African of the unadulterate blood of Ham. A symmetric figure much above the average height. The two ends of a gay silk handkerchief thrown loose about the neck danced upon the displayed ebony of his chest; in his ears were big hoops of gold, and a Scotch Highland bonnet with a tartan band set off his shapely head. It was a hot noon in July; and his face, lustrous with perspiration, beamed with barbaric good humor. In jovial sallies right and left, his white teeth flashing into view, he rollicked along, the centre of a company of his shipmates. These were made up of such an assortment of tribes and complexions as would have well fitted them to be marched up by Anacharsis Cloots before the bar of the first French Assembly as Representatives of the Human Race.[20]

Melville himself had marched such an assortment up before the bar of the American reading public in *Moby Dick* without winning the applause that Cloots did in revolutionary France. But despite his growing conservatism and doubts about the wisdom of Enlightenment political schemes, he never wavered in his Clootsian faith in the essential oneness and equality of the human race. In the detail of the Highland bonnet and the word "barbaric" there is perhaps a passing recollection of Scott and the color-blind Enlightenment stadialist theories which underwrote the universality of the *Waverley*-model.

These environmentalist theories, which would bracket blond Billy with the black Handsome Sailor and other heroic barbarians, were obviously deeply opposed to the theories of inherited racial characteristics which were invoked by the apologists for the American form of slavery. Yet Melville's critique of the progressive civilization of the North was often as severe as Calhoun himself could have wished. In *Benito Cereno* his animadversions are more often indirect and understated, but they are nonetheless damning. When, for instance, Delano's crew board the *San Dominick*, they do so in the true buccaneering style, and we see plainly enough that the usual occupations of the crew –

trading and hunting seals – are not less rapacious, but only more legal, than old-fashioned piracy. This point is brought home in the passage which describes the mangling of the blacks "by the long-edged sealing spears" (p. 61). It is all one: black human beings or seals or whales – and all, thanks to Providence, the spoils of the Yankees. To be sure, much of Melville's strength in his early writings through and including *Moby Dick* was that he was sufficiently coarse-grained to participate enthusiastically in the great cruel commercial adventures of his time and people, rather than to turn aside with a fastidious shudder. Viewed from the perspective of *Moby Dick*, they were great democratic adventures, too. But young Melville knew well enough that they were actuated by motives and appetites which were opposed to the kind of democracy that always mattered most to him – the spontaneous sense of fraternity and interdependence which arose from the shared perils, the shared affections of blood or working relationships. In the long run, a Captain Ahab or a Captain Delano would trample such relationships into the dirt if they interfered with his pursuit of revenge or profit.

As Melville grew older and Reconstruction ran its course, his works gave utterance to criticisms of the North which are increasingly reminiscent of Carlyle and even Calhoun. Perhaps his most powerful onslaught on the "Anglo-Saxons," both Yankees and "John Bulls," occurs in *Clarel* (1876):

> The Anglo-Saxons – lacking grace
> To win the love of any race;
> Hated by myriads dispossessed
> Of rights – the Indians East and West.
> These pirates of the sphere! grave looters –
> Grave, canting, Mammonite freebooters,
> Who in the name of Christ and Trade
> (Oh, bucklered forehead of the brass!)
> Deflower the world's last sylvan glade![21]

Here the target is the continental imperialism of President, once General, U.S. Grant as well as the global imperialism of Queen Victoria. Once again, the speaker is not Melville or Melville's surrogate quite, but it is a speaker who seems to command his intimate respect: the exiled ex-Confederate officer Ungar, now a pilgrim in the Holy Land, to whom the great expansionist secular movements of capitalism and revolutionary socialism are both anathema. Ungar's radical-reactionary position anticipates that of Naptha in *The Magic Mountain* or that of another great character of modern fiction, Ezra Pound in *The Cantos*. From *Mardi* onwards Melville appears to have found this position fascinating and sporadically attractive; perhaps it would have become his own if he had been able to achieve a secure Christian faith. However this may be,

Ungar's denunciations of the English-speaking peoples as materialistic exploiters are consistent with those which Melville had been voicing, from a different ideological base, ever since *Omoo* (1847). And so it is not a little remarkable that he closed his career by writing a kind of paean to England as, in 1797, "a Power then all but the sole free conservative one of the Old World," whose Union Jack stood for "founded law and freedom defined" in opposition to Revolutionary France's "red meteor of unbridled and unbounded revolt" (p. 22).

4

In *Billy Budd, Sailor: An Inside Narrative* the adoptive father-son *topos* dear to historical romancers is given one of its most poignant and meaningful reembodiments. Melville, who lost both of his own sons, knew more than most people what it would cost a man like Captain Vere to reenact the part of Abraham with his son Isaac, "resolutely offering him up in obedience to the exacting behest" (pp. 112–13). That "behest" must have been exacting indeed to drive Vere, like Billy one of "great Nature's nobler order" (p. 113), to act as he did. What is the authority that Vere obeys and makes the drumhead court obey in spite of clear extenuating circumstances, powerful natural feelings, and even the dubious legality of their proceedings? Before trying to answer this question, we must first consider the historical circumstances in which Melville wrote and Vere acted.

Melville began writing his last and most problematic work in 1888, on the eve of the centenary of the French Revolution, with loud public praises of universal Progress echoing in his ears and a quiet conviction in his own mind that very much had been lost. We are aware, as sometimes in his earliest works, of the author's consciousness of a gap between his own beliefs and those which he supposes his readers to hold. Forty, forty-five years earlier, he had written as one who had to those who hadn't seen native life in Polynesia or service aboard a man-of-war. Now he wrote self-consciously as a "graybeard" who had seen the heyday of sailing ships; who had known an era of faith which could still read Genesis literally; and who remembered not so much a century of Progress as a bloody century of civil wars, revolutions, and wars of imperial conquest. Thus Melville is at pains to explain that, however distasteful to men like Edward Vere, impressment was necessary in 1797 because military sailing ships required great numbers of seamen and Britain required great numbers of military sailing ships for her survival. As a concession to "popular" taste among the reading classes of the late nineteenth century, Melville uses Plato's "Natural Depravity" to describe Claggart rather than the biblical "mystery of iniquity." (Significantly, Vere himself uses the biblical phrase later on, during the drumhead court.)

Above all, Melville repeatedly warns us how risky and presumptuous it is to second-guess the judgments passed in those remote times. On the one hand, he insists that, perhaps contrary to appearances, commanders like Vere were right and rational, after the mutinies at Spithead and Nore, to fear recurrences of trouble aboard their own ships. On the other, he reminds us armchair captains that, when men in Vere's position acted in error, they often did so because all their military experience taught them that in an emergency prompt and decisive action – almost any action – was better than delay. More important still, they acted in error sometimes because scarcely anybody in their position could have foreseen what is evident to every schoolboy a century later:

> That era appears measurably clear to us who look back at it, and but read of it. But to the grandfathers of us graybeards, the more thoughtful of them, the genius of it presented an aspect like that of Camoens' Spirit of the Cape, an eclipsing menace mysterious and prodigious. Not America was exempt from apprehension. At the height of Napoleon's unexampled conquests, there were Americans who had fought at Bunker Hill who looked forward to the possibility that the Atlantic might prove no barrier against the ultimate schemes of this French portentous upstart from the revolutionary chaos who seemed in act of fulfilling judgement prefigured in the Apocalypse. (p. 44)

The tone of this passage is difficult to assess since Melville's reference to apocalyptic fears and "an eclipsing menace mysterious and prodigious" could be construed to satirize slyly those "more thoughtful" grand-fathers – for instance, President John Adams – who were misled by their apprehensions into such excesses as the Alien and Sedition Acts of 1798. Like Cooper, several of whose sea romances are set at the very end of the eighteenth century,[22] Melville was drawn to "that era" of revolutionary unrest and shifting political and military alliances precisely because the ambiguous and menacing aspect it presented at the time tested human powers of interpretation, judgment and action as few other periods have. In *Benito Cereno* and *Israel Potter*, Melville's Yankee protagonists muddle through somehow and he does not suggest that more "thoughtful" actors would have done any better. In *Billy Budd*, however, the characters move on an altogether higher plane of thought and action: Nelson, Billy, and even Vere reincarnate the heroic ideal rather than surviving like Cereno as a ghostly vestige or, like Israel, exhibiting heroic qualities in a context where they appear ironically inappropriate. Billy is no more of a thinker than Israel of course, but Melville stresses that the no-less-heroic Nelson is "sagacious" and, "in foresight as to the larger issue of the encounter, and anxious preparations for it" is "painstakingly circum-spect" (p. 27). "Starry" Vere combines these intellectual qualities of a great captain with others which, though they strike his fellow officers as "pedantic" (p. 37) and though they complicate situations for him which would seem simple to most other sailors, obviously earn the respect of the "thoughtful" historian and ex-sailor Melville. His purpose in the passage quoted above therefore seems to have been much less to satirize his grandfathers than to admonish their great- and great-great-grandchildren that historical hindsight is apt to minify the actual dangers quite as much as foresight is to magnify them.

Throughout the narrative, indeed, Melville balances Vere's (and Vere's contemporaries') problems of foresight as a Commander with his own (and his readers') problems of hindsight as a historian. This procedure can be observed in the following, lengthy and disputed but assuredly important, passage.[23]

> The year 1797, the year of this narrative, belongs to a period which, as every thinker now feels, involved a crisis for Christendom not exceeded in its undetermined momentousness at the time by any other era whereof there is record. The opening proposition made by the Spirit of that Age involved the rectification of the Old World's hereditary wrongs. In France, to some extent, this was bloodily effected. But what then? Straightway the Revolution regency as righter of wrongs became a wrongdoer, one more oppressive than the kings. Under Napoleon it enthroned upstart kings, and initiated that prolonged agony of Continental war whose final throe was at Waterloo. During those years not the wisest could have foreseen that the outcome of all would be what to some thinkers apparently it has since turned out to be, a political advance along nearly the whole line for Europeans.
>
> Now, as elsewhere hinted, it was something caught from the Revolutionary Spirit that at Spithead emboldened the man-of-war's men to rise against real abuses, long-standing ones, and afterwards at the Nore to make inordinate and aggressive demands, successful resistance to which was confirmed only when the ringleaders were hung for an admonitory spectacle to the anchored fleet. Yet in a way analogous to the operation of the Revolution at large, the Great Mutiny, though by Englishmen naturally deemed monstrous at the time, doubtless gave the first latent prompting to most important reforms in the British navy.   (pp. 97–8)

Parts of this passage repeat what Melville says about the Spithead and Nore mutinies in chapter 3, but the contention that these mutinies and the Revolution "doubtless gave the first latent prompting to most important reforms" is not stated elsewhere in *Billy Budd*. Coming from Melville, the concession is a notable one which contributes significantly to our sense of him as a cautious, scrupulously fair-minded historian – quite unlike, for instance, the deeply biassed histrionic Ungar of *Clarel*, who acts as a kind of Yeatsian mask for the author, allowing Melville's bitterest resentment against the Anglo-Saxons to pour forth without censorship. The narrator of *Billy Budd* is also a dramatic mask, though in this case we feel that the author takes full responsibility for what the narrator says: for the narrator is not Herman Melville in all his moods and complexities but Melville the historian, who reminds us more than once that he is not (though of course he *is*) writing a romance and therefore cannot achieve the "symmetry of form attainable in pure fiction" (p. 131). The author maintains this mask partly by making himself appear balanced and concessionary even against his own graybeard impulses, as when he speaks of "anybody who can hold the Present at its worth without being inappreciative of the Past" (p. 26). It may be that Melville actually lives the part which he has created – that he tries to be more than commonly fair-minded and concessionary – but my point is that he deliberately dramatizes the role, problems, and advantages of a historian vis-à-vis those of a wartime naval commander, and that he does so with special force when, as in the passages just quoted, he takes the long perspective, available to him and us but not to the actors in his story.[24]

To take the long perspective is not necessarily to be neutral, and Melville quite openly takes sides in *Billy Budd* – with angelic Billy against diabolic Claggart; with Nelson's panegyrists against his detractors ("Benthamites of war," "martial utilitarians"); and with England, "a Power then all but the sole free conservative one of the Old World," against Revolutionary France. How was it that, after firing so many moral broadsides against England and the English-speaking peoples, he ended as their apologist? How, in the face of so many hints in *Billy Budd* itself that English sailors had good reasons for mutinying at Spithead and other Englishmen for listening to the "Jacobin" music of *The Rights of Man*? *Billy Budd* is an unfinished work, a short symbolic romance rather than a discursive novel of "ideas" or a panoramic novel of manners, and so we are not to look in it for a portrait of English society as a whole, much less for a rigorous comparative analysis of the English and French socio-political systems. Still it does provide a fragmentary sketch of English social conditions as well as numerous clues to the moral basis of Melville's rejection of the French system.

So far from picturing England "in the year of the Great Mutiny" as a chiefly just or happy society, Melville refers darkly to rapacious naval contractors; a host of criminal-types ranging from insolvent debtors to the mysteriously depraved Claggart; aristocrats "incensed at the innovators mainly because their theories were inimical to the privileged classes" (p. 37); "press-gangs notoriously abroad both afloat and ashore" (p. 43); and, above all, a nightmare atmosphere of conspiracies and conspiracy-fears. To set in the balance against all these evils there is, in *Billy Budd*, little more than the manifest decency of most of the officers and men of the British Mediterranean fleet and their proven courage and prowess. Possibly the saving remnant would have appeared larger if Melville had not been drawing, besides the English/French contrast, another and more prominent one between the landsman's "crookedness of heart" and the sailor's "frank manifestations in accordance with natural law" (p. 17). (Claggart, it should be noted, is not a sailor at all but a landsman whose affinities are with "Daddy Rat," the thief-turned-thiefcatcher of *The Heart of Mid-Lothian* and with such persecuting detective-figures as Chillingworth, Mr. Forester in *Caleb Williams*, and especially Inspector Javert in *Les Misérables*.) Yet we must bear in mind that Melville in his final years did not hope for much from *any* society because he did not hope for many souls like Billy whose "pristine and unadulterate" virtues seemed "not to be derived from custom or convention, but rather to be out of keeping with these, as if indeed exceptionally transmitted from a period prior to Cain's city and citified man" (p. 17). The corruptions of the England of *Billy Budd* are those of Israel Potter's London, but Melville does not suggest that they are essentially different from those of Bartleby's New York or the Paris of *A Tale of Two Cities*.

Confronted with a choice between highly imperfect socio-political systems, Melville now preferred the one that most frankly recognized the imperfection of man and the inequality of talents. The rule of "custom or convention" or better yet of "founded law and freedom defined" was precisely what citified man required. He also required, what the English system was capable of producing in time of need, heroic leaders like Nelson, patriarchal leaders like Vere. The latter, less brilliant and inspiring than "The greatest sailor since our world began," was more complete as a man and a better governor for all seasons, working good out of the evil of Cain's city and calling the tune to which mankind danced:

> "With mankind," he would say, "forms, measured forms are everything; and that is the import couched in the story of Orpheus with his lyre spellbinding the wild denizens of the wood." And this he once applied to the disruption of forms going on across the Channel and the consequences thereof. (p. 130)

Melville may well have regarded these analogies as hyperbolic from his own viewpoint and yet not indicative of blind reaction in their author Vere – an eighteenth-century aristocrat trained to lead men and accustomed by his reading of various authors, Milton for instance,[25] to make the ancient story of Orpheus a vehicle for contemporary political interpretation. True, "some deemed him" a martinet (p. 130), but everything that the narrator himself says directly about Vere approves him as a wise and conscientious patriarch. Indeed, he is likened both to Jacob and Abraham; and in the Abraham-Isaac relationship between Saxon Budd and Norman Vere we perhaps glimpse a representation in miniature of the English socio-political system as an ideal patriarchy – not as it is or ever could be evolved in the brazen world of history but as it might have been in a Burkean poet-philosopher's golden world of romance.

It is tempting to say that Melville's sketchy picture of a villainous revolutionary France also belongs to romance rather than to history, but we must bear in mind not only that *Billy Budd* does not purport to offer a scholarly assessment of the rival socio-political systems but also that Melville's most substantial statements about the Revolution (quoted above) are concerned less with what happened in France than with what conservative Americans and Englishmen then apprehended from the Spirit of the Age. Still, there is no reason to doubt that Melville approved of Vere's "disinterestedly" opposing revolutionary theories "not alone because they seemed to him insusceptible of embodiment in lasting institutions, but at war with the peace of the world and the true welfare of mankind" (p. 37). The last phrase is crucial to our interpretation of the novel. As early as *Mardi* Melville commented on the tendency of republics (Roman, French, American) to overflow their national boundaries, and in *Billy Budd* one of the charges against "the Revolution" is that it "initiated that prolonged agony of Continental war whose final throe was at Waterloo" (p. 98). Besides being "at war with the peace of the world," the Revolution was opposed to "the true welfare of mankind" in Melville's view because it was "atheistical"; it regarded men not as immortal spirits but as soulless bodies. That is the point of his statement in *Battle-Pieces* that he was among those "who always abhorred slavery as an atheistical iniquity." In *Billy Budd* Vere is killed as a result of a battle between the *Bellipotent* and a French warship, formerly the *St. Louis*, renamed *L'Athée* by the Directory: "Such a name," says Melville, "was yet, though not so intended to be, the aptest name, if one consider it, ever given to a warship" (pp. 131–2). He does not, of course, claim that the Revolution is alone in promoting war, atheism, and their kindred evils. On the contrary, he suggests (through Vere) that the British Mutiny Act which condemns Billy is war's "child" (p. 107); he presents the *Bellipotent*'s surgeon as a Hobbesian materialist; and he speaks of war-contractors "whose gains, honest or otherwise, are in every land an anticipated portion of the harvest of death" (p. 118). But if the evils are universal and even more than commonly active in England at the time of the action of *Billy Budd*, their crusading legions are the "conquering and proselyting armies of the French Directory" (pp. 21–2).

As Melville well knew, this reading of history would not commend itself to the majority of late nineteenth-century readers, and it may appear that even today I do him a disservice by foregrounding what can be ignored easily enough by readers of a different political persuasion. It is true that his questionings of progress and democracy and his caricature of the French Revolution can be shrugged off as mere reactionary crotchets of an isolated old man; or they can be turned on their head as the ironies of a venerable liberal *manqué*. But we have seen that Melville was highly conscious of a gap between his own beliefs and those of most of his potential readers; what is more, he drew attention to his minority "graybeard" position, risking and even inviting antagonism by noticing "the side popularly disclaimed" (p. 87). Perhaps he did so partly because, nearing the end of life and having no readers anyway, he had nothing to lose by being prickly. Yet *Billy Budd* certainly appears to have been written with a general readership in mind, and it is my contention that the "crotchets" are present also because Melville wished to dramatize through his own persona how far we see and judge the same event differently, and often conflictingly, because of differences of role, background, circumstance, and intelligence. In other words, Melville the historian is simultaneously Herman Melville's conservative spokesman and a character whose minority reports function thematically in a novel centrally concerned, after all, with the agonizing difficulty of interpretation and judgment.

A "veritable touch-stone" of another man's "essential nature" (p. 89), Vere intuits immediately that Claggart is false and Billy innocent. But in spite of Vere's swift and prudent action, Claggart's design is ironically fulfilled. A different course of action might have averted the tragedy, but now it is too late to think of the options Vere had when the master-at-arms first approached him. Again he must interpret and act. How are we to interpret and judge what he now does? Studies of *Billy Budd* tend to focus on the action Vere subsequently takes – calling and supervising the drumhead court, presiding over the execution of Billy – and pay too little attention, I believe, to his options and his interpretation of the situation immediately after Billy strikes the fatal blow.

As for options, there can be no doubt that Vere has the legal power, perhaps even the sanction of usage, to place Billy in chains and let higher authority try him after the *Bellipotent* rejoins the fleet.[26] But neither can there be any reasonable doubt that to do so would merely defer inevitable injustice; the outcome for Billy would be the same. (The possibility that Vere might try to cover up what happened is not mentioned and, given both the circumstances and his character, does not seem a serious option anyway.) Still, nobody except a prophet or a madman feels absolutely certain of the future, and therefore injustice deferred conceivably might be injustice averted. What, then, can account for Vere's decision to drive ahead roughshod over his own paternal feelings, the moral misgivings of his senior officers, and even customary procedure by summarily calling the drumhead court?

The most obvious explanation is military expediency – most obvious and surely true as far as it goes. Yet to embark on a course of action of which the foreseen end is hanging the ship's favorite is deliberately to risk provoking the very mutiny which Vere apprehends might result from a show of weakness or indecision. In the event, it does not, and of course there is no way of knowing whether a mutiny would have occurred if Billy had been put in confinement for the time being rather than tried and executed. All we can know is that the ritual slaying of the Handsome Sailor – the champion who incarnates the sailors' own ideal of themselves – results in the opposite of mutiny. Despite ominous murmurings, the ship's company echo Billy's benediction of authority, "God bless Captain Vere!" and later unite in conquering *L'Athée*. Thus the argument from expediency which Vere uses to persuade his officers that Billy must hang proves to be, though a perilous counsel, "right" in its own terms.

Yet these, the terms of the "martial utilitarians" whom Melville mentions contemptuously in chapter 4, are not the ones that Vere uses when he interprets the situation brought about by Billy's fatal act:

> Suddenly, catching the Surgeon's arm convulsively, he exclaimed, pointing down to the body – "It is the divine judgement on Ananias! Look!"
>
> Disturbed by the excited manner he had never before observed in the *Bellipotent*'s Captain, and as yet wholly ignorant of the affair, the prudent Surgeon nevertheless held his peace, only again looking an earnest interrogation as to what it was that had resulted in such a tragedy.
>
> But Captain Vere was now again motionless standing absorbed in thought. But again starting, he vehemently exclaimed – "Struck dead by an angel of God! Yet the angel must hang!" (pp. 94–5)

The surgeon suspects that Vere is unhinged – "not mad indeed, but yet not quite unaffected in his intellect" (p. 96). Such may be the case, but we have to bear in mind that the surgeon is a "scientist" who, when confronted with the unaccountable absence of spasmodic movement in Billy's body during the hanging, declines to consider any explanation except one based on Newtonian mechanical physics. Although Melville suggests that he is able and conscientious at his job, the surgeon is scarcely the man to entertain the possibility that it is because Vere has just experienced a vision or revelation that he behaves with "unwonted agitation . . . and . . . excited exclamations so at variance with his normal manner" (p. 96). Yet his "possessed" physical behavior and words imply just that. Does Vere suddenly see himself as the appointed instrument of Providence – the impresario fated to stage Billy's trial and execution in spite of all the difficulties we have noticed?

Certainly the last acts of Billy's "tragedy" – Melville's oft-repeated word – seem very much willed and directed by Vere alone, who does not so much follow forms as use them (with frequent departures) to achieve a predetermined end. Lest this behavior seem out of character, we should recall that "Starry" Vere is no tame intellectual conformist but one of those whose minds move apart from and beyond the usual human range. "Their honesty," says Melville, "prescribes to them directness, sometimes far-reaching like that of a migratory fowl that in its flight never heeds when it crosses a frontier" (p. 38). That is a wonderful image of Vere's mind in action, suggesting as it does both the speculative freedom and the tactical daring of Melville's intellectual sea-dog. That he believes himself to be acting under divine guidance is the most satisfactory explanation of his conduct. Nor need it be scoffing or unsympathetic to observe that Providence and expediency point out the same course of action. Melville likens a "true military officer" to a "true monk" with respect to their keeping strictly to their vows (p. 99), and I think we may say that Vere becomes more rather than less of a military officer as he becomes a priest. Of course we are not obliged to believe that he actually is following the dictates of Providence. Perhaps, "as the Surgeon professionally and privately surmised," Vere is temporarily the victim of a "degree of aberration" (p. 97). (The surgeon's figure derives, characteristically, either from astronomy or optics, and reduces the problem to one of mechanical regularity: the surgeon, not Vere, is the fanatical conformist.) There is, finally, no way to know whether Vere is mad or inspired. What we cannot doubt is that he acts with complete honesty and self-abnegation, though without being able fully to divulge his motives and meaning to the subordinate actors in the drama.

This interpretation receives support from Melville's poem "Timoleon," a work which belongs to the same period as *Billy Budd* and clearly anticipates some of the themes of the novel.[27] Based on Plutarch's life of Timoleon, the poem portrays a man who in spite of strong fraternal feelings and the weight of "prescriptive morals" slays his own brother, the tyrant of Corinth, because of patriotism and hatred "For crimes of pride and men-of-prey" (p. 212). Like Billy Budd's, Timoleon's name is smeared:

> The whispering-gallery of the world,
> Where each breathed slur runs wheeling wide
> Eddies a false perverted truth,
> Inveterate turning still on fratricide.   (p. 213)

And the question that Melville asks of Timoleon, "Estranged through one transcendent deed" (p. 214), might also be asked of Billy:

> Or, put it, where dread stress inspires
> A virtue beyond man's standard rate,
> Seems virtue there a strain forbid –
> Transcendence such as shares transgression's fate?   (p. 209)

Yet unlike Timoleon's, Billy's "transcendent deed" is unpremeditated, and Billy suffers none of Timoleon's agonies of doubt before and after. The character most like Timoleon in this respect is the thinking man, Vere, and not least in that

> He heeds the voice whose mandate calls,
> Or seems to call, peremptory from the skies. (p. 212)

In the end, Timoleon and the reader are left in the dark as to whether the voice of Providence did call, but not as to whether Timoleon acted in that belief and for the best. So with Vere. Moreover, the question that Melville asks concerning the consequences of Timoleon's deed – predestined or not? – also has a bearing on Vere's role in history:

> If so, and wan eclipse ensue,
> Yet glory await emergence won,
> Is that high Providence, or Chance? (p. 209)

For Vere there is little glory. "Unhappily," says Melville, he is "cut off too early for the Nile and Trafalgar" (p. 132). But glory awaits the British fleet under Nelson, and Melville implies that the sacrifice of Billy may have contributed to it by effecting a species of religious conversion to patriotism and duty in his fellows. Providence, or Chance?

At the end of *Benito Cereno* we are left with a voiceless head rather than with the narrative by Babo which the logic of narrative structure seems to demand. Babo's dead eyes are fixed on a future consummation which he cannot disclose but which we can infer in the light of more recent events and the cyclic theory of history. The inference is a grim one. At the end of *Billy Budd* we are left with three chapters "in way of sequel." Melville tells us (with bold artifice) that "Truth uncompromisingly told will always have its ragged edges; hence the conclusion of such a narrative is apt to be less finished than an architectural finial" (p. 131). At this point the author reestablishes the presence of Melville the historian, a character who does not hold back his interpretations and judgments. Yet instead of offering us the expected concluding interpretation – the "inside" as it were of this "inside narrative" – Melville leaves us, with three impersonally annotated pieces of historical "evidence," to be our own historians. One is an enigmatic eye witness account of Vere's death; the second, a defamatory gazette account of the episode aboard H.M.S. *Bellipotent*; and the third, a dramatic monologue in verse, supposed to be spoken by Billy shortly before his death. Our inside knowledge enables us to gauge the gazette report at its real value; but the irony is partly at our own expense, since we must realize that in normal circumstances we should either have believed the report or been quite unable to measure its degree of falsity. As for Vere's last words, "Billy Budd, Billy Budd" – do these signify that he is like Pontius Pilate, who on his own deathbed reportedly murmured Christ's name? We cannot know, we can only speculate – armed with whatever humility Melville has taught us in the course of this narrative.

But that humility is not to be confused with the incurious scepticism of the surgeon, for it has a positive side to it. We are taught not to despise certain kinds of evidence merely because they are no longer fashionable. Thus we are taught not to despise the wisdom of a girl or of the Hebrew prophets, though neither had much experience of the world. By extension, we are taught not to dismiss the possibility that Vere *did* experience a revelation and *was* guided through the perils of mutiny by true Providence: not, that is, by the moral somnambulism of a Captain Delano, which is the Yankee counterfeit of Providence. At the same time, also by extension, we are taught not to underrate the value of poetic insight, though "rudely" expressed in the broadside ballad "Billy in the Darbies." As Melville says elsewhere of human passion, poetic insight is not the perquisite of kings or of those who watch from the dress circle – and the less so when the subject of the poem is himself an illiterate sailor boy. Though we cannot be sure whether the ballad does reveal the truth about this particular sailor's last thoughts and feelings, it certainly seems to have the authenticity and *representative* truthfulness of literary art. It cannot tell us what *did* happen, but it can give us a vivid recreation of what might or normally would have happened. And, short of revelation, that is as near certainty about moral or spiritual matters as we are ever likely to come. Since Melville does not venture such a recreation of Vere's inmost thoughts and feelings when he exclaims, "fated boy" and "the angel must hang," we must assume that to do so was beyond the reach of his experience or his art, great as both of these were. We are left with a mystery, comparable to the "mystery of iniquity," which the Hebrew prophets might have understood but which neither the modern historian nor the modern fictionalist can penetrate. We may here recall Melville's final comment on the last interview between Vere and Billy: "But there is no telling the sacrament, seldom if in any case revealed to the gadding world . . . There is privacy at the time, inviolable to the survivor; and holy oblivion, the sequel to each diviner magnanimity, providentially covers all at last" (p. 113).

I have stressed Melville's preoccupation with different kinds of knowledge and ways of knowing because it is the central preoccupation not alone of *Billy Budd* but of the historical romance as a genre. In one of the most insightful recent studies of the novella, Rowland Sherrill says that "despite Vere's recognition of the transcendent presence that looms through Billy and the promise there of that which would redeem the man-of-war world, the captain will not meet the demands of the portent he encounters . . . Vere refuses the rule of wonder and resumes the 'spirit of common sense' " (p. 215). On the contrary, so I believe, Vere rejects the "*cold common sense*" that Horace Walpole excoriated and, at a devastating personal cost, submits to the "rule of wonder," which is also the rule of romance. Of all great historical romances, *Billy Budd* is the most a romance because it so boldly confronts its leading character, and us too, with the problem of recognizing and coping with oracles and emissaries from that "wonder-world" where the heroic, the mythic, and the sublime have their proper home.

Critics have, on the whole, done justice to this dimension of the book. But they have paid less heed to Melville's portrayals of other ways of apprehending "what happened": the ways of the lawyer, the scientist, the detective, and, above all, the historian. Although Melville privileges the unworldly knowledge of saints and children, as Hawthorne did before him, it is important not to underrate the seriousness of his dramatization of himself as a historian weighing and sifting the surviving evidence, balancing the present against the past, and inviting us to consider how we, mere humans, would have responded had we been in Vere's shoes "in the time before steamships." Peering "disinterestedly" into the obscurity of the past, as he imagines Vere peering into the even greater obscurity of the future, Melville enables us to glimpse, in the ambivalent light of history, a lost heroic world and the most titanic of all struggles between the forces of progress and reaction. But he will not, or cannot, discover the heart of the mystery about Billy and Vere – the very inside of his "Inside Narrative." As the centennial beat of the *Marseillaise* fades in the distance, he makes us hear the "melancholy, long, withdrawing roar" of the Sea of Faith.[28] In *Billy Budd* the current of historical romance is indeed "extraordinarily rich and mixed, washing us successively with the warm wave of the near and familiar and the tonic shock, as may be, of the far and strange."

7

The hero and heroine of historical romance

1

At the time that Scott decided to abandon the field of extended verse narrative to Byron and Southey, the field of prose fiction was dominated by women authors: most notably by Ann Radcliffe, Maria Edgeworth, and, soon thereafter, Jane Austen. One reason why he hesitated to become, and to become known as, a novelist may have been that during the half century preceding the publication of *Waverley* fiction-writing had been increasingly identified as a female preserve. (A measure of the degree to which novel-writing was feminized during this period is that in 1819 Cooper's first response to his wife's challenge to write "a better novel" was not to imitate Scott but to don a seemingly female persona and produce, in *Precaution*, a novel more reminiscent of Jane Austen's than of any male author's work.) Late eighteenth- and early nineteenth-century male writers, or at least the most talented ones, generally devoted themselves to other kinds of literature, and during this period there was a glorious flowering of historiography and heroic poetry – narrative genres which were more ancient and "serious" than either the novel or prose romance, and which were also traditionally masculine in authorship and even in readership. By assimilating these genres within the novel, Scott created a branch of modern prose fiction which combined the courtship matter of novel and romance with the historical and heroic matter of epic which spoke more directly and exclusively to the experience and aspirations of men. The historical romance therefore appealed strongly to the established readership interests of both sexes and by popularizing history undoubtedly contributed to the gradual breakdown of the distinctions drawn both at home and in school between the educational needs and preferences of boys and girls.

Still, the nineteenth-century historical romance must be regarded as a predominantly masculine genre on two counts. First, although Scott had female as well as male imitators, e.g., Catharine Sedgwick and Lydia Maria Child in America, the most successful historical romancers were men. Not that the great women fictionalists of the period failed to learn from Scott – works as different as *Wuthering Heights* and *Adam Bede* owe much to his example – but rather that, instead of adhering closely to the *Waverley*-model, they made use of his innovations to strengthen and enlarge some of *his* models – notably the gothic romance of Radcliffe and the novel of regional manners of Edgeworth. As for the American female fictionalists who were contemporaries of Cooper and Hawthorne, Nina Baym identifies their principal inspirations as Edgeworth, Fanny Burney, Mrs. Opie, and Mrs. Barbauld, writers whose educative mission led them to focus on manners and morals familiar to their intended, largely female, audience.[1] Eventually, of course, women did write historical romances as fine as the finest written by men, but not before the end of the frontier and the (partial) end of segregated education.

A second reason why the nineteenth-century historical romance must be considered chiefly a masculine genre is that its heroic matter favored the celebration of male feats and male relationships in the tradition of Achilles and Patroclus, David and Jonathan, Roland and Oliver, and tended to consort so awkwardly with the matter of courtship that some writers (e.g., Melville and Stevenson) dispensed with both the "love story" and women characters altogether while others (e.g., Cooper and Simms) frequently retained them at the cost of making both seem peripheral, decorative, and silly. Of course there are important exceptions, like *Satanstoe* and *The Wept of Wish-ton-Wish*, but it is surely no accident that the most imposing women characters in early nineteenth-century historical romances – Hester Prynne and Scott's Jeanie Deans – are the heroines of works in which the "heroes" are disabled or there is little scope for traditional masculine heroic adventure.

Maggie Tulliver, the "dark heroine" of George Eliot's *The Mill on the Floss* (1860), teaches us to recognize two basic stereotypes behind the vast majority of romantic heroines in nineteenth- and twentieth-century Anglo-American fiction:

> "I didn't finish the book [George Sand's *Corinne*] . . . As soon as I came to the blond-haired young lady reading in the park, I shut it up, and determined to read no further. I foresaw that the light-complexioned girl would win away all the love from Corinne and make her miserable . . . If you could give me some story, now, where the dark woman triumphs, it would restore the balance. I want to avenge Rebecca and Flora MacIvor, and Minna and all the rest of the dark unhappy ones. Since you are my tutor, you ought to preserve my mind from prejudices.[2]

George Eliot herself had recently reinforced "prejudice" with Hetty and Dinah, the dark and light heroines of *Adam Bede*; and despite Maggie's protests, novelists of both sexes and all levels of talent went on working with the same old binary pattern as if, despite its lack of correspondence to anything in front of their noses, it enshrined some profound, universal, and inexhaustible truth about human nature. Nor was this assumption altogether mistaken. For the "light" and "dark" stereotypes "behind" these heroines are so in the double, psychological and historical, sense that (1) they translate today's, yesterday's, everyday's private fantasies (of achievement) and anxieties (of failure) into public literary codes and conventions, and that (2) they have been around in a recognizable form since classical antiquity and in something close to their modern shape since the later Middle Ages.

Bold simplification seems to be called for at this point, and so I will try to profile these heroines by reducing their salient features to the lowest common denominators. The "light" heroine of flight-and-pursuit narratives is a virgin and heiress whose marriage to the hero reconciles warring factions of the past and builds securely for the future. The other, the "dark" heroine of siege narratives, is a wife, mistress or betrothed whose sexual allure or infidelity unmans the hero and precipitates the fall of the kingdom. For the ancient patterns of these heroines we may look to Middle High comedy and the *Iliad*.[3] For influential American examples we may turn to Hester Prynne and the heroines of Cooper's frontier novels, especially *The Last of the Mohicans*. The novels of Dickens, Thackeray, Eliot, and Hardy offer a seemingly inexhaustible supply of British examples. However, as Maggie Tulliver's instances suggest, the author most responsible for the light/dark stereotypes of nineteenth-century British and American fiction was undoubtedly Sir Walter Scott.

Scott created no fewer than three pairs of light and dark heroines who captured the imaginations of readers throughout the world and supplied sure-fire models for later writers. Jeanie and Effie Deans, the heroines of *The Heart of Mid-Lothian*, are the pair with whom I will be most concerned in this chapter. Yet we must not overlook the element of truth in the proposition that all of Scott (of Scott the fictionalist, that is) is in *Waverley*: Rose Bradwardine and Flora Mac-Ivor supplied Scott himself with a model for the later pairs and cannot be neglected. Nor should it be forgotten that the pair who probably enthralled the nineteenth century most of all were Rowena and Rebecca, the fair Saxon princess and dark Jewish angel who love Wilfred of Ivanhoe.

That these heroines supplied the patterns for countless fictional Mays and Ellens, Ernestinas and Sarahs, has been widely recognized; but if Scott was more responsible than anybody else for glamorizing the light

and dark stereotypes of nineteenth-century fiction, he was also among
the first to expose their inadequacy. In the Waverley novels may be
found both the sexist and anti-sexist perspectives of American historical
romancers ranging from Cooper to Toni Morrison in our own time. As
we shall see, the crucial mediating figure in this tradition was
Hawthorne. For in *The Scarlet Letter* he created a classic which not only
transmitted and refined Scott's best insights into gender relations but also
commanded the admiration of America's greatest women novelists,
Edith Wharton and Willa Cather.

One critic who offers important insights into the complex nature of
Scott's treatment of gender is Harriet Martineau (1802–76), who, in an
obituary essay on Scott, wrote an analysis of his heroines which has
retained much of its fire and cogency. A feminist, a daughter of the
Scottish Enlightenment, Martineau underrated neither the strength of
Scott's conservatism nor the power of his imagination all unintentionally
to reveal radical truths about the human condition. She begins by
contending that just as the "best argument for Negro Emancipation lies
in the vices and subservience of slaves," so the best argument "for female
emancipation lies in the folly and contentedness of women under the
present system, – an argument to which Walter Scott has done the fullest
justice; for a set of more passionless, frivolous, uninteresting beings was
never assembled at morning auction or evening tea-table, than he has
presented us with in his novels."[4] This contempt for Scott's heroines has
always been shared by some eminent critics, including ones, like Balzac,
who do not sympathize with the feminist viewpoint. A notable
confirmation of Martineau's critique can be found in Edith Wharton's *A
Backward Glance*, where she agrees with John Buchan that Scott was
unable "to create a lifelike woman of his own class" because

> after all, to the men of his generation, gentlewomen were "a toast" and little
> else . . . Child-bearing was their task, fine needlework their recreation, being
> respected their privilege. Only in aristocratic society, and in the most
> sophisticated capitals of Europe, had they added to this repertory a good many
> private distractions. In the upper middle class "the ladies, God bless 'em'", sums
> it up.[5]

The New York upper-middle-class women of the 1870s in *The Age of
Innocence* stitch the same pattern as the gentlewomen of Scott's
generation. The difference is that in Wharton's novel "the ladies, God
bless 'em," have their revenge because the men, captives of their own
leisure-class system, have become every bit as idle and trivial as
themselves.

But critics of all persuasions agree that there are some remarkable
exceptions among Scott's women characters. Martineau identifies four:
Flora Mac-Ivor, Jeanie Deans, Rebecca, and Die Vernon (the spirited

light/dark heroine of *Rob Roy*). Her comments on Jeanie are extremely perceptive and I will return to them later in this chapter; but Rebecca is the Scott heroine who supplies the most telling evidence for her case. As might be expected, Martineau's concern is not with Rebecca's proscribed "dark" sexuality but with the nineteenth-century socio-political implications of her being both a woman and a Jew:

> As a woman, no less than as a Jewess, she is the representative of the wrongs of a degraded and despised class . . . first despised, then wondered at, and involuntarily admired; tempted, made use of, then persecuted, and finally banished – not by a formal decree, but by being refused honourable occupation, and a safe abiding place. Let women not only take her for their model, but make her speak for them to society, till they have obtained the educational discipline which beseems them; the rights, political and social, which are their due; and that equal regard with the other sex in the eye of man, which it requires the faith of Rebecca to assure them they have in the eye of Heaven.   (pp. 456–7)

So far from endorsing the contention of many frustrated readers that Scott should have married Ivanhoe to brilliant Rebecca rather than to dull Rowena, Martineau emphatically approves Scott's appeal to history and probability. It is but too true that, as Scott says, "the prejudices of the age rendered such an union almost impossible" and that "a character of a highly virtuous and lofty stamp, is degraded rather than exalted by an attempt to reward virtue with temporal prosperity . . . a glance on the great picture of life will show, that the duties of self-denial, and the sacrifice of passion to principle, are seldom thus remunerated." Martineau's approval is ironic inasmuch as she recognizes an illustration of the law of unintended consequences in this apologia. For of course Scott himself draws quite different inferences than she does from these reflections on the history of prejudice, the meaning of marriage, and the likely rewards of patience and humility. Despite his own entrenched prejudices, she argues, the tendency of Scott's realism and historicism is to expose and counteract prejudice of all kinds: "He has softened national prejudices . . . he has imparted to certain influential classes the conviction that human nature works alike in all; he has exposed priestcraft and fanaticism . . . and finally, he has advocated the rights of women with a force all the greater for his being unaware of the import and tendency of what he was saying" (p. 457).

Martineau believed that, for all their differences of ideology and intention, she and Scott were both participating in and contributing to a revolution in the popular understanding of the role and nature of women. As her allusion to "Negro Emancipation" reveals, she, like Mary Wollstonecraft before her, conceived of the campaign for "female emancipation" as but an aspect of a much larger battle for human rights which had its origins in Enlightenment social philosophy and the French

Revolution. This long and broad historical perspective not only permitted her to be a generous and perceptive critic of the writings of a political opponent but also enabled her to see that there was hope for far-reaching and enduring changes in attitudes to *women* precisely because the preceding century had introduced a new understanding of *human* nature and history – of the factitious and historically determined character of many distinctions which had previously appeared determined by Nature (or God) and thus of the very possibility of change, for the better or worse. Martineau believed that change in recent times had generally been for the better and expected it to be so in the future as well. We have seen that Scott did too, although he believed that change was better when it was gradual and that many factitious and historically determined distinctions contributed to the happiness and welfare of mankind. However, anybody familiar with Scott will know that his feelings about progress were much more deeply mixed than Martineau's and that, except by a miracle of intuition, neither was likely to be able to enter fully into the other's world of hopes and fears. Martineau could look optimistically towards the advent of a New Eve, but poets of Scott's generation who went to school with Goethe and Schiller saw more disturbing and ambivalent omens when they looked back along the course of progress.

At this point it may be useful to remind ourselves of the basic pattern of opposed characteristics which Scott found in the writings of Young, Goethe, and Schiller, and eventually reembodied in the *Waverley*-model. Some of the key terms are:

feudalism	bourgeois society
country	town
oral	literate
natural	artificial
spontaneous	labored
liberty/wildness	order/boundaries
individual	mass
poetry/mystery	prose/reason
sublimity	correctness

These oppositions reflect a widespread and growing anxiety about the costs which "Progress" and "Enlightenment" were exacting of entire social groups and – even more disturbing because closer to home and less easily diagnosed and remedied – of the individual human psyche right in the midst of the triumphant middle classes. That "Civilization" had its own peculiar and devastating ills was evidenced, in Britain alone, by the consequences for the laboring classes of rural depopulation and the new factory system and by the unprecedented incidence of suicide and madness among greatly gifted writers: the fates of Collins, Smart, Cowper, Chatterton, and Wollstonecraft haunted both fictional and nonfictional portraits of the artist as a young man or woman throughout the later eighteenth and early nineteenth centuries.

A comparatively zestful and resilient soul like Horace Walpole might count on there being "some time hereafter, when taste shall resume the place philosophy now occupies"; but especially in Germany, where such things were taken not more seriously perhaps but more tragically, there were many who anticipated no such counterrevolution. For they inferred that somewhere along the path of progress European man had suffered a second Fall. Among them was Goethe's friend Schiller, whose creative and critical writings did much to ensure that the oppositions recapitulated above would be among the chief staples of the Romantic literature of all nations, of all genres, and of all levels of excellence for the next two hundred years. Most important for the present discussion is his celebrated distinction – yet another Romantic polarity – between the "Sentimental" and "Naive" poet.

Schiller's distinction between "Sentimental" and "Naive" cannot be reduced to a mere opposition of modern to ancient and bad to good. For he includes Euripides and Horace in the Sentimental camp and discovers potentialities in the Sentimental poet which surpass those of the Naive poet. However, according to Schiller, most modern writers *are* Sentimental: estranged from their own nature, they lack the harmonious, spontaneous relationship between feeling and thought, thought and words, which is enjoyed by Naive poets and is, so to speak, the birthright of all mankind. Schiller theorizes that modern writers are attracted to nonhuman nature and to primitive peoples because they are themselves exiles from nature:

> We regret this place of safety, we earnestly long to come back to it as soon as we have begun to feel the bitter side of civilisation, and in the totally artificial life in which we are exiled we hear in deep emotion the voice of our mother. While we were still only children of nature we were happy, we were perfect: – we have become free, and we have lost both advantages.[6]

Carried too far, this longing for unattainable happiness and perfection can lead to disaster; Schiller cites Werther as an example "of the dangerous extreme of the sentimental character":

> a dreamy and unhappy love, a very vivid feeling for nature, the religious sense coupled with the spirit of philosophic contemplation, and lastly, to omit nothing, the world of Ossian, dark, formless melancholy . . . see how all external circumstances unite to drive back the unhappy man into his ideal world; and now we understand that it was quite impossible for a character thus constituted to save itself, and issue from the circle in which it was enclosed.
> (pp. 306–7)

Whether the particular instance be a suicidal extreme like Werther or a more "healthy" individual, the essential trait of the Sentimental character is its estrangement from nature:

> The ancients felt naturally; we on our part, feel what is natural. It was certainly a very different inspiration that filled the soul of Homer, when he depicted his divine cowherd giving hospitality to Ulysses, from that which agitated the soul of the young Werther at the moment when he read the 'Odyssey' on issuing from an assembly in which he had only found tedium. The feeling we experience for nature resembles that of a sick man for health. (pp. 279–80)

What of the "healthy," the Naive, man or woman? What they were like in a prelapsarian society we can know only through the portraits in Naive literature and, by inference, through contrasts with the predicament of the Sentimental character in modern society. When Naive individuals do stray uncomprehendingly into our world,

> Being themselves of a truly good and humane nature, they forget that they have to do with a depraved world; and they act, even in the courts of kings, with an ingenuousness and an innocence that are only found in the world of pastoral idylls. (p. 270)

Such people are bound to seem wanting in wit, hence ridiculous, to shallow observers. But Schiller insists that their guilelessness results from no lack but rather from fullness of nature expressing its *"moral magnitude"*; their spontaneous acts of trust, generosity, and truth-telling exhibit nature obeying *"without let or hindrance* her *moral constitution*, that is, the *law of harmony"* (p. 268). And although we might laugh at him when such a person is easily duped, "we cannot avoid esteeming him, precisely on account of his simplicity. This is because his trust in others proceeds from the rectitude of his own heart" (pp. 269–70).

Had his anatomy of the Naive character followed rather than preceded the publication of the Leatherstocking tales, Schiller might well have cited Natty Bumppo as a splendid example. However, Schiller is careful to stress that "simplicity" of character is a trait that belongs not only to cultural primitives but also to the great men – literary geniuses, philosophers, and generals – of more sophisticated societies: "the egg of Christopher Columbus is the emblem of all the discoveries of genius. It only justifies its character as genius by triumphing through simplicity over all the complications of art" (p. 272). And, as might be anticipated, it is not in the male but in the female of the species that Schiller finds simplicity and nature most becoming and most essential:

> With regard to the other sex, nature proposes to it simplicity of character as the supreme perfection to which it should reach . . . But, as the principles that prevail in the education of women are perpetually struggling with this character, it is as difficult for them in the moral order to reconcile this magnificent gift of nature with the advantages of a good education, as it is difficult for men to preserve them unchanged in the intellectual order: and the woman who knows how to join a knowledge of the world to this sort of simplicity in manners, is as deserving of respect as a scholar who joins to the strictness of scholastic rules the freedom and originality of thought. (p. 273)

This passage demonstrates that, for all his talk of simplicity and good education, Schiller's ideal woman is neither very earthy nor very intellectual. Still, retaining as much of the "magnificent gift of nature" as is possible in modern society, she may be the best hope that the Sentimental male has of regaining health.

Schiller's compelling portrait of the Sentimental character was drawn from recent literature and from the life – his own as well as others' – and is itself a brilliant exemplification of "Sentimental" self-consciousness working its way out of the fatal circle that enclosed Werther. Since his contemporaries recognized their friends and sometimes themselves in this portrait (and had been so well prepared for it by Goethe's early masterpieces), it is only to be expected that Schiller's diagnosis of what ailed the age and its literature soon became famous and influential. Yet for the same reason it is often impossible to say for sure whether that diagnosis directly or even indirectly influenced the delineation of any particular Sentimental protagonist in subsequent fiction. Inasmuch as Scott was translating Schiller's historical drama *The Conspiracy of Fiesco* and otherwise immersing himself as deeply as possible in German literature and thought at the very time that the essay on Sentimental and Naive literature first gained celebrity, the chances are that he did know it and that it had some influence on his conception of the character and fate of Edward Waverley. My contention here, however, is merely that Schiller's thesis has a special pertinence to the treatment of gender in the historical romance.

Taking Schiller as our guide, we can rewrite our lists of opposed characteristics in historical romance to show how these are likely to be associated with gender:

Man	Woman
sentimental	naive
intellect/learning	intuition/instinct
history	myth
art	nature
modern	primitive
fragmentary	whole

Whether this polarization of gender traits in fiction corresponds to anything that might be actually observed in modern men and women and, if so, whether any of these oppositions has its basis in "nature" rather than nurture are not questions we need try to answer here. However, the fact that the qualities associated with women in this scheme are the same as or at least similar to those associated in my earlier lists with subjugated heroic societies raises two other questions which should be briefly addressed at once.

First: who comes off worse by this polarization, the hero or the heroine? The short answer is that neither list adds up to a satisfactory human being or indeed to *any* particular person or fictional character. Probably the "purest" Naive characters in American fiction are not women at all but Natty Bumppo and Huckleberry Finn. Still, it is strikingly often the case that various combinations of the traits listed on the left (which for the sake of brevity, but at the risk of oversimplifying Schiller's meaning, I will call "Sentimental") characterize the principal male protagonists in historical romances while their opposites on the right tend to cluster in the female protagonists. Whether it is better to be dominated by the Sentimental or the Naive characteristics depends on the position of the observer and the extremity of the case. Willa Cather clearly intends us to believe that Ántonia's weaknesses are less serious than Jim's and that her human strengths are more valuable, but other Cather novels (e.g., *The Song of the Lark*) record the frustration experienced by women like herself who defy expectations by being richly endowed with Sentimental traits. The second question, then, is: do not the gender polarities enshrined in the historical romance reinforce "Earth-Mother" stereotypes of women as "naturally" domestic and unintellectual? No doubt they do have that tendency, but they also question many traditional gender-role expectations and in effect propose a new understanding of dependence in relationships between men and women.

Edward Waverley is the first of a long line of historical romance heroes ranging through Pushkin's Pyotr Griniev to Hawthorne's Arthur Dimmesdale to Faulkner's Isaac McCaslin who are powerfully drawn to primitive societies and individuals (sometimes paternal but just as often maternal figures) who possess the Naive qualities missing in themselves. Just as Werther discovers nature in the *Odyssey* and the captivatingly Naive person of Charlotte, so Waverley finds it in Froissart and the Highland clans and at last, assimilably, in thornless Rose Bradwardine. It is true that Rose seems sweet and simple rather than primitive and instinctual, but she may well be as much of nature as a gentle Sentimental soul like Waverley could actually survive. And he is a survivor as well as a romantic. Neither suicide as for Werther and Emma Bovary, nor heart-shriveling scepticism as for Candide, nor brutalizing disillusionment as for Conrad's Kurtz, awaits Waverley when the world fails his youthful assay. He confesses: "The plumed troops and the big war used to enchant me in poetry; but the night marches, vigils, couches under the wintry sky, and such accompaniments of the glorious trade, are not at all to my taste in practice" (p. 290). This discovery does not destroy him or even (so far as can be inferred) destroy his pleasure in Froissart.

Of course there must always be some danger that a fictional "hero" who is both a survivor and an unreconstructed romantic will appear not only unmanly but also immature. What is Scott saying about these qualities in a man? When Waverley retires from military service, he commissions this memorial of his Jacobite adventure:

> It was a large and spirited painting, representing Fergus Mac-Ivor and Waverley in their Highland dress, the scene a wild, rocky, and mountainous pass, down which the clan were descending in the background . . . and the ardent, fiery, and impetuous character of the unfortunate Chief of Glennaquoich was finely contrasted with the contemplative, fanciful, and enthusiastic expression of his happier friend. Beside this painting hung the arms which Waverley had borne in the unfortunate civil war.   (p. 338)

Although not a self-portrait (for Waverley is a poet, not a painter), this picture reflects his new understanding of his own character. At the same time, because his character has been tempered rather than transmuted by his experience, the painting epitomizes for future generations a heroic episode not unworthy of Froissart. And this is to say that, in Scott's view, part of Waverley's hard-earned maturity consists in his not altogether abandoning a romantic perspective on life. For sometimes it is the true one or at least one that cannot be left out of account. So, when we seek to understand Prince Charles Edward's extraordinary initial successes, we have to remember how "the gallant and handsome young Prince . . . threw himself upon the mercy of his countrymen, rather like a hero of romance than a calculating politician" (p. 327). So, when we try to explain the loyalty of the Jacobite adherents after they begin to suffer reverses, we should not forget Waverley's response to the argument that the forces assembled against them were now overwhelmingly superior: "If the cause I have undertaken be perilous, there would be the greater disgrace in abandoning it" (p. 258). Evidently a mature – and realistic – view of life must take account of the power of appeals to a "romantic" ideal of conduct. Scott himself never allows us to settle for one view of the Prince, or the 45, or Waverley's part in it; his current remains, in Henry James's words, "extraordinarily rich and mixed."

As for Waverley's manliness, there is no shrewder judge of it than Flora Mac-Ivor:

> 'For mere fighting . . . I believe all men (that is, who deserve the name) are pretty much alike: there is generally more courage required to run away. They have besides, when confronted with each other, a certain instinct for strife, as we see in other male animals, such as dogs, bulls, and so forth. But high and perilous enterprize is not Waverley's forte. He would never have been his celebrated ancestor Sir Nigel, but only Sir Nigel's eulogist and poet. I will tell you where he will be at home, my dear, and in his place, – in the quiet circle of domestic happiness, lettered indolence, and elegant enjoyments, of Waverley Honour. And he will refit the old library in the most exquisite Gothic taste . . . and he will draw plans and landscapes, and write verses, and rear temples, and

dig grottoes; – and he will stand in a clear summer night in the colonnade before the hall, and gaze on the deer as they stray in the moonlight, or lie shadowed by the boughs of the huge old fantastic oaks; – and he will repeat verses to his beautiful wife, who shall hang upon his arm; – and he will be a happy man.' (pp. 249–50)

This character sketch wittily echoes the myriad eighteenth-century imitations of *L'Allegro* and *Il Penseroso* that Waverley would have read along with Froissart; its imagery is exactly the kind that Waverley, a sentimental poet as well as a Sentimental character, would imitate in his own verses. Flora's satire is very like Scott's own gently Cervantesque satire of Waverley in the opening chapters, but it recognizes a new stage in Waverley's career by modulating from the mock-chivalric to the mock-ruminative mode.[7] The sketch helps us to understand both why Harriet Martineau admired Flora and why Waverley and Flora could never be mates. Waverley is manly enough – he has a sufficiency of the male instincts – but since he is formed for a life of contemplation rather than of action he needs a mate "who shall hang upon his arm." At least so far as Flora is concerned, this picturesque image of female dependence does not symbolize woman's natural and inevitable role in the eternal scheme of things. On the contrary, it is a conventional image of the kind of conventional relationship necessary to the happiness of a man who is "contemplative, fanciful, and enthusiastic" but essentially unoriginal. If he were more original, Rose Bradwardine might be less capable of making him a happy man.

I do not mean to suggest that Waverley is very old-fashioned in his attitudes towards women. It is rather Flora's brother Fergus, a feudal overlord and man of action, who supposes that men have a natural right to dispose of their womenfolk in marriage as if they were chattels. When Waverley announces that he must withdraw from a courtship which plainly displeases Flora, Fergus cannot understand why his erstwhile friend protests that he "would not take the hand of an angel, with an empire for her dowry, if her consent were extorted by the importunity of friends and guardians, and did not flow from her own free inclination" (p. 265). Fergus jumps to the conclusion that Waverley is dissatisfied with Flora's dowry or no longer desires an alliance with the house of Mac-Ivor, and immediately translates what he takes as an insult to his sister into an insult to himself:

> 'But, sir . . . if Flora Mac-Ivor have not the dowry of an empire, she is *my* sister, and that is sufficient at least to secure her against being treated with any thing approaching to levity.'
> 'She is Flora Mac-Ivor, sir, which to me, were I capable of treating any woman with levity, would be a more effectual protection.'

The distinction Waverley draws between "Flora Mac-Ivor" as an independent person and Fergus's "*my* sister" manifests a basically modern outlook. Waverley rejects patriarchalism in personal relations between the sexes for much the same reason that the people of Britain were in the process of rejecting patriarchalism, as represented by the Stuart dynasty, in national politics. Of course neither Waverley nor Sir Walter Scott, Bart., thought that these rejections would or should lead to perfect equality in all social and political relations between men and women. The revolutions in these relations which they approved placed as much emphasis on "consent" (to something proposed by somebody else) as on "free inclination." Taking this view in 1745 was distinctly progressive; taking the same view in 1814 was moderately conservative but, as Harriet Martineau would have recognized, certainly not reactionary.[8]

If we ask where all of this leaves Flora, the answer that *Waverley* gives is: the convent of the Scottish Benedictine nuns in Paris. Flora's true soulmate is Fergus, and when he and their "high and perilous enterprize" are wrecked the world has no further holds on her. More interesting than the incestuous overtones which can be detected in their relationship is the partial reversal of traditional gender roles which Scott emphasizes. It is not just Waverley who fails to measure up to Flora's highest standards of "strength of mind"; neither does Fergus. Fergus, she explains to Waverley in their last interview, was "as volatile as ardent" and therefore "would have divided his energies amid an hundred objects. It was I who taught him to centre them, and to gage all on this dreadful and desperate cast" (pp. 322–3). Thus it is, she concludes, "that the strength of mind on which Flora prided herself has – murdered her brother!"

I believe we misread *Waverley* if we conclude that Scott's conscious or unconscious purpose is to expose and punish Satanic overreaching in a woman who has prided herself on superior, and unnatural because unwomanly, strength of mind. What he does, rather, is to show that the mismatching of natural talents with conventional gender roles can have tragic consequences. In all of his great novels except *Old Mortality* he shows that there is nothing extraordinary about such mismatchings. To be sure, some of his "strong" women are harsh or weird figures; Lady Ashton in *The Bride of Lammermoor* and Helen MacGregor in *Rob Roy* are cases in point. But Flora has the dignity as well as the burden of her strength. She is possessed of sufficient moral intelligence to blame herself (as, I believe, she should) for having directed Fergus into dangers which she knew that she, as a woman, would be able to share only vicariously, and she has enough firmness of character (as Waverley and Rose have not) to be capable of a great and enduring sorrow.

2

When news of the defeat at Culloden reaches Waverley, he is "for a time altogether unmanned" (p. 293) by the thought of what might have become of the Prince, of Fergus, and of the Baron Bradwardine. As for those "who clung for support to these fallen columns, Rose and Flora, – where were they to be sought, and in what distress must not the loss of their natural protectors have involved them?" Although the sentimental figure of the female flowering vines clinging to the male columns may be regarded as Waverley's rather than Scott's conceit, there can be no doubt that the latter shared the former's belief that men were the "natural protectors" of women. This, after all, was the belief of nearly all their contemporaries, women as well as men; and in addition to the various reasons which any educated person might then have adduced in its justification, Scott had the special reason that romancers have always had: the "plot interest," the suspense- and reversal-producing potential, inherent in the questions: "where were they to be sought, and in what distress must not the loss of their natural protectors have involved them?" Since fictionalists from Homer to Richardson to Austen to John Fowles have found one or both of these questions worth asking, it is not especially noteworthy that Scott did, too. But it is worth noting that the protection offered by men inevitably tends to seem more important and more natural in the physical-exertion-and-danger-packed romances which Scott and his followers wrote than it does in novels of manners. Worth noting also is the corollary that such romances tend to highlight the helplessness and vulnerability of women and to school their female readers in grateful dependence.

However, these salutary lessons entail a certain risk of male embarrass-ment. For Waverley's questions to be asked, women's natural protectors must themselves be rendered temporarily helpless. The expedients which romancers have found to disable their male protagonists without making them appear excessively foolish or "effeminate" range from the effects of aging (leaving daughters actual or virtual orphans) to natural catastrophe (leaving wives actual or supposed widows) to incarceration as a result of treachery or force of numbers (leaving sisters or fiancées potential victims of rape, murder, or madness). Of course the male protagonists of such fiction often contribute to their own disablement by being excessively proud, daring or hot-tempered – faults natural, pardonable, and even engaging in "male animals, such as dogs, bulls, and so forth." But not until the later eighteenth century are "heroes" – i.e., male protagonists who are meant to be regarded seriously and sympathetically by readers – immobilized by a high-strung temperament associated often though not invariably with an enfeebled physical constitution. These males could barely look after themselves, let alone a train of sisters, mothers, fiancées or daughters. Not surprisingly, tracts and satires of the time were quick to point out their self-indulgent character and (as Temperance novels were to do a half century later) the ruinous consequences of this self-indulgence both for themselves and their resourceless female dependents.[9]

Schiller was well aware of this new type of hero when he anatomized the Sentimental character. Indeed, one of his main objectives in the essay on Sentimental and Naive Literature was to provide a broad philosophical and historical explanation for the novel kind of temperament manifested most alarmingly and influentially in Goethe's young Werther and identified in English imitations and parallels as "Sensibility." It may therefore be said that a character like Werther is both a Sentimental and Sensible hero – the crucial generic distinction being that although characters who are the victims of a Sensible temperament usually exhibit at least a few of the Sentimental traits listed above, a good many Sentimental characters (Waverley, for example) do not suffer from a debilitating and ultimately self-destructive Sensibility. In the present section I am concerned principally with the former, the Sensible hero, who is in desperate need of succor from a Naive heroine. My examples will be two characters who have, on the face of it, little in common with Werther: the Calvinist ministers Reuben Butler from *The Heart of Mid-Lothian* and Arthur Dimmesdale from *The Scarlet Letter*. Despite many obvious differences, the romances in which they appear share key plotting devices and many details of characterization; more important, they both upset traditional gender-role expectations and explore the nature of dependence in human relationships. Before turning to them, however, I will comment briefly on a contrasting Scott hero who has nothing of the Sensible and little of the Sentimental in his make-up.

Edgar Ravenswood is an unambiguously masculine and dignified figure throughout *The Bride of Lammermoor*. Although he is embarrassed by poverty and anachronistic feudal pretensions and loyalties (not to mention the perplexities involved in loving the daughter of the man who has usurped his family estate), we are allowed to share his frustrations and exasperations but never to laugh at him as we do at the more fortunate Waverley. Scott makes sure that any quixotic risibilities which might arise because of Edgar's circumstances are transferred to the elderly Ravenswood family servant, Caleb Balderstone. Scott likewise takes care that all the "ductile" and Sentimental qualities which abound in Waverley are invested in Edgar's beloved, Lucy Ashton. And as if to confirm that this traditional allocation of gender traits is natural and right, Scott makes the catastrophe result from the reverse allocation in

Lucy's "wavering" father and domineering mother. In this respect, then, as in several others, *The Bride of Lammermoor* is the most purely conventional of Scott's great historical romances.

Yet before we conclude that Harriet Martineau must have disapproved altogether of this novel, we should recall that the incident which gives the romance its title is probably the most stunning and famous act of female retaliation in nineteenth-century fiction. Were Lucy a jot less sweet and submissive, her stabbing "your bonny bridegroom" in the very bridal chamber would seem far less violent, astonishing, and right than it does. Dramatically and symbolically "right," that is, and although her new husband is not smart or wicked enough for his punishment to seem morally right, the wrong he suffers does not alienate our sympathies from Lucy. After all, he survives his injuries whereas she does not survive hers. It might also be argued that she is mad and therefore not responsible for what she does. Yet I question whether any reader who has been moved by her story would wish to deny Lucy some moral credit, hence some responsibility, for throwing off her passive character for a moment and taking up the weapons of a coercive society, which treats its daughters as chattels, against its agent. Conservative though Scott was, the issue of consent flowing from "free inclination" evidently stirred his feelings quite as powerfully as it did Waverley's.

In its happy ending as in its treatment of gender roles, *The Heart of Mid-Lothian* contrasts sharply with *The Bride of Lammermoor*. During the closing chapters of the novel, the great good Duke of Argyle (or rather the great good Sir Walter Scott) transports Jeanie Deans and her menfolk from the vicinity of urban crime and mob violence in Edinburgh to the pastoral island of Roseneath on the edge of the Western Highlands. Here canny, humble Jeanie manages not only the Duke's dairy cattle but also the lives of her aged father David and her husband Reuben and their children – manages them so unobtrusively and successfully that the men suffer no loss of patriarchal face while the children are enabled eventually to move up in the world and become proper ladies and gentlemen. Here too the long-lost bastard son of Jeanie's sister Effie (now Lady Staunton, a brilliant society dame) emerges abruptly from the wild Highlands to slay Sir George Staunton (once, under the alias of Geordie Robertson, a convicted felon), never dreaming that Staunton is his own father.

Indeed, it might appear that only in a wish-fulfillment dream could so many happy alterations be made and so much "poetic justice" dispensed. Despite a rather fatuous concluding address to the reader in which Scott claims that the novel illustrates "the great truth, that guilt . . . can never confer real happiness . . . and that the paths of virtue . . . are always those of pleasantness and peace,"[10] earlier references to dreams and fairy tales imply very distinctly that the last ten chapters make no serious claim to realism. The "great truth" they actually illustrate, by flagrantly defying probability in order to make everything come out as it should, is the fictionality, hence the ultimate plasticity, of the tale in the hands of the Wizard of the North. In contrast to the irremediable doom which governs the characters and events (and seemingly Scott himself) in *The Bride of Lammermoor*, a principle of plasticity – especially with respect to social-class identities and gender roles – makes an astonishing amount of mobility and shape-shifting possible in *The Heart of Mid-Lothian*.

Possible but not necessarily easy. For throughout most of the novel the principle of plasticity encounters an opposing and, at first, much stronger principle of rigidity. Neither Scott nor his characters get their heart's desire until after they have earned it by hard, heroic effort. For this effort to be (and seem) hard and heroic, Scott must first bring his characters up against apparently intractable legal obstacles and unbridgeable gulfs – social-class, national, religious, and geographical. Further, although these particular characters are able to find a way around them, the obstacles and gulfs remain as and where they were and obviously would forestall anybody less determined than Jeanie, adept than Effie, or economically and socially powerful than the Duke of Argyle. Thus the novel as a whole is neither a realistic mirror of British society of any period nor, as I once believed, an escapist fantasy. It is best regarded, rather, as a fable which illustrates Scott's conservative but pragmatic social ideal of flexibility for individuals within a fairly rigid and durable framework of social conventions.

Just as Hawthorne thinks of the Puritan fathers standing up "for the welfare of the state like a line of cliffs against a tempestuous tide," Scott regularly associates the traditional protective roles of males with stone towers and columns. But the principal male characters in *The Heart of Mid-Lothian* are not even fallen columns; they are themselves the clinging vines. Jeanie becomes a heroine because she and her sister are let down by the three men who should be their "natural protectors." At the moment of supreme crisis and need, their affectionate but elderly and unworldly father is shattered by the successive blows of his favorite daughter having an illegitimate child and then being sentenced to death for child-murder. Effie's lover George Staunton is immobilized by a physical accident but still more by the need to avoid detection as an escaped criminal and leader of the Porteus Riots. Jeanie's fiancé Reuben, possessor of a delicate frame and a more delicate temperament, is incapacitated by a frightening encounter with Staunton and still more by his anxiety on behalf of the Deans family.

Jeanie's emergence as the protector of her family is not an unprepared-for event but one which has been in the making since before her birth. In a lengthy comparative portrait of Naive Jeanie and Sensible Reuben,

Scott implicitly returns an ambiguous answer to some fundamental questions about the relative importance of environment, heredity, and natural biological differences in determining an individual's capacity to fulfill traditional gender roles:

> But Douce Davie Deans knew better things, and so schooled and trained the young minion, as he called her, that from the time she could walk, upwards, she was daily employed in some task or other suitable to her age and capacity; a circumstance which, added to her father's daily instructions and lectures, tended to give her mind, even when a child, a grave, serious, firm, and reflecting cast. An uncommonly strong and healthy temperament, free from all nervous affection and every other irregularity, which, attacking the body in its more noble functions, so often influences the mind, tended greatly to establish this fortitude, simplicity, and decision of character.
>
> On the other hand, Reuben was weak in constitution, and, though not timid in temper, might be safely pronounced anxious, doubtful, and apprehensive. He partook of the temperament of his mother, who had died of a consumption in early age. He was a pale, thin, feeble, sickly boy, and somewhat lame, from an accident in early youth. He was, besides, the child of a doting grandmother, whose too solicitous attention to him soon taught him a sort of diffidence in himself, with a disposition to overrate his own importance, which is one of the very worst consequences that children deduce from over-indulgence . . . they went together to school, the boy receiving that encouragement and example from his companion, in crossing the little brooks which intersected their path, and encountering cattle, dogs, and other perils, upon their journey, which the male sex in such cases usually consider it as their prerogative to extend to the weaker. (pp. 114–15)

No doubt about it: Jeanie has been in training from early childhood for the long lonely journey to London which she must take in order to secure a pardon for her sister. As might be expected, Harriet Martineau believed that environment – the plastic factor – accounted for very nearly everything that was special about Jeanie's character. She describes Jeanie as a graduate of "the school of experience" who has developed her human potential more fully than women usually do because she has "escaped the management of men, and been trained by the discipline of circumstance" (p. 456). "When Jeanie is spoken of with tender esteem," Martineau continues, "let it be suggested, that strength of motive makes heroism of action; and that as long as motive is confined and weakened, the very activity which should accomplish high aims must degenerate into puerile restlessness."

Scott on the other hand believed that the factors of heredity and gender-related physical differences, the natural "givens" of the human condition, could not be discounted. From *Waverley* onwards his romances assume that heredity and sexual differentiation inevitably and rightly play a large part in determining both society's expectations and individual capacities and performance. Yet they weigh much less in his calculations than might be expected of a conservative male social thinker.

So far as biological differences are concerned, the reason for his moderation may have been deeply personal. For earlier in life Scott himself had been "a sickly boy, and somewhat lame," and thus knew from his own experience how vulnerable were the human male's natural physical powers and therefore how easily, through no fault of their own, individuals might be deprived of the capacity to fulfill gender-role expectations. He knew and yet did not suppose that those expectations would or could be greatly modified. It was his conservative faith that the British social system could and routinely did accommodate individual variations humanely and that, even if every Reuben Butler did not find his compensating Jeanie Deans, the exceptions caused less suffering than would the "rash and venturous experiments" proposed by radical reformers.[11]

Leaving aside the natural vulnerability to accidents which can make a man lame or a woman incapable of bearing children, *The Heart of Mid-Lothian* shows that each of us has still to contend with the consequences for good or ill, strength or weakness, of heredity. Reuben, we are told, inherited this weak constitution from his consumptive mother. Since Jeanie and Effie have the same father but different mothers, the latter must be at least partly responsible for Jeanie's plainness and Effie's beauty, Jeanie's stern virtue in adversity and Effie's yielding frailty in temptation. In turn, Effie's son, "a born imp of Satan" (p. 770) according to the savage Highland robber who becomes his adoptive father, seems to have inherited his "fierce and vindictive spirit" from Staunton.

However, Scott was both too much of an upstart aristocrat himself and too much of a philosophical historian in the tradition of Adam Ferguson to think of heredity as much more than a wild card in the deck which now and then upset the results that would be predicted on the basis of environmental factors. We have seen that Jeanie's self-reliant character is developed, if perhaps not molded exclusively, by both "the discipline of circumstance" and (*pace* Martineau) "the management of man," i.e., her father. Environment also plays a part in forming and preserving her chaste and family-oriented ways. For her rural occupations tend to secure her from amorous temptation, and when Effie's mother dies Jeanie is obliged to assume the roles of housekeeper and surrogate mother – the more so because their father is an odd, sometimes comic and sometimes touching, mixture of patriarch and child. By contrast, Effie is the pampered daughter of David Deans's old age; she is exposed to more temptation than Jeanie partly because she is more physically beautiful but partly also because she becomes a shop assistant "in the centre of a populous and corrupted city" (p. 144). In Reuben's case the unfortunate effects of the accident that made him somewhat lame in early youth are compounded by the "too solicitous attention" of his "doting grand-mother." George Staunton, we discover, is an only child who "passed the first part of his early youth under the charge of a doting mother, and in the society of negro slaves, whose study it was to gratify his every caprice" (p. 520). Nothing that can be done by his father (a very model of paternal goodness who endeavors to be his son's best friend) can undo the consequences of the mother's "imprudence and unjustifiable indul-gence." In short, so preoccupied is Scott with the effects of environment on character and behavior that *The Heart of Mid-Lothian* is, among other things, a Lockean tract on child-rearing which advocates quite clear principles and kindly but firm methods.

To leave it at that, however, is to take a narrower and less "philosophical" view of the relationship between character and environ-ment than Scott would have expected of his educated readers. Jeanie and her father have the strengths and weaknesses of the Naive character-type: Jeanie's conduct as a witness at Effie's trial perfectly exemplifies the unworldly rectitude and vulnerability described by Schiller. They have these traits not just because of practical upbringing, rural seclusion, or a parochial creed – important though these factors are – but also and especially because they are pastoral folk like the ancient Hebrews. Scott comments that Deans's "wealth, like that of the patriarchs of old, consisted in his kine and herds" (p. 374). He is christened David because it is a good eighteenth-century Presbyterian name and also because Scott wants us to associate him with the most famous shepherd of all. So, too, David's habit of drawing parallels with Old Testament characters and events serves the dual purpose of reinforcing *vraisemblance* and reminding us that he and Jeanie belong to the pastoral stage of social development. This being so, their presence not far from the growing city of Edinburgh has become nearly as anachronous as Natty Bumppo's in the farming community of Templeton. Their removal to a new Canaan on the isle of Roseneath, in itself an improbable action, restores them to a more probable environment and brings the fictional world of *The Heart of Mid-Lothian* into a satisfying harmony with the stadialist scheme of things.

Although Jeanie and Effie are half sisters and Scotswomen, Scott associates them with different stages of social development and, correspondingly, with radically different ancient civilizations. If we knew nothing else about her, Jeanie's Hebraic-pastoral affiliations would lead us to predict her "manly" independence and inability to adapt to the ways of a more "advanced" society. For these are among the traits which stadialist theorists ascribe to peoples at the second stage of social development and which Scott attributes to Helen MacGregor in *Rob Roy* and Cooper to Esther Bush in *The Prairie*.[12] Intimately familiar with Jeanie's pastoral background and habit of employing the Old Testament as a guide to conduct, Butler immediately recognizes the origins of her anachronistic scheme to go to London and appeal directly to the King: " 'Alas! alas!' said Butler, 'the kings now-adays do not sit in the gate to administer justice, as in patriarchal times' " (p. 404). As for traits which are distinctively Hebraic rather than broadly pastoral, the Book of Exodus might cause us to anticipate Jeanie's piety, moral earnestness, and unswerving determination to reach her destination and to hold to the truth.

The Book of Exodus is very likely one of the sources for an extended metaphor which David Deans uses to praise those (like himself) who have remained true to "the gude auld cause," and which also clearly foreshadows Jeanie's journey to London:

> I wish every man and woman in this land had kept the true testimony, and the middle and straight path, as it were, on the ridge of a hill, where wind and water shears, avoiding right-hand snares and extremes, and left-hand way-slidings, as weel as Johnny Dodds of Farthing's Acre, and ae man mair that shall be nameless. (p. 285)

The words "true" and "testimony" echo with several meanings throughout the chapters leading up to and including Effie's trial; indeed, it might be said that the meaning of these two words is what *The Heart of Mid-Lothian*, at its most morally serious, is about. Precisely because he has "kept the true testimony" and is determined to continue doing so despite all temptations, David cannot in good conscience testify before a court appointed by an "uncovenanted" government. Jeanie's conscience permits her to serve as a witness but not to forswear herself by giving other than the "true testimony" which in effect condemns her sister to death. Again and again, other characters condemn David and Jeanie for being stiff-necked and perverse, and Scott himself exposes David's prejudice and vanity and Jeanie's readiness in what might be termed "secular" circumstances to manage situations and people by telling them what they want to hear or by omitting to tell the whole truth. Nonetheless, he expects us to share his admiration for the way both remain true, i.e., "constant and unchanged in . . . [their] testimony" (p. 290), and he makes their conduct wholly credible by reminding us of the heroic models they have ever in view: the Puritan Saints who chose martyrdom over obedience to a false "prelatical" government, and those Saints' own models, the ancient Hebrews who chose the fiery furnace over obeisance before false gods.

What a contrast there is, then, between these stern cultural associations and those evoked by Scott's first description of Effie as a blooming adolescent:

> Her Grecian-shaped head was profusely rich in waving ringlets of brown hair, which, confined by a blue snood of silk, and shadowing a laughing Hebe countenance, seemed the picture of health, pleasure, and contentment. (p. 135)

Goddess of eternal youth, Hebe is associated in Greek and Roman rites with the loosening of constraints of all kinds. She is therefore a deity suitable for the worship of the Porteous rioters, whose invasion of "the Heart of Mid-Lothian," i.e., the Edinburgh city jail, is an act of civil rebellion which Scott both celebrates and deplores. Hebe is also an apt prefiguration of Effie inasmuch as, in contrast to the Hebrew, the Greek mythology to which she belongs is a mythology of the senses whose chief miracles are endless plastic wonders of metamorphosis. Effie, as Lady Staunton, becomes so perfectly metamorphosed that her own sister does not recognize her when she first appears at Roseneath. The very picture of pagan "health, pleasure, and contentment," Hebe-Effie is at once more archaic and more modern than her sister, and so it is a fitting development of her career and personality – Jeanie has a "character," Effie a "personality" – that she should follow Staunton in adopting the Roman Catholic faith and end her days in a convent. Universal romancer that he is, Scott patently delights in this and all the other conversions and ruses – e.g., of Staunton (*alias* Geordie Robertson) disguised as a woman during the Porteous riots – he invents to create variety and surprise. Scottish moralist that he is, he is moved by Jeanie's keeping "the true testimony, and the middle and straight path" and also by Butler's constancy to his pastoral mission in the Highlands when, late in the book, Staunton offers him a comfortable living in the Church of England.

If Hebraic Jeanie and Hellenic Effie are ideal anti-types many of whose traits are reembodied in countless light and dark heroines in nineteenth-century fiction, Reuben Butler and George Staunton are outwardly antitypical as well: in rank, religion, morals, and fate they are as unlike as the lovers of two sisters could well be. However, Scott hints at enough parallels in their predicaments and inward conditions that we might well begin to wonder whether in the course of the novel they do not become each other's light and dark doubles.

Not long after paying a farewell visit to the invalid Butler in his humble Edinburgh apartment, Jeanie finds herself in the chamber of the no-less-invalid Staunton. The immediate occasion of Staunton's disablement is a riding accident, but there are numerous hints that a profligate life has reduced his own constitution to a level with Butler's. That Staunton is a burnt-out case does not become certain, however, until years later when he at last returns to the scenes of his criminal youth:

> Walking at the right hand of the representative of Sovereignty, covered with lace and embroidery, and with all the paraphernalia of wealth and rank, the handsome though wasted figure of the English stranger attracted all eyes. Who

> could have recognized in a form so aristocratic the plebeian convict, that,
> disguised in the rags of Madge Wildfire, had led the formidable rioters to their
> destined revenge!   (pp. 739–40)

The entire account of Staunton's return to Scotland resonates with
ironies – not the least of them being that this "wasted figure" who was
once capable of terrorizing Butler must now lean on him for physical
assistance.

Scott declines to reveal the nature of Staunton's feelings as he walks in
solemn procession down the Edinburgh High Street, but we discover at
the end of the novel that remorse has so affected his conscience that now
he is not only as physically frail but also as temperamentally
hypersensible as Butler was at the time of Effie's trial. Accompanied by
Butler on his fatal journey to Roseneath, Staunton at first finds his
companion's conversation wonderfully restorative but soon begins to
suffer painful shocks as he listens to Butler moralizing upon the longterm
consequences of a dissolute youth and recognizes the Highland scenes
where, as Geordie Robertson, he once smuggled contraband goods. It
transpires that he has undertaken a form of discipline and self-
punishment ironically like and unlike that which Butler experienced as a
university student, "macerating his body with the privations which were
necessary in seeking food for his mind" (p. 118). When Staunton's body
is undressed, it "then appeared, from the crucifix, the beads, and the shirt
of hair which he wore next his person, that his sense of guilt had induced
him to receive the dogmata of a religion which pretends, by maceration
of the body, to expiate the crimes of the soul" (p. 768). The physical
tortures which Staunton inflicts on himself as a penance are also
analogous to the psychological ones which "pressed cruelly hard" on
Butler when, interdicted from holding communications with the
Deanses, he imagines that Jeanie must suppose him to have deserted
them. "This painful thought, pressing on a frame already injured,
brought on a succession of slow and lingering feverish attacks, which
greatly impaired his health" (p. 396).

As Butler becomes progressively less, Staunton becomes progressively
more, morbidly imaginative. Butler's terrifying initial encounter with
Staunton, on a remote and allegedly haunted dueling ground the night
after the Porteous riots, excites apprehensions that the handsome,
aristocratic, and in every other respect conventionally Byronic figure
might be "the Roaring Lion, who goeth about seeking whom he may
devour!"

> The whole partook of the mien, language, and port of the ruined archangel;
> and . . . the effect of the interview upon Butler's nerves, shaken as they were at
> the time by the horrors of the preceding night, were greater than his
> understanding warranted, or his pride cared to submit to . . . It was in such

places, according to the belief of that period (when the laws against witchcraft were still in fresh observance, and had even lately been acted upon,) that evil spirits had power to make themselves visible to human eyes, and to practise upon the feelings and senses of mankind. (pp. 160–1)

The haunted wilderness of North America holds similar spectral encounters for Hawthorne's young Goodman Brown. In less emergent circumstances and in better health, however, Reuben Butler takes a far more "Enlightened" view of such manifestations. As the Pastor of Roseneath, he sometimes even finds himself in conflict with his superstitious father-in-law, a veteran of the heroic age of Puritanism when (as Jeanie diplomatically puts it) "folk were gifted wi' a far look into eternity, to make up for the oppressions whilk they suffered here below in time" (p. 687). Butler protests that, contrary to David's counsels, he "cannot be persecuting old women for witches, or ferreting out matter of scandal among the young ones, which might otherwise have remained concealed" (p. 686).

Staunton, on the other hand, in adopting the religion of the Stuarts has become scarcely less superstitious than the old Covenanter. Shortly before his death, he remarks of the weather that "There is something solemn in this delay of the storm . . . it seems as if it suspended its peal till it solemnized some important event in the world below" (p. 757). "Alas," responds Butler, who has by now assumed a position of moral and intellectual authority not just in his Highland parish but in the novel itself,

> "what are we, that the laws of nature should correspond in their march with our ephemeral deeds or sufferings? The clouds will burst when surcharged with the electric fluid, whether a goat is falling at that instant from the cliffs of Arran, or a hero expiring on the field of battle he has won."

Secure in Jeanie's care and in the knowledge that he has been true to her, to the religion of his fathers, and to the people entrusted to his ministry, Butler has outgrown the egoistical Sensibility of his youth and become in his own modest way a strong column of support for his family and community. And yet Scott does not unambiguously endorse the minister's sensible, as distinct from Sensible, outlook on the relationship between nature, Providence, and human destiny. For Staunton's imaginative apprehension that "some important event in the world below" is about to take place turns out to have been right. Superstition? Veritable omen? Scott characteristically declines to choose betwixt ancient faith and modern incredulity, imagination and common sense, romance and realism.

3

I have stated that *The Heart of Mid-Lothian* and *The Scarlet Letter* share key plot devices and many descriptive details, and that both upset traditional gender-role expectations and explore the nature of dependence in human relationships. To point to these likenesses is not to deny that there are also obvious and major differences of technique, scale, historical setting, moral and aesthetic rigor. Nor is it to contend that Hawthorne absolutely required the example of *The Heart of Mid-Lothian* to be able to develop the *donnée* of "a young woman, with no mean share of beauty, whose doom it was to wear the letter A on the breast of her gown" into his first full-length historical romance.[13] *The Scarlet Letter* is a book at once profoundly personal to Hawthorne and authentically of the New England *patria*. Nonetheless, I do contend that the heroines and especially the heroes of *The Heart of Mid-Lothian* and *The Scarlet Letter* are surprisingly alike and that these likenesses are more significant than might at first appear or than my hedgings now and later might seem to suggest.

That Dimmesdale, Butler, and Staunton all belong to the genus Sensible or Wertherian Man presumably requires no further demonstration. Certainly all three exhibit the frail health and hypersensitive temperament which characterize the Sensible hero, and both Dimmesdale and Butler appear to be attracted to "nature" in Hester and Jeanie for the same reason that, in Schiller's analysis, Werther is drawn to Charlotte. Dimmesdale is a far more gifted individual than nearly any of Scott's Sensible or Sentimental protagonists, but this is only to say that Hawthorne cleaves closer to Romantic myth by investing his doomed Sensible hero with the gift of inspiration. (The closest that Scott comes in *The Heart of Mid-Lothian* is the fleeting "Sense and Sensibility" juxtaposition of Butler's Newtonianism with Staunton's moment of clairvoyance before his death.) Nor is Dimmesdale's resemblance to the "brothers" Staunton–Butler merely a matter of general conformity to the Sensible character-type. So striking is the resemblance in a few particulars that we might wonder whether Hawthorne ever asked himself: what if the secret criminal Staunton had been a minister like his own father – or like the morbidly sensitive Reuben Butler – instead of an aristocratic youth without significant communal responsibilities? All the greater, surely, would have been the moral interest and irony of his predicament when as an honored public figure he returned, wasted by guilt, to the scenes of his crimes? Would it not have been more in character, more psychologically plausible, for such a pastoral sinner to be so obsessed by his guilt that he begins secretly to punish himself physically and to discover ominous signs in the heavens addressed personally to himself? I do not suppose that Hawthorne ever asked himself precisely these questions, but the literary historian may legitimately ask them as a way of pointing not merely to Hawthorne's probable indebtedness but also to his originality.

For although Scott's conception of the sisters' lovers as each other's double is bold and effective, the characters themselves are almost stock figures. Bourgeois moralist and Protestant nationalist, Scott wanted Jeanie's lover to be as admirable as was consistent with his also being "unmanned" by the crisis which brought out all of her latent heroism – to be, despite his pardonable frailties of body and temperament, the very model of a Presbyterian minister: good, true, learned, pious, and yet not fanatical. And Scott wanted Effie's seducer to be an English aristocrat in the mold of Richardson's Lovelace who at last shows his true moral and political colors by converting to Roman Catholicism. Hawthorne too was a bourgeois moralist and Protestant nationalist and, as an allegorist, was generally more inclined even than Scott to make use of stock character-types. However, although he was probably not a closer student of the *whole* of Puritan psychology than Scott, stories like "Young Goodman Brown" and "The Minister's Black Veil" show that he early understood better than Scott or any other historical fictionalist how hypocrisy and paranoia were the inevitable and mutually reinforcing consequences of a religion which instilled an inward conviction of personal guilt while effectively enforcing an outward show of purity. Thus he was uniquely able to see how the traits which Scott had carefully parceled out between Butler and Staunton might be recombined with far greater literary impact and moral import.

Tempting though it is to dwell on the resemblances and differences between Scott's and Hawthorne's treatments of the gothic matter of – literally – breast-baring at the point of death and of "practices, more in accordance with the old, corrupted faith of Rome" (p. 144), a less specific but more important likeness between Dimmesdale and the "heroes" of *The Heart of Mid-Lothian* is their mutual failure to act as the "natural protectors" of their womenfolk and children. It is more important because, irrespective of what the failure does to the men themselves (little to Staunton and Butler, much to Dimmesdale), it puts on trial not only the strength of their women but also the wisdom and compassion of their respective communities. And of course it raises quite as many fundamental questions about the "place" and natural capacities of women in *The Scarlet Letter* as it does in Scott's novel.

Why were Hawthorne's answers less liberal or at least more troubled than Scott's? While it is beyond the scope of the present study to go very deeply into the elusive connections between particular authors' lives and works, we may profitably remind ourselves of a few comparative biographical data and of their likely bearing on Scott's and Hawthorne's feelings about gender roles and responsibilities.

I have already commented on the parallel between Reuben Butler's and Scott's own lameness and ill health as a boy. Although the lameness proved a life-long disability, Scott overcame it so well that he was able to pursue the masculine field sports of his class and to officer a company of militia. Still, he knew from the inside how it was with a man like Butler, and it is hard to believe that the many instances of male entrapment or disablement in the Waverley novels have nothing whatever to do with the author's own early and lingering fears of incapacity to perform the traditional manly part adequately. Hawthorne too was a frail boy who experienced two years of lameness on the eve of adolescence, and it is tempting to argue for a close connection between this experience and his later refusal to make use of physical feats and courage either as a proof of his characters' virtue or as a snare for literary popularity. But what may have been a more determinative factor for his greatest achievement as a fictionalist was that he lost his father early in childhood and grew up as the respectful but unloving foster son of his mother's brother, Robert Manning. For, again, it is hard to believe that the powerful sense of the missing father – and, equally, of the missing husband – which he creates in *The Scarlet Letter* owes nothing to this early deprivation.[14]

Whether their boyhood experiences made Scott and Hawthorne less prone than other romancers simply to take the gender demarcations of their age for granted must remain a matter of guesswork, but there can surely be no doubt that their contrasting attitudes to female competition were strongly influenced by the very different receptions accorded their early fiction and also by the very different social-intellectual milieux in which they wrote.

Because Scott achieved immense and almost instant fame and financial reward as a romancer and in any case wrote a different brand of fiction, he could afford to be, and in practice was, generous in his appreciations of his principal women predecessors and rivals. Nor does this readiness to appreciate their work appear to have had much to do with broad national or political biases. For the same can be said of the American Democrat Cooper, who although a blatant sexist in many other respects, was perfectly ready to salute the achievements of Austen and Edgeworth and other, much less gifted, women fictionalists. Moreover, in their romances as in their own social intercourse, Scott and Cooper generally preferred "spirited" and "cultivated" women and stuck by the principle that, at least in the most important decision of her life, a woman's consent should never be "extorted by the importunity of friends and guardians" but should always "flow from her own free inclination." Of course this was not the whole story: perhaps sensing the risks that even such limited freedom entailed, they also took care that a heroine who was both spirited and intellectual, like Die Vernon or Eve Effingham (the heroine of *Homeward Bound* and *Home as Found*) should be a daddy's girl, devoted to him and his causes, and that female characters who actually exercised considerable independent authority, like Jeanie or Helen MacGregor or Esther Bush, should be decidedly unintellectual and beyond the pale of modern genteel society. Whether these patterns were consciously meant to be exemplary is hard to say, but I do not think that they reflect any grave anxiety about contemporary trends: Scott and Cooper seem to have regarded the "female Jacobins" of their day – Mary Wollstonecraft, say, or Margaret Fuller – as aberrations so queer and unattractive to the majority of women as to require no public reproof.[15]

With Hawthorne it was otherwise. Until the publication of *The Scarlet Letter*, he enjoyed scant popular success; and since neither by experience nor temperament was he cut out to write the romances or autobiographical narratives of male adventure on the frontier and high seas which won fame and fat royalties for Cooper, Henry Dana, Jr., old Irving and young Melville, he came much more directly into early competition with the authors, many of them women, who earned pin money by selling essays, sketches, and tales to gift books and magazines. Add to this that no American woman appeared to have written fiction at all comparable in talent or artistic seriousness to that of the great British women novelists, or to that which he himself had published with meager reward for nearly twenty years, and it becomes easier to forgive Hawthorne's notorious, exasperated, and inaccurate remark that "America is now wholly given over to a d––––d mob of scribbling women."[16]

Especially after his experience of Brook Farm, he could not warm to the radical reform movements – Abolition, Temperance, Women's Suffrage – which had their home in Boston and had many Bostonian women among their most energetic supporters. One of these women, Hawthorne's admirable sister-in-law, Elizabeth Peabody, considered him her very own discovery and did everything she could to promote his career and personal happiness. Everything, that is, from arranging for Thoreau to dig a vegetable garden for the Hawthornes at the Old Manse to arranging the publication of Nathaniel's history books for children. Wholly characteristic of her and the age was her regret that he could not be brought to give *The Scarlet Letter* a happy ending. Although he valued her good qualities, it is evident that she and others who shared her sunny radical faith got on Hawthorne's nerves badly and deepened both his pessimism and his sense of social guilt.[17]

Perhaps Hawthorne is most at one with the Puritan fathers in their mislike of Hester in chapter XIII, "Another View of Hester," where she emerges for the first time as a free-thinking intellectual: "She assumed a freedom of speculation . . . which our forefathers, had they known of it, would have held to be a deadlier crime than that stigmatized by the scarlet letter" (p. 164). If she had not had Pearl's education upon which to "wreak" her "enthusiasm of thought," Hester

> might have come down to us in history, hand in hand with Ann Hutchinson, as the foundress of a religious sect. She might, in one of her phases, have been a prophetess. She might, and not improbably would, have suffered death from the stern tribunals of the period, for attempting to undermine the foundations of the Puritan establishment.   (p. 165)

When Hester does eventually prophesy the coming of a greater (because purer) prophetess than herself who would reveal a new truth "in order to establish the whole relation between man and woman on a surer ground of mutual happiness" (p. 263), Hawthorne declines to speculate whether the new truth predicted by Hester will be merely an old illusion or whether, true or not, it will threaten to undermine the foundations of the modern establishment. He declines to speculate, but he gives us little reason to confide in Hester's oracles on any topic – especially the topic of "the whole relation between man and woman." More interesting than Hawthorne's judgment on these matters, however, is his hint that nineteenth-century feminism reincarnates the schismatic and "enthusiastic" impulses of seventeenth-century Puritanism.

What can a character who is an intellectual overreacher as well as a practical transgressor of one of the most sacred of human laws have in common with either Jeanie or Effie Deans? It is obvious that Hester differs widely from either Jeanie or Effie in several major and many minor respects, and we do well to remember that Hawthorne almost certainly had in mind the *donnée* for her character and plight long before he conceived those of her clergyman-seducer. Therefore, while Dimmesdale is unmistakably a Sensible hero like Butler and Staunton and recapitulates particular aspects of their behavior so closely as to argue for Scott's direct and by no means trivial influence on Hawthorne's original conception of the character, the examples of Jeanie and Effie must have had an impact both later and lighter. In short, I do not suppose that Hawthorne ever had the occasion to ask: what if Jeanie had been not only constitutionally strong and capable but also beautiful, passionate, and tempted like Effie? Still, if Hawthorne was the close reader of *The Heart of Mid-Lothian* I have supposed him to be, he must have been interested in Scott's characterization of the two sisters as personal and cultural antitypes, each other's opposites and complements, and likewise interested in Scott's depiction both of what women can do and what can be done to them when the men whose role it is to protect them do not measure up. Let us first consider how Scott's characterization of the heroines of *The Heart of Mid-Lothian* might have provided Hawthorne with suggestions for developing his original conception of a heroine doomed to wear a scarlet letter A on her breast.

Scott's strategy of characterization is to disentangle and externalize the traits of individuals so that both his main and subordinate characters typify large classes of people. Regarded as products and representatives of cultural history, the characters in *The Heart of Mid-Lothian* are therefore rich and complex; their interactions mean far more than could possibly have been guessed by the millions of people who have read the book for its gripping romantic story.

Regarded as mimetic representations of individual human beings, these characters and their dilemmas are sufficiently convincing and moving for Scott's purposes. Indeed, inasmuch as her true testimony and pedestrian achievements demonstrate the extraordinary strengths sometimes latent in people who in more commonplace circumstances would seem – and by and large actually *are* – pretty ordinary, Jeanie Deans is a character who magnificently vindicates Scott's mixed form. Familiar fibber and heroic truth-teller, canny domestic economist and bold strategist, she is the great character that Harriet Martineau and other, less ideologically actuated critics have claimed her to be. Morally and psychologically speaking, however, Jeanie and her fellow characters are quite simple. Scott made them so simple chiefly because he aimed to render the complexity of national communities rather than of individuals, and, extensive though his sympathies were, beyond a certain point he was not very interested in the agonies and exultations of romantic individualists, however exceptionally gifted. Although he liked and admired his fellow Scotsman Lord Byron, he was himself the least "Byronic" of writers.[18]

Hawthorne shared Scott's "patriotic" ambition to depict the national community in epic fictions. However, the infant community which is the setting and in considerable measure the subject of *The Scarlet Letter* is much more narrow, egalitarian, and primitive than the one depicted in *The Heart of Mid-Lothian*; and, as if in reverse ratio, Hester and Dimmesdale are correspondingly less narrow, less ordinary, and less morally and psychologically simple, than Scott's main characters. Everything that James has to say about the poverty of manners and richness of inner life in Hawthorne's Puritan world is pertinent here, and I would add that the claustrophobic closeness and stasis of Boston in 1642–9 – so unlike the spaciousness and mobility of Scott's fictional world – magnifies Hester and Dimmesdale's guilt-ridden sense of being constantly exposed to public scrutiny and has the paradoxical effect of making them all the more self-preoccupied and estranged from the people with whom they have to rub shoulders. However, since their experience in this respect is but an intensified epitome of the lives led by many other citizens of this isolated Calvinistic theocracy, it has the typicality necessary to epic fiction. Neither does Hawthorne's shift of emphasis from action to interpretation, from simplicity to moral and psychological complexity, from the ordinarily to the extraordinarily gifted, mean that his characters are much less "typical" than Scott's or fail to betray the effects of historical conditioning.

Although he seems never to have subscribed to stadialism, Hawthorne embraced an older and more picturesque form of environmental determinism. On the showing of his historical fiction from "The Gentle Boy" onwards, the harsh conditions imposed by the soil and climate and natives of New England gradually made the Puritan settlers as severe and gloomy as the land itself was – in its prevailing mood. In "The Custom-House" Hawthorne goes so far as to allege that the Salem witchcraft craze of 1692 can be attributed to this transformation of the original English character. Yet he also suggests that when the chilly winds of Massachusetts first touched the westward-gazing immigrants aboard the *Mayflower*, these Puritans met a Wordsworthian "corresponding breeze within": in other words, that the prevailing mood of Puritanism had always been sable: and therefore that New England was indeed the true Canaan for the Endicotts and Bellinghams. But not for Hester and Dimmesdale. Although Dimmesdale dies of an inner wasting disease, it is apparent that these frosty conditions are scarcely congenial either to his genius or Hester's except insofar as suffering and Puritan discipline have altered *their* "native" characters.

Almost from the beginning of the romance, Hawthorne associates Hester with the Mediterranean and matriarchal cult of Mary:

> Had there been a Papist among the crowd of Puritans, he might have seen in this beautiful woman, so picturesque in her attire and mien, and with the infant at her bosom, an object to remind him of the image of Divine Maternity, which so many illustrious painters have vied with one another to represent; something which should remind him, indeed, but only by contrast, of that sacred image of sinless motherhood, whose infant was to redeem the world.
>
> (p. 56)

The key word here is "picturesque." Not only is the passage – and the entire book – strikingly visual and painterly, but its subject has through her sartorial artistry turned herself (as she later turns Pearl) into an icon, reminding us, "but only by contrast," of the icon-busting heritage of the Puritan fathers which Hawthorne himself had been picturing ever since "The May-Pole of Merry Mount." When, later in the romance, "the scarlet little figure" of Pearl reminds good old Mr. Wilson of "golden and crimson images" projected by stained glass "in the old land" (pp. 109–10), his recollection should carry with it an ironic reminder to the reader that, at that very time in England, Puritan zealots were breaking as much of that glass as they could reach. And inasmuch as Puritan iconoclasm is traditionally linked with, and drew its scriptural justification from, the Hebrew prohibition of graven images, these and other passages already discussed in chapter 4 should direct us to think of Hester and her persecutors as associated not just with the hostile factions contemporaneously fighting a civil war in England but also with those factions' "types" in earlier civilizations: the civilizations of ancient Southern Europe and ancient Israel. In "one of her phases," Hester was perhaps not unlike Hebe, the goddess associated with the unbinding of constraints: or so she appears fleetingly in a flood of sunshine near the end of the book.

On the face of it, of course, there cannot be any very close parallel between the Hester who emerges from prison at the beginning of *The Scarlet Letter* and the joyous Effie-Hebe we see near the beginning of Scott's romance, many months before she too is placed in prison by the civil authorities. The many burdens Hester must then and later bear – of personal guilt, of public ostracism, of single parenthood, of conflicting loyalties to Chillingworth and Dimmesdale – combine to repress and distort the passionate, sensuous, and enthusiastic nature which surfaces in her behavior from time to time. It does not seem possible that she could ever recover the pagan freshness and spontaneity of Effie, whom Scott describes as an "untaught child of nature, whose good and evil seemed to flow rather from impulse than from reflection" (p. 139). Yet Hawthorne asserts that such a miracle, or one very like it, is possible: "She who has once been a woman, and ceased to be so, might at any moment become a woman again, if there were only the magic touch to effect the transfiguration" (p. 164). When the reunion with Dimmesdale does effect a brief transfiguration, in defiance of history and probability, we know that we are in the presence both of romance and divinity:

> By another impulse, she took off the formal cap that confined her hair; and down it fell upon her shoulders, dark and rich, with at once a shadow and a light in its abundance, and imparting the charm of softness to her features. There played around her mouth, and beamed out of her eyes, a radiant and tender smile, that seemed gushing from the very heart of womanhood. A crimson flush was glowing on her cheek, that had been long so pale. Her sex, her youth, and the whole richness of her beauty, came back from what men call the irrevocable past, and clustered themselves, with her maiden hope, and a happiness before unknown, within the magic circle of this hour. (p. 202)

It is not merely to her own days of free impulse and maiden hope that Hester magically reverts at this moment. However stained and dimmed she might be in her seventeenth-century New England incarnation, luminous qualities survive in her which belonged to mankind at the dawn of civilization.

On a lower or at least less mythic plane, instinctual nature is strong in the woman Hester as a mate and mother. Unlike the male intellectuals Chillingworth and Dimmesdale, she feels naturally rather than feels what is natural. So it is that the heterodox intellectual questioning which Hawthorne attributes to her is most convincing when, as in the forest scenes, it appears less a matter of speculating dangerously about (among other topics) biblical and patriarchal authority than of simply rationalizing the heterodox conduct to which the "wild, heathen Nature of the forest" (p. 203) impels her:

> Her intellect and heart had their home, as it were, in desert places, where she roamed as freely as the wild Indian in his woods. For years past she had looked from this estranged point of view at human institutions, and whatever priests or legislators had established; criticizing all with hardly more reverence than the Indian would feel for the clerical band, the judicial robe, the pillory, the gallows, the fireside, or the church.   (p. 199)

Hawthorne rarely sounds like a stadialist, but he does here. In likening her viewpoint to that of a displaced Indian, Hawthorne suggests that the experience which appears to have repressed nature in her has actually brought her much closer to the rootless "savage" nature which, of necessity, looks to the needs of the family rather than of the state. Her most "advanced" and radical arguments – "The past is gone! Wherefore should we linger upon it now?" – serve the most "primitive" and conservative instincts.

Yet if Hester manifests some of the cardinal traits of the Naive character, she nonetheless fails to display the authenticating sign of that character's "moral magnitude." Never could it be said of her, as it could of Jeanie Deans, that she acts "even in the courts of kings, with an ingenuousness and innocence that are only found in the world of pastoral idylls." Having sinned herself, and with one of the community's holy men, she never makes the Naive character's error of forgetting that she has "to do with a depraved world." Her new access to creaturely wisdom and moral sympathy with others is at the expense of her own openness and candor. Thus she is unable to live up to the moral principle which Hawthorne extracts from Dimmesdale's experience: "Be true! Be true! Be true! Show freely to the world, if not your worst, yet some trait whereby the worst may be inferred!" (p. 260). Like *The Heart of Mid-Lothian*, *The Scarlet Letter* is very centrally concerned with what it means to be "true."

To be sure, Hester shows the world her emblem of adultery long after the world would have allowed her to put it aside, and Hawthorne not only has her say that she has been "disciplined to truth" by the letter (p. 173) but himself also says that "In all the seven bygone years, Hester Prynne had never before been false to the symbol on her bosom" (p. 181).

But does it show freely to the world Hester's worst? From the moment she is false to her marriage vows she enters upon a course of systematic suppression of the truth, refusing to reveal her lover's identity to the community or to her husband and agreeing to hide the latter's "true character" (p. 173) from everybody else in Boston. Doubtless she is sincere when, at the moment she at last reveals Chillingworth's identity to Dimmesdale, she says: "In all things else, I have striven to be true! Truth was the one virtue which I might have held fast, and did hold fast through all extremity; save when thy good, – thy life, – thy fame, – were put in question! Then I consented to a deception" (p. 193). But, as she immediately adds, "a lie is never good," and the result of this one – whatever the precise degree of blame which Hester herself must finally bear – is Chillingworth's and possibly Dimmesdale's moral destruction and damnation. In another sense, however, Hester does obey Hawthorne's injunction: "Be true!" For seven joyless years she is true, i.e., constant and loyal, to her child and to its father. In this sense of the word she certainly does much better than Dimmesdale, of whom Pearl truly says: "Thou wast not bold! Thou wast not true!" (p. 157).

Because Dimmesdale is neither bold nor true, Pearl and Hester must look to others to fill the roles of father and husband. Thus the community itself is put on trial. According to kindly Mr. Wilson, "every good Christian man hath a title to show a father's kindness towards the poor, deserted babe" (p. 116). But although Mr. Wilson's doctrine regarding orphans is considerably more hopeful than that of David Deans (who says that "God is the only father of the fatherless" [p. 124]), in practice the elders of this well-regulated community show less of the kindness than of the strictness traditionally associated with fathers. Only an ingenious appeal by Dimmesdale (when threatened by Hester, "Look thou to it!") prevents them from taking Pearl away from her mother. For this deserted babe to find satisfactory surrogate fathers appears as hard as for her deserted mother to find satisfactory substitutes for those who should have been her "natural protectors." By contrast, despite the harsh laws and violent lawlessness which characterize eighteenth-century Scottish society in Scott's portrait, the community responds quickly and hospitably to the needs of orphans and unprotected women. Despite a strong sense of *meum* and *teum* which reaches to family as much as to property, David Deans is "like a father" to fatherless Reuben Butler. In addition to her role as Reuben's protector, Jeanie takes on the part of mother to Effie. So rigid in some ways, she is a model of plastic adaptability to the needs of her loved ones.

And in this respect she also epitomizes her nation: for on her pilgrimage to the Queen, Scottish people from lowly tavern-keepers to the patriarchal Duke of Argyle extend a family's shelter and support simply because she is their countrywoman in need. Scott defends "this national partiality" on the grounds that, as "an additional tie, binding man to man, and calling forth the good offices of such as can render them to the countryman who happens to need them, we think it must be found to exceed, as an active and efficient motive to generosity, that more impartial and wider principle of general benevolence, which we have sometimes seen pleaded as an excuse for assisting no individual whatever" (p. 417). In *The Scarlet Letter*, we observe the sinister side of the principle of national partiality in operation: intuiting a foreign presence in their new *patria*, the Puritans reject Hester and Pearl just as, in Hawthorne's first significant work, "The Gentle Boy," they turn away the Quaker mother and the fatherless son of God, Ilbrahim.

4

During the present century women have broken the male hegemony over historical romance. Margaret Mitchell's *Gone with the Wind* is the most famous and best-selling twentieth-century American historical romance. Wharton's *The Age of Innocence* has a claim as strong as Faulkner's *Absalom, Absalom!* to be the greatest. Measured by her total *oeuvre* rather than by any single work, Cather may well be the preeminent American historical romancer-novelist of our century. And there are other women fictionalists whose best historical romances are little inferior to those of Wharton and Cather. Ellen Glasgow, Esther Forbes, Elizabeth Madox Roberts, and Janet Lewis belong in this group.

I do not mean to suggest that men simply or suddenly abandoned the field of historical romance to the "opposite" sex. Allen Tate and Robert Penn Warren are among the distinguished twentieth-century male writers besides Faulkner who have responded to the powerful appeal of the traditional matters of the frontier and the Civil War. More recently, historical fictions by native-American and black-American writers of both sexes – e.g. Forrest Carter's *Watch for Me on the Mountain* and Ernest Gaines's *The Autobiography of Miss Jane Pittman* – have ensured that those matters can never look quite the same again. The cases of Carter and Gaines suggest that the shifts which have occurred in the authorship of fiction in America should not be seen as startling reversals but rather as aspects of an overall equalization of performance which follows from the gradual equalization of educational and professional opportunities. Still, social progress by itself cannot adequately explain why (if I am correct in believing that) a higher percentage of gifted women writers than of comparably gifted men writers devoted themselves to the historical romance during the early decades of this century.

A second explanation seems to be that after the Civil War writers and readers began to feel differently about the *gender* of historical romance. Although great historical romances continued to be written during the later nineteenth century, e.g., by Robert Louis Stevenson, the genre came increasingly to be associated with escapist adventure stories and an adolescent readership. The greatest American fictionalist and literary theorist of the period, Henry James, loved, championed, and learned from Hawthorne and Stevenson; but he also saw them as charmingly archaic, and not altogether unlike one of his own American innocents in Europe, when measured against Balzac, Flaubert, and Zola. The French models of James, William Dean Howells, and Frank Norris were accessible but less useful to the rising generation of women fictionalists, because a host of taboos continued to bar women from experiencing or writing about much of the matter of contemporary realistic fiction. Wharton and Cather might write their own very powerful, and yet also very reticent, versions of *Madame Bovary* in *The House of Mirth* and *O Pioneers!*, but it seems obvious that social restraints on experience and expression dragged harder on them than on their male contemporaries. Of course many of them, including Wharton, did work extensively and profitably in the vein of contemporary realism; but historical fiction, especially because of the preoccupation with gender roles and character-istics which Scott gave it from the outset, offered patent opportunities and advantages.

However, rather than belabor a case which is perhaps self-evident, I will merely illustrate it briefly with two symptomatic instances of authorial characterization in the fiction of the period. My first instance, Hank Morgan's beloved compulsive talker and fantasist Alisande (*alias* Sandy) la Carteloise in *A Connecticut Yankee at King Arthur's Court* (1889), is a portrait of the historical romancer as a young woman which contrasts her green inexperience and willful anti-empiricism with Hank's practical wisdom and lucidity. Of course Sandy's male Camelot contemporaries also exhibit quixotic traits to some degree, but she so epitomizes this aspect of Arthurian civilization as to turn a division of genres into a division of genders. Such a division is quite consistent with Mark Twain's satirical critiques of Scott and Cooper as absurdly out of touch with social reality, and his "Victorian" views on the proper roles of middle-class women as uncontaminable mothers superior and literary censors – precisely the roles which Olivia Clemens had in his own household. The saving irony of the book is that, notwithstanding Hank Morgan's Enlightenment perspective on "superstition" and romance, both author and narrator come increasingly under the Camelot spell and therefore increasingly delight, as Sandy does, in invention for extrava-gant invention's sake. Finally separated from Sandy by the unbridgeable chasm of centuries, the bereft Yankee dwindles to silence and death – a conclusion whose implied verdict on the life-sustaining importance of, and inextricable relationships between, imagination, female, and romance Mark Twain cannot have originally intended to deliver.

My second and later instance, Sherwood Anderson's apprentice newshound George Willard in *Winesburg, Ohio* (1919), is a portrait of the American fictionalist as a young man which is truly representative of an age that counted many investigative newspaper reporters among its leading male fictionalists and which tended to regard the vast Naturalistic novel of Zola – himself a journalist of genius – as the modern epic form. Although the best of them, including Anderson, were little more concerned to achieve "realism" in a merely reportorial sense than Henry James had been, they placed an extraordinarily high valuation on firsthand observation. In this connection, it is significant that another representative figure in Anderson's Book of Grotesques, George Willard's culturally and sexually starved mentor, schoolteacher Kate Swift, is denied the young journalist's chance to leave Winesburg.

If we turn from fiction to biography, an instructive contrast can be drawn between Cather and Ernest Hemingway, writers of comparable talent and seriousness who began their careers as journalists and held remarkably similar views about the art of fiction but employed their tip-of-the-iceberg method to very dissimilar ends.[19] After a brief experience of reporting, Cather worked her way up the editorial ladder, whereas Hemingway, who loathed editorial work, reverted to the role of field correspondent from time to time long after he became a successful novelist. Similar contrasts appear in their fictional presentations of life. In particular, although sexual passion and its consequences are just as important in her work as in his, she generally deals with sexual encounters obliquely or metonymically – so tactfully at times, as in the account of Jim and Lena's affair in *My Ántonia,* that we cannot be sure whether consummation actually occurs. No doubt she might have been less shy if she had been born in 1899 as Hemingway was rather than 1874, but the difference surely has as much to do with gender as with generation.

Although the exemplary instances I have cited can prove nothing, they may help us to understand why, if Hawthorne had been transported in imagination to the mid-twentieth century as he arranged for Dimmesdale to be transported to the mid-nineteenth, he would have confronted the irony that as often as not his most distinguished successors have belonged to "a d————d mob of scribbling women." What is more, he would have discovered that one of their favorite books was *The Scarlet Letter.*[20] A wanderer all his life and yet as true to the domestic hearth as man or woman could be, Hawthorne felt and gave paradigmatic expression to the conflicting drives to nest and to migrate, to remember and to forget, which our greatest women historical romancers have also felt. In his portrait of Dimmesdale, moreover, he created an American version of the Sentimental (and Sensible) male protagonist whose weaknesses and strengths rang true to the experience of women whose own professional careers brought them into conflict with traditional gender-role expectations and made them unusually sensitive to the frequent failures of men to live up to *their* assigned parts in society, including their familial responsibilities as husbands and fathers. In the remaining pages of this chapter I will discuss two great historical romances authored by American women which develop the themes and insights of *The Scarlet Letter* in ways which surely would have both pleased and disturbed its author.

I have chosen to write about *My Ántonia* and *The Age of Innocence* rather than about some of the other fine and more recent works which belong to the tradition I have been tracing – Janet Lewis's *The Invasion* (1930) is one, Toni Morrison's *Sula* (1973) is another – because I believe that Cather and Wharton were the first American women to write fiction which measures up to the highest international standards, and that, despite many intelligent appreciations of their achievements, they are still undervalued by the literary-critical community. Introducing *Edith Wharton: A Biography*, R. W. B. Lewis "wondered, with other admirers of her work, whether her reputation might today stand even higher if she had been a man" (p. xiii). Who can say? Who, at least in this case, can disentangle sexist bias from literary fashion and social-class prejudice? When *The Age of Innocence* was awarded the Pulitzer Prize in 1921, two of the judges, Stuart P. Sherman and Robert Morss Lovett, announced that their own votes had been in favor of Sinclair Lewis's *Main Street*.[21] It is difficult today to understand how anybody ever supposed that *Main Street* was a better novel than *The Age of Innocence*. But the better part of valor is probably not to try to scrutinize Sherman's and Lovett's motives, but rather to rejoice that, after all, other members of the committee were able to recognize a masterpiece and vote accordingly. For my own part, I suspect that Wharton's and Cather's reputations would stand higher today if only they had more crudely, more instantly, satisfied *or* rejected our century's prevailing political and literary demands to "Make it New." As a matter of fact, they were considerable innovators both as artists and feminists; but, like their admirable heroines, they stood a little apart and declined to don the uniform of any movement.

One of the ways that Cather creates variety, parallel, and counterpoint in her novels is by the lavish use of inset stories ranging in length from a few sentences to tens of thousands of words. *The Professor's House* contains the longest and probably best known of these tales, "Tom

Outland's Story," but none of her works is more richly diversified with them that *My Ántonia*. Nearly every notable visitor to Black Hawk and every immigrant group on the nearby prairies comes with a story redolent of another *patria*: of Bohemian forests, of a Louisiana plantation, of a Colorado silver mine – of a host of strange ways and places that become part of narrator Jim Burden's well-remembered Nebraska. The most haunting, certainly the most archetypal, of these inset stories concerns the Russians Peter and Pavel, outcasts from their native land who once on a winter's night returning home with a wedding party on sledges, saved themselves from imminent death by throwing the bride and bridegroom to pursuing wolves. The story of "the two men who had fed the bride to the wolves" follows them from place to place, and when they seem at last to have escaped it Pavel feels compelled like an Ancient Mariner to tell the story himself. Indeed, this compulsion, like the ostracism which follows them, becomes part of their story: only in death are they able to escape the wolves.

The retelling of this strange tale of Russia on a wintery night in the familiar setting of Nebraska has the metaphorical effect of making the familiar place strange and the strange place familiar. It is also one (and perhaps the most Hawthornean) of many emblematic acts or objects in the book which make the past present and the present past. The story thus epitomizes much that this great historical romance says about place and time. It likewise epitomizes, albeit with extraordinary violence, the many failures of Cather's men to be strong in defense of their women and children.

Unable to cope with the harsh and lonely life on the treeless frontier, Ántonia's gentle and cultivated father commits suicide. His grave, on which the red prairie grass survives long after it has been plowed under everywhere else, becomes the community's principal memorial to the sacrifices exacted of the pioneer generation. After Mr. Shimerda's death, Ántonia is exploited by a series of "strong" men: by her selfish and unfeeling elder brother Ambrosch, who forces her to labor in the fields like a man; by the usurer Wick Cutter, who tries to rape her; and by the railroad conductor Larry Donovan, who promises to marry her but soon deserts her and their illegitimate child. Fatherless, foreign, and female, she is exceptionally vulnerable but also exceptionally strong in her character and commitment to life, and so she does not go the way of Mr. Shimerda or the several other suicides in the novel. Her story turns out to be not the tragic exemplum of female victimization it might easily and Naturalistically have been but rather an almost hagiographical legend of matriarchal triumph concluding with Ántonia in charge of her own life, her own prosperous farm, and her own abundant family (including an appreciative and dependent husband).[22] Thus described, *My Ántonia* sounds like an upbeat female-chauvinist tract, but anybody who has read the book knows that it is wonderfully sympathetic and evenhanded in its treatment of men as well as women. If the novel concludes with Ántonia emerging from her trials as the ideal matriarch, it opens with a portrait of the ideal patriarch: Jim Burden's grandfather, a man whose wisdom and goodness make him a moral touchstone. If Ántonia's brother Ambrosch is a domestic male bully who makes dependent women his drudges, the reason is not far to seek: their mother, a "strong" woman who so dotes on her firstborn son that she compels the rest of the family, including her husband, to sacrifice their interests for his. To set in the balance against Wick Cutter and Krajiek (a predator on the Shimerdas whom Jim likens to a rattlesnake) are the neighborly Bohemians Jelinek and Cusak and the Burden farm hands Jake and Otto, as vulnerable in their way as young Ántonia in hers:

> I can see them now, exactly as they looked, working about the table in the lamplight: Jake with his heavy features, so rudely moulded that his face seemed, somehow, unfinished; Otto with his half-ear and the savage scar that made his upper lip curl so ferociously under his twisted moustache. As I remember them, what unprotected faces they were; their very roughness and violence made them defenceless. These boys had no practised manner behind which they could retreat and hold people at a distance. They had only their fists to batter at the world with. Otto was already one of those drifting, case-hardened labourers who never marry or have children of their own. Yet he was so fond of children! (pp. 84–5)

That is the true Cather note. What is easily misread as sentimentality is rather moral compassion, the product of a great and rare gift of "negative capability" which enables her to get behind the defenses and to share the viewpoints of an extraordinary range of human types. I believe that no other American fictionalist quite equals Cather in this respect. But Scott does, and that is one reason why *The Heart of Mid-Lothian* manifests, as *The Scarlet Letter* does not, a fictional world on the same generous scale and with a diversity as rich as that of *My Ántonia*.

Cather's fictional world likewise reminds us more of Scott's than of Hawthorne's in that it premises a great deal of plasticity and mobility in human roles and relations. From one perspective, *My Ántonia* is a book about the geographical, economic, and social mobility of Americans; it begins with Jim's and the Shimerdas' journeys to Nebraska and ends with the "arrival" of Ántonia and her friends as middle-aged and, in their different ways and places around the country, successful and respected citizens. It is also a book about the plasticity of gender roles. Three of Ántonia's women friends – Frances Harling, Tiny Soderball, and Lena Lingard – pursue careers which make them independent and, in Tiny's and Lena's cases, highly mobile.

Let us take a closer look at Frances Harling, who in some ways is very
like Cather herself. Although she does not figure as prominently in the
action of the novel as Lena or even Tiny, Frances is drawn with
considerable care as a positive example of what a single woman can
achieve in a traditionally male occupation and male-dominated society.
Tall as a man and bearing the feminine version of a man's name, she is the
oldest Harling child and is obliged to assume the responsibilities in the
family grain-marketing firm which would normally be the right (or
duty) of the eldest son. Unlike most Black Hawk sons, however, she uses
her considerable business power and acumen unselfishly, allying herself
with patriarchal Grandfather Burden in community benefactions:

> Sometimes she came over to see grandfather after supper, and her visits
> flattered him. More than once they put their wits together to rescue some
> unfortunate farmer from the clutches of Wick Cutter, the Black Hawk
> money-lender. Grandfather said Frances Harling was as good a judge of credits
> as any banker in the county. The two or three men who had tried to take
> advantage of her in a deal acquired celebrity by their defeat. She knew every
> farmer for miles about: how much land he had under cultivation, how many
> cattle he was feeding, what his liabilities were. Her interest in these people was
> more than a business interest. She carried them all in her mind as if they were
> characters in a book or a play.
>
> When Frances drove out into the country on business, she would go miles
> out of her way to call on some of the old people, or to see the women who
> seldom got to town. She was quick at understanding the grandmothers who
> spoke no English, and the most reticent and distrustful of them would tell her
> their story without realizing they were doing so. She went to country funerals
> and weddings in all weathers. A farmer's daughter who was to be married
> could count on a wedding present from Frances Harling.   (pp. 150–1)

They could count on a wedding present from her precisely because, free
of the family obligations of a young wife and mother, she is able to make
her neighbors her family. Clearly, her career represents not only a
worthy practical counterpart of that of the literary artist Cather (who sets
down in a book the characters Frances carries in her mind) but also a
worthy nondomestic alternative to that of the matriarch Ántonia. I
should add that Frances, whose "masculine" habits and physique contrast
sharply with Lena's conspicuous "femininity," does eventually marry –
an event which contradicts nothing I have said but simply underscores
this character's and this author's unwillingness to submit to the fates built
into gender stereotypes.

Ántonia has none of Frances's business skills, but as a young woman
she is able to take on "man's work" on the farm because she is physically
and psychologically robust. Here is middle-aged Jim Burden's recollection of how she appeared to him when he was a twelve-year-old boy:

> She kept her sleeves rolled up all day, and her arms and throat were burned as
> brown as a sailor's. Her neck came up strongly out of her shoulders, like the
> bole of a tree out of the turf. One sees that draught-horse neck among the
> peasant women in all old countries. (p. 122)

A sailor, a tree, a draught-horse – these ambivalent analogies are at least
partly celebrative and prepare us for Jim's later, adult vision of Ántonia as
a woman who renaturalizes human nature and puts us back in touch with
the primitive experience of the race:

> She lent herself to immemorial human attitudes which we recognize by
> instinct as universal and true . . . She had only to stand in the orchard, to put her
> hand on a little crab tree and look up at the apples, to make you feel the
> goodness of planting and tending and harvesting at last . . . It was no wonder
> that her sons stood tall and straight. She was a rich mine of life, like the founders
> of early races. (p. 353)

As we have seen, the discovery of such timeless and universal – in a word,
mythic – traits in intensely local and historical contexts is highly, indeed
generically, characteristic of historical romances. But it occurs in other
kinds of fiction as well, and the book most likely to have impressed
Cather with the mythic potential of regional scenes and characters is
Sarah Orne Jewett's *The Country of the Pointed Firs*.

Jewett's Maine folk remind her constantly of prehistorical Greece, of
the Cumaean Sibyl, of Jason and Medea, of the procession on Keats's urn
brought back to perishable and yet eternally recurrent life:

> The plash of the water could be heard faintly, yet still be heard; we might have
> been a company of ancient Greeks going to celebrate a victory, or to worship
> the god of harvests in the grove above . . . The sky, the sea, have watched poor
> humanity at its rites so long; we were no more a New England family
> celebrating its own existence and simple progress; we carried the tokens and
> inheritance of all such households from which this had descended, and were
> only the latest of our line. We possessed the instincts of a far, forgotten
> childhood; I found myself thinking that we ought to be carrying green
> branches and singing as we went.[23]

Cather must have felt that there was also a miracle of reincarnation
involved in her ability to do for Nebraska and its "ordinary" people
what Jewett had done for Maine. The procession in which Ántonia
walked along with the Maine Bowden family in company with ancient
Greeks had appointed places likewise for Cather and Jewett, writers who
like the Virgil of the *Georgics* had brought the muse into their own
countries.

Turning from heroic visions back to quotidian reality, we notice that
the analogies which Jim draws in his description of Ántonia also imply

reservations which say as much about his own boyhood anxieties concerning family and gender as they do about the fifteen-year-old girl. An orphaned only-child and several years younger than Ántonia, Jim resents both her superior "mannish" physical strength and close involvement with her own family. At this point in their lives, she cannot give him what he needs by confirming his masculine identity and providing unfettered companionship. Nor is she able to do so when they move to Black Hawk, since although their friendship is revived and confirmed, their differences of age and education pull them in very different directions.

In his classics teacher, Gaston Cleric, Jim discovers a surrogate father, a mind- and character-shaping figure who draws him to the East Coast. But no woman appears to replace his mother – or Ántonia. Although Jim is reticent about his affair with Lena Lingard in Lincoln and his childless marriage in New York, it seems clear that he never quite finds a mature and independent masculine identity. Returning to the American heartland as a middle-aged man, however, he is at last able to accept Ántonia's generous involvement with others and to take advantage of it by finding a surrogate mother in her and an avuncular role for himself in relation to her children. So much is perhaps obvious to readers accustomed to modern psychological readings of gender and familial relations, but I believe it has not been remarked how perfectly the relationship between Jim and Ántonia recapitulates that between the Sentimental hero and Naive heroine of earlier historical romances.

A few pages back I said that a major reason for the largeness and diversity of the fictional worlds of *My Ántonia* and *The Heart of Mid-Lothian*, as compared with Hawthorne's in *The Scarlet Letter*, was Cather's and Scott's more abundant endowment of "negative capability." Why should we be reluctant to concede with Hawthorne himself that he was, in this respect, as deficient as the great majority of fictionalists, most of whom were also far more deficient than he in moral insight and artistic integrity? To leave it at that, however, would still be unjust to Hawthorne and miss the point of his greatest literary achievement. For – I repeat – a major theme of the book, as of tales like "The May-Pole of Merry Mount" and "The Gentle Boy," is the Puritan's rejection of largeness and diversity in the interests of purity and survival. If Cather's fictional world is an image of plenitude, the reason is partly that late-nineteenth-century Nebraskans were more open to human variety and also less well-organized to exclude it than Hawthorne's Puritans. Still, Cather does not ignore the fact that national and religious prejudices abounded in that society and that the native-born, English-speaking citizens of small-town Nebraska had the same xenophobic feelings that communities always have when their identities, their privileges, and their customs are threatened by an influx of strangers. Book II of *My Ántonia, entitled "The Hired Girls," shows how some of* the descendants of the Puritans discovered the signs of election in qualities denied the daughters of recent immigrants: affluence, female indolence, and "good English."

That his analysis of xenophobic behavior might be applied to later societies is suggested, perhaps unintentionally, by Hawthorne himself in his comments on changing ideals of feminine beauty in America. When Hawthorne first presents Hester to us and to the Puritan crowd waiting for her outside the Boston town jail, he sounds for all the world as if he were reporting a beauty contest:

> The young woman was tall, with a figure of perfect elegance, on a large scale. She had dark and abundant hair, so glossy that it threw off the sunshine with a gleam, and a face which, besides being beautiful from regularity of feature and richness of complexion, had the impressiveness belonging to a marked brow and deep black eyes. She was lady-like, too, after the manner of the feminine gentility of those days; characterized by a certain state and dignity, rather than by the delicate evanescent, and indescribable grace, which is now recognized as its indication. (p. 53)

The heroines of other Hawthorne romances who conform to Hester's "dark" style of beauty, Zenobia and Miriam, are doubly suspect, because they are not only uncommonly beautiful like her "from regularity of feature and richness of complexion," qualities associated with feminine beauty in most periods, but also beautiful after a fashion that has become foreign to the culture. (The name "Zenobia" may include a punning reference to the Greek *xenos*, stranger.)

The same is true of Cather's hired girls – Ántonia, Lena, Tiny, the three Bohemian Marys – who are not European aristocrats *manqués* like Hester but rather magnificent peasants: "Physically they were almost a race apart, and out-of-door work had given them a vigour which, when they got over their first shyness on coming to town, developed into a positive carriage and freedom of movement, and made them conspicuous among Black Hawk women" (p. 198). Black Hawk women, who think of themselves as "refined," still aspire to the "manner of feminine gentility" which was the ideal in 1850. No wonder that

> The country girls were considered a menace to the social order. Their beauty shone out too boldly against a conventional background. But anxious mothers need have felt no alarm. They mistook the mettle of their sons. The respect for respectability was stronger than any desire in Black Hawk youth. (pp. 202–3)

Yet they dally with desire just a little. Using a phrase that echoes down the historical romance tradition, Cather says that a dancing tent in Black Hawk "brought the town boys and the country girls together on neutral ground" (p. 203). However, Waverley-like Jim is the only town boy who risks his good name by regularly and openly consorting with the "wild" country girls rather than with girls of his own set. Frances Harling remarks shrewdly of Jim that "in some ways" he is older than boys of his age but that he puts "a kind of glamour over" the country girls: "The trouble with you, Jim, is that you're romantic" (p. 229).

His "trouble" is also his great strength. It is the romantic in Jim that enables him to penetrate through the superficial blemishes and eccentricities of a middle-aged, turn-of-the-century, Bohemian-American farmwoman to discover "immemorial human attitudes which we recognize by instinct as universal and true." It also vouchsafes him visions, at once alluring and threatening, of Lena as a harvest-field Aphrodite:

> One dream I dreamed a great many times, and it was always the same. I was in a harvest-field full of shocks, and I was lying against one of them. Lena Lingard came across the stubble barefoot, in a short skirt, with a curved reaping-hook in her hand, and she was flushed like the dawn, with a kind of luminous rosiness all about her. She sat down beside me, turned to me with a soft sigh and said, "Now they are all gone, and I can kiss you as much as I like." (pp. 225–6)

On the one hand, Jim's "vision" is no more than an adolescent sexual dream. On the other, Homer's and Virgil's Aphrodite is also "flushed like the dawn, with a kind of luminous rosiness all about her," and after Lena's first visit to the young scholar in Lincoln Jim sees the connection:

> When I closed my eyes I could hear them all laughing – the Danish laundry girls and the three Bohemian Marys. Lena had brought them all back to me. It came over me, as it had never done before, the relation between girls like those and the poetry of Virgil. If there were no girls like them in the world, there would be no poetry.   (p. 270)

This "revelation" soon reminds Jim of his dreams of Lena in a short skirt, but although Cather is gently satirizing the young scholar's distractable state of mind she is likewise recalling ancient doctrine concerning the relation between *eros* and poetry. How does this doctrine apply to Cather's novel? We do not think of My Ántonia as a "love story," and of course it is not one in the way that *The Age of Innocence* so movingly and frustratingly is. But Book II, "The Hired Girls," affirms the power of *eros* to create and destroy; it shows that the country girls are indeed "a menace to the social order" and also goes some way towards validating the claim that if there were no girls like them in the world, there would be no poetry. Cather believed this as earnestly as any medieval troubadour, but she also believed that to write that poetry a person might have to sublimate her sexual drives or find some expression for them outside a conjugal relationship.

The anxieties of Black Hawk mothers are shared by the New York matrons of *The Age of Innocence*, and I believe that Cather and Wharton both profited from Hawthorne's example when they wrote about the quite different varieties of American beauty and "exclusiveness" which they had personally observed as young women. That they had anything in common besides their nationality, gender, and literary talent and vocation is somewhat surprising, since in other respects the disparity between them was as wide as it is obvious today. Cather (1873–1947) was just young and obscure enough at the time that Wharton (1862–1937) enjoyed her first great publishing success, with *The House of Mirth* in 1905, that she thought of Wharton as a contemporary and peer of James. Recalling the state of American fiction at the time she wrote her own first masterpiece, *O Pioneers!* (1913), she explains that she was obliged to ignore "all the situations and accents that were then generally thought to be necessary . . . Henry James and Mrs. Wharton were our most interesting novelists, and most of the younger writers followed their manner, without having their qualifications."[24]

Although Cather and Wharton agreed in their admiration for James and Hawthorne, it is inconceivable that, if asked to name three American books "which have the possibility of a long, long life," Wharton would have followed up *The Scarlet Letter*, as Cather did, with *"Huckleberry Finn*, and *The Country of the Pointed Firs*. I can think of no others that confront time and change so serenely."[25] Nor is it conceivable that she would have turned for critical maxims, as Cather did throughout her career, to Robert Louis Stevenson.[26] Whereas Cather in her mature fiction aimed for the "significant simplicity" extolled by Stevenson and the seemingly artless intimacy with "ordinary life" achieved by Jewett, Wharton's greatest fiction, like James's and Hawthorne's, is conspicuously "made" and charged with ironic complexity. Of course there is irony in *My Ántonia*, too, and considerably more of it in post-war novels like *A Lost Lady* and *My Mortal Enemy*; but one can, as I just have, write at some length about her fiction without having occasion to use the word "irony" once. It is hard to imagine writing as many pages about *The Age of Innocence* without referring to ironic incongruities, ironic deflations, or ironic reversals.

Rather than stress what Wharton does not share with Cather, however, I want to begin my discussion of *The Age of Innocence* by identifying the common ground between it and *My Ántonia*. The most obvious resemblance is between their Sentimental heroes, Jim Burden and Newland Archer. Like Jim's, Newland's travels and reading have familiarized him with alien standards; they have even led to contacts outside the circle where New Yorkers of his social class normally move. He is therefore an acute though silent critic of that circle; at the same time, he has internalized so many of its standards that he is more deeply confused than Jim Burden about what he most values, what he most desires from life. His is, therefore, a much more advanced stage of Sentimentality. His fiancée, May Welland, shrewdly intuits that Archer wants to "behave like people in novels."[27] And that is the way he does behave – like people in novels rather than like heroes in romances – for his projections of passionate assignations and elopements with the dark heroine, Ellen Olenska, come to no more than Waverley's dreams of military glory. Because he does not know his own mind and yet is perceptive enough to recognize that something is missing from his life which May cannot supply, he creates disappointment and heartache not only for himself but also for the two women who depend on him.

Since other characters in the novel are registered chiefly through Archer's consciousness, it is difficult to judge where his fantasy of May and Ellen ends and where their actuality begins, how far they fit and how far his imagination makes them conform to the light and dark heroine pattern. May he repeatedly sees as "Diana-like," hence virginal by nature, "primitive and pure" but with a "classic grace" (pp. 189, 193, 210, 306). Is she cool like the moon or a Greek statue only because she kindles no lust in him? To her, during their engagement, he gives a daily gift of dewy lilies of the valley; to Ellen he sends yellow roses – "sun-golden" rather than moon-silver:

> his first impulse was to send them to May instead of the lilies. But they did not look like her – there was something too rich, too strong, in their fiery beauty.   (p. 80)

Incorrigible subjective reshaper of reality, Archer deifies persons as readily as he personifies flowers.

Is Ellen's beauty "rich," "strong," and "fiery" in anybody's eyes except those of erotically aroused Newland Archer? As their unconsummated affair develops, her beauty comes to seem increasingly wan and haggard rather than sun-golden. On the other hand, we know that it appeals (as May's does not) to the experienced sensualist Julius Beaufort, a somewhat shady "outsider" whose business and amatory dealings are equally dubious. A judge less expert but with sound instincts, Newland's mother, scents trouble in Ellen and, half-consciously associating her with several "fast" women, reflects that, since "young men are so foolish and incalculable – and some women so ensnaring and unscrupulous . . . it was nothing short of a miracle to see one's only son safe past the Siren Isle and in the haven of a blameless domesticity" (pp. 37–8).

Whether or not Ellen's beauty is a menace to the social order, there is at least ample evidence that she strikes everybody as "foreign." As a child, her "dusky red cheeks" and dress of crimson merino with amber beads remind New Yorkers of a gipsy foundling – the more so because she is in fact an orphan and in the charge of a wandering eccentric aunt. Raised and disastrously married abroad, she has acquired a cultivation as well as a bruised knowledge of "life" altogether beyond the range of her New York friends and relatives. She cannot help being "different." In Newland Archer's eyes, being different after Ellen's fashion means being superior. He is fascinated by the "abominations" and "temptations" he supposes her to have experienced in the European Heart of Darkness (p. 243), and he takes "a secret pride in his own picture of her" as someone who "doesn't care a hang about where she lives – or about any of our little social sign-posts" (p. 123). They will pay a high price for this superior in*difference*.

When she returns "home" to New York as an adult, separated but undivorced from her brutal husband, Ellen wants "to cast off all my old life, to become just like everybody else here" (p. 108). That she imagines such a repatriation desirable and possible points to traits which are invisible to Archer and in conflict with his image of her. For all that she has "had to look at the Gorgon" (p. 288) – her figure for the traumatic experiences she has suffered in Europe – she is the least worldly, the most Naive, character in the book. If she "doesn't care a hang about where she lives," it is because she has no sense of American social geography and yet is American enough to suppose, like Daisy Miller, that the purity of her intentions will be granted by all people of good will (meaning everybody she knows in New York) and that she can therefore simply "be herself."

And at first she is not mistaken in her trust. When she returns, she is perceived still to have an orphan's claim to a father's kindness and protection from the community. Like the Scots who come to the aid of orphan Reuben Butler and vulnerable Jeanie Deans, the New Yorkers do rally around their kinswoman. But despite good intentions on both sides, she is hopelessly out of place because of her status as an attractive but unmarriageable young woman. Perhaps she could survive if she were capable of practicing hypocrisy, as do, among others, the unscrupulous Beaufort and Lawrence Lefferts, the fatuous and hypocritical womanizer who envisages, as the worst possible event, a time when "we shall see our children . . . marrying Beaufort's bastards" (p. 338). But Naive Ellen simply cannot read the local "little social sign-posts." She should not dress as she does; live where she does; entertain married men like Beaufort and Archer as she does. Her gifts of relaxed social intercourse and graceful conversance with the arts and manners of Europe are badly needed by a neurotically "tasteful" provincial society in whose drawing rooms books are thought to be "out of place" (p. 104). But they are gifts which, coming from such a compromised and compromising source, cannot be accepted, and so she must be gently but inexorably "eliminated from the tribe" (p. 334). Writing as an expatriate and veteran observer of New York manners, Edith Wharton is at her most deft and telling when she explicates the meaning of the seating arrangements at May's farewell dinner for dear cousin Ellen:

> It was only at an entertainment ostensibly offered to a "foreign visitor" that Mrs. van der Luyden could suffer the diminution of being placed on her host's left. The fact of Madame Olenska's "foreignness" could hardly have been more adroitly emphasized than by this farewell tribute.   (p. 334)

So, like Hawthorne's Pearl, Wharton's Ellen sets sail for Europe and takes with her something that might and should have been cherished by others besides Newland Archer.

Of course it is not *New York* that rejects her, but only its most "select" set.'By living where she does and consorting with questionable people like writers and musicians, Ellen begins to build a frail bridge between New York's aristocracy and its artistic bohemia and, beyond that, its teeming, threatening multitudes of American and foreign immigrants – the people who fill Willa Cather's pages with such energy and variety. Newland's mother recalls a time when "society" had included writers, "gentlemen" like Washington Irving and Fitz-Greene Halleck: "perhaps the unknown persons who succeeded them had gentlemanly sentiments, but their origin, their appearance, their hair, their intimacy with the stage and Opera, made any old New York criterion inapplicable to them" (p. 102). We cannot suppose that Mrs. Archer has Whitman specifically in mind, but Mrs. Wharton (who shared Henry James's love of *Leaves of Grass*) surely does. So remote from such hairy amative people, so "choice" is the society in which May, Newland, and Ellen move that its acknowledged leaders, the van der Luydens, make exclusiveness and reclusiveness synonymous by spending most of their time in a Hudson River retreat. Decent and loyal after its fashion, but narrow, effete, and functionless, this elite inner circle within New York society makes the "exclusive" society of Hawthorne's seventeenth-century Boston seem open and hospitable as well as vigorous and purposeful.

Archer survives his loss and goes on to lead a useful and not unhappy life; Ellen also survives and, we gather, makes a rewarding life for herself in Paris. Since both are survivors and Archer is, as well, a fantasist whose schemes for trysts and confessions are invariably and almost comically frustrated, it might appear that Wharton punctures their romantic balloon beyond hope either of rescue or tears. Despite and perhaps partly because of these deflationary developments, however, their love story is one of the most moving in American literature. One reason why it is so moving is that they really do seem to be soul-mates, equally adrift between cultures and doomed to remain so. Another is that Archer has the virtues as well as the vices of a "romantic" temperament.[28] Like Waverley and other Sentimental protagonists, he is able, as most of his fellow citizens are not, to imagine something finer and greater in life than it has been his lot to encounter; and when he does encounter it in Ellen he is able to recognize its worth. Whether or not Ellen is sun-golden, she is a character whose plight – capped as it is by her hopeless love for Archer – engages our own and the author's sympathies. She is the only character in the book, including even the formidable but generally sympathetic matriarch Catherine (the Great) Mingott, who entirely escapes the lash of Wharton's irony.

The scene in *The Age of Innocence* which is at once most and least "romantic" is Ellen and Newland's last meeting alone, in the Cesnola gallery of the Metropolitan Museum:

> His mind, as always when they first met, was wholly absorbed in the delicious details that made her herself and no other. Presently he rose and approached the case before which she stood. Its glass shelves were crowded with small broken objects – hardly recognizable domestic utensils, ornaments and personal trifles – made of glass, of clay, of discolored bronze and other time-blurred substances.
>
> "It seems cruel," she said, "that after a while nothing matters . . . any more than these little things, that used to be necessary and important to forgotten people, and now have to be guessed at under a magnifying glass and labeled: 'Use unknown.'"
>
> "Yes; but meanwhile – "
>
> "Ah, meanwhile – " (pp. 309–10)

They are gazing at "the recovered fragments of Ilium." The ironic perspective which this scene opens up on the unhappy lovers seems, at first sight, so desolate and diminishing that we cannot possibly view them as other than brazen figures in a brazen world. Certainly Newland Archer is no Paris, Wharton's genteel Gilded Age New York neither Achaia nor Ilium. But suddenly we recognize that, for all that she is "herself and no other," in this novel where every character's name is charged with significance Ellen *is* Helen – "meanwhile." Or so Wharton implies, compounding betwixt the romancer's faith and novelistic incredulity.

This unanticipated glimpse of Ellen as a character who comes to Archer and to us from the timeless, spacious world of epic has the extraordinary effect of tempering the ironies that lash, or at least play wickedly around, nearly all the characters and institutions depicted in *The Age of Innocence*. They are further tempered, while also being multiplied, by the last chapter of the novel where, miming the conclusion of Flaubert's *L'Education Sentimentale*, Wharton returns to her characters at a date much later than that of the main action. In this chapter, some of the main characters and actions of the main narrative are recapitulated in a new key.

At the age of fifty-seven, Archer reflects on the successes and failures of his life, on the strengths and blindspots of his recently deceased wife, and on the good and bad points of the past as compared with the present. With his beloved son Dallas, who is engaged to Julius Beaufort's daughter Fanny, Archer visits Paris where Ellen Olenska still lives. When Dallas creates the opportunity for his father to meet Ellen again after a space of nearly thirty years, Archer considers the possibility longingly but, in the end, sends his son in his place and walks "back alone to his hotel" (p. 361). This disappointing non-event looks like a repetition of earlier projected trysts which came to nothing, and Archer's failure to seize his opportunity when there are no longer any moral or social impediments can be taken as proof that, inveterate Wertherian romantic, he was always more in love with his image of Ellen than with Ellen herself and that, had there been no impediments, there would have been no passion. This reading may be right as far as it goes, and in any case it cannot be effectively disputed without a more thorough examination than I can give it here. However, it is possible to point to a few developments in the concluding chapter which argue for a more sympathetic view of Archer.

Like other examples of the genre, *The Age of Innocence* reveals the timeless in the temporal, the romance in the historical: in this instance, the eternal Helen in Ellen Olenska. Since our seeing Ellen in this light depends not on Archer's inflamed imagination but rather on Wharton's adroit juxtapositions, I think we may take this visitation from the wonder-world as confirming the value and significance of this particular "love story." Yet the story would not have the meaning and poignance it has except for the lesson of transience, hence of the need to adapt to change, conveyed by the "time-blurred substances" labeled: "Use unknown." We have no way of knowing how well Ellen heeds this lesson after her departure from New York. But if Archer's appraisal of his wife can be trusted at all, May has ignored it entirely. By the time of her recent death, Archer reflects, "the world of her youth had fallen into pieces and rebuilt itself without her ever being conscious of the change . . . Her incapacity to recognize change made her children conceal their views from her as Archer concealed his" (p. 348). Whatever his defects as a husband and lover, Archer clearly does recognize and, up to a point, welcome change. To be sure, he belongs to his own generation and has feelings which Dallas, in his generation, cannot understand. But Archer cherishes the companionship of his frank, up-to-date son, and is even pleased that Dallas is going to marry (thus ironically fulfilling Lawrence Lefferts's gloomy prophecy) one of "Beaufort's bastards."

On his side, Dallas is an affectionate and sensitive son who is able to catch a glimpse of Archer's secret life and even to teach him something worth knowing about the eternal return. He asks his father whether Ellen wasn't "most awfully lovely":

> "Lovely? I don't know. She was different."
>
> "Ah – there you have it! That's what it always comes to, doesn't it? When she comes, *she's different* – and one doesn't know why. It's exactly what I feel about Fanny."
>
> His father drew back a step, releasing his arm. "About Fanny? But, my dear fellow – I should hope so! Only I don't see – "
>
> "Dash it, Dad, don't be prehistoric. Wasn't she – once – your Fanny?"
>
> (p. 355)

Orphaned early in life and befriended as a schoolgirl in Paris by Ellen herself, Fanny is a kind of reincarnation of the "different" woman Archer loved nearly three decades earlier. And so, for all his differences of style and temperament, is Dallas a reincarnation of Newland Archer as a young man. (People say that "his boy 'took after him' " [p. 361].) This is why, instructed by his son's question, Archer does not go to Ellen but has Dallas go in his stead. In sending this bright image of his former self, he not only preserves his memory of Ellen in her beauty but also, generously, preserves her memory of him. No doubt there are other reasons as well, viz., that Dallas, the child whose conception put an end to the affair, is "the pride of his life" (p. 252) and represents the good that Archer has been able to make of that life since Ellen's departure. Thus, while doubtless still believing that he has missed "the flower of life" (p. 347), he yet affirms the value of what he has had. With its note of almost Pirandelloesque compassion and its unwillingness to come down unambiguously on the side of realism or romance, the temporal or the timeless, the near or the strange, this scene supplies a supremely fitting conclusion to a book which reprises so many of the themes, situations, and character-types that belong to historical romance.

8

The historical romance of the South

1. Was Scott responsible for the American Civil War?

> Sir Walter had so large a hand in making Southern character, as it existed before the war, that he is in great measure responsible for the war. It seems a little harsh toward a dead man to say that we never should have had any war but for Sir Walter; and yet something of a plausible argument might, perhaps, be made in support of that wild proposition. The Southerner of the American revolution owned slaves; so did the Southerner of the Civil War; but the former resembles the latter as an Englishman resembles a Frenchman. The change of character can be traced rather more easily to Sir Walter's influence than to that of any other thing or person.[1]

Mark Twain's "wild proposition" has a certain plausibility and attractiveness. For to pin the blame for the war on Scott's "enchantments" is to make an ambitious claim for the power and importance of literature. I am going to argue in favor of a somewhat more modest version of this claim later on, but it must be said at the outset that of course Mark Twain's proposition *is* wild.[2] Many factors, both literary and non-literary, contributed to the formation of Southern character and to the act of secession which brought on the war. With the non-literary factors I cannot be much concerned here; I trust that anybody who takes the trouble to read this book will be at least broadly familiar with the socio-political contexts of the Southern historical romances which are my primary concern. On the other hand, to make sense of Mark Twain's proposition, let alone to formulate a useable counter-proposition, I will be obliged to construe "literary" broadly and to make further use of Allen Tate's helpful concept of a "lower myth." Just as the Puritans had their lower myth of the Old Testament Hebrews, so the settlers of the Southern colonies had their myth – or, rather, myths; for "the South" has always been a conglomeration of diverse peoples, topographies,

272

climates, economies, and religions, and therefore has always needed a variety of myths to live by, some of which were bound to come into conflict with each other as well as with the myths of "the North."

Now, it is obvious that the Southern character was not simply frozen in plaster during the years between the Revolution and the Civil War, but that the changes were even remotely as great as Mark Twain alleges would have been vehemently disputed by the Southerners who fought in the second of America's major fratricidal wars. When the Confederate states at last seceded, their leaders composed a new Constitution which began:

> We, the people of the Confederate States, each State acting in its sovereign and independent character, in order to form a permanent federal government, establish justice, insure domestic tranquillity . . .[3]

This preamble of 1861 avoids the word "union" and highlights the doctrine of state sovereignty, but it also pointedly echoes the original phrasing of 1789. Jefferson Davis's Inaugural Address likewise mimes Thomas Jefferson's First Inaugural and invokes the language and principles of the Declaration of Independence. The reason for this elaborate display of filial piety was not that men like Davis and his vice president, Alexander Stephens, lacked words and ideas of their own or borrowed them only as a rhetorical ploy designed to create the appearance of continuity and legality for their new government. The hall in Montgomery, Alabama, where the Confederacy was born was a theater as well as a political forum, and the founding fathers of the Confederate States of America thought of themselves as reenacting the parts not of Ivanhoe and Robin Hood but rather of General Washington and Mr. Jefferson, General Marion and Mr. Madison.

Still, the Confederate leaders are unlikely to have had only one heroic model in mind. During the course of their history Southerners have identified with, have sought to interpret themselves and their predicaments by discovering parallels with, many characters and conflicts out of history books, oral legends, and romances. The character of the American rebel against British tyranny and usurpation was easily reconciled and conflated with the character of Scott's chivalrous rebel against King John, and both have points in common with a character which, if it did not absolutely possess the Southern imagination, certainly buttressed and appealed to its deepest prejudices and loftiest aspirations. I refer, of course to the character of the "Cavalier" which William R. Taylor elucidates so well in *Cavalier and Yankee: The Old South and American National Character* (1961).[4] Taylor is required reading for anybody who wishes to understand the relationship between antebellum Southern politics and literature – especially the historical romances of Caruthers, Kennedy, and Simms – and I will not attempt to summarize the findings of his rich and complex book. However, a few reminders and comments are in order.

First, the historical romancers he discusses are more interesting and important figures from his perspective than they are from mine: for although they undoubtedly helped to create and sustain the myths by which the Old South lived and eventually perished, their best work is clearly inferior to that of Cooper, Hawthorne, and Melville, and also to that of later Southern fictionalists. Second, as Taylor himself emphasizes, the Yankee/Cavalier opposition was believed in both north and south of the Mason-Dixon line, and it was widely attractive at least partly because it transposed internal social-class tensions and hostilities which afflicted both the North and the South into conveniently external sectional terms. (The North was not so democratic nor the South nearly so aristocratic in its social forms and distribution of political power as residents of the other section wanted to believe.) A third point is that although Taylor's subtitle accurately indicates his emphasis on Southern sources and experience, his main title conveys what I consider the most crucial point about his subject: that, whatever their mimetic relationship to social reality may have been, the "Cavalier" and "Yankee" characters were inextricably linked as polar opposites which existed both despite and because of each other and which had a profound and enduring appeal to writers and readers because they simplified, organized, and moralized matters which even today appear bewilderingly complicated and ambiguous.

With the origin of this polarity Taylor is not much concerned, but we should recall that it is antecedent to Scott, to the American Revolution, to the beginning of slavery in the British colonies, and even to the establishment of the colonies themselves. The Yankee and Cavalier characters are largely secularized versions of Puritan and Cavalier types which developed in British literature and popular iconography during the course of the social and religious conflicts of the sixteenth, seventeenth, and eighteenth centuries. When Hawthorne has John Endicott order his "Roundhead" followers to crop the Lord of the May's love-lock and long glossy curls, "and that in the true pumpkin-shell fashion," he reminds us of the − in effect − official uniforms which members of the hostile factions in seventeenth-century Britain and America were expected to don in order to identify themselves to friends and give affront to opponents. These value-charged externals of dress and hair style constituted a language as fetishistic and inflammatory as the hippy costume and crew cut have been in recent times, and because they were not only easily hated but also easily copied, in actual cloth as well as in portrait paintings and funeral statuary, they were powerful transmitters of the Puritan/Cavalier antinomy from generation to generation. Their influence was reinforced by the images of artistic literature. I have already mentioned the long series of masterly caricatures of Puritans and Puritanism, from Malvolio to Burns's Holy Willie, which their opponents had drawn well before Scott created the wonderfully eloquent, courageous, and bigoted Covenanters of *Old Mortality* and *The Heart of Mid-Lothian*. But we must not forget that myth-making Puritan writers countered the high and low forms of pro-Stuart propaganda with a thousand images of Cavalier libertinism, papistry, atheism, luxury, frivolity, cynicism, francophilia, etc. A master-image of the Cavalier stands behind and in turn is magnified by the great villains, Satan and Lovelace, of the two greatest works of seventeenth- and eighteenth-century English narrative fiction. Hawthorne's descriptions of Governor Andros in "The Gray Champion" and Thomas Morton in "Main Street" have a long, long history behind them.

Preserved and reinforced not only by the conservative reading habits consequent upon America's remoteness from the cultural capitals of Europe but also by powerful regional auxiliaries, Puritan/Cavalier factionalism was bound to linger on in provincial America both as an actual continuation of ancient religious and political conflicts and as a fiction whereby to interpret and judge new ones. This being so, Americans who were not backward and provincial but, on the contrary, ahead of their time and comparatively free of sectional prejudice themselves had to reckon with and make use of the polarity when they tried to understand their countrymen's behavior. In 1785, looking back on America from the vantage point of Paris, Thomas Jefferson agreed with his philosophical friend the Chevalier de Chastellux that Southerners were "aristocratical, pompous, clannish, indolent, hospitable."[5] Then, warming to the subject, he drew up two lists to give his "idea of the characters of the several states":

in the North they are	*in the South they are*
cool	fiery
sober	voluptuary
laborious	indolent
persevering	unsteady
independent	independent
jealous of their own liberties, just to those of others	zealous of their own liberties, but trampling on those of others
interested	generous
chicaning	candid
superstitious and hypocritical in their religion	without attachment or pretentions to any religion but that of the heart

Evidently the enchantments which Mark Twain attributed to the Wizard of the North had bewitched the American South thirty years or more before the Waverley novels began to appear.

The eclectic product of shrewd observation, mild regional astigma-
tism, traditional Puritan and Cavalier typology, stadialist abstraction,
and the dichotomizing process itself, Jefferson's characters of the
Northerner and Southerner strikingly resemble some of the opposed
characters, notably the chief protagonists of *Goetz von Berlichingen*, who
were Scott's models.[6] "Influence" as such is not in question here. It is
highly unlikely that Jefferson knew Goethe's play or that Scott knew
Jefferson's letter to Chastellux. But because Jefferson was a cosmopolitan
thinker as well as a Southern patriot and American nationalist, he shared
Goethe's and Scott's late Enlightenment ways of seeing and explaining.
And what he shared with them he likewise shared largely with his fellow
educated Americans. Although his opposed characters of the Northerner
and Southerner are singular inasmuch as they are the earliest fully
developed American anticipations of Scott's leading antithetical characters that I have been able to discover, they point to a growing consensus
about the nature of the regional traits, interests, and tensions with which
the new political union would have to cope – a consensus which must
have made the Waverley novels, when at last they arrived, seem both
very strange and very familiar.

Jefferson's analysis also helps us to understand why the first major
American fictionalist to follow Scott in throwing these basic characters
into opposition was a New Yorker rather than a Southerner. For
Jefferson goes on to maintain that, although "these characteristics grow
weaker and weaker by gradation from North to South and South to
North . . . Peculiar circumstances [i.e., the Dutch patroon system] have
given to New York the character which climate would have given had
she been placed on the South instead of the North side of Pennsylvania."
It was in New York, therefore, that the Northern and Southern
characters came directly into contact and conflict with each other well
before the Revolution. Cooper understood these geo-cultural matters so
well that he placed the Revolutionary War action of *The Spy* in New
York's Westchester County and subtitled this prototypical story of
fratricidal strife in America "A Tale of the Neutral Ground." On this
ground between geographical and cultural extremes, Yankee peddlers
meet the Virginian cousins of New York "aristocrats" – but meet
fraternally because the primary division for the time being is not between
them but rather between Britons and Americans and between American
"Whigs" and "Tories." Partly because Cooper was still learning how to
write fiction and partly because this particular fiction had a strong
nationalist motive behind it, the Yankee and Cavalier characters of *The
Spy* are not so sharply or suggestively contrasted as those of Jefferson's
letter or as the Cavaliers and Covenanters of *Old Mortality*. But the first
American historical romance shows what riches of regional character

and conflict were ready to hand and awaiting further development in works like *Satanstoe* and *A Connecticut Yankee at King Arthur's Court.*

Reviewing *The Spy* in 1822, New Englander W. H. Gardiner directed attention to these riches and proceeded to draw a bolder contrast between the Cavalier and Yankee characters than Cooper himself had:

> Did any one . . . ever cross the Potomac, or even the Hudson, and not feel himself surrounded by a different race of men? Is there any assimilation of character between the highminded, vainglorious Virginian, living on his plantation in baronial state, an autocrat among his slaves, a nobleman among his peers, and the active, enterprizing, moneygetting merchant of the East, who spends his days in bustling activity among men and ships, and his nights in sober calculations over his ledger and day-book?[7]

Although very much a nationalist himself, Gardiner is honest enough to acknowledge that the variety of American character which is such a potential boon to the aspiring fictionalist is, from another perspective, a dangerous legacy of "those conflicting sectional interests, which sometimes perplex us at the present day" (p. 61). It can be argued that by following Scott's example, i.e., keeping the Cavalier and Yankee characters alive in fiction, American historical romancers also helped to keep sectional conflict alive.

What " assimilation of character" could there be, after all, between the cunning Yankee Jason Newcome of Cooper's *Satanstoe* and the improvident Cavalier Colonel Porgy of Simms's *Woodcraft* (1851)? And even when regional character and conflict were not directly at issue, portraits of Cavaliers and Puritans like those in the Waverley novels may have contributed to misunderstanding and ill will between the North and South. Consider, for instance, the implications of Hawthorne's use of Puritan/Cavalier typology. In "The Gray Champion," he depicts the 1689 rising against Andros as a sequel to the English Puritan revolution against Charles I and a "type" of the New England colonists' future revolt against British tyranny in 1775. This "explanation" of late eighteenth-century events inevitably leads to warps and omissions in Hawthorne's version of American colonial history. One is that, although he pays his respects to George Washington in *Grandfather's Chair*, his fictional and historiographical accounts of the Revolution generally suggest that it was an exclusively New England affair – largely, no doubt, because his historical interests were centered in his own region; but partly also because he tended to associate the Yankee revolutionaries' Virginian allies with the very Cavaliers who, as the hereditary foes of the Puritans, were the types of British tyranny.[8] Besides being misleading about the part which the South played in the Revolution and about the freedom-loving character of the Puritan fathers, these associations must also have strengthened mid-nineteenth-century Northerners' suspicions of the motives and inclinations of their Southern fellow countrymen.

Yet we cannot hold Scott responsible for the historical errors and stereotypical thinking of his followers and their readers. The political message of the Scottish Waverley novels, and most explicitly of *Redgauntlet*, is that Cavalier/Puritan factionalism was a great evil for Britain, that the Cavalier outlook was hopelessly anachronistic as far back as 1745, and that political union and compromise were necessary to avert invasion from abroad and revolution at home. Nor was this message so deeply buried as to be detectable only through the scanning techniques of late twentieth-century literary scholarship. Thoughtful readers of the Waverley novels have always recognized that Scott was a reconciler and proponent of the *via media* even though his subject was revolution and imperialistic conflict. It was, for instance, in the conciliatory spirit of Scott that W.H. Gardiner advised would-be American historical romancers to look especially to three epochs – "the times just succeeding the first settlement . . . the aera of the Indian wars . . . and the revolution" (pp. 59–60). For these were epochs which all of the former colonies had experienced: by concentrating on them, writers could help consolidate that unity within diversity which the fathers of the American republic had envisioned. On the same principle, Scott, although as loyal to his own *patria* as Jefferson to Virginia, was ever a champion of the *United* Kingdom.

Another thoughtful reader of Scott, who lived late enough in the nineteenth century to be able also to reflect on the causes, course, and consequences of the Civil War, was Herman Melville. In the "Supplement" to *Battle-Pieces and Aspects of the War* (1866), Melville at one point asks rhetorically:

> If George IV. could, out of the graceful instinct of a gentleman, raise an honorable monument in the great fane of Christendom over the remains of the enemy of his dynasty, Charles Edward, the invader of England and victor in the rout at Preston Pans – upon whose head the king's ancestor but one reign removed had set a price – is it probable that the grandchildren of General Grant will pursue with rancor, or slur by sour neglect, the memory of Stonewall Jackson?[9]

Continuing the parallel between Unionists and Hanoverians, Confederates and Jacobites, Melville speculates that

> in the generation next to come, Southerners there will be yielding allegiance to the Union, feeling all their interests bound up in it, and yet cherishing unrebuked that kind of feeling for the memory of the soldiers of the fallen Confederacy that Burns, Scott, and the Etterick Shepherd felt for the memory of the gallant clansmen ruined through their fidelity to the Stuarts – a feeling whose passion was tempered by the poetry imbuing it, and which in no wise affected their loyalty to the Georges, and which, it may be added, indirectly contributed excellent things to literature.   (p. 262)

Battle-Pieces and Aspects of the War itself gives a more honest and historically insightful account of the Civil War than does any nineteenth-century historical romance that I have read. Yet Melville's reflections proved prophetic; for, when 'Twas Sixty Years Since Appomattox, the feeling inspired by memory of the fallen soldiers of the Confederacy also " contributed excellent things to literature." Conspicuous among them were historical romances which, in the true Waverley tradition, could honor the prowess and heroism of a Stonewall Jackson while acknowledging the evil and anachronism of a cause whose objective was, in Melville's words once again, "the erecting in our advanced century of an Anglo-American empire based upon the systematic degradation of man" (p. 261).

I wish it were possible to turn Mark Twain's wild proposition on its head and maintain that, so far from being "in great measure responsible for the war," Scott presented a compelling example of moderation and historical realism which held extremists on both sides in check for a long time and eventually redeemed the literature of the South. The fact, rather, is that the great early twentieth-century Southern writers found inspiration and example not in Scott but rather in such modern masters as Conrad, James, and Proust, and to a lesser extent in intermediary figures like Poe, Hawthorne, and the "rediscovered" Melville.[10] As for the antebellum readers who may have been influenced for good or ill by the Waverley novels, do not the mass of readers in any age generally take what they want from literature and heed only those lessons of history which they have been schooled to heed by one master or another? The truth of this deflationary proposition certainly seems to be borne out by responses to many fictional masterpieces besides the Waverley novels. Readers of the kind who were drawn more to Milton's Satan than to his Messiah, who wanted a reformed Lovelace to marry Clarissa, who regretted the "unhappy ending" of *The Scarlet Letter*, who persuaded Dickens to alter the conclusion of *Great Expectations* – such readers, of whom the American South presumably had its share, doubtless regretted the failure of Bonny Prince Charlie's "gallant" expedition and longed for a successful sequel. Small wonder, therefore, if many Southerners actually did continue to pattern themselves after the Jacobite Cavaliers even though the Waverley novels showed how those Cavaliers went on fighting and losing, fighting and losing, precisely because they refused to learn from the auguries and plain evidence of recent history.

Even so, the Waverley novels and later historical romances would not exist as we know them if Scott and his successors had despaired of their readers' capacity to learn from the past. Indeed, as I pointed out in the previous chapter, the early Waverley novels may be considered Lockean treatises on education – treatises which, in effect, divide mankind into those who are historically uneducable and therefore doomed to repeat the past, and those like Edward Waverley who are capable of modifying their behavior in the light of historical evidence which runs counter to their ideals and expectations. It is partly because the characters and readers of historical romances belong to both camps that history goes on recycling itself stupidly and catastrophically and yet does go on, so their authors have believed, slowly and generally improving.

Can anything be said, then, in favor of Mark Twain's Wildean contention that Southern life imitated Scottish art and that Scott was somehow responsible? I believe that Mark Twain was perversely wrong but that some grains of truth can be sifted from his bushels of rhetoric. It is true that Scott himself was ambivalent enough about the claims of romance and realism that he often made his uneducable characters more glamorous than his learners and survivors: readers less intelligent and reflective and Northern than Gardiner or Melville might be pardoned for failing to draw all the correct moral and historical inferences. Moreover, although the conservatism which Scott espouses is comparatively moderate and flexible, it does nevertheless promise a hereditary ruling class which stands in a paternalistic relation to other classes. The antidemocratic ethos of the Waverley novels, which observers like Cooper and Emerson early diagnosed as political poison, surely was a tonic for those who needed to feel good about the "Southern way of life." Finally, the example of Scott's own career – his prodigious rise by virtue of immense individual talent and industry from comparative obscurity to a hereditary baronetcy and estate, climaxed by his stunning financial failure and legendary recovery – may well have spoken even more beguilingly than his fiction to Southern readers. For it was a career which seemed to prove that the Old South's contradictory desires for democratic mobility and aristocratic permanence could both be fully gratified, and which did in fact bear some resemblance to the careers of many prominent Southerners from Andrew Jackson and John Calhoun to the Secessionist leaders William L. Yancey and James Henry Hammond.[11] It is of more than anecdotal interest that Hammond, William Gilmore Simms's good friend, visited not only Abbotsford but also the grave of his favorite novelist at Melrose Abbey, and that Hammond's biographer has recently observed a close parallel between the famous "Design" of Thomas Sutpen and – art imitating life this time around – Hammond's equally aspiring and disastrous "Design for Mastery."[12]

One more word about Scott's "enchantments" and their influence on the form of Southern historical fiction, including Mark Twain's. If one of the unintended consequences of the Waverley novels was to reinforce the Southerners' notion that they could successfully impersonate the Cavaliers of yesteryear, an intended one was to make readers sensitive as never before to the immense practical difficulties that historians and indeed everybody faces in the constantly necessary task of recovering the past: from recollecting where the car keys were left to accounting for the decline and fall of the Roman Empire. This pervasive concern of the Waverley novels is most apparent in Scott's formula of alternative possibilities, whose "some saw this . . . others reported that" pattern calls attention to the problematic nature of witnessing and thus of reconstructing historical events. In the final section of this chapter we will see that the greatest Southern fictionalists, Mark Twain and Faulkner, go a stage farther by turning the historical romance into a version of the detective novel. Summoning up witness after witness in an effort to solve some of the outstanding mysteries of the Old South, they are as interested in the process of historical reconstruction as in its product.

2. Epics and mock-epics of the Old South

During their long history, I have remarked, Southerners have identified with, have sought to interpret themselves and their predicaments by discovering parallels with, many characters and conflicts out of history books, oral legends, and romances. It would be surprising if recollections of such characters and conflicts did not crop up fairly regularly in the literary genre which, more than any other, has celebrated (or exposed the falsity of) the heroic codes, character-types, and actions which Southerners have especially associated with their own region and identity. In the present section, I will discuss some of these moments of epic reminiscence as they appear in a group of historical romances by Elizabeth Madox Roberts, Ellen Glasgow, Allen Tate, and William Faulkner which, taken together, trace the historical development of the South from exploration and early settlement through the Civil War and Reconstruction down to more recent times. On the showing of these books by leading figures of the "Southern Renaissance," Southerners have always been engaged in the difficult, perhaps impossible, task of reconstructing the patterns – some "mythic," in Allen Tate's sense, and some not – of a previous existence, while simultaneously adapting to the changed circumstances of a new land, a new era.

To reconstruct after what pattern? That the first permanent English settlement in North America was christened "Jamestown" (or "James Cittie"), in the mapless wilderness of "Virginia" (or "New England" as Captain John Smith called it), tells us plainly enough that the initial pattern could only be English. And since that initial pattern was determined in England by "The Treasurer and Company of Adventurers and Planters of the City of London for the First Colony in Virginia," it was bound to be as strictly and uniformly English as possible. In *Notes on the State of Virginia*, Jefferson recalls that the earliest charters established governmental units and offices with such ancient English names as "hundreds" and "burgesses" and charged Virginia's General Assembly to "make laws for the behoof and government of the colony, imitating and following the laws and policy of England as nearly as might be."[13] There were many reasons why anglicizing everything "as nearly as might be" was (*pace* William Carlos Williams) a necessary and by-and-large productive strategy during the early years of settlement, but one reason continued to be of vital importance to colonial prosperity and self-esteem down to the time of the Revolution.

In the words of a solemn convention signed on 12 March 1651 by commissioners representing the Puritan Parliament, the people of Virginia "shall have and enjoy such freedoms and privileges as belong to the free borne people of England"; in particular, they shall "have free trade as the people of England do enjoy to all places and with all nations according to the laws of that commonwealth" (p. 108). Only by preserving the fiction that they were Englishmen first and Virginians (or anything else) second, could the colonists preserve their practical economic and political independence from England. This familiar paradox of American political history applied in the northern colonies as well, but it is significant that, in treating with Cromwell's commissioners, the Virginians added the rider that "Virginia shall enjoy all priviledges equall with any English plantations in America" (p. 108). For unlike the Massachusetts colony, Virginia had neither publicly welcomed the deposition of Charles I nor immediately recognized the political authority of Parliament; when it eventually compounded with Parliament, it did so warily and with a jealous eye on other "English plantations in America." American colonists might all be Englishmen, but there was more than one English pattern to follow.

No extant English pattern, however, was shaped for survival in the American wilderness; the pattern or the wilderness or both would have to be altered; and of course both were. A region of extremes, of extraordinary social and geographical diversity, the Old South was the stage for more, and probably more ambitious and persistent, attempts to replicate the life styles of the English gentry than could be seen in any other part of the country, while it was also the region that gave America its first great "Western" hero in Filson's Daniel Boone, the white man who succeeded in making the red man's way of life his own without being brutalized by it.[14] To produce a Boone took a century and a half of British presence in America, and thus chronologically he arrives upon the scene much later than the earliest Virginian "Cavaliers." As the prototypical American pathfinder, however, he has a strong and logical claim to precedence in my scheme of Southern heroic patterns. Besides,

with the special exception of Simms's Porgy, the Cavaliers who are of
abiding fictional interest are those who come late enough in the historical
romance of the South to be able to ride with Bedford Forrest, Jeb Stuart,
or Jubal Early.

One of the characters in *The Great Meadow* (1930) calls Boone "a man
you could take for a pattern to make men by."[15] Boone appears in the
novel only once, but his short conversation with Diony Jarvis, Elizabeth
Madox Roberts's admirable heroine, eloquently sums up the different
viewpoints of the pathfinder and pioneer woman and recalls the toil and
danger experienced by those who first settled the Dark and Bloody
Ground:

> "Like all the balance I walked to Kentuck, or rode my nag, over your road,"
> she said, "marched here over the trace you made out for us. I'm obliged to you
> for a road, right obliged and beholden."
>
> "You're right welcome to it," Boone said. "If I marked out the way, you
> had to go it with your two feet, and so the road's yours too for the trouble you
> took to walk it. And the danger was yours whilst you went the way."
>
> "A right perilous journey," she said.
>
> "An Indian says to me, at Watauga when Colonel Henderson made his
> treaty, says he, 'Brother, we give you a fine land, but I believe you'll have a
> trouble to settle it. Trouble,' says he."
>
> "A fine country though. I reckon I have been a-hearen about Kentuck or
> Caintuck, by whatever name you please to call it, ever since I was that high, and
> report always said a fine land. And a heap of unexplored corners there must be.
> Places a body could get lost in and never find himself again."
>
> "Parts you could explore, yes, boundaries of land not yet spied out, I
> reckon," Boone said. "Yes, I could find new ways to go and creeks to travel,
> falls to spy out, caves and wonders to see. But I don't reckon I'd get lost in e'er
> one. Not to say lost. I never was lost. I was bewildered right bad once for as
> much as a week, but not lost. I never felt lost the whole enduren time."
>
> "You always felt at home in the world," Diony said. "You felt at home with
> what way the sun rises and how it stands overhead at noon, at home with the
> ways rivers run and the ways hills are. It's a gift you have, to be natured that
> way."
>
> "Elbow room is what a man wants," he said. (pp. 111–12)

Boone's self-assurance that borders on boastfulness and Diony's words
"gift" and "natured" reinforce the suspicion that Roberts's version of the
original pathfinder derives not only from Filson's portrait but also from
the intermediary character of Leatherstocking. Still, we must feel that it
is the authentic Boone who comments sententiously, "Elbow room is
what a man wants."

Moreover, the brevity of his appearance in *The Great Meadow* means
that Boone has a very different role and "feel" as a character than
Leatherstocking has. Like Cooper, Elizabeth Madox Roberts follows

Scott's practice of introducing famous historical figures only very sparingly and usually well on in the action when a few words or deeds can achieve maximum resonance. For, to reformulate a point made by Lukács, historical fictions in the Waverley tradition are celebrations not of the genius of "world-historical" figures like Boone but rather of the pluck and sweat and humankindness of women and men who do "get lost" sometimes and yet who also make the road blazed by a pathfinder their own by virtue of the "trouble" and "danger" they have in walking it. No doubt Boone would have been a man of remark, and some of his exploits might have been chronicled by local historians, even if nobody had traveled his Trace during his lifetime. But his place in regional and national history and legend was conferred on him by the masses of "unremarkable" people who were ready to follow – and eventually to leave him with no unexplored "new ways to go." Indeed, for all her lyrical appreciation of Boone, Diony lives to discover the shortcomings of heroes made after his pattern.

The Great Meadow, then, is the story of Boone's followers and especially of Diony Jarvis, who by her own reckoning is "not the Boone kind" (p. 112). Of her own kind, however, Diony is quite as heroic as the pathfinder, and her story would have an epic largeness and appeal for most American readers even if Roberts were less skillful in exploiting its potential. Like many of Cooper's historical romances, notably *The Wept of Wish-ton-Wish* and *The Last of the Mohicans*, *The Great Meadow* has two main actions of roughly equal length. The first is concerned with Berk Jarvis's courtship of Diony Hall in Albemarle County, Virginia, and their trek over the Cumberland Gap to Kentucky. The second deals with Diony's attempt to make a home in the wilderness – an attempt soon frustrated by Berk's disappearance in pursuit of revenge on the Indian murderers of his mother, then revived with her marriage as a presumptive widow to Berk's friend Evan Muir, and at last temporarily confounded by Berk's return after three years of captivity in the wilderness.

These events occur during the Revolutionary War years 1774–81. While the primary focus of the novel is clearly and consistently on the challenges which the characters face as pioneers rather than as partisans of American independence, the British policy of encouraging Indian attacks on the Kentucky settlements means that the war directly affects their lives on the frontier and in fact precipitates the catastrophe of Elvira Jarvis's murder and Berk's vendetta. Thus the issue of fratricidal strife becomes of major importance in the second half of the book, finally manifesting itself very personally and powerfully in the confrontation between Berk and Evan, erstwhile companions but now rival husbands of one woman. Frontier precedent supplies the solution that Diony should choose one of them and that the other should "go away in peace and never show his face here again to darken their door whilst life lasts" (p. 185). Clearly, this device is a personal analogue of the political device – a plebiscite – which would have been the best way to settle the dispute between Britain and her American colonies and which Roberts, writing in 1928–9, would have chosen to resolve all conflicts over sovereignty or territorial possession. As Roberts explains early on, the name of her double-husbanded heroine is that of an earth goddess, Dione, "one of the Titan sisters, the Titans being earth-men, children of Uranus and Terra" (p. 15).

The Great Meadow begins as it ends with Diony's choice of Berk Jarvis. Her choice is free inasmuch as Berk is not the only man available and keen to be her husband. But a husband she must have, since the family farm will go to her brothers and the only way for her to get a place of her own is to marry. "Iffen a woman isn't married she has a poor make-out of a life" (p. 17), her brother Sam advises her. Roberts makes no bones about the limited options which Diony and other frontier women have, but her message is much less that women are the victims of patriarchalism and biology than the independence in its various forms is a good which does not come easily or unconditionally to most people of either sex. When Diony's father, Thomas Hall, is lamed by an accident, he remains the respected head of his family, but along with the labor the actual management of the farm passes to the eldest son, Reuben. Reuben himself is among the men who are willing to fight for American political independence and is in fact preparing to journey east to join Washington's army at the very time that Berk and Diony are preparing to journey west over the Wilderness Road to make a home for themselves in "a promise land . . . a well-nigh sort of Eden" (p. 13). Underscoring the independence theme, Roberts records how, during the autumn of 1776 while the young people make ready for their journeys, Thomas Hall "would read aloud the Declaration of Independence, the great words of Thomas Jefferson thundering through the house at evening. 'We hold these truths to be self-evident: That all men are created equal, that they are endowed by their Creator with certain unalienable Rights' " (p.61).

Jefferson's words are immediately followed by a more down-to-earth revelation concerning human nature and inalienable rights: Reuben's remark that "when he could market his tobacco he would buy himself two black servants, men to labor for him in the fields." Although the juxtaposition cannot but be ironic, Roberts withholds editorial comment both here and a few pages later when Diony's mother, pleading the territorial rights of the Indian, is silenced by a male chorus which concludes simply and brutally: "Strong men will go in and take" (p. 67). While Roberts does not endorse this might-makes-right morality, neither does she protest against it except by formulating it in terms which expose how frail the garment of the white pioneers' civilization is when push comes to shove. Regrettable but true: the brave independent yeomen who settled Kentucky were as "strong" as Vikings and had to be to fulfill their individual and national destiny. More critical than this of her frontiersmen she cannot be without calling into question the ultimate rightness and grandeur of their democratic exodus. In this as in many other respects an instructive contrast is offered by Faulkner's Mississippian pioneer patriarchs, notably Carothers McCaslin and Thomas Sutpen. They are not necessarily more ruthless than Roberts's frontiersmen; but because they aspire to be aristocratic (which means slaveholding) planters on a grand scale rather than modest farmers like the Halls and Jarvises, their ambitions are at odds with both national destiny and common humanity. And therefore, although Faulkner clearly admires Sutpen's heroic individualism and justifying dream of hospitality, he makes us recognize that Sutpen's ends – and those of the Old South as a whole – are ruinously flawed by the "strong" means employed.

Since Roberts's frontiersmen are more practiced in shoeing horses and growing corn than in meditating on philosophical history or absorbing impulses from a vernal wood, the elementary level of their moral reasoning is very much in character. However, historical realism does not require that all of these pioneers be uneducated and unreflective. Since Thomas Hall is related to the Virginian gentry which nurtured Jefferson, Mason, and Madison, it is credible that he reads their literary productions and also some of the works that they would have read, e.g., Gray's "Elegy Written in a Country Churchyard," the Homeric epics, the *Aeneid*, and Berkeley's *Principles of Human Knowledge*. He is evidently responsible for his daughter's name, and he teaches her that the goddess Dione "was the mother of Venus by Jupiter, in the lore of Homer, an older report than that of the legendary birth through the foam of the sea" (p. 15). While her mother instructs her to weave a mantle to "fold about her knees on the long march," her father intones in Latin the opening lines of Virgil's epic and then translates: "I sing of arms and the hero who, fate driven, first came from the shores of Troy to Italy and the Lavinian coast, he, *vi superum*, by the power of the gods, much tossed about, *multum jactatus*, much tossed about on land and sea" (p. 75). So it is sufficiently plausible that Diony herself combines the practical mastery and traditionary wisdom of her mother – "seems like hit's the women has got insight and is natured to hold fast to the old customs" – with the Romantic reflectiveness of her crippled father. In effect, the one side of her psyche balances and corrects the other, enabling her to be, in her own generation, both a wholehearted participant in and imaginative observer of the epic migration of her people.

I say "in her own generation" because she has a profound sense of herself as historical product and representative, not just the daughter of Thomas and Polly Hall but

> the daughter of many, going back through Polly Brook through the Shenandoah Valley and the Pennsylvania clearings and roadways to England, Methodists and Quakers, small farmers and weavers, going back through Thomas Hall to tidewater farmers and owners of land. In herself then an infinity of hopes welled up, vague desires and holy passions for some better place, infinite regrets and rending farewells mingled . . . These remembrances were put into her own flesh as a passion, as if she remembered all her origins, and remembered every sensation her forebears had known, and in the front of all this mass arose her present need for Berk and her wish to move all the past outward now in conjunction with him. (p. 85)

At times her sense of the presence of the past is so strong that, half recalling her father's Berkeleyan Idealism, Diony feels that she more than rehearses ancestral deeds, she actually reembodies eternal forms:

> Her whole body swayed toward the wilderness, toward some further part of the world which was not yet known or sensed in any human mind, swayed outward toward whatever was kept apart in some eternal repository, so that she leaped within to meet this force halfway and share with it entirely. (p. 60)
>
> She had a sudden overwhelming sense of this place as of a place she had known before. Feeling that she had been here before, that these events were the duplicate of some former happening, she left her little mare to graze by the trail and walked cautiously into a meadow. (p. 104)
>
> She was a tall strong woman and a child clung to her breast . . . She helped Anne Pogue to make cloth of the buffalo wool or to make a thin cloth of the wild nettle fiber, or she tended her child to keep him free of the vermin. Remembering some phrase from a book which was now more than half forgotten she had a sudden sense of herself as eternal, as if all that she did now were of a kind older than kings, older than beliefs and governments. (p. 149)

Mere psychological tricks of *déjà vu* or obscure validations of the system of Thomas Hall's favorite philosopher? No more than Hawthorne or Cather in similar situations does Roberts opt firmly for one of the alternative possibilities.

Elizabeth Madox Roberts was widely read and acclaimed during the 1920s and '30s, but, like the work of many other historical romancers who deserve a better fate, hers now seems to be read, if at all, chiefly for its regional interest. No doubt *The Great Meadow* sometimes smacks more of Carl Sandburg than is good for it, and that its characterization lacks psychological complexity. Despite Roberts's close attention to her chief protagonist's education in Virginia and, later, on the Kentucky frontier, even Diony seems a little abstract, her representative function threatening to crowd out her individual identity. Still, it is to be expected that an epic tale of the matriarch (or patriarch) will be short on character and long on scene and fable. Such is the case with *The Heart of Mid-Lothian* and *My Ántonia*. Diony has as much depth and individuality as is requisite in the principal character of a work which aspires to the condition of a heroic poem. And if Roberts's rhetorical climaxes are sometimes disappointing, the staple of her prose is an innovative combination of Appalachian folk idiom and stately though simple syntactical patterns, an instrument worthy of the epic story she has to tell. Despite the deficiencies noticed here and earlier, then, *The Great Meadow* is a minor classic of its kind. It is a work richer in substance and finer in execution than, for instance, the remarkable yarn of Civil War and Reconstruction Georgia which Margaret Mitchell published only a few years later and which, partly because of the enduring charm and marketability of the movie based on it, has long enjoyed a very special popular status as *the* Southern historical romance.[16]

Similar claims to superiority can be fairly made, I believe, for two historical romances of the Civil War by Ellen Glasgow (1874–1945) and Allen Tate (1899–1977) which, because of the matter they share with *Gone with the Wind*, might appear more appropriate works to stack up against it. Qualitative issues aside, however, even a cursory comparison of Mitchell's book with *The Battle-Ground* (1902) and *The Fathers* (1938) reveals nearly as many important differences as resemblances in their portrayals of the Southern experience of the war. The resemblances are most apparent in the opening and early-middle chapters of the novels where all three writers exhibit the eve-of-war social rituals and mores of representative upper-class white Southerners (*arrivistes* as well as scions of "old families"), the attitudes of these characters towards slavery and secession, their fears and hopes for military glory and triumph, and their inevitable enlistment when the war finally comes. As has been customary in civil war fiction since *Waverley*, the "rebels" in these books include both fire-eaters and reluctant warriors. As in *Waverley*, too, something archaic and factitious clings to their military as to their peacetime social enterprises; hence the central action of all three works involves a gradual exposure of this unreality and a sorting out of survivors from dinosaurs and belles.

In *Gone with the Wind*, however, the sorting-out process continues well into the Reconstruction era and ends only with Scarlett's development into an ambivalent representative of the New South. By contrast, *The Battle-Ground* concludes with the hero's homecoming after Appomattox, and the main action of *The Fathers* is over almost before the main action of the war gets started. Another major difference is that Glasgow's and Tate's books are Civil War romances of Virginia, where history as well as geography dictated that, both before and during the early years of the conflict, divisions of loyalty would be more numerous and painful and the threat of invasion ever more present than in the deep South. The famous legend of Robert E. Lee's heroic soldier's struggle of conscience between loyalty to the federal union created by his grandsires and love of a home state at war with that union, ensured that Virginian writers – even those less intelligent and informed than Tate and Glasgow – would appreciate some of the riches and complexities inherent in their Civil War matter.[17]

The Battle-Ground comes early in the Glasgow canon and, like many greater historical romances, belongs partly to the world of serious artistic literature and partly to that of popular sentimental fiction. Allen Tate was therefore unkind but not wholly unjust when, reflecting on the parochialism of early twentieth-century Southern novelists, he asked, "who cannot bring himself to wish that Miss Glasgow had studied James and Flaubert in her apprenticeship, and spared herself and us her first three or four novels?"[18] The principal heroines of this book have all the genteel attributes which Scarlett was to envy in Melanie. They are patrician but kindly, beautiful but well-read, demure but tender, graceful but gritty in adversity; and their contrasting love stories cleave faithfully to the stock patterns of saber-and-magnolia fiction. After Virginia Ambler dies, an inadvertent casualty of the war, her cavalryman husband seeks death by riding headlong at the enemy lines in battle after battle, and is finally felled at the Battle of Brandy Station. Her younger sister Betty stays behind to care for the plantation and the elderly and to keep the home fires burning for her infantryman lover. (He joins her at last, physically and financially broken but resolute to begin again: "and this time, my dear, we will begin together.")[19] As the names Virginia and Betty (Elizabeth) suggest, these heroines are closely identified with each other and with the land for which their lovers and other male Virginians are fighting. Thus the death of Virginia and her unborn child anticipates, in little, the death of the old way of life in the state; but Betty's survival and marriage to Dan Montjoy mean that the *matria* will also survive and prosper again some day.

If the Commonwealth of Virginia is the ultimate heroine of *The Battle-Ground*, her destined spouse is the patriarchal hero General Lee. Dan decides that Lee's ability to keep the shredded remnants of his army together as an effective fighting force owed little to the authority or glamor of his position:

> No, the charm lay deeper still, beyond all the factitious aids of fortune – somewhere in that serene and noble presence he had met one evening as the gray dusk closed, riding alone on an old road between level fields. After this it was always as a high figure against a low horizon that he had seen the man who made his army. (p. 447)

Although Montjoy is the ostensible recorder of this reverential image – the symbolic details of the scene all so romantically apt and evocative –

nothing elsewhere in the book disallows our impression that Glasgow shares in his worship of "the Commander." Like most other Southern historical writers or like Cooper when he contemplates Washington in *The Spy*, Glasgow is herself disarmed by this new Gray Champion, seemingly bereft of both her sense of humor and her considerable gift for ironic distancing. Although she manages his departure from the army of Northern Virginia with dignified simplicity and brevity similar to that which actually distinguished the historical Lee's words of farewell to his troops, she cannot resist adding, as a last serio-comic touch to the picture, a report of the Common Soldier's emotional response:[20]

> " 'I've done my best for you,' that's what he said," sobbed Pinetop. " 'I've done my best for you,' and I kissed old Traveller's mane."   (p. 483)

To most Southern readers at the turn of the century, this childish gesture must have been an affecting evidence of the Confederate soldier's simple-hearted devotion not only to Lee but to something greater than any individual: to "the cause" or to a *patria* which (as is acknowledged elsewhere in the book) had done little for such men as Pinetop. But to readers who cannot participate uncritically in the nostalgic rituals of confession and redemptive suffering which Southern romances of the Civil War rehearse for communicants, the transfer of so much feeling to Lee's horse says more than Glasgow can have fully intended about the dehumanizing effects of a social code which elevated Cavaliers and their animals above both black and poor-white human beings.

Yet it is evident that Glasgow herself was far from a wholehearted communicant of the Southern Rite. She does more than justice to the attractive qualities – the courtesy, hospitality, kindliness, public-spiritedness, military prowess and valor – of the slave-holding gentry at its legendary best; and in Lee at a distance and the heroines' father Peyton Ambler up close, she depicts patriarchal figures of that class who are paragons of affectionate solicitude and rational authority. But *The Battle-Ground* also has a subversive agenda and calls into question the wisdom and worth not just of the governing class of the Old South but also of the male ascendency at home. And, contrary to Allen Tate's suggestion, this historical romance of the Old South supplies a critique of romantic literature and its social effects which is very much in the tradition of James and Flaubert – and Scott.

Peyton Ambler's neighbor, and Dan Montjoy's grandfather, is Major Lightfoot, a gentleman of the old school whose provincial manners and views illustrate many of the best and worst traits of his class and sex. A genial host, a reader of Horace and Addison, an advocate of slavery and secession, an ex-soldier who is sure that an army of Virginian gentlemen will beat the Yankees in two weeks, he is impulsively generous and indulgent as a master and parent but choleric and unforgiving when his will is thwarted. As a young man the Major was hard-riding, hard-drinking, and reckless with his fortune after the style of eighteenth-century English squires. That the model had defects is shown by his having gambled away much of his patrimony one night; but, being one of historical romance's dinosaurs and incapable of learning from experience, he is determined to bring up his grandson after the same pattern. Dan predictably rebels and, as his mother Jane Lightfoot had done twenty years earlier, runs away from home. Thus history repeats itself, but not in the way that the broken-hearted Major designed. Although the idolatrous filial loyalty and affection inspired by Lee and Peyton Ambler give the lie to the Major's sad dictum that "youth is always an enemy to the old" (p. 271), the Lightfoot family history does argue that the rebellious child is but the youthful image and just desert of the despotic parent. The political corollary is not (as might be expected from a historical romance of the Old South) that the rebellion was the consequence of Northern despotism but, on the contrary, that it was the twisted expression of the South's own despotic spirit.

Glasgow metes out punishments to her fictional despot-rebels almost as severe as those which Sherman and Sheridan actually visited upon the South Atlantic states. The Major loses a loved only-child and only-grandchild and witnesses the destruction of the hospitable Lightfoot house, Chericoke. Jane Lightfoot runs away with a man who beats and eventually abandons her; she dies young, leaving her son an orphan to be misraised by the Major. Dan suffers four years of danger, privation, illness, injury, and final defeat with Lee's army. In the end, it is true, Glasgow concludes Dan's ordeal by restoring him to his grandfather and Betty, purged of his despotic-rebellious temper, to rebuild Chericoke. This upbeat ending might seem a concession to the sentimental demands of her audience such as Glasgow would not have made in her later fiction, but she concedes less than first appears. For she not only carries her fictional action into homes to which no sons will ever return but also makes plain that the peace will go hard for the South as a whole and that the remnants of the Lightfoot and Ambler families will have to face a life of greatly diminished resources and expectations. The question which *The Battle-Ground* poses is not whether these survivors deserve a little happiness or, from the standpoint of historical probability, would have been able to find it. It is, rather, whether the terrible punishment experienced by the Civil War generation is not in excess of their sins.

Early in the novel, when the prospect of disunion is still remote and Dan and Betty are still children, Peyton Ambler is obliged to abandon his dinner in order to save Dan from being punished for Betty's act of mischief. Although the incident is comic in intention and effect,

Ambler's wry joke that "The sins of the children are visited upon the father" (p. 55) inverts the biblical sentence which, as the action unfolds, seems increasingly to be the sentence of history and biology on the Virginian gentry irrespective of individual guilt or innocence, of individual stands for or against slavery and secession. Ambler himself works actively and publicly against secession, and his wife openly disapproves of slavery; but the war kills Ambler and his daughter Virginia and nearly kills his wife. Dan is expelled from university and jailed overnight for defending a mere bartender's daughter from abuse, and the ensuing disgrace leads to his breach with Major Lightfoot, who blames his grandson's wildness and "lowness" on the "dirty" Montjoy blood. However, Glasgow leaves us in no doubt that Dan's misdemeanor manifests his basic humanity and generous spirit and that the unbridled temper which later causes him to storm out of Chericoke (and thus eventually to go through the purging fire with Lee's infantry) is the inherited mirror image of, as it is an immediate response to, his grandfather's own unbridled temper. What these and many other examples of unmerited suffering argue for is not a malevolent deity but rather an Ibsenian scheme of delayed retribution on a class which owes its accumulated wealth, leisure, and romantic self-image to generations of deprived black slaves and poor whites. The Civil War generation of this class must bear much more than its fair share of the punishment. But *The Battle-Ground* leaves no doubt that the punishment is due and also necessary for the changes of heart and mind which alone can build a more just society in the South.

No character in the book suffers more or experiences more far-reaching changes, especially to his romantic self-image, than Dan. "Dandridge Montjoy" is the perfect name for a Virginian Cavalier, and Glasgow suggests that during his reckless university years he does indeed reembody a Jacobite hero in modern dress:

> He let the reins fall loosely on Prince Rupert's neck, and as the hoofs rang on the frozen road, thrust his hands for warmth into his coat. In another dress, with his dark hair blown backward in the wind, he might have been a cavalier fresh from the service of his lady or his king, or riding carelessly to his death for the sake of the drunken young Pretender.   (pp. 136–7)

That the young Pretender is drunken rather tarnishes the glamor of the picture and also hints that the Southern "cause" for which a later generation of cavaliers will ride to their deaths might be equally dubious. But Dan entertains no such sobering reflections at this stage of his career: the romantic image is not only a description of his physical appearance but also an objectification of his aspirations. Later, when Dan is at the front, Betty looks through his favorite books:

> Among them there was a copy of the "Morte d'Arthur," and as it fell open in
> her hand, she found a bit of her own blue ribbon between the faded leaves . . .
> Behind her in the dim room Dan seemed to rise as suddenly as a ghost – and that
> high-flown chivalry of his, which delighted in sounding phrases as in heroic
> virtues, was loosened from the leaves of the old romance.   (pp. 335–6)

From the Major we discover that Dan's mother also had a quixotic love
of popular romances:

> but it's a dangerous taste, my dear, the taste for trash. I've always said that it
> ruined poor Jane, with all her pride. She got into her head all kind of notions
> about that scamp Montjoy, with his pale face and his long black hair. Poor girl,
> poor girl! I tried to bring her up on Homer and Milton, but she took to her
> mother's bookshelf as a duck to water.   (p. 198)

Since Major Lightfoot personifies parental unwisdom in this novel, I
think we may infer not just that Glasgow had doubts about bringing up a
girl on Homer and Milton but also that she sympathized with Jane's and
Dan's "taste for trash."

An odd intertextual feature of this debate about the effects of reading –
and an ironic comment on the archaic and provincial character of the
Lightfoot household and, by implication, of all too many other Southern
households – is that it recapitulates, a half century later, debates in
Waverley and *Northanger Abbey* about the corrupting influence of the
very same books: *Morte Darthur, Evelina*, and *The Mysteries of Udolpho*.
Glasgow's implied diagnosis is that the "trash" is contagious chiefly
because the Lightfoot home is so unventilated, so closed to outside and
recent literary as well as political influences. This interpretation is
confirmed by two "reading" incidents which occur late in the action of
the book and the war, long after Dan's experience as an infantryman has
cured him of many of the romantic Cavalier (= cavalryman) illusions of
his class.

The first is Dan's discovery of his comrade Pinetop struggling with the
word "RAT" in a child's primer:

> For the first time in his life he was brought face to face with the tragedy of
> hopeless ignorance for an inquiring mind . . . Until knowing Pinetop he had,
> in the lofty isolation of his class, regarded the plebeian in the light of an alien to
> the soil, not as a victim to the kindly society in which he himself had moved – a
> society produced by that free [i.e., slave!] labour which had degraded the white
> workman to the level of a serf . . . To men like Pinetop, slavery, stern or mild,
> could be but an equal menace, and yet these were the men who, when Virginia
> called, came from their little cabins in the mountains, who tied the flint-locks
> upon their muskets and fought uncomplainingly until the end. (pp. 442–3)

This democratic epiphany prompts Dan to instruct Pinetop and to begin
reading aloud from

a garbled version of "Les Miserables," which, after running the blockade with a daring English sailor, had passed from regiment to regiment in the resting army. At first Dan had begun to read with only Pinetop for a listener, but gradually, as the tale unfolded, a group of eager privates filled the little hut and even hung breathlessly about the doorway in the winter nights. They were mostly gaunt, unwashed volunteers from the hills or the low countries, to whom literature was only a vast silence and life a courageous struggle against greater odds. (p. 445)

Hugo's story of Jean Valjean, the brutal galley-slave who rose against all odds to wealth, public honor, and goodness, is both a democratic parable of the power of education and a historical romance of the revolutionary movement in early nineteenth-century France. As we have seen, Glasgow is quite explicit about the irony that Lee's foot soldiers are fighting on behalf of a social system which denied them economic and educational opportunities. One of the implicit ironies of this scene is that the book which speaks so directly and compellingly to these humble defenders of a reactionary society is (among the many things it is) a work of incendiary propaganda for the forces of social progress. If we chart the development of moral consciousness in *The Battle-Ground* by the books which are important to its characters, we might say that the shift is not principally from romance to realism (although that is part of the story) but from a reactionary to a progressive version of romance. To a critic who objected that in its action and implied view of human capabilities *Les Misérables* was as out of touch with reality as any romance of chivalry, Glasgow might have replied that the loyalty and heroism of the Army of Northern Virginia during the closing stages of the war were also "unrealistic" and that the improbable and unintended result of the war was a new sense of the value of the South's poor "white trash."[21]

I have tried to show that neither the political liberalism nor the literary artistry of *The Battle-Ground* is nearly so ingenuous, so provincially limited, as Tate's dismissive comments on Glasgow's early fiction would lead us to suppose. Yet it must be allowed that his own lone venture into the field, *The Fathers*, sets a standard in comparison with which Glasgow's and nearly all other romances of the American Civil War seem deficient in artistic maturity and still more in historical mass and imaginative energy. The Southern peers of Tate's masterpiece are neither Civil War romances aimed at the mass market like *The Battle-Ground* and *Gone with the Wind* nor even such highbrow treatments of the same matter as those of his first wife Caroline Gordon and his Fugitive colleague Robert Penn Warren: they are, rather, *Absalom, Absalom!* and the greatest of the stories gathered in *The Unvanquished* and *Go Down, Moses*. Nor need the comparisons be limited to the works of Tate's Southern contemporaries. When *The Fathers* was reissued in 1960, Frank

Kermode paralleled its achievement with that of another recent historical novel richly preoccupied with the passing of a feudal order, Giuseppe di Lampedusa's newly translated *The Leopard*.[22] Like *The Leopard*, like *Doctor Zhivago* too, *The Fathers* is the "first novel" of a writer who had pondered his subject and his fictional craft for many years before showing the world what he could do in that line. In Tate's case the prolegomena included several volumes of excellent poetry, biographies of Stonewall Jackson and Jefferson Davis, an abandoned family-chronicle novel, and a series of essays and reviews which demonstrated that he had read not only Flaubert and James but also Ford Madox Ford and Faulkner. Probably just as important for the gestation of a major work of historical fiction, Tate's early involvement with the Fugitive and Agrarian groups meant that he had gone to school with some of the brightest and best-informed conservative social philosophers, historians, and men of letters of the '20s and '30s – not just his eminent Nashville friends and mentors but also such foreign elders as T. S. Eliot and Ford.

Compared with the author of *The Fathers*, then, Glasgow was a very unseasoned writer when she brought out *The Battle-Ground*. But since it is the 'prentice work of a writer of formidable talent, we should not be surprised that her Civil War romance of Northern Virginia anticipates many of the major themes, configurations, and insights of Tate's. Both make much of contrasts between pedestrians and men on horseback and, following Mark Twain, of the problematic influence of literature on life. More important, both take the "sins of the fathers" theme with utmost seriousness and require us to view the great historical action in which their characters are involved as one in which the South was long since foredoomed to defeat. And justly foredoomed, because in both novels the governing class of the old South is shown to be incapable of remedying (when it is even capable of recognizing) the social evils to which it owes its wealth and leisure. Although both writers discover much to admire in this class, in Glasgow's Lightfoots and Tate's Buchans and Poseys we witness an aristocracy in decline, creating unawares the conditions of its own supersession. This theme is also Scott's theme, and we do not need the cues of Glasgow's allusion to the Young Pretender and Tate's to *Ivanhoe* to recognize that both authors are working in the Waverley tradition.

However, *The Battle-Ground* belongs to the Waverley tradition in a state of genteel decay whereas Tate's book represents an astonishing twentieth-century revivification. Janet Adam Smith's summary of the affinities between *The Fathers* and *Waverley* may help us to see why, in defiance of chronology, Tate is closer to Scott than Glasgow is:

> Both write of the last days of an order – the clan system in the Highlands, the half-feudal order of antebellum Virginia; both are realists. As there was no

room in the Scotland of David Hume and the agricultural improvers for the chieftain Fergus MacIvor and his 500 claymores, so in the America of the Pennsylvania steel-mills and the spreading railroads there was no room for Major Buchan supporting, on his conservatively cultivated estate of Pleasant Hill, the ever-increasing families of his Negro servants. Yet the old orders had a style, a set of values – rating honour above personal advancement, hospitality above wealth – to which their commercially minded successors looked back with nostalgia.[23]

Scott and Tate are "realists" because both create a historical context of controlling (especially economic) social realities which their feudalistic characters either fail to gauge accurately or choose to ignore. Tate's firm grasp of these realities means, in turn, that the mimetic texture of his novel includes a host of practical and sensory details of life – a whiff of salt fish, a young bull ineffectually mounting the Buchan cows – such as never appear in *The Battle-Ground*. (Glasgow generally reserves her "realism" for the war scenes, but even these focus on Dan Montjoy's psychological reactions and leave the butchery and burning pretty much to the reader's imagination.) Yet to call *The Fathers* a "realistic" novel would be misleading. For the violence in Part III – three murders, a sudden onset of white hair and madness, an alleged rape, a suicide – is carried to a gothic extreme which is likewise at odds with Glasgow's sense of propriety and of "the way things happen." Extremes of realism and romance are perhaps to be expected of a historical fiction that presents antebellum Virginia as a revolutionary society armed to the teeth and yet not at all monolithic or homogeneous but, on the contrary, fragmented within by contending loyalties and interests which divide black from white, planter from merchant, man from wife, father from son, brother from brother.

Although the most conspicuous and destructive polar oppositions in Civil War romances are those which divide the South from the North and eventually assume the shape of armies colored gray and blue, Southern historical romancers from Simms and Kennedy onwards have also regularly discovered a host of polarities within Southern society itself, some of which mirror, on a smaller scale, those usually associated with sectional (Cavalier *vs.* Yankee) conflict. In particular, G. W. Cable's uneven but powerful novel of doubling and miscegenation, *The Grandissimes* (1880), exposes conflicts and contradictions within the Southern social structure which occasioned violence at the beginning of the nineteenth century and were bound to lead to greater violence later. Still, Tate was right to maintain that, by and large, nineteenth-century Southern writers assumed a defensive posture in relation to their *patria* and that it was left to writers of his own generation to act on the important insight which he later formulated in "A Southern Mode of the Imagination" (1959):

W.B. Yeats's great epigram points to the nature of the shift from melodramatic rhetoric [characteristic of Southern letters before World War One] to the dialectic of tragedy: 'Out of the quarrel with others we make rhetoric; out of the quarrel with ourselves, poetry.'[24]

In a prefatory note added in 1975, Tate remarks that *The Fathers* has two heroes: "Major Buchan, the classical hero, whose *hubris* destroys him; George Posey, who may have seemed to some readers a villain, is now clearly a modern romantic hero."[25] This "clarification," though suggestive, I take to be somewhat tongue-in-cheek, and I believe we can gain a more revealing perspective on Tate's heroes by temporarily replacing his critical terms with Schiller's "Naive" and "Sentimental."

Despite his social status and abundant family, Major Lewis Buchan of Pleasant Hill is as Naive as Natty Bumppo, as out of touch with modern social trends and the wisdom of the hour as Cooper's hero is when confronted with the "wasty ways" and unfamiliar laws of Judge Temple's settlement. While his daughter Susan marries the Georgetown merchant George Posey, and his three sons join the rebel forces, Major Buchan keeps the Jeffersonian faith: tilling the soil and adhering to the Union until, at last directly faced with the fact of Northern invasion, he hangs himself just before General Blencker's New York Dutch troops burn down the family house. Clearly, Major Buchan is a good and courageous man, and, just as clearly, Tate means us to admire him and to regard the highly ritualized life at Pleasant Hill – "a house / Where all's accustomed, ceremonious" – as offering rewards peculiar to a traditional, semifeudal agrarian society.[26] However, it is no accident that Tate makes his chief representative of the old Virginian landed gentry as aged as Natty Bumppo in *The Pioneers* or Major Bradwardine in *Waverley*. Like theirs, his wonderful integrity cannot be distinguished completely from mere geriatric incomprehension of newfangled ways of thinking and feeling.

Moreover, the wasty ways in *The Fathers* are the Major's; for the Buchan farm can no longer support his gentleman's life style (modest though this is shown to be) or the uneconomically numerous slaves whom he refuses to sell and cannot afford to manumit with necessary "starting" gifts of land or money. Of course Tate does not represent Major Buchan as a "typical" Southern planter; for he understood perfectly well (and wrote on more than one occasion) that by 1860 agriculture throughout much of the South was highly capitalized, men and land being for sale or not according to the demands of the market. In areas such as the northern Virginia of *The Fathers*, however, the economy and the society supported by it remained rather more "primitive," and Tate was able to make the most of this Jeffersonian survival. But the survival is short-lived. Just before the outbreak of war, the actual owner of Pleasant Hill becomes the man of business George Posey, and it is through his skill, ruthlessness, and liberality that Major Buchan is permitted to go on residing in his ancestral home. This is a generous arrangement for sure, but under George's influence the Major's sons agree to sell not only their family home but also the "surplus" family slaves.

Like Werther, Tate's "modern romantic hero" is a man estranged from nature. Unable to bear the sight either of death or copulation, he flees from his mother-in-law's funeral in the opening scene of the novel and subsequently turns beet-red when he witnesses cattle breeding. Later, Tate demonstrates Posey's estrangement from nature by means of a favorite device of historical romancers from Scott and Cooper onwards – a landscape observed from two radically opposed viewpoints:

> "We were coming over here. Last summer. We passed the prettiest stand of tobacco you ever saw, in Cyarter's big field. Why, man, every leaf was pea-green and the light played on it like it does on a tropical sea. I called George's attention to it. 'Yes,' he says, 'old Cyarter's got it over his whole damn farm.' Charlie, it ain't natural for a man not to like to see a fine stand of tobacco."
>
> (pp. 82–3)

As a town-dweller and merchant, "George Posey of Georgetown" is also an alien presence among the landed Virginian families – "the Carters of Ravensworth, the Carys of Vaucluse, the Buchans of Pleasant Hill" (p. 135) – with whom his marriage to Susan allies him and by whom he obviously longs to be accepted. An outsider possessed of more energy, more practical capacity, and fewer scruples than the gentry he both adulates and despises, George has obvious, and tragic, affinities with Thomas Sutpen. However, George's social antecedents are far different from Sutpen's. For within living memory the Poseys themselves were landed proprietors in Maryland, and it was only during George's boyhood that "the family left the land and settled permanently in Georgetown, in a tall brick house on Vista Avenue" (p. 5). (Houses are important in this novel: Major Buchan's is made of wood, of course, and enjoys a view rather than a "vista.") In *The Fathers*, then, the intrusion of mercantile capitalism into the agrarian pastoral of the Old South comes about not through an invasion by outsiders but through a process of internal transformation. The dislocated product of this process, George is an immensely successful entrepreneur at whose touch everything turns readily into cash; but, unsatisfied by his business triumphs, he seems ever to be wistfully in search of the lost security of his boyhood home and of a firm sense of social identity.

Although we learn a good deal about George Posey, he remains in some ways a shadowy and elusive character – to the narrator, Lacy Buchan, as well as to the reader. Lacy's confusion is understandable. Only a boy of fifteen at the beginning of the novel, he idolizes George as the dashing husband of his sister Susan, best friend of his brother Semmes, general benefactor of the Buchan family, and kindly adoptive elder brother. (To Lacy, Posey is "Brother George" and not only because of his marriage into the Buchan family.) Yet it can be shown that George is directly or indirectly responsible for nearly all of the misfortunes that befall the Buchans during the tragic year 1861. Perhaps the closest Lacy gets to the truth about George's character comes to him when he is furthest from rational understanding, in a hallucinatory vision in which his dead grandfather recounts an ancient story:

> Jason was a handsome young blade of royal descent who had suffered much from a violent family in his youth, so that nothing ordinary interested him; and he called together a great party of heroes and went off after the wool of a remarkable ram; but before he could get it he had to master certain rituals, and it was there that he failed, and showed the white feather. For the king of the country where lived the golden ram commanded him to subdue a certain number of savage bulls, a feat that he at last accomplished with the aid of the king's daughter, Medea, a high-spirited girl of a more primitive society than that from which the arrogant Jason came. He married this girl and carried her and the Fleece back to Hellas . . . It was Jason's misfortune to care only for the Golden Fleece and the like impossible things, while at the same time getting himself involved with the humanity of others, which it was not his intention but rather of his very nature to betray. For he came to love another woman, or he thought that he did, but he was actually repudiating, as we should now say, the very meaning of human loyalties and ties. It is said . . . that Jason desecrated his fathers' graves. I have no doubt that he did. And when Medea discovered his perfidy she killed her children, and went mad, becoming evil; whereas Jason caused all the evil by means of his own privation of good. He was a noble fellow in whom the patriarchal and familial loyalties had become meaningless but his human nature necessarily limited him, and he made an heroic effort to combine his love of the extraordinary and the inhuman with the ancient domestic virtues. If the Fleece had been all-sufficing would he have taken Medea back with him to Greece? My son, I do not think so, my grandfather said. (pp. 268–9)

Just as Cooper must have been conscious of Maria Edgeworth's usurping steward Jason Quirk when he created his own Jason Newcome in the Littlepage trilogy, so Tate must have thought of Faulkner's humanly deficient man of business Jason Compson when he invoked the Jason story to "explain" George Posey. Like the Jason figures of Edgeworth, Cooper, and Faulkner, George is an acquisitive "new man" whose outlook puzzles those who belong to "a more primitive society." Unlike those Jasons, however, he is in no sense mean-spirited or venally dishonest, and in this respect he is much closer to his adventurous legendary prototype. Some of the details of Jason's story as recounted by Grandfather Buchan (mastering certain rituals, subduing savage bulls with Medea's help) bear an almost ludicrous correspondence to events already mentioned; a few details (a violent family in his youth, falling in love with another woman, desecrating his fathers' graves) find only distant parallels in George's career; but on the whole Grandfather's version of the Jason story does nicely as a kind of parable of the modern bourgeois, Sentimental hero.

That George Posey is estranged from nature is true in ways more sinister and destructive than any so far mentioned. However, his native vigor and daily involvement with getting and spending prevent him from becoming effete and withdrawn like other members of his family – his hypochondriacal mother, Jane Anne, and peeping aunt Milly George, his pretty but infantile sister Jane, and his mole-like uncle Jarman Posey, a literary man and, as Lacy says, "a recluse, a kind of Roderick Usher, whose nerves could bear whatever reality they received from the dormer windows at the top of the house, which looked out upon the river. There is much less fantasy in Poe's creation than most people think: Usher was just like Mr. Jarman – Poe had a prophetic insight – for Mr. Jarman, like Usher, had had so long an assured living that he no longer knew that it had a natural source in human activity" (p. 178). Lacy makes an acute philological and social-historical distinction when he goes on to comment that "the Poseys were more refined than the Buchans, but less civilized" (p. 179). In Lacy's usage "civilized" retains something of its Enlightenment sense of citizenship and the public virtues, whereas "refined" refers to an essentially private quality of the leisure classes and even implies disengagement from the political and economic activities of "the world." If George were only an unworldly recluse like Mr. Jarman Posey, his refinement would render him useless but also harmless to others and himself; but he is both refined, i.e., sensitive and imaginative even to the point of morbidity, and, as a businessman, dross, of the world worldly. In good times the divided sides of his personality work well in harness: there is almost always money handy to maintain a handsome style of chivalrous living and giving. But in bad times, and in the absence of the kind of civilized code that constrains while it supports the Buchans, his refined sensibility can do nothing to curb either the cold ruthlessness of his pursuit of the Golden Fleece or the unpremeditated outbreaks of violence that cause the deaths of his best friend and worst enemy.

Most of the tragic events of *The Fathers* can be traced back to a single generative episode at the beginning of the novel, the tournament in which, as a guest of the Buchans, George Posey bests all the members of the Fairfax County Gentlemen's Tournament Association, including the brutal hard-drinking, hard-riding squire John Langton, winner of the previous competitions. A fairly recent innovation – Tate's social history is accurate – the tournament includes a "Parade of Chivalry," ladies wearing their knights' colors, knights lancing rings while riding at full gallop, a crown of laurel, and a speech proclaiming: "It is beyond disputation that the chivalry of this County is unsurpassed in our state, which in turn is unsurpassed in the world for cultivation of the manly arts of Nimrod and of Mars" (p. 66). Anachronistic and absurd, the tournament revival goes some way towards validating Mark Twain's "wild proposition"; and Tate makes sure that Lacy's reading matter shortly before the great event is *Ivanhoe*. For his part, George mimes Scott's black knight by competing anonymously, the only "knight" who wears a hood, and since he wins with a spectacular display of skill and strength the romantic imitation is a great success. Thus he outdoes the Virginians at their own game and appears to take their values and conventions with utmost seriousness and respect. But then, disconcertingly, he reacts as a modern reader would to the actions in which he has been an earnest participant by suddenly finding them antic or merely stupid. When the time comes for him solemnly to crown Susie Buchan with the wreath of laurel, he drops it into her lap and bursts out laughing. When, minutes later, he responds to John Langton's challenge to a duel, he takes a practice shot to demonstrate his prowess with a pistol and then violates protocol by abruptly felling Langton with a mighty right cross to the chin. No wonder that Major Buchan and his neighbors are baffled by Posey, who at one moment appears to be one with them and at the next to be a complete outsider with wholly alien laws and logic. So when the time comes to choose officers for the new Army of the C.S.A., they put the familiar leader John Langton in the saddle and the outsider George Posey in the ranks even though they dislike Langton's coarseness and recognize Posey's superior abilities.

No wonder, too, that to Lacy Buchan at the age of fifteen George is a hero: "I wanted to ask him if there was something I could do, some errand for him, something I might perform that would lift me out of ordinary life" (p. 76). A half century later, Lacy recalls his boyhood worship of George Posey in an image that proves prophetic: "In my boyish delight I would have any day followed him over a precipice, just for his bidding. I know distinctly that I thought of him always boldly riding somewhere, and because I couldn't see where, I suppose I thought of a precipice" (p. 10). The glamorous figure that George cuts at the tournament requires a splendid mount, and this he obtains by trading the Posey family household slave Yellow Jim for a fine bay mare (renamed "Queen Susie") and some cash. Yellow Jim himself explains the deal: "I'm liquid capital, that's what I is, that's what Marse George say when he say he got to sell me." (p. 54). This transaction in which a man becomes "liquid capital" later prompts "Cousin John" Semmes (Major Buchan's cousin), in conversation with "Brother Charles" (Lacy Buchan's brother), to another startling trope:

> "I can't figger that feller out – no, sir . . . He don't think it's right to own Negroes. I don't either." He slapped his leg. "By God, I don't own any. And I didn't sell the Negroes I had."
>
> "Has George sold any Negroes?" Brother Charles spoke in a low voice.
>
> "He rode away from here today on the back of a bay Negro." (p. 82)

We eventually discover that Yellow Jim is Rozier Posey's son by a household slave, hence George's half brother. And as surely as Charles Bon appears at the gate of Sutpen's Hundred to claim his father's recognition or to be the agent of retribution for Sutpen's renunciation of Bon's "black" mother, so Yellow Jim returns home to precipitate the series of catastrophic events which conclude the novel. When Jim is accused, falsely but with appearances against him, of attempting to rape his white half sister, Jane Posey, Lacy recalls the tournament scene and John Semmes's remark:

> As we continued to look at the poor girl I knew that here at last was the night that followed the brilliant day in May when the gay party rode away from Pleasant Hill for the gentlemen's tilt in the west meadow of Henry Broadacre, Esq., that rolled away into the distance green as the sea. I saw Brother George charging down the course, his lance perfectly balanced; only I saw him sadly astride, not Queen Susie, but the man Yellow Jim whose face was as white as his master's. (p. 227)

In the night that follows that brilliant day, Jim is slain by Jane's fiancé, Semmes Buchan, who in turn is shot and killed in a spasm of fraternal feeling by Jim's half brother, and his own best friend and brother-in-law, "Brother George" Posey. Susan Posey goes mad and Major Buchan, confronted with the destruction of the persons and institutions he had most cherished, elects to die like a Roman.

I say "like a Roman" because, although a younger generation may be enamored by Sir Walter Scott and the medieval revival, Tate unmistakably identifies his "classical hero" with those Virginians of the late Enlightenment whom he described as "the noblest Romans of them all" in an address delivered at the University of Virginia in 1936, i.e., while he was writing *The Fathers*:

> men of the early American Republic had a profound instinct for high style, a genius for dramatizing themselves at their particular moment of history . . . The Virginian of the 1790's might have found a better part in the play than that of the Roman in *toga virilis* . . . but it was the easiest role to lay hold upon at that time, and it was distinctly better than no imaginative version of himself at all. A few years ago Mr. T. S. Eliot told an audience at this university that there are two kinds of mythology, a higher and a lower. The Roman *toga* of our early Republic was doubtless a sort of lower mythology, inferior to the higher mythology of the Christian thirteenth century . . . But we must remember that the rationalism of the eighteenth century had made myths of all ranks

exceedingly scarce, as the romantic poets were beginning to testify . . . Men see
themselves in the stern light of the character of Cato, but they can no longer see
themselves under the control of a tutelary deity.[27]

Major Buchan plays the part of Cato with total conviction and dignity;
but George Posey, the sole masked rider at the tournament, can assume
any number of *personae* briefly and brilliantly and yet can find no
permanent role or identity in life. Another passage from the address
"What Is a Traditional Society?" in which Tate comments on *The Waste
Land*, can serve as a final gloss on the "modern romantic hero" of *The
Fathers*:

> It means that in ages which suffer the decay of manners, religion, morals, codes,
> our indestructible vitality demands expression in violence and chaos; it means
> that men who have lost both the higher myth of religion and the lower myth of
> historical dramatization have lost the forms of human action; it means that they
> are no longer capable of defining a human objective, of forming a dramatic
> conception of human nature; it means that they capitulate from their human
> role to a series of pragmatic conquests. (p. 554)

Tate's insistent repetition of the word "human" may remind us that
the Nashville Agrarians were no less concerned about the dehumanizing
effects of the cash nexus than their Marxist contemporaries and, further,
that their radical-right critique of Northern capitalism revived the
charges not just of Calhoun and Carlyle but also of earlier and more
liberal thinkers, the Enlightenment philosophical historians, who
influenced the social thought of Sir Walter Scott *and* Marx and Engels. In
his meditation on the nature of the "traditional society," Tate remarks
that Thomas Jefferson, the greatest American philosophical historian,
"was trying to revive the small freeholder who had been dispossessed by
the rising capitalist of the eighteenth century" (p. 548) and also that
Jefferson "could not have built Monticello had he not been dominated
by the lower myth of the *toga virilis*" (p. 551). The link between these two
propositions is a familiar eighteenth-century analogy (which the
Nashville group wished, with certain qualifications, to revive and
extend) between the agrarian virtue of the Roman republic and
precapitalist "yeoman" England on the one hand and, on the other,
between the urban vice of imperial Rome and imperial "fourth-stage"
London. Tate's use of the Roman analogy – explicitly in "What Is a
Traditional Society?" and implicitly in his characterization of Major
Buchan – prompts two concluding observations about *The Fathers* and
its place in the historical romance tradition.

First, this analogy, with a Tacitean emphasis on the fall from
republican grace and on the oppressiveness and corruption of a
centralizing imperial state, haunted the writings which shaped the
Waverley-model as, in turn, it troubled the political thought of those late

eighteenth- and early nineteenth-century Americans who were not yet wholly converted from a cyclical to a linear-progressive view of historical development. Tate's Major Buchan, a man who was young during the war of 1812 and whose favorite authors are Gibbon and Robertson and the author of *The Vanity of Human Wishes*, is precisely such an American. So were Cooper, Hawthorne, and Melville; although obviously their cosmopolitan range of observation and reading gave them a perspective on modern socio-economic history which was both more encompassing and more "romantic" (in a Goethean or Words-worthian as distinct from a Poseyan or Poe-esque sense) and therefore closer to Tate's than to Major Buchan's. Indeed, Melville's understand-ing of modern history coincides very closely with Tate's, and in his writings the Roman analogy crops up again and again. If Melville was one of the anachronistic "graybeards" mentioned in *Billy Budd*, surely Tate and his Agrarian friends of the 1930s were graybeards of a yet longer growth. But historical romance has a way of giving graybeards like Cooper's Leatherstocking and Cather's Grandfather Burden the last and wisest word.

Second, it is evident that Tate preferred the "lower myth" of the Roman *toga virilis* to that of the romantic medievalism he dismissed in "What Is a Traditional Society?" as "only picturesquely and not sufficiently revived" (p. 548) and which he portrayed in the tournament episode of *The Fathers* as something homemade and verging on the Quixotic. Nevertheless, he might well have responded to Mark Twain that it was better to cast one's self in the role of an Arthurian knight than, like George Posey (and Sam Clemens, too, for that matter), to have no consistent "imaginative version of himself at all." Not to be dominated by any myth, as Jefferson and Major Buchan were by that of the *toga virilis*, also means having no consistent imaginative version of others or of one's human relationship and responsibility to them. Depending on his needs at the moment, Posey can see Yellow Jim as a person and a brother, or as a mere chattel, "liquid capital."

Which is the more dehumanizing in its consequences – to "have lost both the higher myth of religion and the lower myth of historical dramatization" and thus, like George Posey, to "have lost the forms of human action"? Or, like Thomas Sutpen, to have been so dominated by the compound lower myth of the Virginian Planter-Cavalier that any person or thing that gets in the way must be put aside or, if necessary, run over? So much absurdity and appalling evil is perpetrated in the name of one compelling "Design" or another, in the fictional world of *Absalom, Absalom!* and the more unreal worlds of Hitler, Stalin, and Star Wars, that we must surely feel it is better to have too little than too much myth. We must, at any rate, until we recall the evils of a world in which the cash nexus replaces the human relation – in which the metamorphoses of Ovid are supplanted by the metamorphoses of capitalism and, thanks to the all-dissolving agent money, a man becomes "liquid capital" becomes a bay mare.

I do not contend that we must accept Tate's premise that myth cannot survive in a world dominated by capitalist values, or, much less, that we ought to endorse the jeremiadic historical scheme implicit in Tate's tribute to the Virginian Founding Fathers in "What Is a Traditional Society?": "They were so situated economically and politically that they were able to form a definite conception of their human role: they were not ants in an economic ant hill, nor were they investigating statistically the behavior of other ants" (p. 550). I do contend that reading history in terms of a lessening of the power of myth to control men's lives is characteristic of the Waverley tradition and that in *The Fathers* and *Absalom, Absalom!*, Tate and Faulkner follow the tendency of earlier historical romancers to ascribe man's inhumanity to man at a given moment in history to one or the other, to an excess *or* a deficiency of myth. Broadly speaking and without allowance for submerged ambivalences, Scott, early Cooper, and Mark Twain are of one mind about the dangers of too much myth; later Cooper, Melville, and Tate, about the dangers of too little. Hawthorne vacillates between these viewpoints according to whether he is ruminating over the evils of the past (excess) or the present (deficiency).

We have seen that *The Fathers* is a realistic and historical as well as a mythic novel. Indeed, the myths which dominate the lives of Major Buchan and his neighbors are constitutive of the reality they experience and thus essential to our historical understanding of these characters and their world. By contrast, many critics maintain that myth flourishes in *Absalom, Absalom!* at the expense and even in lordly defiance both of realism and history. A perceptive recent commentator, Richard H. King, is at his least original when he says that in *Flags in the Dust* and *Absalom, Absalom!* historical reality is "transformed by the action of memory into high tragedy – and farce. Faulkner's are less historical novels than novels about the workings of memory and the varieties of historical consciousness."[28] One of Faulkner's finest readers, Albert J. Guerard, rightly points to the comparative thinness of concrete socio-economic detail in the novel and maintains that "the reality is the obsessed giant of myth, traveling with the enormous gravestones."[29] King and Guerard speak for many able critics of Faulkner, and I would be the last to deny that *Absalom, Absalom!* is best regarded as a romance. In my view, however, it is distinctly a *historical* romance inasmuch as the principal characters, especially Thomas Sutpen, are at once mythic fashionings of "memory" (or, better, the historical imagination) and figures whose deeds, values, and psychological problems have a representative historical significance. I will go a step further and contend that one of the main reasons why it is such a great book is that Faulkner never entirely releases the tension, characteristic of historical romance, which is created by the book's pulls towards the contrary poles of romance and realism, myth and history. To the extent that reconciliation is achieved, it is through the mediating agency of the Planter-Cavalier myth.

To argue for Sutpen's representativeness is not, however, to claim that a social historian of the Old Southwest would consider him, or that Faulkner ever meant him to be considered, a representative member of the planter class. As Cleanth Brooks points out, those characters in *Absalom, Absalom!* who clearly do belong to that paternalistic class are puzzled and repelled not just by Sutpen's style but by his proto-capitalist values.[30] Eric Sundquist clinches Brooks's case for Sutpen's *Americanness* with an analogy – implausible at first sight but very telling when closely examined – between Sutpen and Abraham Lincoln.[31] But one can concede the main points of Brooks's and Sundquist's well-documented arguments without abandoning the belief that Sutpen's career is in important respects historically representative of antebellum Southern experience. As David Levin says, the question of representativeness can be framed somewhat differently: "The question ought not to be whether most planters were as ruthless as Thomas Sutpen, but whether the system required of any white man who wanted to find a dignified place in it the outrageous waste of land, humanity, and labor . . . The test of Sutpen's representativeness is that he found it necessary to imitate the gentry of Virginia."[32] Faulkner's portrait of Thomas Sutpen does not give us an undistorted image of the typical Southern planter, but it does teach us a great deal about the human condition of the Southern poor white.

The case that Sutpen is a representative Southerner can be usefully carried somewhat further. Cleanth Brooks suggests this possibility when he remarks that, after Sutpen is turned away from the front door of the Virginian mansion, he experiences a species of revelation which, like Paul's on the road to Damascus, alters his whole life: he sees that he must become one of *them*, and, "like the convert, he outdoes in his vehement orthodoxy those generations old in the faith" (p. 293). Although we learn comparatively little about the origins and beliefs of Sutpen's Virginian mountain ancestors, it appears that they are of Scotch-Irish stock and evangelical-Protestant faith. This people had many affinities with the Puritan settlers of New England, including a proneness to egalitarianism, rambling, and religious enthusiasm, which made them – for historical novelists like Tate, Roberts, and Faulkner – ideal cultural opposites of the stable English and Episcopal stock of the Tidewater.[33] So it is very much in character, Southern character, that Sutpen should experience conversion, in this case to the secular "lower" myth of the Cavalier-Planter, and also that he should seek to realize that myth in his own life with a combination of zeal and calculation usually associated with the Cavalier's cultural opposite: the Puritan or Yankee.

Possessed by the justifying myth of the ruling class of his society, but untouched by it in his essential self, Sutpen is able to build a monument in Sutpen's Hundred which exceeds anything the Compsons, de Spains, and Sartorises could build – and which is thereby but the greater tribute to their superior caste and culture. Despite this deflationary irony (which Sutpen himself never registers) and the terrible injustices which the "Design" exacts, we are surely meant to appreciate the magnitude and even grandeur of his achievement. For it is also a tribute to the power of ideas, of myths, of the word. Sutpen's plantation had to be a "Hundred" not just because that number was large and round and swaggering, but likewise, we may infer, because as a youth he had heard the term which the original planters of Virginia brought with them from England and used to designate a division of a county. Never mind that the term, as a territorial unit, properly belongs to the public rather than the private domain: there is something breathtaking about the way that it, misunderstood or not, abruptly materializes as a plantation ten miles wide by ten miles long. Without that word – or, for sure, without the associated myth of the Virginian Cavalier-Planter – Sutpen's Hundred would have been no more possible than Monticello without the myth of the *toga virilis*.

The myth that animates Sutpen and drives him to his doom has a second and equally important function in *Absalom, Absalom!*: it helps the four historians in the novel to get a fix on the characters and actions not only of Sutpen and his children but also of Yoknapatawpha society as a whole. This method of mythic reconstruction seems to be premised on a principle of eternal return which Quentin enunciates well into the novel:

> *Maybe nothing ever happens once and is finished. Maybe happen is never once but like rippling maybe on water after the pebble sinks, the ripples moving on, spreading, the pool attached by a narrow umbilical water-cord to the next pool which the first pool feeds, has fed, did feed, let this second pool contain a different temperature of water, a different molecularity of having seen, felt, remembered, reflect in a different tone the infinite unchanging sky, it doesn't matter: that pebble's watery echo whose fall it did not even see moves across its surface too at the original ripple-space, to the old ineradicable rhythm.*[34]

So when Quentin and his father try to imagine the advent of Rosa Coldfield's "demon," they reconstruct the event as if Sutpen had "been spontaneously generated there . . . with the silent completeness of a mythological manifestation."[35] The words are Vladimir Nabokov's, not Faulkner's, and refer to a first glimpse of a beautiful girl in a birch wood south of St. Petersburg; but they also exactly describe what happened in Jefferson, Mississippi, on a morning in 1833

> when the other men sitting with their feet on the railing of the Holston House gallery looked up, and there the stranger was. He was already halfway across the Square when they saw him, on a big hard-ridden roan horse, man and beast looking as though they had been created out of thin air and set down in the bright summer sabbath sunshine in the middle of a tired foxtrot – face and horse that none of them had ever seen before, name that none of them had even heard, and origin and purpose which some of them were never to learn.
>
> (pp. 31–2)

A mention of the way that "the stranger's name went back and forth . . . in steady strophe and antistrophe" (p. 32) universalizes the occasion by suggesting the arrival of a disguised demigod or a hero like Oedipus in an ancient Greek play. A page later "the stranger" assumes the legendary attributes of a Wild West gunman whose pistols have "butts worn smooth as pickhandles and which he used with the precision of knitting needles; later Quentin's grandfather saw him ride at a canter around a sapling at twenty feet and put bullets into a playing card fastened to the tree" (p. 33). But when Quentin and Shreve try to fathom the mysteries of Sutpen's later career, they (and *their* creator) turn for parallels to the tragic stories of imperial Rome, Camelot, the Faust legend, and the biblical romance of kingship and filial rebellion which supplies Faulkner's wonderful title.

Viewed thus mythically, the Civil War cast of characters seem possessed of a grandeur and intensity lacking in subsequent generations of Southerners. Nonetheless, the provincial drama in which Sutpen plays out his role is charged with an overplus of myths that exalt egocentric mastery and passion at the expense of human kindness. Shreve and Quentin in their Harvard room may only be students, historians of other men's actions in distant times and places, but the reconstruction they accomplish through imaginative sympathy and the time- and space-transcending insights enshrined in myth is something far better finally than Sutpen's Hundred and represents an advance in civilization as well as refinement. At no point in the novel are the gains more apparent than in Shreve's closing prophecy, where a combination of "transport" and sympathetic identification is achieved that is comparable in effect to that of Dimmesdale's Election Sermon prophecy or, more closely still, to that of Whitman's address to his reader in *Crossing Brooklyn Ferry*:

> I think that in time the Jim Bonds are going to conquer the western hemisphere. Of course it won't quite be in our time and of course as they spread toward the poles they will bleach out again like the rabbits and the birds do, so they won't show up so sharp against the snow. But it will still be Jim Bond; and

so in a few thousand years, I who regard you will also have sprung from the
loins of African kings.   (p. 378)

This positive expansion of consciousness and sympathy – an expansion
on which the historical and narrative methods of *Absalom, Absalom!* are
premised – gives the concluding sections of the novel more light and air,
more hope for resurrection, than is implied by Faulkner's original title:
"Dark House."[36] Still, from another perspective, the expansion that
makes *Absalom, Absalom!* a more hopeful (though no less tragic) book
than *The Fathers* is a rhetorical diversion of attention from the actual
condition of the modern South. For the creative achievement which
completes the narrative so satisfyingly takes place in the Yankee
heartland, Cambridge, Massachusetts, and requires the collaboration of a
Canadian from Alberta. Without a shift of venue and a transfusion of
fresh foreign blood, such as Odysseus provides the shade of Tiresias in
Hades and such as Shreve provides here, what hope that poor Quentin
could give true speech to the "sonorous defeated names . . . stubborn
back-looking ghosts" (p. 12) who make him their barracks?[37] In the
formal design of *Absalom, Absalom!*, Quentin's journey from Jefferson
(via Sutpen's Hundred) to Cambridge stands in genteel counterpoint to
Sutpen's earlier one from western Virginia to the Tidewater and thence
(via Haiti) to Jefferson. And it is no less necessary to the fulfillment of his
destiny – as Sutpen's recreator, as a suicide – than Sutpen's longer and
harder journey is to the creation of Sutpen's Hundred and to his death
appropriately at the hands of an avenger who is "white trash" like
himself and whose name, Wash (Washington) Jones, speaks melancholy
volumes about the aspirations and degradations of Southern poor whites.
Despite the liberating burst of creativity that occurs when he takes his
Southern ghosts north, Quentin is no more able than Sutpen to escape or
rise above his origins.

During and shortly after the writing of *Absalom, Absalom!*, Faulkner
conceived, at least in outline, nearly all of the major elaborations of the
Yoknapatawpha saga which were to occupy him during the remainder
of his life. Probably the most important of these was the Snopes trilogy,
provisionally entitled in 1938 "The Peasants," "Rus in Urbe," and
"Ilium Falling" but eventually published as *The Hamlet* (1940), *The
Town* (1957), and *The Mansion* (1959).[38] The later titles are less
pretentious and image the trajectory of Flem Snopes's career more
clearly; but "Ilium Falling" has epic resonances which remind us that
Flem's rise coincides with, and contributes to, the final decline and fall of
a once powerful aristocratic society. Flem is Thomas Sutpen's
demythicized alter ego, stripped of all glamor and heroism and largeness
of vision; incapable of tragedy but, in the way of business and politics,
more capable than anybody the town of Jefferson has ever seen.

Readers familiar with Cooper's Littlepage trilogy must be struck by the likenesses between the Snopeses and the Newcomes ("the locusts of the west") and their respective chiefs, Flem and Jason. I do not suppose that Faulkner was aware of Cooper's trilogy when he planned his own, or of Thomas Jefferson's remark that, contrary to what one might expect from their climatic differences, the Southern states and New York state had very similar social structures and characters. Nor did he need to be aware of such "anticipations" to be able to design a jeremiadic family-chronicle novel sequence which strikes us today as remarkably "reminiscent." It is reminiscent but it is not directly reflective. Even if he had lacked eyes to observe a process of social change parallel to the one Cooper observed a century earlier in New York, Faulkner could not but have known novels from his own region which made the dispossession of the "old" landed families by bourgeois upstarts their theme. For a fear of decay and dispossession haunts the fiction, and especially the historical romances, written by the Southern gentry from well before the Civil War, as, decades earlier, it also does some of the Northern and British models for that fiction: e.g., *Castle Rackrent*, *Waverley*, and *The Pioneers*.

Similar fears haunted Faulkner himself during the later 1930s as increased financial responsibilities and poor royalties from the novels we now recognize as his greatest obliged him to defer work on the Snopes sequence and resort to cash crops – screen plays and short stories for mass-circulation magazines. Many of these stories were rewritten and brought together in two books, *The Unvanquished* (1938) and *Go Down, Moses* (1942), which could be advertised as novels rather than short-story sequences. This strategy proved moderately lucrative and yielded volumes of fiction that contain not only some of Faulkner's finest stories but also stories which, despite considerable unevenness, do add up in context with each other to something more than the sum of their respective parts. But this expedient could yield only limited success, and therefore when we consider also the financial harassment that drove him to it and consider also the architectonic triumphs of which *Light in August* and *Absalom, Absalom!* had proven him capable when he could muster the time and concentration necessary for a single extended work of fiction, it is tempting to identify just one, immediately personal, reason why the fiction he began at that time became increasingly preoccupied with the fundamental inhumanity of the cash nexus and the decline of moral and spiritual values associated with the rise of capitalism. It is tempting and doubtless partly right to do so, but of course Faulkner was not the only one in financial difficulties during the late 1930s. The social and political circumstances which prompted twelve other Southerners to take a stand in 1930 had worsened so gravely that every serious writer felt the need to respond in some way to their charges, or to those of the political Left, against the capitalist system. Although Faulkner apparently did not reciprocate Tate's admiration and even wrote disparagingly of the cloistered Vanderbilt intelligentsia, *Go Down, Moses* is so "Agrarian" in outlook that its author might well be called the Thirteenth Southerner.[39]

We should therefore expect at least one of the major characters in *Go Down, Moses* to share some of the Naive attributes of Tate's Major Buchan. And such a character is Isaac McCaslin, although his heroic Naive prototype is not Cato but rather Daniel Boone or Leatherstocking. What does it mean for a Mississippian born in 1867 to have affinities with these pathfinder figures out of the eighteenth century and parts east? Of course the original pathfinder, Boone, is first of all an authentically regional and national type, redolent of the Kentucky cane brakes and forever associated as a young man with Boone's Trace and as an old one with an act which must strike us as quintessentially American: his removal beyond the Mississippi when his success as a colonizer made Kentucky too crowded for comfort. Yet although the Boone both of history and legend was a figure shaped by peculiarly Southern and American conditions, he was no more "purely American" than the Virginian and Carolinian planters of more settled parts of the Old South were perfect English Cavaliers. Understanding the enduring pathos of Boone and Leatherstocking – for Frenchmen and Englishmen and Russians as well as for Americans – means reckoning with the European element in his and our own constitutions. The heroic type represented variously by Boone and Leatherstocking and the Lone Ranger has survived in literature and in the juvenile movies and radio serials of yesteryear partly because he enables us to expiate our specifically white and American transgressions against others but equally because he permits us to acknowledge a more general human tragedy in the wounds inflicted on all humankind, and not least on ourselves, in the name of progress. Through him we can memorialize the strengths and virtues which, from the early Romantics onwards, have been associated with pre-capitalist, pre-industrial, pre-novelistic man. Like Tate's Major Buchan, the pathfinder in his old age is a historically displaced Naive man. Supreme courage and candor, as well as woodcraft, this hero must of course have; but his crucial test of character typically occurs when he must reject all the domestic and material temptations which are the objects of pursuit in the bourgeois novel.

Pathfinders come first, or should. It is their common fate to be overtaken by the armies of progress. But Ike McCaslin is a double loser in that he is also born too late to be among "the foremost in that band of Pioneers, who are opening the way for the march of the nation across the continent."[40] Nonetheless, he is born early enough to experience a surviving island of the Mississippi wilderness as it was before the arrival of white men, and also to be marked by Sam Fathers (the son of a Chickasaw chief and black slave woman), "not as a mere hunter, but with something Sam had had in his turn of his vanished and forgotten people."[41] With his forest prowess and "native" relation to American nature, then, he is indeed a true descendant of Boone and Leather-stocking; but he likewise conforms to type in his youthful refusal to assume ownership of – i.e., inherited family responsibility for – the McCaslin plantation.

He still refuses when his young wife tries to bribe him sexually to reclaim possession of "Our farm" and then, failing, deserts him. Thus, denying his patrimony also turns out to mean losing love and prospects of paternity. The seduction is perhaps too stylized, the nameless "lost" wife with the "passionate heart-shaped face" too simply a Yokna-patawpha Eve, for the temptation/prostitution scene in *The Bear* to be as dramatically effective as it might have been. Thematically, however, it is of a piece with greater scenes in this and the other stories which comprise *Go Down, Moses*. (Faulkner rightly insisted that it was a novel, not just a collection of stories.)[42] For the book returns time and again to the master evil of using either human beings or land as chattels. This is the evil on which the McCaslin plantation is founded and from which Ike declines to profit. In this he is like Major Buchan, who could not look upon black slaves as "liquid capital" and "could not think of the house that Dr. Buchan had built in 1791, 'for the enjoyment of the heirs forever,' not, mind you, for their profit, had any money value at all" (p. 134). Surely Faulkner approves of this attitude just as much as Tate does. What is much less clear is how far Faulkner endorses Ike's pathfinder strategy of retreat from the perils of civilization and to what extent he proposes any positive – never mind practical – alternative to the doctrine of possessive individualism.

That Ike repudiates the McCaslin property but is himself repudiated by his wife is an important distinction which points to a possible further distinction between him and his celibate pathfinder prototypes. For although "The Old People" and most of *The Bear* deal with the exclusively male "club" of hunter–initiation rites and wilderness pursuit of Leviathan which we normally associate with pathfinders, and although Faulkner generalizes roundly that, despite Ike's marriage, "still the woods would be his mistress and his wife" (p. 326), it is not for nothing that the next-to-longest story in the book is entitled "The Fire and the Hearth." *Go Down, Moses* as a whole is much less concerned with male-bonding activities than with heterosexual relationships and the ways that they are debased and distorted by racism and acquisitiveness. Whatever the consolations of the woods, Faulkner leaves no doubt that

Ike is fully capable of experiencing the sexual joys of married love and that losing his wife is a harrowing sacrifice for him:

> and they were married, they were married and it was the new country, his heritage too as it was the heritage of all, out of the earth, beyond the earth yet of the earth because his too was of the earth's long chronicle, his too because each must share with another in order to come into it and in the sharing they become one: for that while, one: for that little while at least, one: indivisible, that while at least irrevocable and unrecoverable, living in a rented room still but for just a little while and that room wall-less and topless and floorless in glory for him to leave each morning and return to at night. (pp. 311–12)

It is the privilege of the pathfinder to discover "the new country" which is also paradoxically "his heritage" because it is not his alone but rather "the heritage of all, out of the earth." Unlike the country which is subject to the limits of space and time, of geography and history, the "country" of sexual union can ever be – for pathfinders – as new as it was for the first couple, as unbounded by time as the rented room is spatially "wall-less and topless and floorless in glory." The climactic and key word here is "glory," for it is a word out of the vocabulary of religious vision and in this context links primal sexual joy with spiritual ecstasy. What passes from the earth when material values supervene – when a price tag is put on land, on people, on love – is "glory." This passage may remind us of Lawrence, but it is "Lawrentian" chiefly inasmuch as both Faulkner and Lawrence subscribe to the central perceptions and convictions of the early Romantics.

In a book called *Go Down, Moses*, however, the immediate referential context is more likely to be a black spiritual or even "The Battle Hymn of the Republic" than the Intimations ode or *The Rainbow*. Although the black characters do not experience much earthly glory, the best of them are, like Ike, Naive souls who have kept faith with basic human and spiritual values. So it is that the enduring love matches in the novel are between blacks: Tomey's Turl and Tennie in "Was," Lucas and Molly in "The Fire and the Hearth," and Rider and Mannie in "Pantaloon in Black." The last of these stories, although it has no direct connection with the McCaslin family saga, throws an oblique but revealing, ironic crosslight on that saga and especially on the significance of Ike's pathfinder role.

From the alien point of view of the white sheriff's deputy who recounts the end of the story to his bored wife, the chief protagonist, Rider, is merely a big black sawmill hand who runs amuck after the death of his own wife, inexplicably murdering a crooked white gambler with a razor and, after breaking out of jail by sheer physical force, predictably dies at the hands of a lynch mob. But from the "inside" omniscient point of view of the narrator who relates the events leading up to the murder,

Rider is something else again. First of all, he is a man half-crazed with grief and overwhelmed by a sense of helplessness in the face of unaccountable injustice. But second, he is a virile hero out of popular legend who combines something of John Henry, the great black heavyweight champions, and the magnetic ladies' man of more local repute. Although this potent black hero is superficially as unlike the womanless white pathfinder as is well possible, there is common ground or, rather, common blood between them in Melville's Handsome Sailor, who assumes the Naive forms both of a "black pagod" and blond "angel." Taking us back to Rider's beginnings, Faulkner tells us that "Spoot" was "the name he had gone by in his childhood and adolescence, before the men he worked with and the bright dark nameless women he had taken in course and forgotten until he saw Mannie that day and said, 'Ah'm thu wid all dat,' began to call him Rider" (p. 151). Its sexual connotations aside, the name "Rider" implies a degree of mastery in relation to other men more commonly associated with white landowners ("Cavaliers") or overseers than with black workers. But the prodigies of physical strength which Faulkner ascribes to Rider convince us that within his own sphere he is truly what his name, like that of an epic hero, claims for him. Yet the greater his mastery within the sphere of present physical beings and objects, the more baffled and bereft he is when he confronts Mannie's removal to another sphere.

Like "The Old People" and *The Bear*, "Pantaloon in Black" entertains the possibility of supernatural visitations with complete seriousness. After describing Mannie's burial, Faulkner comments on the black cemetery's abundance of "shards of pottery and broken bottles and old brick and other objects insignificant to sight but actually of a profound meaning and fatal to touch, which no white man could have read" (p. 135). This story – and indeed the entire novel – revolves around events as objects "which no white man" or at least very few "could have read." Rider is warned by a friend not to go home for fear of "the dead who either will not or cannot quit the earth yet although the flesh they once lived in has been returned to it, let the preachers tell and reiterate and affirm how they left it not only without regret but with joy, mounting toward glory: 'You dont wants ter go back dar. She be wawkin yit' " (p. 136). Nevertheless, he returns to a strange meeting:

> Then the dog left him. The light pressure went off his flank; he heard the click and hiss of its claws on the wooden floor as it surged away and he thought at first that it was fleeing. But it stopped just outside the front door, where he could see it now, and the upfling of its head as the howl began, and then he saw her too. She was standing in the kitchen door, looking at him. He didn't move. He didn't breathe nor speak until he knew his voice would be all right, his face fixed too not to alarm her. "Mannie," he said. "Hit's awright. Ah aint afraid."

Then he took a step toward her, slow, not even raising his hand yet, and stopped. Then he took another step. But this time as soon as he moved she began to fade. He stopped at once, not breathing again, motionless, willing his eyes to see that she had stopped too. But she had not stopped. She was fading, going. "Wait," he said, talking as sweet as he had ever heard his voice speak to a woman: "Den lemme go wid you, honey." But she was going. She was going fast now, he could actually feel between them the insuperable barrier of that very strength which could handle alone a log which would have taken any two other men to handle, of the blood and bones and flesh too strong, invincible for life, having learned at least once with his own eyes how tough, even in sudden and violent death, not a young man's bones and flesh perhaps but the will of that bone and flesh to remain alive, actually was.   (pp. 140–1)

To appreciate how convincing and powerful this preternatural encounter is, one must of course traverse the pages which lead up to it. Faulkner's mastery of traditional narrative style and device is nowhere more brilliantly demonstrated than here in his portrayal of Rider's weird homecoming, of Ike's initiatory glimpse of the ghost buck in "The Old People," and of Ike's later and more famous meeting with Ben at the conclusion of Part 1 of *The Bear.*

To what end beyond a short-lived *frisson* for ghost-story aficionados is all this technical mastery dedicated? Unlike many masterpieces of the genre, such as *The Turn of the Screw*, these stories in *Go Down, Moses* are not studies in hysteria, i.e., in the abnormal behavior of super-Sensible individuals. They are, rather, renderings of a kind of experience which, although unusual and awesome, is perfectly "normal" within pre-Enlightenment cultures. This is not to say that Faulkner obliges us to credit the objective existence of a ghost or specter; for, like Hawthorne, he supplies all the psychological and religious circumstances requisite for an alternative sceptical, or "realistic," explanation. But Faulkner's critique of the materialist world view that finds such an explanation necessary is more radical than Hawthorne's (although not more so than Melville's) just as the "passion in him for extremes" of romance and realism is far more "rich." In social terms, Faulkner's passion for the "Terrible Graces of magic and enchantment" and the "sublime and alarming images" of romance translates less as a will to believe in the existence of a nonhuman Other than as a willingness to embrace, *as human*, that experience of the demonic which is one of the marks by which we too commonly identify other peoples as superstitious, subhuman, or demonic themselves.

On the showing of *Go Down, Moses*, the range of experience of which "civilized" white people are capable is extensive in some directions but correspondingly limited in others and likely to grow more so with the disappearance of the wilderness and of "the old people," and with the inevitable atrophy of certain sensory and psychological faculties. Instructing Cass Edmonds to allow Ike to stay behind with the body of Sam Fathers, General Compson accurately recognizes that the great change had been in the making decades before the deaths of Sam and Old Ben:

> You've got one foot straddled into a farm and the other foot straddled into a bank; you aint even got a good hand-hold where this boy was already an old man long before you damned Sartorises and Edmondses invented farms and banks to keep yourselves from having to find out what this boy was born knowing and fearing too maybe but without being afraid, that could go ten miles on a compass because he wanted to look at a bear none of us had ever got near enough to put a bullet in and looked at the bear and came the ten miles back on the compass in the dark; maybe by God that's the why and the wherefore of farms and banks.   (pp. 250–1)

Despite the farms and banks, the wilderness of the Big Bottom remains an island intact in the sea of history, and the long-delayed end of the heroic era does not come until the deaths of Ben, the dog Lion, and Sam Fathers. The event is marked not only by ritualized interments but also by a solemn flourish of elegiac rhetoric reminiscent of Icelandic saga, Arthurian romance, or Anglo-Saxon heroic verse:

> They came up mounted and on foot and in wagons, to enter the yard and look at him [the slain bear] and then go to the front where Lion lay, filling the little yard and overflowing it until there were almost a hundred of them squatting and standing in the warm and drowsing sunlight, talking quietly of hunting, of the game and the dogs which ran it, of hounds and bear and deer and men of yesterday vanished from the earth, while from time to time the great blue dog would open his eyes, not as if he were listening to them but as though to look at the woods for a moment before closing his eyes again, to remember the woods or to see that they were still there. He died at sundown.   (p. 248)

This echo of the heroic narratives of the past reminds us that specters and monsters and prodigious feats of strength and skill belong to the genre and that, as a romance within a novel, *The Bear* is an island against time and familiar social routine like the Big Bottom itself. However, fully committed though he is to the ideals and conventions of heroic romance, Faulkner knows as well as Malory or the *Beowulf* poet that it is the nature and fate of the finest heroic fellowships as of the fairest marital unions to be touched, to be irradiated by "that brief unsubstanced glory which inherently of itself cannot last and hence why glory" (p. 326).

When the spell of romance is broken, subtle changes take place in the characters themselves and in their relations to each other and nature. Major de Spain sells the timber rights in the Big Bottom to a Memphis lumber company; and although his former companions still go on hunting trips together, they go to new places and with a new spirit – a spirit born of farms and banks. The transformation is registered most powerfully not in any pithy sentence but rather in two juxtaposed "treeing" episodes in Part 5. The second of these episodes is the celebrated conclusion of *The Bear* which recounts Ike's coming upon Boon Hogganbeck, his back against a tree alive with forty or fifty trapped and desperate squirrels, hammering at the jammed breech of his dismembered gun with its barrel, and shouting, "Get out of here! Dont touch them! Dont touch a one of them! They're mine!" (p. 331). Taken by itself, this is an unforgettable cartoon image of modern acquisitive man, incapable of controlling his own machines but all too capable of driving nature berserk. However, some of the point of the episode is lost unless it is read in the light of an earlier episode in which a young bear, frightened by a locomotive, rushes as far up a tree as it can go:

> and when the engine returned three hours later with the first load of outbound logs the bear was halfway down the tree and once more scrambled back up as high as it could and clung again while the train passed and was still there when the engine went in again in the afternoon and still there when it came back out at dusk; and Boon had been in Hoke's with the wagon after a barrel of flour that noon when the train-crew told about it and Boon and Ash, both twenty years younger then, sat under the tree all that night to keep anybody from shooting it and the next morning Major de Spain had the log-train held at Hoke's and just before sundown on the second day . . . it came down the tree after almost thirty-six hours without even water and McCaslin told him how for a minute they thought it was going to stop right there at the barrow-pit where they were standing and drink, how it looked at the water and paused and looked at them and at the water again, but did not, gone, running, as bears run, the two sets of feet, front and back, tracking two separate though parallel courses. (pp. 319–20)

The last evocative detail, of the parallel track the bear makes, is extraordinarily poignant, for it helps explain why earlier in the story Faulkner likens Ben to a locomotive. At the same time, it reinforces our awareness of the actual unlikeness of iron machines and flesh-and-blood bears, hence of the sad vulnerability of the latter.

Not only squirrels and bears, but also foxes and human beings are treed in *Go Down, Moses*. In the opening story, "Was," the McCaslin slave Tomey's Turl is the object of a chase which nine-year-old Cass Edmonds considers "the best race he had ever seen" (p. 8). " 'I godfrey, we've got him,' " says Uncle Buck, i.e., Theophilus McCaslin, uncle of Cass Edmonds, twin brother of Amadeus (Uncle Buddy), father-to-be of Isaac, and half brother of Tomey's Turl. " 'He's going to earth. We'll cut back to the house and head him before he can den' " (pp. 17–18). Like that of all the other white adult characters in "Was," Uncle Buck's level of moral sophistication is barely, if at all, more elevated than that of the child from whose point of view the story is told. And because Faulkner does not permit himself any of the explosive authorial surrogates through which Mark Twain denounces similar Southern provincials as stupid, cowardly, cruel, absurd, and contemptible, we have to see for ourselves that this is not the message of "Was." Of course it *is* shocking that Turl is chased like an animal and that the outcome of a game of five-card stud poker decides whether Turl will be able to marry Hubert Beauchamp's slave Tennie and also whether Uncle Buck will have to marry Hubert's sister Sophonsiba. Faulkner means us to be shocked but not to condemn the participants in these games, whose humane instincts are privately and, by and large, unconsciously at odds with the public laws, social rituals, and cultural models – the "lower myths" – which are supposed to govern behavior in antebellum Mississippi society.

In "Was" the Planter-Cavalier myth is still, in 1859, a power to which all of the characters pay homage, even though the gap between this ideal and the life that is actually lived on the McCaslin and Beauchamp places is almost as risibly wide as that between ideal and actuality in *A Connecticut Yankee at King Arthur's Court* and *The Tragedy of Pudd'nhead Wilson*. And it is as true of "Was" as of these novels that the actuality is sufficiently somber, or at least humanly urgent, to give their comedy a very sharp satiric bite – to expose the governing myths of Southern society (or its Arthurian counterpart) as grotesquely inadequate to human needs and even dehumanizing inasmuch as they effectively divide races, genders, and classes from each other in order to enfranchise a few preposterous F.F.V.'s (F.F.V. = First Family of Virginia), knights errant, and Mississippi belles.

When Uncle Buck and Cass arrive at the entrance to the Beauchamp farm,

> there was no gate there; just two posts and a nigger boy about his size sitting on one of them, blowing a fox-horn; this was what Miss Sophonsiba was still reminding people was named Warwick even when they had already known for a long time that's what she aimed to have it called, until when they wouldn't call it Warwick she wouldn't even seem to know what they were talking about and it would sound as if she and Mr Hubert owned two separate plantations covering the same area of ground, one on top of the other. Mr Hubert was sitting in the spring-house with his boots off and his feet in the water, drinking a toddy.   (p. 9)

According to Miss Sophonsiba, Hubert is probably the true Earl of Warwick, "only he never even had enough pride, not to mention energy, to take the trouble to establish his just rights" (p. 5). These claims to illustrious antecedents remind us of Mark Twain's King and Duke, but of course Miss Sophonsiba is not a rogue but a fantasist. And it is true in a way that "she and Mr. Hubert owned two separate plantations." Hers is "Warwick" as it should be – or as it might be conjured up in hazy romantic outline by one of her favorite "historical" fictions. (Soph-onsiba, *alias* Sophy, is very like Mark Twain's Alisande, *alias* Sandy, and it is possible that Faulkner picks Warwick rather than some other romantic touristic site because it is there that the "editor" of *A Connecticut Yankee* obtains the story of Hank Morgan.) Hubert's is the plantation as it is in material reality – a perplexing mixture of the unfinished (two gate posts with neither a gate nor a fence) and the dilapidated (broken windowpanes and rotting floorboards). "Warwick," it transpires, is like Sophonsiba herself: a lonely decaying virgin with a roan-colored tooth and roached hair who would appear merely homely and sadly neglected in other circumstances but is made grotesque by the fine airs and flounces of a conventionally irresistible Mississippi lady.

This pattern of two realities covering the same ground is not limited to the Beauchamp place. Buck and Buddy's cover of gentility amounts to little more than a few scanty tokens – hastily donning a necktie before calling on neighbors, dragging a foot (bowing) when greeting a lady – but the tokens matter and apparently suffice. The same is true of the aged bachelor twins' dealings with their slaves. By the end of the story, it is evident that Tomey's Turl is smarter and stronger than his masters, and that he is essentially able to get what he wants so long as both parties observe the external niceties and regulations of the master-slave relation. In fact, Buck and Buddy are in some respects the victims of an ironic role reversal.

Nowhere in "Was," or indeed in the whole range of Faulkner's fiction, is this kind of reversal (or chiasmus, one of the characteristic forms of Hawthorne's irony) more tellingly imaged than in the account of how, after the death of their father, the founding McCaslin, the twins built a house of their own and "moved all the niggers into the big house which his [Cass's] great-grandfather had not had time to finish" (p. 6). To complete this parodic system within the official system of slavery, Buddy and Buck solemnly fasten the front door of the great unfinished house after dinner every evening but always forget to lock the back door. This benign arrangement – so topsy-turvy and yet so perfectly representative of the accommodations by which human beings in every society manage to gain a little freedom while maintaining outward respectful conformity to the most restrictive codes – is a satiric invention worthy of Mark Twain himself. Of course it is an invention, and when I say that it is representative I do not mean that any antebellum plantations were run with as much permissiveness and ironic humor as the McCaslin twins run theirs.

I have mentioned Mark Twain several times in connection with "Was." How could one do otherwise in any account that looks beyond its immediate Faulknerian context? However, we do both writers an injustice if we suppose that "Was" is simply an exercise in the Southern Cervantesque mode which Mark Twain perfected, patented, and pretty well exhausted in *The Adventures of Huckleberry Finn, A Connecticut Yankee*, and *Pudd'nhead Wilson*.

In the first place, it is obvious that in importing and fostering the Cavalier myth the South also inevitably saddled itself with an unwelcome mock-heroic companion version of the myth which could be kept out of sight and mind most of the time, but not always. Leaving aside some of the peculiar manifestations of latter-day chivalry they might have run into in "real life," Southern readers would have encountered some of the Don's descendants in the eighteenth-century French and English comic novelists – especially Le Sage, Fielding, Smollett, and Goldsmith – whose influence is manifest in the opening chapters of *Waverley* and in a work somewhat less important in the history of letters, but written by a neighbor in Pennsylvania, Hugh Henry Brackenridge's *Modern Chivalry* (1792–1815).

So it is not surprising that we discover quixotic foibles in (for instance) Simms's Carolinian cavalier Porgy and G. W. Cable's Creole Grandissimes as well as in the choice Missourian specimens collected in *Pudd'nhead Wilson*, nor that they reappear in Tate's bombastic Mr. Broadacre, master of ceremonies for the Fairfax County Gentlemen's Tournament Association, and in Faulkner's "Mississippi lady," Miss Sophonsiba Beauchamp of "Warwick." I do not mean to suggest that these characters and the stories in which they figure are as like as blackberries from the same bush. Porgy's subdued quixotry, for instance, sometimes makes him vulnerable and funny but never silly and subhuman like Mark Twain's F.F.V.'s; and Faulkner's experiments in the Cervantesque mode are at once more earthy and grotesque, hence closer to the original, even than those in *A Connecticut Yankee*. Still, their common ancestry is evident; and as is eloquently illustrated by the genealogical romance with which Roxy tries to shame her cowardly son, Tom, ancestry was just about everything in the Old South:

> "Whatever has come o' yo' Essex blood? Dat's what I can't understan'. En it ain't on'y jist Essex blood dats in you, not by a long sight – 'deed it ain't! My great-great-great-gran'-father en yo great-great-great-great-gran'-father was ole Cap'n John Smith, de highest blood dat Ole Virginny ever turned out, en *his* great-great-gran'mother, or somers along back dah, was Pocahontas de Injun queen, en her husbun' was a nigger king outen Africa – en yit here you is, a slinkin' outen a duel en disgracin' our whole line like a ornery low-down hound! Yes, it's de nigger in you."[43]

3. *Mysteries of the Old South*

I do not suppose that Southerners have had more skeletons in their closets than other Americans or that much should be made of the fact that a Virginian invented the detective tale – unless it be that the failure of antebellum Southern society to recognize and patronize a serious literary artist obliged Poe to try to make art, remunerative art, out of the journalistic exposés of family homicide, criminal conspiracy, and urban vice that were as popular during the 1840s as they are today. So little did Poe associate the lurid matter of this literature with the farms and towns of the American South that he set his most famous mystery stories in Paris. It was Hawthorne, not Poe, who wrote our early classic tales of secret sin and inescapable detection; and we need only recall the seventeenth-century witchcraft trials to realize that New England, much more than the South, was the land with a guilty conscience and that it was Northern, not Southern, writers of the antebellum period who inherited the keenest sense of ancestral or neighborly criminality as well as the most refined machinery for searching it out. When Thomas Jefferson sought an explanation for the "witch-hunting" excesses of which the Adams administration was guilty at the time of the XYZ affair, he pointed to the New England origins of the majority of Federalists, but expressed a characteristic conviction that Enlightenment would prevail: "A little patience, and we shall see the reign of witches pass over, their spells dissolved, and the people recovering their true sight, restoring their government to its true principles."[44]

Although the mystery novel has never been associated with any Southern location in the way that it was with Paris and London during the nineteenth century and New York and California during the twentieth, it is perhaps not coincidental that the greatest Southern fictionalist of each century organized his greatest historical romance around the reconstruction of a crime. *Pudd'nhead Wilson* and *Absalom, Absalom!* are both versions of the "whodunnit," and Part IV of *The Bear* makes *Go Down, Moses* another. That this should be true in the cases of the authors of *Tom Sawyer, Detective* and *Intruder in the Dust* is hardly surprising. For they were not only historical romancers but also frequent consumers and producers of the detective novel in its familiar and conventional form.[45] As for the regional connection, it may well be that – among intellectuals – a delayed consequence of the devastating defeat of the South's social experiment was not just a guilty conscience about slavery but also a pressing need to discover crimes sufficient to account for the terrible protracted punishment which the Civil War and Reconstruction generations had suffered. An unverifiable thesis, but one which the historical romances of Glasgow, Tate, and Faulkner go far to support.

Leaving aside, temporarily, the regional affiliations and special generic interests of particular authors, there are several obvious reasons why historical romances have often taken the narrative shape of a "mystery." From the perspective of the present study, the most important one is that the epistemological concerns and procedures of the (fictional) detective are related in quite fundamental ways to those of the historian and historical romancer, and have a common origin in the Enlightenment quest to carry the light of reason and scientific method into all spheres – and especially into those where privileged forms of knowledge were reserved to a priestly or bardic caste and shielded by "superstition" and its ally, the poetic imagination. Such, at any rate, was what Horace Walpole and many of his successors apprehended the agenda of Enlightenment "philosophy" to be. Simultaneously fascinated by the methods and findings of a new, investigative kind of history, and yet anxious to preserve the privileged status of certain "mysteries," historical romancers from Scott and Cooper onwards have constantly flirted with the role of the ratiocinative detective and at other times have rejected it as morally obtuse or worse. The result of this fascination–repulsion pattern is an extraordinary case of generic doubleness, notably in the work of Faulkner, which bears some further investigation here.

Actually, more than doubleness is involved. For while all mystery novels may have a remote ancestor in Greek tragedy, and do have a distinguishing generic preoccupation with the exposure of something hidden because of its sacred or criminal nature, this kind of fiction appears in several interrelated yet distinct forms during the nineteenth and twentieth centuries. A paragraph or two about each of them will help us to recognize their more than mere traces in the historical romances of Tate, Faulkner, and Mark Twain.

I have already had occasion to discuss the gothic mystery novel which Horace Walpole invented and rationalized and which Ann Radcliffe brought to a kind of perfection in *The Mysteries of Udolpho*. The abiding center of interest in Radcliffe's romance is the heroine's apprehensions of, and stratagems to circumvent, rape – i.e., the violation of her own sexual mystery. Compared to this ever-present threat, the mysteries to which Radcliffe's title refers are intense but short-lived and ultimately trivial. They send a shiver up the spine because they partake of the inexplicable and ghastly, but they are easily exposed as so much waxwork just as soon as missing evidence is supplied and the characters stop running long enough to examine it calmly. Fictions which follow the Radcliffe pattern dramatize the final – but deliciously delayed – victory of Enlightenment empiricism over gothic superstition. Cooper liked the pattern and regularly used it, as for instance when he clears up the mystery of the Angel of Hadley in *The Wept of Wish-ton-Wish*.

Older than the gothic mystery tale is the sensational exposé story which discloses the appalling secrets of urban "dens," of allegedly conspiratorial organizations, and of rich and famous individuals. Examples are Eugene Sue's *The Mysteries of Paris*, Ned Buntline's *The Mysteries and Miseries of New York*, and Joseph Berg's *The Great Apostasy, Identical with Papal Rome; or an Exposition of the Mystery of Iniquity, and the Marks and Doom of Antichrist*. The literature that deals in such revelations has an unmistakable family likeness, but may or may not assume an overtly novelistic form, be sincere in its moralistic aims and rhetoric, or have "mystery" in the title. ("Secrets" or "Awful Disclosures" will do, but "mysteries" promises something more horrible.) As Berg's title suggests, one irresistible target of this form of mystery literature in democratic Protestant America during the nineteenth century was any organization, such as a conventual or fraternal order, which actually had a secret rite − a *mysterium* − that it protected by excluding curious neighbors and journalists. Not only hack writers and fraudulent "ex-nuns" like Maria Monk but eminent divines like Lyman Beecher revived the reign of witches with their discoveries of a "Catholic menace." Beecher's own daughter followed his example (albeit in a far better cause) by romancing the horrors of slavery in the most successful exposé fiction of all time. Harriet Beecher Stowe entitled her book *Uncle Tom's Cabin, or, Life among the Lowly*; had she been a few degrees less genteel and earnest, she might have called it "The Mysteries of the Deep South."[46]

Mystery stories of the exposé variety are typically more concerned with the product than the process, i.e., with instant gratification rather than Radcliffean suspense, and with authenticating tokens rather than the personality and procedures of the investigator. Poe's personal obsession with method enabled him to see that whereas the story of a crime was likely to be banal, the story of its detection had a potential for sustained interest which Radcliffe's last-minute disentanglements did not begin to exploit. More, that the combination of these stories − the one "low" and brutal, the other aristocratic and cerebral − had a piquancy which increased in direct proportion to the contrast between them. Hence, in stories presided over by his elegant detective, C. Auguste Dupin, Poe incorporates some of the most gruesome elements from exposé literature. In the *Mystery of Marie Roget*, the narrator counterpoints Dupin's disquisitions on method with rapt descriptions of the decomposing body of a brutally strangled woman. Poe's picture of the corpse may excite a *frisson* of mingled fear and disgust; the sight is one from which, in real life, we would avert our eyes. But this is as close as we usually come in detective fiction to the ancient sense of *mysterium* as a rite or doctrine revealed only to initiates, precious and yet fearful to know, which Poe himself registers in the juvenile poem "Dreamland":

> But the traveller, travelling through it,
> May not – dare not openly view it;
> Never its mysteries are exposed
> To the weak human eye unclosed.[47]

Dupin's cool ratiocinative exploits may be said to propose and celebrate a rival mystery – viz., how deeply and into what secret passages of human history and the natural universe may not the inquiring intelligence penetrate if it only be sufficiently patient to observe and daring to infer?

Although Roger Chillingworth obviously shares many traits with Dupin, we do not ordinarily think of *The Scarlet Letter* as a murder mystery. But a mystery novel of some species it certainly is, and we should recall that one of Hawthorne's sources (the Overbury case) involved a most foul murder and that Dimmesdale is surely thinking of himself when he asks hypothetically, "Why should a wretched man, guilty, we will say, of murder, prefer to keep the dead corpse buried in his own heart, rather than fling it forth at once, and let the universe take care of it!" (p. 132). We are correct to understand him as speaking metaphorically of his "buried" sin and also as registering obliquely his agonized conviction that he has murdered his own soul by living a hideous lie. Yet if we permit the allusions to murder mysteries to stay buried in the text, we may fail to see that one of the projects of *The Scarlet Letter*, as later of *Benito Cereno* and *Billy Budd*, is to reclaim a meaning for the word "mystery" which was fast being lost – at least partly because of the uses to which it had been put by writers like Radcliffe, Sue, and Poe.

Like "sympathy," "mystery" is one of the recurrent keywords of *The Scarlet Letter*, and, also like "sympathy," it is misappropriated by Chillingworth:

> "Never, sayest thou?" rejoined he, with a smile of dark and self-relying intelligence. "Never know him! Believe me, Hester, there are few things, – whether in the outward world, or, to a certain depth, in the invisible sphere of thought, – few things hidden from the man, who devotes himself earnestly and unreservedly to the solution of a mystery . . . There is a sympathy that will make me conscious of him." (p. 75)

The word "mystery" is associated especially with Dimmesdale but also with his pursuing demon, whose "first entry on the scene, few people could tell whence, dropping down, as it were, out of the sky, or starting from the nether earth, had an aspect of mystery, which was easily heightened to the miraculous" (p. 121). To Chillingworth himself, however, who has no more natural or acquired piety than Dupin, a mystery has no kinship with the miraculous; it is merely something to which one finds a "solution." Although he boasts that sympathy will help him detect Hester's lover, his actual method is close observation, skilled inference, interrogation which disarms while it probes, and a kind of intuition which counterfeits the invisible accords of sympathy. When Dimmesdale discovers that the "leech" has used this method to gain access to his secret, he exclaims that Chillingworth has "violated, in cold blood, the sanctity of a human heart" (p. 195). Coming as it does from the minister during his brief reunion with Hester, "violated" has strong sexual overtones, but its primary meaning is "desecrated" or "profaned."

It is on the same principle that the narrator of *Billy Budd* declines to comment further on what happened during Vere's last interview with Billy, concluding that "there is no telling the sacrament, seldom if in any case revealed to the gadding world, wherever . . . two of great Nature's nobler order embrace. There is privacy at the time, inviolable to the survivor, and holy oblivion, the sequel to each diviner magnanimity, providentially covers all at last" (p. 113). Melville does not use the word "mystery" here, and need not, for it is clear that the love described is the polar opposite of the antipathy which he (and Vere, too) categorizes earlier among the "mysteries of iniquity" (pp. 61, 104). Denying that any previous "romantic incident" can be produced to explain why Claggart (himself a detective in the Chillingworth mold) is "down" on the Handsome Sailor, Melville asserts that "the cause . . . is in its very realism as much charged with that prime element of Radcliffian romance, the mysterious, as any that the ingenuity of the author of the *Mysteries of Udolpho* could devise" (pp. 57–8). Intuitive understanding of the moral and spiritual mysteries was the kind of knowledge that Melville came to rate most highly and saw most threatened by the positivistic trends in science, historiography, and realistic fiction. Just as, for W. H. Seward and other opponents of the Fugitive Slave clause, there was a "higher law than the Constitution," so for Melville there was a higher realism than that of W. D. Howells and the Goncourt brothers. "Realism" was another word whose ancient meaning he wished to reclaim.[48]

Very soon after death brought work on *Billy Budd* to a premature conclusion, Francis Galton's *Finger Prints* (1892) supplied Mark Twain with the solution to problems he had been having with a story provisionally entitled "Those Extraordinary Twins." Yet while *Billy Budd* and *Pudd'nhead Wilson* belong to the same period, it would be difficult to find two "mystery novels" less alike in tone and attitude. Nowhere are their differences more apparent than in the contrast between Melville's lightly veiled contempt for the materialist philosophy of the *Bellipotent*'s surgeon and Mark Twain's delight in the brand-new scientific key to identity which enables his Northern outsider hero to demonstrate that the murderer of Judge Driscoll is not the foreigner Count Luigi and that the homegrown real murderer, Tom Driscoll, is actually a "nigger" and a slave rather than the unsullied F.F.V. whom everybody (except his mother Roxy) has always taken him for. To Mark Twain, a transplanted Southerner whose perspective on the cultures of New England and the South almost exactly reverses that of Jefferson at the time of the XYZ affair, Pudd'nhead's achievement represents the triumph of Northern science over Southern prejudice. More broadly still, it represents the triumph of Enlightenment philosophy over medieval superstition, or, to revert once more to Scott's terms, of modern incredulity over ancient faith. Although Wilson's clever but rather elementary performance in the Dawson's Landing courtroom might appear too slight to bear the weight of so much intellectual history, we should not underrate Mark Twain's ability to make the translations I have suggested or his tendency, from *A Connecticut Yankee* onwards, to make them habitually.[49]

We are quick to see the literary joke and sly social commentary implicit in the exclamations of "great Scott!" which echo through his works at this time and in the characterization of "widow Cooper – affectionately called 'aunt Patsy' " and her daughter "Rowena, who was nineteen, romantic, amiable, and very pretty, but otherwise of no consequence" (p. 87). But we may fail to recognize the parodic use of the language of religious vision to describe the process by which Wilson arrives at an explanation of the discrepancy between Tom Driscoll's fingerprints as an adult and as an infant:

> "It's no use – I can't understand it. They don't tally right, and yet I'll swear the names and dates are right, and so of course they *ought* to tally. I never labelled one of these things carelessly in my life. There is a most extraordinary mystery here."
>
> He was tired out now, and his brains were beginning to clog. He said he would sleep himself fresh, and then see what he could do with this riddle. He slept through a troubled and unrestful hour, then unconsciousness began to shred away, and presently he rose drowsily to a sitting posture. "Now what was that dream?" he said, trying to recall it. "What was that dream? It seemed to unravel that puz – "
>
> He landed in the middle of the floor at a bound, without finishing the sentence, and ran and turned up his light and seized his "records." He took a single swift glance at them and cried out –
>
> "It's so! Heavens, what a revelation!"   (pp. 209–10)

Because the solution to a "most extraordinary mystery" comes to Wilson in a dream and surfaces to consciousness with abrupt force, his immediate unconsidered response is, in effect, to betray his hard-won

scientific discovery with a supernaturalist explanation of how he arrived
at it. This irony, aimed not just at poor Pudd'nhead but at the whole of
the damned human race in its struggle to rise above misery and
superstition, is one that Voltaire would have relished.

Still, in *Pudd'nhead Wilson* scepticism tempers rather than undermines
faith in reason, hence in science and progress, and for this cause too its
author reminds us of the *philosophes*. Although Mark Twain's personal
faith in these supreme goods of the Enlightenment did not outlast his
own prosperity, it is characteristic of the works by which he is and should
be chiefly remembered. In them, the South (or its counterpart, Camelot)
is the locus of everything that is "backward," the North of everything
"forward." This scheme, the more important to Mark Twain because it
projected his personal history in national dimensions, is so reductive that
it seems an unintentional parody of the *Waverley*-model, and surely
would be ruinous for his fictions if his power to schematize consistently
were half so great as his power to recall and record the felt life of the Old
Southwest. That power to recall, developed while he was a riverboat
pilot, had another consequence which is of special pertinence here: it
reinforced a confidence, characteristic of progressivists, that just as a
satisfying future for mankind could be built, so could the past be
satisfactorily reconstructed – given the necessary cleverness and (Northern) tools. This confidence, which he shares with early Cooper, Simms,
and Poe, (and also with Hawthorne's Chillingworth,) distinguishes his
sense of history-making very sharply from that of Hawthorne and
Melville, Tate and Faulkner. Unlike the latter writers, Mark Twain
identifies the historian very closely with the detective of "whodunnit"
fiction.

As noticed earlier, detective novels have two stories: the story of the
crime and the story of its detection. This is true of "history" as well. In his
presidential address to the American Historical Association in 1931, Carl
Becker drew an elementary distinction between two histories:

> the actual series of events that once occurred; and the ideal series that we affirm
> and hold in memory. The first is absolute and unchanged – it was what it was
> whatever we do and say about it; the second is relative, always changing in
> response to the increase or refinement of knowledge. The two series
> correspond more or less; it is our aim to make the correspondence as exact as
> possible; but the actual series of events exists for us only in terms of the ideal
> series which we affirm and hold in memory.[50]

Setting aside the fictitiousness of both stories in a detective novel, it seems
clear that there is close structural parallel between those stories and the
two histories differentiated by Becker. But Becker's insistence on the
changing and relative nature of "the ideal series which we . . . hold in
memory," and of its uncertain correspondence to "the actual series of

events," points to a radical difference between his conception of history-making and the classic detective novel's model of mystery-solving. For the contract that the detective novelist makes with his reader is that by the end of the book there will be a perfect correspondence between the two series: the story of detection will reveal the whole story of the crime. In common with many professional historians of the time, Mark Twain apparently believed that the "science" of history would be able to do something very similar. Becker, writing at a time when economic progress had gone into reverse gear and academic historians seemed somewhat beside the point being made by the actual series of events, reacted against this faith in science and specialization, and it is his view that prevails in the historical romances which Tate and Faulkner were to write a few years later.

Tate had already published biographies of Stonewall Jackson and Jefferson Davis by the time he began work on *The Fathers*. Its account of public attitudes and events in northern Virginia at the outset of war is as detailed as could be desired in a historical novel, and I believe that its essential accuracy would be confirmed by Civil War historians. But the private and fictitious part of the book, in which the narrator seeks to recover the motives of individuals, the ambience of "houses," is full of problems and mysteries that refuse to be solved.

Perhaps it is to be expected that "mystery" and "mysterious" would be among Lacy Buchan's favorite words. For one of his favorite authors is Poe, whose works are echoed ("A Dream within a Dream") and explicitly cited ("The Fall of the House of Usher") for their "prophetic insight" into weird over-refined Southern families like the Poseys. Moreover, the story he has to tell has many of the stock ingredients of a gothic mystery tale – the alleged rape of Jane, the double murder of Yellow Jim and Semmes Buchan, the swift removal of the "violated" girl to a convent. Something unexplained and maybe inexplicable clings to these events. What exactly *did* Yellow Jim do to Jane, and what were his motives? What, since there seems to have been some kind of complicity involved, were hers? Retreating from the riddle presented by Jane's part in the tragedy, Lacy simply concludes that "what it all meant was one of those mysteries that never come into the light." (p. 217). There is no doubt that Semmes killed Yellow Jim and that George Posey killed Semmes immediately thereafter, but what drove them to these deeds?[51] Of Semmes, Lacy comments that

> in spite of the simplicity of his part in it, if you looked at it logically, something remained that would always be mysterious . . . That was the mystery about Semmes: he was logical. An engaged man had to see that a Negro who insulted his affianced bride got properly killed. Logic in human conduct is the hardest thing of all to understand, and people are never more mysterious than when

they are being rational. I mean rational without passion; for if you get the
passion behind it then the reason is only a screen through which a sharp eye
may discern what it is that people really do. (p. 270)

Lacy's concluding observation invites us to try to pierce through the
screen of his own reason. To do so is necessary partly because he was an
adolescent at the time of the action and therefore sometimes failed to
understand the motives of his elders simply because of his inexperience. It
is necessary, too, because although he is an elderly and sage man at the
time of the narration, he disclaims any ability to explain his story or even
to recover some of its most important components:

> there is not an old man living who can recover the emotions of the past; he can
> only bring back the objects about which, secretly, the emotions have ordered
> themselves in memory, and that memory is not what happened in the year
> 1860 but is rather a few symbols, a voice, a tree, a gun shining on the wall –
> symbols that will preserve only so much of the old life as they may, in their own
> mysterious history, consent to bear. (p. 22)

In short, the seemingly modest aim of this Gerontion is not to interpret
but to make an "objective correlative" out of the symbolic objects stored
in his memory whereby the reader might share otherwise irrecoverable
and incomprehensible feelings – about money, say, or honor or a slave's
"unspeakable fault" (p. 270). Like the reader of an Eliot poem –
"Gerontion," let us say – the reader of *The Fathers* is obliged to bring
considerable resourcefulness and information to the task of glossing what
young Lacy did not and old Lacy does not understand. So I mention
"Gerontion" advisedly; for, besides, being another literary masterpiece
whose presiding consciousness is that of an aged, culturally adrift
monologist, *The Fathers* is likewise centrally concerned with the loss of
faith, of meaningful contact with the past, and therefore of direction in
the present and future.

The novel appropriately begins with a funeral, mother Buchan's, and
Lacy recalls the Episcopalian pastor Dr. Cartwright intoning the burial
service and seeming to be

> just a voice, in the *ore rotundo* of impersonality, no feeling but in the words
> themselves. I stared at his round face.
>
> "Behold I shew you a mystery: we shall not all sleep, but we shall all be
> changed, in a moment, in the twinkling of an eye, at the last trump; for the
> trumpet shall sound and the dead shall be raised incorruptible." (p. 105)

To Major Buchan, Dr. Cartwright is "the kind of pastor a gentleman can
talk to" (p. 97); to Lacy, remembering the minister's "wide generous
mouth," he is only a "pleasant worldling" who deals in mysteries he is
able to "shew" (thanks to the words of the church's various services)
without having had a glimpse of them himself. Although Lacy does not

claim much more for his own powers of penetration, it is obvious that on any scale of spiritual and moral insight he would have to be ranked several notches higher than this Fairfax County "divine." For, notwithstanding his disclaimers, he is able to evoke the scenes and emotions of the past – to raise the dead in all their mystery – and, up to a point, to supply a very shrewd retrospective interpretation of them. Perhaps he is most revealing about his dead and himself when he recalls what George meant to Semmes and Semmes to George:

> I always come back to the horseman riding off over a precipice . . . And that is what he gave to Semmes – mystery and imagination, the heightened vitality possessed by a man who knew no bounds. What Semmes gave to him was what he most needed but never could take: Semmes gave him first of all Susan, and then – papa being absolutely wrong about this – he tried to give him what the Poseys had lost: an idea, a cause, an action in which his personality could be extinguished, and it seemed as if George had succeeded in becoming a part of something greater than he: the Confederate cause.   (pp. 179–80)

What George meant to Semmes he also meant to the boy Lacy and, to some extent, still does mean to the old retired doctor ruminating over all the gone Poseys and Buchans. Oddly, however, the mystery of this "man who knew no bounds" apparently baffles and troubles Lacy *now* far less than the mystery of a brother Buchan whose every action was dictated by a code of conduct which their family and society had evolved over many generations. Contrary to old Lacy's analysis, there was nothing "logical" or "mysterious" in Semmes's carrying out the execution of Yellow Jim: he was simply playing his assigned part in the drama – putting on his *toga virilis* – and Lacy misreads his brother's actions because he has himself partly forgotten the script. His hero, George Posey, learned the words of the script but never understood what they meant.

Although Faulkner does not join in the verbal reclamation projects of Hawthorne, Melville, and Tate, his sense of the mysterious is very close to theirs. This kinship is probably closest in *Go Down, Moses* where Faulkner's critique of the white materialist world view coincides with the spectral visitations of "Pantaloon in Black," "The Old People," and *The Bear*. As for murder mysteries, murderers are executed both in "Pantaloon in Black" and the novel's title story; but the only mystery about their crimes is why, in the white deputy sheriff's words, Rider "comes straight back to the mill and to the same crap game where Birdsong has been running crooked dice on them mill niggers for fifteen years, goes straight to the same game where he has been peacefully losing a probably steady average ninety-nine percent of his pay ever since he got big enough to read the spots on them miss-out dice, and cuts Birdsong's throat clean to the neckbone five minutes later" (p. 156). It is beyond the

deputy's powers of sympathy or ratiocination to infer that Rider has just
been cruelly cheated in a bigger game than the one Birdsong runs, but
that Birdsong is accessible to a razor blade whereas God is not. However,
if murder does not out in *Go Down, Moses*, incest does – and does as a
result of a precocious feat of historical detective work by Isaac McCaslin
at the age of sixteen.

As is appropriate in a novel so much concerned with the expansion and
contraction of various zones of moral and spiritual consciousness over a
period of more than a century, Ike is able to reconstruct his grandfather's
crime against "*His own daughter His own daughter. No No Not even him*" (p.
270) because he is more capable than any previous McCaslin of entering
into the feelings which drove the girl's mother to suicide. Old Carothers
could not enter into them for the same reason that he could not
acknowledge Tomey as his own daughter and their union as incest – the
same reason that (as Ike perceives) he leaves a large legacy of money to
their child rather than say "*My son to a nigger . . . Even if My son wasn't but
just two words*" (pp. 269–70). With their hearts and deeds his white sons
repudiate both the Peculiar Institution and the justifying Planter myth,
but with their heads and words they can do little better than old
Carothers. When Buck finds Buddy's cryptic note, "Drownd herself,"
in the commissary ledger, he responds incredulously, "Who in hell ever
heard of a niger downding him self" (p. 267). Although Ike's insight and
sympathy are later tested and found wanting in "Delta Autumn," they
clearly represent a considerable improvement over those of his progenitors and also something hopeful to balance against the triumph of Flem
Snopes and the material interests. Certainly as we read *Go Down, Moses*
we are more aware of the downward than of the upward trajectory, of
the Romantic lament for lost wonders and worlds of feeling than of the
Enlightenment paean to the ultimate perfectibility of human institutions;
but it is a flicker of the old faith in moral progress, which cheered Thomas
Jefferson and Mark Twain too for a while, that brings Carothers
McCaslin's worst deed to light.

Although old Carothers leaves mysteries behind for his descendants to
solve, he is himself a much less mysterious figure than Thomas Sutpen
and, partly on that account, a much less imposing one. When Sutpen first
appears in Jefferson, his advent has, like Chillingworth's, "an aspect of
mystery, which was easily heightened to the miraculous." This
"demonic" Sutpen – the creation partly of the slighted virgin Rosa
Coldfield, partly of the idle choral bystanders in Jefferson – is also partly
Sutpen's own creation. Because, as he says, his time is short, his works
must be prodigious if he is to realize his design; and because his past is a
liability instead of an asset to that design, he must impress with the
mystery rather than the respectability of his origins.

This mystery leads, in turn, to a murder mystery: not about *who* Charles Bon's murderer was but about *why* Henry Sutpen killed his sister's fiancé and his own best friend. The rest, the bulk, of *Absalom, Absalom!* is concerned with the demystification of the demon and of the motives behind Sutpen's rejection and Henry's murder of Bon. In the course of what amounts to a collaborative investigation by Miss Rosa, Shreve McCannon, and three generations of Compsons (counting the deceased General Compson, Sutpen's sole confidant and thus a crucial witness), new evidence is brought to light and plausible inferences drawn. The "ideal series" held in the memory is brought into a more exact correspondence with the "actual series of events," and the story of the detection comes closer to the story of the crime. Since the search for Sutpen and his heirs is something of a game, Shreve can say, "Let me play a while now"; and Faulkner, drawing on Poe, can describe the students Shreve and Quentin "in the cold room (it was quite cold now) dedicated to that best of ratiocination which after all was a good deal like Sutpen's morality and Miss Coldfield's demonizing – this room not only dedicated to it but set aside for it and suitably so since it would be here above any other place that it (the logic and morality) could do the least amount of harm" (p. 280). But, as the last clause suggests, the Sutpen family history cannot be reconstructed after so many years without something more than ratiocination.

That something more is the gift of imaginative sympathy which Chillingworth lacked but which Hawthorne himself brought to the task of historical reconstruction. In *Absalom, Absalom!* it is the outsider, Shreve, who brings it. He is, as it were, able to vibrate so well to Quentin's frequency that they achieve "some happy marriage of speaking and hearing wherein each before the demand, the requirement, forgave condoned and forgot the faulting of the other – faultings both in the creating of this shade whom they discussed (rather, existed in) and in the hearing and sifting and discarding the false and conserving what seemed true, or fit the preconceived – in order to overpass to love, where there might be paradox and inconsistency but nothing fault nor false" (p. 336). The strong sense of sympathy, amounting almost to identification, with each other and with Sutpen (in whom they "existed") becomes most powerful as the two friends take up the story of two other friends:

> So that now it was not two but four of them riding the two horses through the dark over the frozen December ruts of that Christmas Eve: four of them and then just two – Charles-Shreve and Quentin-Henry, the two of them both believing that Henry was thinking *He* (meaning his father) *has destroyed us all,* not for one moment thinking *He* (meaning Bon) *must have known or at least suspected this all the time . . .*   (p. 334)

The history that Shreve and Quentin create is the product of a sympathy which connects human with human (irrespective of race or space) and the living present with the future and the past. They thus join the roles of historian and poet, as the latter is profiled by Wordsworth:

> Emphatically may it be said of the Poet, as Shakespeare hath said of man, 'that he looks before and after.' He is the rock of defence for human nature; an upholder and preserver, carrying everywhere with him relationship and love. In spite of difference of soil and climate, of language and manners, of laws and customs; in spite of things silently gone out of mind, and things violently destroyed; the Poet binds together by passion and knowledge the vast empire of human society, as it is spread over the whole earth, and over all time.[52]

To fulfill this role might seem a tall order even for a Wordsworth or a Shakespeare and an impossible one for a historian, who is, after all, constrained in ways that a poet is not. But a role very like this is envisaged for the humane historian by Carl Becker in the address, entitled "Everyman His Own Historian," from which I have already quoted:

> memory of things said and done (whether in our immediate yesterdays or in the long past of mankind), running hand in hand with the anticipation of things to be said and done, enables us, each to the extent of his knowledge and imagination, to be intelligent, to push back the narrow confines of the fleeting present moment so that what we are doing may be judged in the light of what we have done and what we hope to do. In this sense all *living* history, as Croce says, is contemporaneous. (p. 227)

Admirable as is Becker's aim to restore history to its "natural function" and to "Mr. Everyman," we may feel a greater need than he did to defend the dignity of "cloistered" scholarship and its associated values of detachment and of love of the past for its own sake and for its *difference* from the present. But, if we do feel this, we should be the better able to respond sympathetically to his sense of a more urgent need, in the dead of the very dead winter of 1931–2, to open commerce between the cloister and the street, history and "imaginative literature." Faulkner, working at the same time but from the other side of the barrier, felt the same need and in *Absalom, Absalom!* created a historical fiction which answers to the descriptions of both Wordsworth and Becker – nowhere more tellingly than when, at the end, Shreve shifts from the past present to the future present: "and so in a thousand years, I who regard you will also have sprung from the loins of African kings." Paradox and inconsistency there may be here, but it is a great and yet characteristic moment in historical romance and imaginative history.

9

Retrospect: departures and returns

Throughout this study I have resorted to lists of opposed terms as a means of representing the debate about, and with, the modern world which historical romances have been conducting, with more or less consistency and explicitness, over the past century and a half:

novel	romance
history	myth
science	mystery
progress	reaction
bourgeois	feudalistic
culture	nature
Sentimental	Naive
change	recurrence

Such lists can never be very satisfactory, but they have the advantage that their shortcomings are patent to everybody. The terms included in the lists have varied significantly as the discussion has moved from Europe in the eighteenth century to New England in the mid-nineteenth and then back to the American South of Thomas Jefferson. However, some of the terms have remained constant or found close synonyms, and so they help substantiate the claims for generic identity and constancy which I made at the beginning. If the lists were brought together, they might add up to a not unhelpful synthesis or overview of the ground covered in this book. But to do so would run the risk of turning a useful device into a methodological gimmick and, in any case, would pitch the discussion at a higher level of abstraction than seems appropriate at this point.

If these lists have any value, one set of opposed terms should be capable of implicating and standing for the rest. I therefore propose to conclude by reviewing the ways that recurrence has consorted with change in American historical romances. For the most part, recurrence in this study of a fictional genre with epic aspirations has meant some form of heroic reembodiment, and I will have something to say here about the way that historical romances present such reembodiments plausibly and positively, for our admiration and emulation. But as Faulkner's historical fiction illustrates with special force, recurrence can also mean a heart-withering drive to replicate the monumental, or a neurotic-compulsive need to repeat the failures of the past again and again. I will come to this negative form of recurrence at the end of the chapter. By then it may be possible to see somewhat more clearly why a genre which, as I said at the outset, makes more of continuities and reversions to type than is usual among the various forms of the novel, has been so immensely popular in this most changeful of nations.

We have noticed that from Virgil onwards literary epic has claimed kinship with the oral epics of Homer by means of imitations or allusions which highlight heroic parallels and invoke a universal heroic standard. Historical romancers sometimes follow this practice of literary-epic poets quite closely and openly. In *The Last of the Mohicans*, for instance, Cooper reincarnates the heroes of Homer and the Hebrew Bible in the wilderness of upstate New York, and there is no mistaking the kinship of this narrative prose fiction with a Romantic epic in verse like Southey's *Roderick the Last of the Goths*. But the heterogeneous reading public which Scott captured for historical romances has never been one which could be expected to relish learned allusions such as those with which Southey garnishes *Roderick* or Milton *Paradise Lost*. And so historical romancers have tended to draw their heroic types from more "available" sources – notably from *Paradise Lost* itself, the Bible, and from popular history at the point where it merges with legendary *topoi*. Scott's Balfour of Burley, the half-crazed Puritan leader in *Old Mortality*, is the first of a series of sublime yet degraded Satanic figures – Magua, Chillingworth, Babo, Claggart – in the historical romance tradition. David figures include Scott's David Deans, Cooper's Uncas, Hawthorne's Gray Champion, and (less transparently) Faulkner's Thomas Sutpen.

As for fictional heroes who embody the traits of personages out of popular history and legend, Leatherstocking is surely the prime example. Of course he is, in the first place, very singularly himself, a character with individual features who is firmly located in a particularized geographical and historical upstate New York milieu. If this were not so, the displacement he suffers in *The Prairie* would not be nearly so poignant. Still, the first three Leatherstocking tales belong to Cooper's expansive nationalist phase, and his reference to "the patriarch of Kentucky" early in *The Prairie* is the plainest hint that Natty is not just himself but also a national "pathfinder" type in the tradition of Daniel Boone. Besides being idealized representatives of the kind of backwoodsman who could be found in every region of the United States at one stage of its historical development. Cooper's and John Filson's heroes also exist on a plane with the heroes of ancient epic – most convincingly, perhaps, when there are no obvious allusions and the contexts are most concretely local. Thus Boone is a grander figure in Elizabeth Madox Roberts's *The Great Meadow*, where his appearance is brief but rendered in the idiom of his time and place rather than in the "literary" English of his early biographers. Leatherstocking is most Homeric or Arthurian in *The Deerslayer* where the action never strays far out of sight of Lake Otsego or, rather, to give the lake its proper epic-epithetical name, the Glimmerglass. Perhaps there is no moment in the Leatherstocking series when character, scene, and action seem at once so authentically native and so reminiscent of ancient heroic literature as at the sombre conclusion of *The Deerslayer* when, returning to the Glimmerglass after many years' absence, Natty discovers one of Judith's ribbons and ties it around the barrel of his weapon, Killdeer.

Leatherstocking, then, – the Gray Champion, too, for that matter – perfectly exemplifies the kind of popular-legendary figure who, like the sacrificial revolutionary heroes of Yeats's "Easter 1916," suddenly impinges upon scenes governed by change, where only motley is worn, and invests the casual comedy – albeit only for a moment – with tragedy or romance. However, while encomiastic poetry has always enjoyed a broad licence to endow ordinary mortals with the features of gods or heroes, heroic archetypes do not recur in novelistic fiction as a matter of course. For their presence implicitly challenges the scientific and historicist world view – what Edward Young called the "mere Prose-reason" – of the novel form. As James cautions in the preface to *The American*, much ingenuity is needed to accommodate these and other departures from the familiar norms of the novelistic world of "all our vulgar communities" lest "the sacrifice of community, or the 'related' sides of situations" be "too rash." To achieve this accommodation, historical romancers use various tactics, often in combination, of two basic kinds. First, they appeal to certain widely accepted and even "scientific" explanations of reversions to type, of "repeats" in history. Second, where the recurrences involve departures from historical probability or natural law too wide to be covered by such explanations, historical romancers so manipulate point-of-view or testimony that only a provisional faith is required of their readers. This manipulation, so essential to the supernatural returns in Hawthorne, Melville, and Faulkner, claims our attention first.

Scott does not require us to believe that the aged figure who rescues the village of Hadley is a champion returned from the dead, but he provides eye-witnesses to the event who we are required to believe are true testifiers albeit prejudiced observers. Scott's American successors make frequent use of such earnest yet biassed witnesses to testify to the existence not just of history-defying reincarnations but also of other sorts of improbable or marvellous happenings with which we are not presently concerned. In my main example of this use of "colored" testimony, "The Gray Champion," Hawthorne withholds his own opinion but invests the aged Puritan spokesman with the patriarchal authority of a David, a regicide *redivivus*, by "reporting" the ejaculations and opinions of the credulous folk who witnessed the champion's wonderful intervention. These witnesses have a typological theory of history to explain the event and a predisposition to discover divinely authored portents and retributions where unbelievers can see nothing. Possessed by the myth of the ancient Hebrews and therefore taking themselves and their American Exodus with utmost seriousness, they are capable of seemingly superhuman feats of courage and perseverance. Hence they and their testimony are open to a variety of interpretations, attitudes, and fictional treatments. They can be presented with the grave respect which belongs to such epic fictions as the first half of *The Wept of Wish-ton-Wish*; with the Romantic irony that throws a passing shadow across even the most flattering of Hawthorne's portraits; or with the satirical mock-epic exposure of Knickerbocker's *History of New York*.

It is tempting to speculate that the seventeenth-century Puritans might have been given fewer opportunities to return from the grave if they had lent themselves less rewardingly to the varied narrative purposes of historical romancers. Certainly this seems to have been true of another type of witness favored by historical romancers – the romantic or Sentimental protagonist from Scott's Edward Waverley to Tate's Lacy Buchan – who serves some of the same narrative purposes but exhibits rather more conspicuously the noble and absurd ancestral features of that champion of all modern fictional champions, Don Quixote. Like the "superstitious" Puritans, these bookish romantic observers may see more (or less) than is actually present; but there is always the possibility that their visions are truer and more searching than anything a camera or a more "objective" human witness could record. Although Frances Harling says that the "trouble" with Jim Burden is that he is romantic and puts "a kind of glamour over" girls like Ántonia and Lena (p. 229), who is to say that he sees falsely when he perceives an earth mother in the one and an Aphrodite in the other? The same goes for Wharton's Newland Archer and the several historian-detectives of *Absalom, Absalom!*

However, history-defying recurrences in historical romance need not always or entirely rely on the eye of the beholder. The most common-sensical explanation for them is simply that, when life or the novel is "*démeublé*" (as Cather says) or stripped down to a "significant simplicity" (as Stevenson says), there are only a few human types and situations, the truly universal ones, worth writing about. As Cather has a character in *O Pioneers!* observe:

> Isn't it queer: there are only two or three human stories, and they go on repeating themselves as fiercely as if they had never happened before; like the larks in this country, that have been singing the same five notes for thousands of years.[1]

Cather requires no more complicated theory than this – neither Daedalean metempsychosis nor Nietzschean Eternal Return – to lend realistic support to Jim's romantic visions of Ántonia and Lena. However, it is significant that we begin to encounter such figures in Cather's work chiefly after she abandons the urban and contemporary settings of her early Jamesean phase in favor of more primitive scenes and more naked encounters between human beings and nature in frontier Nebraska, the old Southwest, and the Canada of Francis Parkman. In effect, she follows what has been one of the favored paths of historical romance ever since Waverley was despatched to the wild mid-eighteenth-century Highlands of Scotland.

Sending a representative of our novelistic world into such a region meant that he would encounter an authentic heroic society whose mode of subsistence produced attitudes, skills, and actions similar or identical to those in Homer or Ossian. Friend and disciple of Adam Ferguson, Scott believed – and as a historical romancer must have been all the readier to believe – that the clans gathered by Fergus Mac-Ivor were truly like those assembled by Agamemnon at Aulis three millennia earlier. An American stadialist could follow Scott's procedure or reverse it by showing the survivors of a heroic society, e.g., Leatherstocking and Indian John in *The Pioneers*, overtaken and engulfed by the westering tide of white agriculturalists. (Scott anticipates the latter strategy in *The Heart of Mid-Lothian* by locating the pastoral Deans family on the outskirts of Edinburgh, thereby staging an inevitable conflict between a corrupt urban society and, in Jeanie, a reincarnation of heroic ancient Hebrew traits and values.) These displacements help to create the "rich and mixed" character of historical romances and do so with a minimum of "rashness" because they employ historicist theory to license epic reincarnations.

Stadialists generally believed that when the history of society was traced from its savage beginnings to the technological triumphs and humanitarian reforms of modern times it manifested overall a linear and "upward" trajectory: it was, in a word, progressive. But stadialists also suggested why those who were displaced or dispossessed by societies which were more "advanced," hence more economically and militarily powerful, were likely to interpret such progress as regress and to take refuge in an old-fashioned cyclical theory of history. This is exactly what Leatherstocking does in *The Prairie*, and it is what Leatherstocking's creator, grown old and disillusioned with the behavior of American democracy, does in *The Crater* (1847). Disillusioned somewhat earlier in the game than Cooper, Melville responds to American expansionism (and specifically to American aggression against Mexico) with a warning in *Mardi* to heed the fates of "Romara" and other great empires. The warning and the cyclical theory on which it is based are precisely the same as those which Thomas Cole paints into *The Course of Empire*. If the shape of history (especially the history of empires) is cyclical, as Melville implies rather than contends in *Israel Potter* and *Benito Cereno*, then it is plausible to discover a Roman in Ethan Allen and to augur a fate as bloody as that of Santo Domingo for the American South.

It is not necessary to invoke these overarching theories of history, abstract and remote from everyday experience as they must be, to explain the reappearance of physical traits in individuals. Direct observation confirms that reversions to physical type are the legacy of "blood," i.e. biological inheritance. But does blood also cause the reappearance of *character* traits? Does family and racial inheritance determine character quite as much as (or even much more than) physical and social environment does? These questions take us back to the nature *vs.* nurture debate which, in one version or another, crops up in most nineteenth-century novelistic fiction and especially in the historical romance. All of Scott's major novels reflect his deep interest, and unwillingness to take a side, in this debate; they all balance Harriet Martineau's – every liberal social reformer's – premise that human nature is essentially plastic against the conservative premise that the grain or bias of character is in important respects fixed before birth by the combined influences of gender and blood.

The Bride of Lammermoor is of special interest here because it portrays both parties to the nature *vs.* nurture controversy in the four principal characters. Upwardly mobile Sir William Ashton and his daughter Lucy represent the "ductile" side and are mismatched in their respective generations with the "hard" hereditary aristocrats Lady Ashton and Edgar, dispossessed Laird of Ravenswood. In Lady Ashton's case, blood counts for more than gender; in Edgar's, blood finally overrides all of his inclinations as an educated man and Lucy's lover. For blood or fate, which are virtually the same thing, makes him a "throwback," a reincarnation of his feudal ancestor Malise of Ravenswood, and hence casts him as the destined avenger of his family. So powerful was Scott's treatment of the perils of family inheritance – involving not merely transmission of likeness but virtual possession by rebirth – that it was bound to be adopted with local modifications by Scott's successors. Hawthorne in particular developed a democratic New England version of the same *topos* in *The House of the Seven Gables*, making "hard" and "aristocratic" Jaffrey Pyncheon not an avenger-figure like Edgar but rather a usurper in the physical and moral image of his evil Puritan ancestor, Colonel Pyncheon.

The House of the Seven Gables is an appropriate work with which to end this study of the American historical romance; for in it Hawthorne did at last forge an alternative to the "worn-out mould that has been in use these thirty years." Most obviously, of course, he departed from the *Waverley*-model by situating the narrative present of the romance in his own era. Just as important in the present context, he created a fable of founding and "blood" which, while it mimes Scott's characteristic themes and devices, implicitly attacks the Laird of Abbotsford, his conservative ideology, and the historical romance itself.

Not only is Jaffrey the spitting image of Colonel Pyncheon as Edgar is of Sir Malise Ravenswood, but in each case the reembodiment is recognizable because of an ancestral portrait which, so far from being an inert image, seems actively to witness or preside over the final catastrophe. In Scott's romance, Sir William Ashton relegates the portrait of Malise of Ravenswood to the lumber room and replaces it with portraits of his Puritan mother "with a book of devotion in her hand" and of his father wearing "a black silk Geneva cowl, or skull-cap."[2] But shortly before their discovery of Lucy mad and her bridegroom Bucklaw horribly wounded, the wedding guests are shocked to see the portrait of Malise mysteriously restored to its place. In *The House of the Seven Gables*, Colonel Pyncheon so identifies with his heirs, his mansion, and his portrait – in which he wears a skullcap and holds a Bible in one hand and a sword in the other – that he stipulates in his will that all those who inherit the house must keep the picture in his study. It is in this room, with the portrait impotently looking on, that his descendant Jaffrey dies of the hereditary disease which killed the Colonel and his reembodiments in succeeding generations. Each suffers a hemorrhage at the point of death and thus fulfills the prophecy of Matthew Maule, the man Colonel Pyncheon had dispossessed and then persecuted for witchcraft: "God will give him blood to drink."[3] Maule's own descendant, Holgrave, provides a gloss on the meaning of "blood" and the Pyncheon family history which, as it echoes remarks in "The Custom-House" about the desirability of frequent transplantation, may be considered a somewhat hyperbolic reflection of Hawthorne's views as well:

> To plant a family! This idea is at the bottom of most of the wrong and mischief which men do. The truth is, that, once in every half-century, at longest, a family should be merged into the great, obscure mass of humanity, and forget all about its ancestors. Human blood, in order to keep its freshness, should run in hidden streams. . . .   (p. 185)

Whether or not Holgrave speaks for Hawthorne in a Jeffersonian mood, the pointed recurrence of *topoi* drawn from *The Bride of Lammermoor* is managed so as to challenge many of the principles which Scott lived by and defended in his fiction. On the showing of *The House of the Seven Gables*, those who found houses or "plant families" are not to be venerated but rather suspected of egocentricity and readiness to stop at nothing to realize a dynastic "design." (We associate that word with Thomas Sutpen, but Hawthorne uses it in connection with Colonel Pyncheon almost a century earlier.) So far from being strengthened and ennobled, as is the premise of apologists for hereditary aristocracy, succeeding generations are likely to be made evil or weak by their material and blood inheritance. For besides the "hard" Pyncheons who reincarnate the founder, there are others in each generation who recognize that their inheritance is tainted but cannot bring themselves to repudiate it and therefore, by "doing over again some deed of sin," "incur all its original responsibilities" (pp. 20–1). Thus Hawthorne associates the hereditary principle of aristocracy with the doctrine of Original Sin rather than with the champion *redivivus* who belongs to heroic legend and epic, and who is the secular counterpart of the god reincarnate of sacred literature. The blood of the Pyncheons is death. Clearly, the implications of this critique extend to the genre which Scott invented, a revived form of epic for an age of novelty and revolution: the historical romance is the Jaffrey Pyncheon of literature.

In *The House of the Seven Gables*, then, Hawthorne joins Cooper, Emerson, Mark Twain, and many other nineteenth-century critics in finding Scott and his fictions deeply subversive of American political and social ideals. Although Scott's surpassing popularity in the Old South was much more the effect than the cause of the region's conservative social code, the fact of his popularity there serves to substantiate the complaints of readers who wished the New England village rather than Abbotsford to be the model for local development in the young nation. So it is scarcely surprising that, within a few years of the sensational international success of *Waverley*, reviewers and orators were clamoring for an "American Scott" who would create books like the Waverley novels but committed to distinctively American principles. That was Cooper's literary–political agenda and also, with some qualifications, Hawthorne's, Simms's, and Paulding's – to mention but the leading figures in the American historical romance tradition during its nationalist phase. Conscientiously, vigorously, and sometimes movingly, they celebrated Revolutionary War leaders like Washington and Marion and fictitious heroes from "the people" like Leatherstocking and Horse-Shoe Robinson; they pilloried the selfish pride of aristocrats like Lady Eleanore and various British governors and generals; they anticipated the doctrine of Manifest Destiny in a hundred purple passages. At the popular didactic level, the campaign to counter Scott's anti-democratic subversions by Americanizing his genre was won well before Hawthorne exposed the sins of the Pyncheons.

At other levels, however, Scott's influence was more pervasive and consequential, and much less easily checked, because it went with the genre and was channeled through historical romances written by American authors with motives which were no less patriotic for also being socially conservative. Thus when the heir of Judge William Cooper was greeted on his return to Cooperstown with sentiments like those expressed by Holgrave, and witnessed those sentiments translated into mob violence by tenants on the Hudson River estates of his friends, he did not have far to look for a fictional model with which to defend the claims of the American gentry and to attack the character and legitimacy of the usurping class. In *Satanstoe* and *The Chainbearer* Cooper is more truly the "American Scott" – equal weight being given to both words – than in the more popular books which earned him that sobriquet.

But Scott's most telling and enduring influence was exerted at yet deeper levels and in forms less amenable to scholarly verification. Throughout the nineteenth century, the historicism of the Waverley tradition (which may be fairly extended here to include America's great Romantic historians: Motley, Prescott, and Parkman) was in all likelihood the single most important educative counterforce to the anti-historical tendencies of the national creed of progressivism. What is more, the polar form of the *Waverley*-model obliged American historical romancers to represent the viewpoints of the losers in the long succession of contests between the forces of progress and reaction: the native American Indians, the New York Dutch, the Virginia planters. It is easy enough today to find those representations inadequate, preju-diced, or even self-serving; but they gave a hearing to cases which must otherwise have never reached, let alone touched, a large public. Cooper's heroic Mohicans are among the ancestors of such minority heroes as the black champions who are reincarnated in each of five generations in Ernest Gaines's fine historical romance *The Autobiography of Miss Jane Pittman* (1971). Almost as important, the regionalism of the Waverley tradition, by causing Americans to cherish their respective *patriae*, has been a powerful force of resistance against the centralizing, unionizing, and standardizing pressures of American government and commerce. Scott was not responsible for the Civil War, but the generic tradition he began has had far-reaching, if incalculable, consequences for good and ill in American life.

I have been writing about Scott as if he and his current of influence were strongly and invariably conservative; but while that was undoubt-edly their prevailing direction, he was no more a pure and simple reactionary than Hawthorne was a pure and simple progressive. Scott would not permit Waverley to have a wife on any terms less liberal than mutual inclination; Hawthorne, in a moment of disconcerting but convincing irony, makes newly married and affluent Holgrave decide that, after all, stone is a better building material than wood. The great historical romancers, Melville himself certainly included, have never completely endorsed either Captain Delano's progressivist admonition to forget the past or Captain Vere's counterrevolutionary dictum: "With mankind . . . forms, measured forms are everything; and that is the import couched in the story of Orpheus with his lyre spellbinding the wild denizens of the wood" (p. 130). The tune they would have mankind dance to calls for recurrence, as all tunes must, but also for variation and improvisation. Cather, revising the proposition that there are only a few human stories that go on passionately repeating themselves like the songs of larks, has Jim Burden express a preference which applies to much more than styles of dancing:

> To dance "Home, Sweet Home," with Lena was like coming in with the tide. She danced every dance like a waltz, and it was always the same waltz – the waltz of coming home to something, of inevitable, fated return. After a while one got restless under it, as one does under the heat of a soft, sultry summer day.
>
> When you spun out into the floor with Tony, you didn't return to anything. You set out every time upon a new adventure. I liked to schottische with her; she had so much spring and variety, and was always putting in new steps and slides. She taught me to dance against and around the hard-and-fast beat of the music. (pp. 222–3)

Notes

PREFACE

1. The books referred to are *James Fenimore Cooper: The Novelist* (London: Routledge & Kegan Paul, 1967) and *Coleridge and the Literature of Sensibility* (London: Vision Press, 1978).
2. Whether Scott is a "canonical author" is open to debate. My own informal inquiries persuade me that he is read and taught little more than, say, Maria Edgeworth or Elizabeth Gaskell. If Edgeworth and Gaskell are not canonical, then neither is Scott.

I THE AMERICAN HISTORICAL ROMANCE: A PROSPECTUS

1. C. Hugh Holman, *The Immoderate Past: The Southern Writer and History* (Athens, Ga.: Univ. of Georgia Press, 1977). This valuable little book, which is stronger on contexts and theory than on particular novels, can be profitably read in conjunction with Holman's excellent studies of William Gilmore Simms and William Faulkner in *The Roots of Southern Writing: Essays on the Literature of the American South* (Athens, Ga.: Univ. of Georgia Press, 1972). David Levin, *History as Romantic Art: Bancroft, Prescott, Motley, and Parkman* (Stanford: Stanford Univ. Press, 1959) and *In Defense of Historical Literature: Essays on American History, Autobiography, Drama, and Fiction* (New York: Hill and Wang, 1967). Harry Henderson, *Versions of the Past: The Historical Imagination in American Fiction* (New York: Oxford Univ. Press, 1974). Roy Harvey Pearce, *Historicism Once More: Problems & Occasions for the American Scholar* (Princeton: Princeton Univ. Press, 1969), pp. 159–60. Ernest Leisey, *The American Historical Novel* (Norman: Univ. of Oklahoma Press, 1950).
2. Michael Davitt Bell, *Hawthorne and the Historical Romance of New England* (Princeton: Princeton Univ. Press, 1971).
3. Recent examples of the kind of resourceful contextual scholarship I have in mind are Jay Fliegelman's *Prodigals and Pilgrims: The American Revolution Against Patriarchal Authority, 1750–1800* (Cambridge: Cambridge Univ. Press, 1982) and Michael J. Colacurcio's *The Province of Piety: Moral History in Hawthorne's Early Tales* (Cambridge, Mass.: Harvard Univ. Press, 1984). For my reservations about Colacurcio's methods, see my discussion of Hawthorne's tales in chapter 5.
4. The broad literary culture of great Americanists like Perry Miller and F.O. Matthiessen is evident in nearly everything they wrote, and Miller in particular made major contributions to our understanding of the relationship between American literary and intellectual traditions and those of Britain and Europe. But a parochial or nationalistic strain sometimes surfaces in American literary scholarship (as, for example, in Howard Mumford Jones's *The Theory of American Literature* [1948; revised edn., Ithaca: Cornell Univ. Press, 1965]), and is the more worrying today because the pressure to generate substantial publications as early as possible creates pressures in graduate school to specialize prematurely.
5. I refer to Sacvan Bercovitch's *The Puritan Origins of the American Self* (New Haven:

Yale Univ. Press, 1975) and *The American Jeremiad* (Madison: Univ. of Wisconsin
Press, 1978); Richard Slotkin's *Regeneration Through Violence: The Mythology of the
American Frontier* (Middleton, Conn.: Wesleyan Univ. Press, 1973); and Robert
Ferguson's *Law and Letters in American Culture* (Cambridge, Mass.: Harvard Univ.
Press, 1984).

6. Mark Twain, *Life on the Mississippi* (1883; New York: New American Library,
   1961), pp. 265–6.
7. Georg Lukács, *The Historical Novel*, trans. Hannah and Stanley Mitchell (1937;
   London: Merlin, 1962). Lukács wrote this great book in exile and under conditions
   which made perfect accuracy impossible.
8. *Billy Budd, Sailor*, ed. Milton R. Stern (Indianapolis: Bobbs-Merrill, 1975), p. 44.
9. Donald Davie, *The Heyday of Sir Walter Scott* (London: Routledge & Kegan Paul,
   1961). Avrom Fleishman, *The English Historical Novel: Walter Scott to Virginia Woolf*
   (Baltimore: Johns Hopkins Univ. Press, 1971). Harry Shaw, *The Forms of Historical
   Fiction: Sir Walter Scott and His Successors* (Ithaca: Cornell Univ. Press, 1983).
10. Shaw's categories are: "history as pastoral" (novels in which history is used primarily
    to elucidate the moral or social problems of the present); "history as drama" (novels
    in which history is used primarily to provide an effective setting for a "timeless"
    story); and "history as subject" (novels in which "historical milieux or great
    historical figures or the workings of historical process itself" form the center of
    interest). Provided they are not applied insensitively, these categories can help us
    locate the center of authorial interest in a historical novel. I say "center" because it
    must be obvious on reflection that many (maybe most) significant historical novels
    "use" history in all three ways but not at the same time or to the same degree.
11. I have written about some of the documentary sources of *The Wept of Wish-ton-Wish*
    in "Sir Walter Scott, the Angel of Hadley, and American Historical Fiction,"
    American Studies, 17, (1984), 211–27.
12. Northrop Frye, *Anatomy of Criticism: Four Essays* (Princeton: Princeton Univ. Press,
    1957).
13. Henry James, "The Art of Fiction," rpt. in *The House of Fiction*, ed. Leon Edel
    (London: Rupert Hart Davies, 1957), p. 35.
14. Probably the most influential study of the novel–romance in America is Richard
    Chase, *The American Novel and Its Tradition* (Garden City, N.Y.: Doubleday, 1957).
    Also important are Perry Miller, "The Romance and the Novel," *Nature's Nation*
    (Cambridge, Mass.: Harvard Univ. Press, 1967), pp. 241–78; Joel Porte, *The
    Romance in America: Studies in Cooper, Poe, Hawthorne, Melville, and James*
    (Middletown, Conn.: Wesleyan Univ. Press, 1969); and Michael Davitt Bell, *The
    Development of American Romance: The Sacrifice of Relation* (Chicago: Univ. of
    Chicago Press, 1980). In *American and English Fiction of the Nineteenth Century: An
    Antigenre Critique and Comparison* (Bloomington: Indiana Univ. Press, 1973),
    Nicolaus Mills agrees with Henry James that the distinction between novel and
    romance is itself a fiction. Albeit limited in historical purview, a shrewd analysis of
    the conflicting values behind the novel/romance debate is Robert Post's "A Theory
    of Genre: Romance, Realism, and Moral Reality," *American Quarterly*, 33 (Fall 1981),
    367–90. For a recent historical survey, see Sergio Perosa, *American Theories of the
    Novel: 1793–1903* (New York: New York Univ. Press, 1983), pp. 3–83.
15. *Pamela*, ed. George Saintsbury (London: J.M. Dent & Sons, 1914), II, iv.
16. .Ian Watt, *The Rise of the Novel* (London: Chatto & Windus, 1957).
17. *Joseph Andrews*, III, i, rpt. in *The Criticism of Henry Fielding*, ed. Ioan Williams (New
    York: Barnes & Noble, 1970), p. 258.
18. *The Writings of Jonathan Swift*, ed. Robert A. Greenberg and William Bowman Piper
    (New York: Norton, 1973), p. 384.

19. Thomas Warton, *Observations on the Faerie Queene*, rpt. in *Eighteenth-Century English Literature*, ed. Geoffrey Tillotson, Paul Fussell, Jr., and Marshall Waingrow (New York: Harcourt, Brace, & World, 1969), pp. 934–5.

20. *The Castle of Otranto*, ed. Caroline Spurgeon with Sir Walter Scott's Introduction (London: Chatto & Windus, 1937), p. li. For a compatible but somewhat different account of the relationship between bourgeois novel, gothic romance, and historical romance, see Wolfgang Iser's "Fiction and the Filter of History: A Study of Sir Walter Scott's *Waverley*," *The Implied Reader: Patterns of Communication in Prose Fiction from Bunyan to Beckett* (1972; English edn., Baltimore: Johns Hopkins Univ. Press, 1974), pp. 81–100.

21. Scott, "Romance," *Miscellaneous Prose Works of Sir Walter Scott* (Edinburgh: Robert Cadell, 1847), VI, 129.

22. Heine, "Don Quixote" (1837), trans. Fleishman, *The Prose Works of Heinrich Heine*, ed. Havelock Ellis (London: n.d.), pp. 259–60.

23. E. T. Channing, *North American Review*, VIII (July 1818), rpt. in *Scott: the Critical Heritage*, ed. John O. Hayden (London: Routledge & Kegan Paul, 1970), p. 164.

24. Nassau Senior, *Essays on Fiction* (London, 1864), pp. 2–3.

25. *The American* (New York: Charles Scribner's Sons, 1907), p. xiv.

26. Commenting on this passage in *The Romance in America*, p. 193, Joel Porte says that James supposed himself "unlike" Scott, Balzac, and Zola inasmuch as he committed himself in both directions while they did not. But surely James is saying that they *did* so commit themselves.

27. Fredric Jameson, "Magical Narratives: On the Dialectical Use of Genre Criticism," *The Political Unconscious: Narrative as a Socially Symbolic Act* (Ithaca: Cornell Univ. Press, 1981), p. 141.

28. In *The Development of American Romance*, pp. 7–8, Bell claims that James characterizes Romance as essentially escapist. As I read the preface to *The American*, however, James seems to be saying that the "liberation" with which romance deals has the potential for both irresponsible (escapist) and supremely responsible acts.

29. James used the phrase quoted to describe Balzac in "Honoré de Balzac" (1902), rpt. in *The Art of Fiction and Other Essays*, ed. Morris Roberts (New York: Oxford Univ. Press, 1948, p. 27).

30. William Gilmore Simms, "History for the Purposes of Art" (1845), *Views and Reviews in American Literature, History, and Fiction*, First Series, ed. C. Hugh Holman (1845; Cambridge, Mass.: Harvard Univ. Press, 1962), pp. 76, 56. The "neutral ground" metaphor, also employed by (among others) Cooper and Hawthorne, comes from Scott and is central to all early theorizing about historical romance.

31. Tzvetan Todorov, *The Fantastic: A Structural Approach to a Literary Genre*, trans. Richard Howard (1970; Ithaca: Cornell Univ. Press, 1975), p. 42. Todorov explains that a state of uncertainty is characteristic of "the fantastic" and that once it is given a natural explanation it becomes "the uncanny"; given a supernatural one, "the marvellous." Although such explanations are usual and in effect explode "the fantastic," it has a powerful life while it exists. I return to Todorov's discussion of this "evanescent genre" in chapter 5.

32. For an example of what a "myth-crit" reading of a historical romance can disclose, see H. Daniel Peck's interpretation of *The Last of the Mohicans* in *A World by Itself: The Pastoral Moment in Cooper's Fiction* (New Haven: Yale Univ. Press, 1977), pp. 120–45. Peck, it should be noted, has gone to school not only with Frye and Campbell but also with, among others, Eliade and Foucault.

33. Allen Tate, "What Is a Traditional Society?" (1936), rpt. in *Essays of Four Decades* (Chicago: Swallow Press, 1968), pp. 550–1. I discuss this passage further in chapter 8.

2 THE *WAVERLEY*-MODEL AND THE RISE OF HISTORICAL
ROMANCE

1. Hugh Trevor-Roper, "Sir Walter Scott and History," *The Listener*, 86 (19 August
   1971), 227. In preparing this account of the rise of historical romance and especially of
   Scott's contribution, I have drawn on a host of books and articles. None of them
   offered precisely the perspective I required for a study concerned primarily, after all,
   with the Waverley tradition in American historical fiction. But I could not have
   arrived at that perspective without their help. The general studies by Lukács, Davie,
   and Fleishman cited in the previous chapter were of special importance to me and
   should be acknowledged again here. I have, I believe, read most of the important
   modern studies of Scott and many even of the notes and letters concerned with the
   minutiae of Waverleyana. Those which have most affected my own approach or
   proved indispensable guides are David Daiches, "Scott's Achievement as a Novelist"
   (1951), rpt. in *Scott's Mind and Art*, ed. A. Norman Jeffares (New York: Barnes &
   Noble, 1970), pp. 21–52. Francis Hart, *Scott's Novels: The Plotting of Historic Survival*
   (Charlottesville: Univ. Press of Virginia, 1966). Edgar Johnson, *Sir Walter Scott: The
   Great Unknown* (New York: Macmillan, 1970). Alexander Welsh, *The Hero of the
   Waverley Novels* (New Haven: Yale Univ. Press, 1963). As will become evident from
   citations in the following chapter, I also owe a great debt to Duncan Forbes's
   groundbreaking studies of Scott's connections with the Scottish Enlightenment.
2. Thomas Carlyle, "Sir Walter Scott" (1838), *Critical and Miscellaneous Essays*, IV
   (New York: Charles Scribner's Sons, 1899), p. 77.
3. Thomas Babington Macaulay, review of Henry Neele's *The Romance of History*,
   Edinburgh Review, xlvii (May 1828), 365.
4. Trevor-Roper, 229.
5. For Scott's international influence on historians, see G.P. Gooch, *History and
   Historians in the Nineteenth Century* (second edn., London: Longmans, Green, 1952).
   For the American Romantic historians, see David Levin, *History as Romantic Art*.
6. Robert Wood, *An Essay on the Original Genius and Writings of Homer* (London, 1775),
   p. 5.
7. Friedrich Meinecke, *Historism: The Rise of a New Historical Outlook*, trans. J.E.
   Anderson (1936; London: Routledge & Kegan Paul, 1972), pp. 208, 485.
8. Robert Louis Stevenson, "Victor Hugo's Romances," *Cornhill Magazine*, xxx
   (August 1874), 182.
9. Letter to Thos. Allsop dated 8 April 1820, *Collected Letters of Samuel Taylor Coleridge*,
   ed. E.L. Griggs (Oxford: Clarendon Press, 1971), v, 34–5.
10. Scott, *Life of Napoleon Buonaparte, Miscellaneous Prose Works*, 11, 63.
11. Scott, "On the present state of historical composition," ed. William Baker and J.H.
    Alexander, *The Scott Newsletter*, No. 5 (Autumn 1984), 11–12.
12. Marilyn Butler, *Romantics, Rebels and Reactionaries: English Literature and its
    Background 1760–1830* (Oxford: Oxford Univ. Press, 1981), p. 110.
13. Thomas Kuhn, *The Structure of Scientific Revolutions* (2nd edn., Chicago: Univ. of
    Chicago Press, 1970), p. viii. Scientific paradigms have been successful, writes Kuhn,
    when they "shared two essential characteristics. Their achievement was sufficiently
    unprecedented to attract an enduring group of adherents away from competing
    modes of scientific activity. Simultaneously, it has been sufficiently open-ended to
    leave all sorts of problems for the redefined group of practitioners to resolve" (p. 10).
    Substitute "literary" for "scientific" and Kuhn's description fits the *Waverley*-model
    precisely. Kuhn's account of scientific paradigms has not gone unchallenged, but the
    point I am making about its relevance to the *Waverley*-model has principally to do

with Enlightenment ideas about science, society, and literature rather than with the findings of historians of science since 1970.

14. T. S. Eliot, *"Ulysses,* Order, and Myth," *The Dial* (November, 1923).

15. Claudio Guillén, *Literature as System: Essays toward the Theory of Literary History* (Princeton: Princeton Univ. Press, 1971), p. 415. On binary oppositions and their transcendence, see pp. 405–18.

16. Howard Erskine-Hill, *The Augustan Idea in English Literature* (London: Arnold, 1983).

17. John Gibson Lockhart, *Memoirs of Sir Walter Scott* (London: Macmillan & Co., 1900), I, 257–8. Full documentation of Scott's indebtedness to Goethe is provided in G. H. Needler, *Goethe and Scott* (Toronto: Oxford Univ. Press, 1950). For a succinct placing of *Goetz* in the history of historical literature, see Herbert Lindenberger, *Historical Drama: the Relation of Literature and Reality* (Chicago: Chicago Univ. Press, 1975), pp. 114–15.

18. *The Criticism of Henry Fielding,* p. 251.

19. *Elements of Criticism,* ed. Abraham Mills (New York: 1855), p. 414. The edition from which I quote was supplied with "analysis and translations of ancient and foreign illustrations" (i.e., quotations) for the benefit of American readers. That there was a market for Kames's post-Lockean treatise on aesthetics nearly a century after its initial publication is further evidence of the widespread and lingering influence of Scottish Enlightenment thought on America.

20. Cooper, review (1838) of Lockhart's *Memoirs of Sir Walter Scott,* rpt. in *American Romanticism: A Shape for Fiction,* ed. Stanley Bank (New York: Capricorn Books, 1969), p. 126.

21. Simms, *The Yemassee: A Romance of Carolina* (1835; reprint of revised edition of 1853; Boston: Houghton Mifflin, 1961), pp. 5–6.

22. Cooper, preface to the Leatherstocking Tales (1850), rpt. in Bank, *American Romanticism,* p. 139.

23. Porte, *The Romance in America,* pp. 39–44.

24. Ker, *Epic and Romance* (2nd edn., London: Macmillan & Co., 1908), p. 25. I summarize the argument of Ker's first and last chapters. For a somewhat different approach to the epic characteristics of novelistic fiction, see E. M. W. Tillyard, *The Epic Strain in the English Novel* (London: Chatto & Windus, 1958).

25. Scott, "Henry Fielding," *Miscellaneous Prose Works,* II, 78. Byron's eulogy of Fielding is quoted by Scott's editor on p. 116.

26. Scott, General Preface to the 1829 edition of the Waverley Novels, rpt. in *Waverley; or, 'Tis Sixty Years Since,* ed. Claire Lamont (Oxford: Clarendon Press, 1981), p. 353.

27. Scott, "Romance," *Miscellaneous Prose Works,* VI, 134–5.

28. For an informed account of Simms's place in the American literary tradition, see the five essays on Simms gathered in C. Hugh Holman's *The Roots of Southern Writing.*

29. A sound pioneering account of the encouragement which reviewers and orators gave writers to become "the American Scott" may be found in G. Harrison Orians, "The Romance Ferment after *Waverley,*" *American Literature,* III (January 1932), 408–31. A useful recent study is Neal Frank Doubleday, "Doctrine for Fiction in the *North American Review*: 1815–26," *Literature and Ideas in America: Essays in Memory of Harry Hayden Clark,* ed. Robert Falk (Ohio Univ. Press, 1975), pp. 20–39. James D. Hart has a helpful chapter on the vogue of Scott and his followers in America in *The Popular Book: A History of America's Literary Taste* (New York: Oxford Univ. Press, 1950), pp. 67–84. Of course there are many studies of Scott's "influence" on specific books, authors, or regional literatures in America. Some of these are mentioned by

Hart in his bibliographical checklist (p. 293), others by me in notes to subsequent chapters.

30. In a perceptive review of *The Spy* which I shall discuss more fully in chapter 4, W. H. Gardiner identified "three great epochs" for the American historical romancer to mine: "the times just succeeding the first settlement – the aera of the Indian wars, which lie scattered along a considerable period – and the revolution." (*North American Review*, xv [July 1822], rpt. *Fenimore Cooper: The Critical Heritage*, ed. George Dekker and John McWilliams [London and Boston: Routledge & Kegan Paul, 1973], pp. 59–60.) A century later, Carl Van Doren turned Gardiner's prospectus into a retrospective classification of "The Three Matters of American Romance": the Revolution, the Settlement, and the Frontier. (*The American Novel 1789–1939* [1921; revised edn., New York: The Macmillan Co., 1940], pp. 14–20.) As Michael Davitt Bell suggests in *Nathaniel Hawthorne and the Historical Romance of New England*, pp. viii–ix, some system of "matters" based on categories of place and/or period is helpful and perhaps inevitable when one discusses this kind of fiction. I do so myself, in effect, when in chapters 4 and 8 I discuss the regional romances of New York and the South. But given the scope and starting point of the present chapter, I require broader and more flexible terms of reference than Gardiner could have envisaged or than would have been useful to Bell or earlier scholars like Van Doren, Leisy, and Cowie. From my perspective the American historical romance has two great matters corresponding to the two major types of conflict in *Waverley*. The first matter, of fratricidal civil war, includes both the Revolution and the American Civil War. The second, of colonial conquest, joins "Settlement" and "Frontier" under the single heading "frontier" or "times of frontier hardship." Throughout this study I think of the American frontier as existing when and wherever the encroaching European peoples or their descendants met primeval America, the land and/or the people, face to face.

31. C. Hugh Holman, "The Influence of Scott and Cooper on Simms," rpt. in *The Roots of Southern Writing*, pp. 50–60.

32. *The Sketch Book of Geoffrey Crayon, Gent.*, ed. Haskell Springer (Boston: Twayne Publishers, 1978), p. 235.

33. *Political Justice in a Republic: James Fenimore Cooper's America* (Berkeley and Los Angeles: Univ. of California Press, 1972), pp. 238–58. Other important discussions of the novel are Yvor Winters, "Fenimore Cooper, or the Ruins of Time," *Maule's Curse: Seven Studies in the History of American Obscurantism* (Norfolk, Conn.: New Directions, 1938), pp. 42–3, and Warren Motley, *The American Abraham: James Fenimore Cooper and the Frontier Patriarch* (New York: Cambridge Univ. Press, 1987), ch. 1.

34. *Love and Death in the American Novel* (New York: Criterion Books, 1960), pp. 200–2.

35. McWilliams, p. 262. Winters, p. 43.

3 HISTORICAL ROMANCE AND THE STADIALIST MODEL OF PROGRESS

1. Mill, *A System of Logic Ratiocinative and Inductive*, ed. J. M. Robson and R. F. McRae (Toronto: Univ. of Toronto Press, 1973), pp. 913–14. The secondary literature dealing with the meaning and history of the idea of progress is vast. Two works which I have found especially useful are Ernest Lee Tuveson's *Millennium and Utopia: A Study in the Background of the Idea of Progress* (Berkeley: Univ. of California Press, 1949) and W. Warren Wagar's *Good Tidings: The Belief in Progress from Darwin to*

Marcuse (Bloomington: Indiana Univ. Press, 1972). For specifically American developments, see Tuveson's *Redeemer Nation: The Idea of America's Millennial Role* (Chicago: Univ. of Chicago Press, 1968).

2. de Tocqueville, *Democracy in America*, trans. Henry Reeves, revised by Bowen and Bradley (New York: Vintage, 1945), II, 35.

3. For further information about the impact of Scottish thought and literature in America, see Andrew Hook, *Scotland and America: A Study of Cultural Relations, 1750–1835* (Glasgow: Blackie, 1975).

4. My discussion of stadialism is greatly indebted to Ralph Meek's excellent survey of the subject in *Social Science and the Ignoble Savage* (Cambridge: Cambridge Univ. Press, 1976).

5. Robertson, *History of the Reign of the Emperor Charles V* (1769), quoted by Meek, p. 139.

6. Forbes, "The Rationalism of Sir Walter Scott," *Cambridge Journal* (October 1953), VII, 20–35. Fleishman, *The English Historical Novel* (Baltimore: Johns Hopkins Press, 1971), pp. 37–50. More recent developments of Forbes's ground-breaking approach are P. D. Garside, "Scott and the 'Philosophical' Historians," *Journal of the History of Ideas* (1975), XXX, 497–512, and David Brown, *Walter Scott and the Historical Imagination* (London: Routledge & Kegan Paul, 1979), pp. 196–205. For a somewhat different reading of the relationship between Scott and the Scottish historians, see David Daiches, "Sir Walter Scott and History," *Etudes Anglaises* (1971) xxiv, 458–71. A valuable recent overview of Scott's debts to Scottish Enlightenment thought can be found in Graham McMaster, *Scott and Society* (Cambridge: Cambridge Univ. Press, 1981), pp. 49–77.

7. Fleishman, p. 50.

8. John Dryden, "To My Honor'd Friend, Dr. Charleton," lines 11–14.

9. J. G. Lockhart, quoted more fully above, pp. 1, 21–2.

10. Charles and Mary Beard, *The American Spirit: A Study of the Idea of Civilization in the United States* (New York: Macmillan, 1942). Henry Nash Smith, *Virgin Land: The American West as Symbol and Myth* (1950; reprinted New York: Vintage, 1957), pp. 253–60. Roy Harvey Pearce, *The Savages of America: A Study of the Indian and the Idea of Civilization* (revised edn., Baltimore: Johns Hopkins Press, 1965).

11. Ferguson, *An Essay on the History of Civil Society, 1767*, ed. Duncan Forbes (Edinburgh: Univ. of Edinburgh Press, 1966), p. 75.

12. Beard, pp. 84–7. However, *pace* the Beards, it remains debatable whether the French or Scottish influence was strongest. For the pervasive influence of Scottish thought and the Scottish educational system in America, see Andrew Hook, *Scotland and America: A Study of Cultural Relations* (Glasgow: Blackie, 1975).

13. Pearce, p. 49. Also see David Levin, *History as Romantic Art*, pp. 126–59.

14. Letter to William Ludlow (6 September 1824), *The Writings of Thomas Jefferson*, ed. Andrew A. Lipscomb (Washington, D.C.: Thos. Jefferson Memorial Assn., 1904), XVI, 74–5.

15. *Democracy in America*, II, 78.

16. *Notions of the Americans Picked up by a Travelling Bachelor* (Philadelphia, 1828), I, 252.

17. *NAR* (July 1822), rpt. Dekker and McWilliams, *Fenimore Cooper: The Critical Heritage*, pp. 59–60. As McWilliams shows (pp. 2–4), Cooper was familiar with Gardiner's review.

18. *An Inquiry into the Nature and Causes of the Wealth of Nations*, ed. R. H. Skinner, A. S. Skinner, and W. B. Todd (Oxford: Clarendon Press, 1976), II, 564–5. Or, according to the customary numbering system: IV, vii, b, 1–2.

19. *Waverley*, p. 340.

20. *The Pioneers, or the Sources of the Susquehanna; a Descriptive Tale*, ed. James Franklin Beard, Lance Schacterle, and Kenneth M. Anderson, Jr. (Albany: State Univ. of New York Press, 1980), p. 16.
21. Preface to the first English edition of *The Prairie* (London, 1827), pp. vii–viii.
22. Ferguson, pp. 95–6.
23. These pages on the pace of social change, obsolescence, and the overall form of the Leatherstocking series develop ideas first published in my *James Fenimore Cooper the Novelist* (London: Routledge & Kegan Paul, 1967), pp. 254–9. What is new in the present discussion is my belated recognition of the full extent of Cooper's debt to stadialist thought.
24. *The Pioneers*, p. 476.
25. Ferguson, p. 121.
26. Fleishman, pp. 45–6.
27. *The American Democrat*, ed. George Dekker and Larry Johnston (Harmondsworth: Penguin, 1969), p. 186.
28. *The Prairie*, ed. Henry Nash Smith (New York: Rinehart, 1963), pp. 63–4.
29. *Commentaries on the Laws of England* (14th edition; London, 1803), II, 7.
30. E. Soteris Muszynska-Wallace, "The Sources of *The Prairie*," *American Literature* (1949), XXI, 191–200. Henry Nash Smith, Introduction to *The Prairie*, pp. xii–xx. Orm Overland, *The Making and Meaning of an American Classic: James Fenimore Cooper's The Prairie* (Oslo and New York: Universitetsforlaget and Humanities Press, 1973).
31. Quoted by Forbes, "The Rationalism of Sir Walter Scott," p. 33.
32. See Thomas Philbrick's Introduction to *The Crater* (Cambridge, Mass.: Belknap Press, 1962).
33. Cooper's restatement of the stadial thesis in its American (spatialized) form appears at the beginning of chapter 6, p. 69.
34. David Howard, "James Fenimore Cooper's Leatherstocking Tales: 'Without a Cross'", *Tradition and Tolerance in Nineteenth-Century Fiction* (London: Routledge & Kegan Paul, 1966), p. 20.
35. The compromise appears in, for example, Turgot. See Donald Ringe, *The Pictorial Mode: Space and Time in the Art of Bryant, Irving and Cooper* (Lexington: Univ. of Kentucky Press, 1971), p. 164.
36. Henry Nash Smith, *The Prairie*, p. xii.
37. In *Wealth of Nations*, v, i, a, 3, Adam Smith explains that among herding peoples warfare is not the exclusive preserve of males. "They all go to war together, therefore, and every one does as well as he can. Among the Tartars, even the women have been frequently known to engage in battle." According to Smith and other stadialists (Cooper of course included), this is not the normal practice of other, less or more advanced societies. Ferguson is a mine of information about the Bush family: "They are fond of fantastic ornaments in their dress, and endeavour to fill up the listless intervals of a life addicted to violence, with hazardous sports, and with games of chance. Every servile occupation they commit to women or slaves. But we may apprehend, that the individual now having found a separate interest [i.e., property], the bands of society must become less firm, and domestic disorders more frequent" (p. 98). Yet in spite of alternating periods of sloth and violence, such men "are generous and hospitable to strangers, as well as kind, affectionate, and gentle, in their domestic society. Friendship and enmity are to them terms of the greatest importance: they mingle not their functions together; they have singled out their enemy, and they have chosen their friend . . . Nations and tribes are their prey: the solitary traveller, by whom they can acquire only the reputation of generosity, is

suffered to pass unhurt, or is treated with splendid munificence" (pp. 101–2).

38. *The Prairie*, p. 400. The great arbitrary power of the pastoral chieftain is a byword of stadial literature. See, for instance, *Wealth of Nations*, v, i, b, 7.

39. The most important studies of Cooper's pictorialism and of the Cooper–Cole relationship in particular are by Donald Ringe in *The Pictorial Mode* and "James Fenimore Cooper and Thomas Cole: An Analogous Technique," *American Literature*, XXX (March, 1958), 26–36; by James T. Callow in *Kindred Spirits: Knickerbocker Writers and American Artists, 1807–1855* (Chapel Hill: Univ. of North Carolina Press, 1967); and by Blake Nevius in *Cooper's Landscapes: An Essay on the Picturesque Vision* (Berkeley: Univ. of California Press, 1976).

40. I discuss Cooper's pessimism about the future of the republican form of government in America in *James Fenimore Cooper the Novelist*, pp. 236–59.

41. Cooper to Louis Legrand Noble, dated 6 January 1849, reproduced by Noble in *The Life and Works of Thomas Cole*, ed. Elliot S. Vesell (1853; Cambridge: Belknap Press of Harvard Univ. Press, 1964), p. 167.

42. Cole's pessimism about the ability of republican government to survive the growing power of the moneyed interests in America is discussed by Matthew Baigell in *Thomas Cole* (New York: Watson–Guptill Publications, 1981), p. 22.

4 THE REGIONALISM OF HISTORICAL ROMANCE

1. *My Ántonia* (Boston: Houghton Mifflin, 1918), p. 264. Many historical romancers declare their "patriotic" motives in phrases that echo Scott's or anticipate Cather's. In *The Roots of Southern Writing*, p. 38, C. Hugh Holman quotes such a declaration from Simms's *Katharine Walton* (1851): "I summon to my aid the muse of local History – the traditions of our own home – the chronicles of our own section – the deeds of our native heroes – the recollections of our own noble ancestry."

2. *Castle Rackrent*, ed. George Watson (London: Oxford Univ. Press, 1964), p. vii.

3. *Memoirs of Sir Walter Scott*, II, 486.

4. "A Book of Autographs," *The Snow-Image and Uncollected Tales*, ed. J. Donald Crowley (Columbus: Ohio State Univ. Press, 1974), p. 362.

5. "Edward Randolph's Portrait," *Twice-Told Tales*, ed. J. Donald Crowley (Columbus: Ohio State Univ. Press, 1974), pp. 256–7.

6. W.H. Gardiner, review of *The Spy*, rpt. in Dekker and McWilliams, *Fenimore Cooper: The Critical Heritage*, pp. 56–7.

7. The nationalist historian George Bancroft was one of the commentators who doubted that the American past was rich enough in romantic associations to yield a healthy crop of historical romances. The white communities were too short-lived, such pessimists alleged, and even the red American tribes that the English colonists had displaced were comparative nomads, too primitive and too light in their passage to leave any imposing monuments behind. As for the American landscape, though doubtless sublime, it was inhuman and devoid of moral associations. The optimistic party replied that, on the contrary, the effect of rapid progress, of crowding many incidents into a few years, was to make brief-lived American communities seem positively venerable and their beginnings romantically remote; American Indians were as sublime as the wilderness they inhabited and by no means deficient in legends or artifacts; and it was the duty of American writers to humanize the American landscape and create the moral associations which might be lacking. This debate was joined in journal articles, orations, and prefaces during the early nineteenth century when the interest in Scott was at its height, when Cooper, Paulding, Simms, and Hawthorne began publishing their regional–historical fiction, and when Cole was

torn between the impulse to continue painting Catskill landscapes or to turn to religious allegories. For the influence of associationist aesthetics during this period, see William Charvat, *The Origins of American Critical Thought: 1810–1835* (Philadelphia: Univ. of Pennsylvania Press, 1936), chapter 3, and Robert E. Streeter, "Association Psychology and Literary Nationalism in the *North American Review*, 1815–1825," *American Literature*, XVII (Nov. 1945), 243–54.

8. Tate, "Faulkner's *Sanctuary* and the Southern Myth" (1968), rpt. in *Memoirs and Opinions, 1926–1974* (Chicago: Swallow Press), p. 152.

9. *Quarterly Review*, 22 (1814), 356. The reviewer (John Wilson Croker), it should be said, doesn't have epic in mind when he speaks of a "much higher strain"; he is thinking of more genteel fictions by Edgeworth herself, e.g., *The Absentee*.

10. "Roger Malvin's Burial," *Mosses from an Old Manse*, ed. J. Donald Crowley (Columbus: Ohio State Univ. Press, 1974), p. 337.

11. The classic study of the Yankee is Constance Rourke's *American Humor: A Study of the National Character* (New York: Harcourt Brace, 1931), pp. 3–32. William R. Taylor's *Cavalier and Yankee: The Old South and American National Character* (New York: George Braziller, 1961) is concerned primarily with the "Cavalier" of the Southern Plantation legend but has insightful comments on his fictive opposite, the Yankee, on pp. 95–109. Useful studies of regional tensions in the "New York" fiction of Irving and Cooper are Kay Seymour House's *Cooper's Americans* (Columbus: Ohio State Univ. Press, 1965), pp. 93–145, and Donald A. Ringe's "New York and New England: Irving's Criticism of American Society," *American Literature*, 38 (1967), 455–67.

12. *Satanstoe*, ed. Robert L. Hough (Lincoln: Univ. of Nebraska Press, 1962), p. 47.

13. Still the best account of Irving's historical imagination is William L. Hedges's *Washington Irving: An American Study, 1802–1832* (Baltimore: The Johns Hopkins Press, 1965).

14. *A History of New York*, ed. Michael L. Black and Nancy B. Black (Boston: Twayne Publishers, 1984), p. 121. This volume of the new *Complete Works of Washington Irving* uses the 1848 edition as copy text. Several of the felicitous phrasings from Knickerbocker's *History* which I discuss do not appear in early editions, but passages which express the same sentiments can be found in the first (1809) edition.

15. *The Sketch Book*, p. 40.

16. *Bracebridge Hall, Or, The Humorists: A Medley by Geoffrey Crayon, Gent.*, ed. Herbert F. Smith (Boston: Twayne Publishers, 1977), p. 296.

17. *The Last of the Mohicans: A Narrative of 1757*, afterword by James Franklin Beard (New York: New American Library, 1962), p. 362.

5 HAWTHORNE AND THE IRONIES OF NEW ENGLAND HISTORY

1. *The Scarlet Letter*, ed. William Charvat, *et al.* (Columbus: Ohio State Univ. Press, 1962), pp. 38, 11, 12.

2. Quoted by Edward Wagenknecht, *Nathaniel Hawthorne: Man and Writer* (New York: Oxford Univ. Press, 1961), p. 130. For further information about Hawthorne's attitude to the Union, see Randall Stewart, "Hawthorne and the Civil War" (1937), rpt. in *Regionalism and Beyond*, ed. George Core (Nashville: Vanderbilt Univ. Press, 1968), pp. 94–112.

3. Michael Colacurcio delivers a spirited case for taking the history in Hawthorne's fiction seriously in *The Province of Piety: Moral History in Hawthorne's Early Tales*, pp. 1–28. While differing with him about how this should be done, I agree with his general argument and am much indebted to his scholarly findings and readings.

Others who take much the same position and who also have contributed much to my own historical understanding of Hawthorne are the following. Michael Davitt Bell's *Hawthorne and the Historical Romance of New England* (Princeton: Princeton Univ. Press, 1971) is an invaluable study of theme and characterization in Hawthorne's historical fiction which comes at its subject mainly through his minor American contemporaries. Scholarship dealing with Hawthorne's knowledge of New England history is extensive. I have profited especially from David Levin's *In Defense of Historical Literature* (New York: Hill & Wang, 1967), pp. 78–87 and 98–113, on the use Hawthorne made of that knowledge in "Young Goodman Brown" and *The Scarlet Letter*. Also notably useful on *The Scarlet Letter* is Charles Ryskamp's "The New England Sources of *The Scarlet Letter*," *American Literature*, 31 (November 1959), 257–72. I have learned much about Hawthorne's political attitudes and his relationship to the popular historians of his own era from John P. McWilliams, Jr., *Hawthorne, Melville, and the American Character: A Looking-Glass Business* (Cambridge: Cambridge Univ. Press, 1984), p. 90.

4. "P.'s Correspondence," *Mosses from an Old Manse*, p. 369.

5. Quoted by David Levin, *In Defense of Historical Literature*, p. 98.

6. Neal F. Doubleday, *Hawthorne's Early Tales: A Critical Study* (Durham: Duke Univ. Press, 1972), pp. 5, 14–18 is good on the relevance of Scott's example to young American writers bent on supplying their *patria* with a literature.

7. The pioneering research on this subject was done by G. Harrison Orians, "The Angel of Hadley in Fiction: A Study of the Sources of Hawthorne's 'The Gray Champion,'" *American Literature*, 4 (November 1932), 257–69. For further information and interpretation, see Bell, pp. 27–33, 47–53; Doubleday, pp. 22–3, 85–92; and Ursula Brumm, "A Regicide Judge as 'Champion' of American Independence," *Amerikastudien*, 21 (1976), 177–86. The most comprehensive study of the various versions of the Angel of Hadley story, from Thomas Hutchinson's in 1764 to Hawthorne's in 1835, is my "Sir Walter Scott, the Angel of Hadley, and American Historical Fiction," *American Studies*, 17, (1984), 211–27. Michael Colacurcio, *The Province of Piety*, pp. 208–20, offers a challenging reading of the tale to which I respond later in this chapter.

8. *Peveril of the Peak*, ed. Andrew Lang (London: John C. Nimmo, 1899), p. 223. Bridgenorth's anecdote is related in Ch. xiv.

9. "The Gray Champion," *Twice-Told Tales*, ed. J. Donald Crowley (Columbus: Ohio State Univ. Press, 1974), p. 17.

10. Yvor Winters, "Maule's Curse, or Hawthorne and the Problem of Allegory" (1938), reprinted in *In Defense of Reason* (London: Routledge & Kegan Paul, 1960), pp. 170–2.

11. *Sir Walter Scott on Novelists and Fiction*, ed. Ioan Williams (London: Routledge & Kegan Paul, 1968), pp. 115–16. Since Hawthorne alludes to "Rip Van Winkle" in this tale and Scott himself felt that Irving would be the ideal person to do something with the Angel of Hadley story, it should be noted that Irving's handling of supernatural occurrences sometimes anticipates that of both Scott and Hawthorne.

12. In *The Fantastic*, p. 41, Todorov comments that the *fantastic* "appears to be located on the frontier of two genres, the marvelous and the uncanny, rather than to be an autonomous genre . . . Indeed, we generally distinguish, within the literary Gothic, two tendencies: that of the supernatural explained (the "uncanny"), as it appears in the novels of Clara Reeves and Ann Radcliffe; and that of the supernatural accepted (the "marvelous") which is characteristic of the works of Horace Walpole, M. G. Lewis, and Maturin." Todorov doesn't mention the authors I am discussing, but it is clear that his observations apply to them and that Scott's apply to the authors

Todorov does discuss. On p. 46, Todorov explains that "the *fantastic* refers to an ambiguous perception shared by the reader and one of the characters."

13. Jefferson addresses himself to the degenerative theories of Buffon and Raynal in his answer to Query VI in *Notes on the State of Virginia*. Natty Bumppo responds to Obed Batt's garbled version of these theories in Chapter XXII of *The Prairie*.

14. The spiral figure is used by Clifford in Chapter XVII of *The House of the Seven Gables*, by Miriam in Chapter XLVII of *The Marble Faun*. Neither, however, is a speaker who can be confidently identified with Hawthorne's viewpoint. For the use that Hawthorne's contemporaries made of the spiral as a figure for progress, see David Levin, *History as Romantic Art*.

15. Coleridge, *The Stateman's Manual* (1816), reprinted in *Imagination in Coleridge*, ed. John Spencer Hill (London: Macmillan Press, 1978), pp. 151–2.

16. As will be seen below, many critics discover "subversive" irony in one passage or another in Hawthorne's fiction. A good example of such criticism is Frederick Newberry's "'The Gray Champion': Hawthorne's Ironic Criticism of Puritanic Rebellion," *Studies in Short Fiction*, 13 (1976), 363–70. Others, dealing with Dimmesdale's Election Sermon, are cited below. The most uncompromising and learned advocate of this approach to Hawthorne's historical fiction is Michael Colacurcio in *The Province of Piety*, passim.

17. "The Gentle Boy," *Twice-Told Tales*, p. 68.

18. *Old Mortality*, ed. Andrew Lang (London: John C. Nimmo, 1898), pp. 4–5.

19. A brilliant comparison of Scott and Galt, which argues for Galt's superiority as a historian and moralist, is Charles Swann's "Past into Present: Scott, Galt and the Historical Novel," *Literature and History*, 3 (1976), 65–82.

20. My comments on myth and history in "Edward Randolph's Portrait" owe much to Colacurcio's fine reading of the tale in *The Province of Piety*, pp. 406–23.

21. "Edward Randolph's Portrait," *Twice-Told Tales*, pp. 262–3.

22. Thomas Hutchinson, *The History of the Colony of Massachusetts Bay* (Boston, 1764), I, 294, 219.

23. Anne Mellor, *English Romantic Irony* (Cambridge, Mass.: Harvard University Press, 1980), p. 14. In *The Compass of Irony* (London: Methuen, 1969), pp. 186–215, D.C. Muecke links Romantic irony with the practice of structuring fictional worlds by means of unresolved or only partially resolved contraries. As we have seen, such contraries abound in – are, indeed, at the heart of – the historical romance. One of the devices of the Romantic ironist which both Scott and Hawthorne employ is that of the framed narrative in which the frame implicitly and ironically contradicts the spirit if not the letter of the main narrative. I discuss their use of framed narratives in the final section of this chapter. For help in understanding Romantic irony, I am also indebted to my colleague W. B. Carnochan whose forthcoming book on Gibbon shows how this kind of irony crops up in one of the greatest Enlightenment historians.

24. Neither Barker nor McHenry was a New Englander, nor were *Superstition* or *The Specter of the Forest* published in New England. There is no evidence of which I am aware that they enjoyed a wide circulation. Given Hawthorne's interests and appetites as a reader, he may well have come across one or both; but it would have been uncharacteristically incautious of him to count on *his* readers knowing them – unless, of course, the readers he had in view were literary scholars of the following century.

25. Michael Bell defines "the great theme of Hawthorne's historical fiction" somewhat differently. In that fiction, he says, Hawthorne seeks to "set forth the ways in which these groups and their original motives are altered by the conditions of their survival

(or failure to survive) in the New World environment" (p. 112). The characteristic tension in that fiction is "between Old World values and New World conditions" (p. 117). These definitions are accurate and useful but not, I believe, quite adequate. They do not suggest how *teleological* Hawthorne's historical fiction is – how much it is written with future nationhood and national character in view. Nor do they suggest how, in transposing the traditional conflicts of historical romance to a new testing ground, Hawthorne shows a doubleness (native roses as well as pumpkins) in "New World conditions" that answers the doubleness (roughly, Cavalier *vs.* Puritan) in "Old World values," or how he balances admiration for the Puritan achievement with regret for the precious potentialities in American nature and European culture that the Puritans were unwilling or unable to nurture.

26. "The May-Pole of Merry Mount," *Twice-Told Tales,* p. 54.
27. See John P. McWilliams's "Fictions of Merry Mount," *American Quarterly,* 29 (Spring 1977), 17–19.
28. "Main-Street," *The Snow-Image and Uncollected Tales,* ed. J. Donald Crowley (Columbus: Ohio State Univ. Press, 1974), p. 62.
29. Pound, "Date Line" (1934), *Literary Essays of Ezra Pound,* ed. T.S. Eliot (Norfolk, Conn.: New Directions, 1954), p. 75.
30. "Roger Malvin's Burial," *Mosses from an Old Manse,* p. 337.
31. "Endicott and the Red Cross," *Twice-Told Tales,* p. 438.
32. Among the studies which might be cited in support of an "ironic reading" of Dimmesdale's last acts are the following. John T. Frederick, *The Darkened Sky: Nineteenth-Century American Novelists and Religion* (Notre Dame Univ. Press, 1969), pp. 51–2, maintains that Dimmesdale's "inspiration" is an illusion and that the Election Sermon is of a piece with his previous hypocritical sermons. Michael Davitt Bell, *Hawthorne and the Historical Romance of New England,* p. 142, describes the Election Sermon as "to all intents and purposes a ranting political oration" and Dimmesdale's audience as "less a seventeenth-century congregation than a nine-teenth-century mob." David H. Hirsch, *Reality and Idea in the Early American Novel* (The Hague: Mouton, 1971), pp. 148–50, argues that the Election Sermon is a soft false prophecy – "one of the high points of Hawthorne's ironic method." John McWilliams, *Hawthorne, Melville, and the American Character,* p. 68, contends that "By such an amassing of ironies, Hawthorne suggests that, in 1649 and possibly in 1849, oratory about the progress of God's favored community is a lie that the people will continue to believe."
33. In *Puritanism in America: New Culture in a New World* (New York: Viking Press, 1973), pp. 122–3, Larzer Ziff offers a cogent explanation of the relationship between the later seventeenth-century Puritan sermons and prayer. Dimmesdale's Sermon has many of the "inspiriting" qualities of a prayer.
34. "Self Reliance," *Essays: First Series* (1841); Boston: Houghton, Mifflin, 1904), p. 50.
35. *The Poems of John Milton,* ed. John Carey and Alastair Fowler (London: Longman, 1980), p. 146. Another work in which Hawthorne draws heavily on World Music metaphors is "Young Goodman Brown." I discuss the Romantics' use of World Music lore in Chapter IV of *Coleridge and the Literature of Sensibility.*
36. *Leaves of Grass.* Comprehensive Reader's Edition, ed. Harold W. Blodgett and Sculley Bradley (New York: New York Univ. Press, 1965).
37. "My Kinsman, Major Molineux," *The Snow-Image and Uncollected Tales,* p. 231.
38. Jay Fliegelman, *Prodigals and Pilgrims.*
39. For an informative general introduction to the historical literature of the American Revolution, see Michael Kammen, *A Season of Youth: The American Revolution and the Historical Imagination* (New York: Alfred A. Knopf, 1978). To my mind, the

classic study of "My Kinsman, Major Molineux" remains that of Roy Harvey Pearce, "Hawthorne and the Sense of the Past: or, The Immortality of Major Molineux," *ELH* 31 (1954), 327–49. More recent commentaries which deal specifically with the tale's political meaning are those of McWilliams and Colacurcio in, respectively, *Hawthorne, Melville, and the American Character* and *The Province of Piety*.

40. *The Works of John Adams*, ed. Charles Francis Adams (Boston, 1856), x, 184. Letter to Jedediah Morse written in 1815.

41. The phrases "modern Tory" and "thoroughgoing Democrat" are ones which (on different occasions) Hawthorne, or his *persona*, uses to describe himself. John McWilliams employs both phrases in the title of an article which anatomizes Hawthorne's shifty, or at least shifting, attitudes to the Revolution: "'Thoroughgoing Democrat' and 'Modern Tory': Hawthorne and the Puritan Revolution of 1776," *Studies in Romanticism*, 15 (Fall 1976), 549–71.

42. "Howe's Masquerade," *Twice-Told Tales*, p. 249. Further page references to this and the three other "Legends of the Province-House" gathered in *Twice-Told Tales* (i.e., "Edward Randolph's Portrait," "Lady Eleanore's Mantle," and "Old Esther Dudley") will be given in the text.

43. See note no. 23, on the subject of Romantic irony and framed narrative.

44. *True Stories from History and Biography*, ed. William Charvat, *et al.* (Columbus: Ohio State Univ. Press, 1972), p. 173.

45. *Billy Budd, Sailor: An Inside Narrative*, p. 26.

6 MELVILLE: THE RED COMETS RETURN

1. Melville alluded to *Ivanhoe* in "Fragments from a Writing Desk" (1839) and again in "The Paradise of Bachelors" (1855); had a copy of Scott's *Tales of a Grandfather* in his library; visited Abbotsford in 1856; and, on the day he returned Howells's *A Hazard of New Fortunes* to the New York Society Library, 13 June 1890, borrowed *Peveril of the Peak* and *Quentin Durward*. Most of this information is gleaned from Jay Leyda's invaluable *The Melville Log: A Documentary Life of Herman Melville 1819–1891* (New York: Harcourt, Brace, 1951), 2 vols. I think it is a safe inference from the surviving evidence that Melville had more than a passing acquaintance with Scott's work, and one might argue that there is something of Scott in Melville's conception of character as culturally representative; in his delight in the variety of human types created by racial, regional, social-class, etc., differences; in his conception of incident as historically synecdochic; and in the extreme contrasts between "real" and "ideal" which are present in all his great works from *Moby Dick* onwards. But these traits are characteristic of (although not exclusive to) the historical romance genre as a whole and are lavishly exemplified in models closer to hand, notably Cooper's romances, which Melville is known to have admired. And while Melville must have responded warmly to the range and generosity of the fictional world of the Waverley novels, he was also an admirer of two of Scott's serverest critics, Hawthorne and Carlyle, and probably shared their misgivings about Scott's spiritual and aesthetic seriousness.

2. *Memorial of Fenimore Cooper* (New York: G.P. Putnam, 1852), p. 30. Melville reviewed *The Sea Lions* in 1849 and referred to Cooper as "our National Novelist"; a year later he reviewed a reissue of *The Red Rover*, remarking on the pleasure it had given him when "Long ago, and far inland, we read it in our uncritical days." Those reviews and the full text of Melville's Cooper Memorial letter are reproduced in Dekker and McWilliams, *Fenimore Cooper: The Critical Heritage*.

3. Thomas Philbrick, *James Fenimore Cooper and the Development of American Sea Fiction* (Cambridge, Mass.: Harvard Univ. Press, 1961). The speculation that Cooper's example may have been almost as important to Melville as Hawthorne's is my own, not Philbrick's.

4. Melville's famous appreciation of Hawthorne's "blackness" appears in the review of *Mosses from an Old Manse* he published in 1850. This review is reprinted in J. Donald Crowley, *Hawthorne: The Critical Heritage* (London: Routledge & Kegan Paul, 1970).

5. "To Ned," *Selected Poems of Herman Melville: A Reader's Edition*, ed. Robert Penn Warren (New York: Random House, 1967), pp. 319–20. Originally published in *John Marr and Other Sailors* (1888). As these lines show, Melville was an uneven and sometimes scarcely competent poet; but like Hardy, another great fictionalist turned poet, Melville rarely wrote a dull or empty poem and in a couple of dozen instances wrote poems which will bear comparison with the best of the Victorian era.

6. *Mardi and a Voyage Thither*, ed. Harrison Hayford, Hershel Parker, and G. Thomas Tanselle (Evanston and Chicago: Northwestern Univ. Press and Newberry Library, 1970), p. 526.

7. *His Fifty Years of Exile (Israel Potter)*, intro. Lewis Leary (New York: Sagamore Press, 1957), p. vi. First "forlornly published on sleazy gray paper" in 1824 in Providence, Rhode Island, the *Life and Remarkable Adventures of Israel R. Potter* has been reprinted by Corinth Books (New York: 1962) with an introduction by Leonard Kriegel.

8. To George Palmer Putnam (? June 7, 1854). Quoted in *Log*, I, 488. John McWilliams believes that Melville's design in *Israel Potter* was subversive from the beginning: "To have selected so forgotten a tale of woe indicates that Melville sought to subvert contemporary assumptions of heroic grandeur by placing an unknown historical victim at the center of a narrative that would picture culture heroes as tainted, ineffective, or peripheral." *Hawthorne, Melville, and the American Character*, p. 184.

9. For the political significance of such stories of paternal "tyranny," see my discussion of "My Kinsman, Major Molineux" in the preceding chapter. Potter himself tells the story of parental interference but Melville exploits its potential as political allegory by introducing phrases like "the tyranny of his father." Ironically, both Melville's Israel and the historical Potter discover George III to "possess a disposition less tyrannical . . . than what had been imparted to him" (*Life*, p. 45). Arnold Rampersad discusses Melville's embroiderings on the Potter life story in *Melville's Israel Potter: A Pilgrimage and Progress* (Bowling Green: Bowling Green Univ. Popular Press, 1969).

10. Quoted in *Log*, I, 486.

11. For the relationship between "Augustan" political literature in Rome and later on in England, see Howard Erskine-Hill, *The Augustan Idea in English Literature*.

12. In *Israel Potter* (p. 182) Melville draws a sinister analogy between the "mechanical magic of discipline" exhibited by the gunners of the *Serapis* and that of the "Lowell girls" tending looms in a cotton mill. The latter are described wryly and compassionately in "The Tartarus of Maids."

13. Pope's lines may be found in the third Moral Essay ("Of the Use of Riches") of the *Epistles to Several Persons*, ed. F. W. Bateson (London: Methuen & Co., and New Haven: Yale Univ. Press, 1951), p. 117:

> Where London's column, pointing at the skies,
> Like a tall bully, lifts the head, and lies;

Like Melville, Pope introduces the image of the opulent monument in a passage where he is moralizing on the acute poverty and lack of charity which subsist in a society where the capitalist ethic rules.

14. See "Absalom and Achitophel," *The Poems of John Dryden*, ed. James Kinsley (Oxford: Clarendon Press, 1958), I, 223:

> Thy longing Countries Darling and Desire;
> Their cloudy Pillar, and their guardian Fire:
> Their second *Moses*, whose extended Wand
> Divides the Seas, and shows the promis'd Land:

15. The historical incident occurred in 1805. Melville moved its date back a half-dozen years to the period when the United States was still greatly agitated by fears that Jacobinism might catch on here and that the black revolution in progress in Santo Domingo might spread to the American South. By 1805 Napoleon had negotiated the Louisiana Purchase and executed the black liberator Toussaint L'Ouverture, and so these fears were temporarily tranquilized.

16. G. W. Curtis to J. H. Dix, quoted in *Log*, II, 500–501. Though critical of Curtis and Dix for their handling of Melville, Leon Howard agrees with their criticism of Melville's handling of his narrative: *Herman Melville: A Biography* (Berkeley: Univ. of California Press, 1951), pp. 220–2.

17. I quote from the useful transcription of Delano's *Narrative* reproduced in *Melville's Benito Cereno: A Text for Guided Research*, ed. John P. Runden (Boston: D. C. Heath, 1965), p. 80. My quotations from *Benito Cereno* are also taken from this book. Runden's copy-text is the version of the story published in *The Piazza Tales* (1856), which incorporates numerous minor revisions of the story as it first appeared in *Putnam's Monthly Magazine* the year before. Runden also gives a good overview of the main critical controversies which the novella has inspired and anthologizes representative pre-1965 studies of it. For more recent accounts of Melville's attitudes to race and slavery, see Carolyn L. Karcher, *Shadow over the Promised Land: Slavery, Race, and Violence in Melville's America* (Baton Rouge: Louisiana State Univ. Press, 1980), especially pp. 128–43. Also helpful is Joyce Sparer Adler's perceptive *War in Melville's Imagination* (New York: New York Univ. Press, 1981), pp. 85–110. A book which ranges more widely and is excellent on Melville and the larger Civil War context is George Forgie's *Patricide in the House Divided: a Psychological Interpretation of Lincoln and His Age* (New York: Norton, 1979). Good on Melville's audience and "subversive" strategy is Marvin Fisher's *Going Under: Melville's Short Fiction and the American 1850s* (Baton Rouge: Louisiana State Univ. Press, 1977), pp. 104–17. My own interpretation owes much to Bruce Franklin's pioneering study of the historical implications of Melville's allusions, cited in the next note. This is only a sampling of the vast secondary literature which has grown up around *Benito Cereno*.

18. *The Wake of the Gods: Melville's Mythology* (Stanford: Stanford Univ. Press, 1963), chapter 5, traces detailed parallels between Melville's story and Stirling's *Cloister Life*. Franklin's argument has been challenged by, among others, Hershel Parker in "'Benito Cereno' and Cloister-Life: A Re-Scrutiny of a 'Source,'" *Studies in Short Fiction*, 9 (1972), 221–32.

19. "The Portent," *Battle-Pieces and Aspects of the War*, intro. Sidney Kaplan (Gainesville: Scholars' Facsimiles & Reprints, 1960), p. 13.

20. *Billy Budd, Sailor: An Inside Narrative*, ed. Milton R. Stern (Indianapolis: Bobbs-Merrill, 1975), pp. 3–4. Like every other student of the work, I have found that the indispensable edition of *Billy Budd* is that by Harrison Hayford and Merton M. Sealts, Jr. (Chicago: Univ. of Chicago Press, 1962), since the "genetic text" they establish provides our main, and most reliable, evidence concerning Melville's intentions. However, my own efforts to understand those intentions have led me, as they have Professor Stern, to conclude that some passages which Professors Hayford and Sealts exclude from their "reading text" have enough authority to be kept. I have therefore

preferred to use Professor Stern's more inclusive reading text. See note no. 23.

21. *Clarel: A Poem and Pilgrimage in the Holy Land*, ed. Walter Bezanson (New York: Hendricks House, 1960), p. 434.

22. The most important of Cooper's sea romances which have a 1797–1802 setting is *Afloat and Ashore*, one of his best and least read fictions.

23. The passage quoted was printed as the "Preface" to *Billy Budd* by editors before Hayford and Sealts on the questionable (but not dismissable) authority of a note by Melville's wife. Whether the passage should be included in the "reading text" and, if so, where, are questions which cannot be answered succinctly. I find Stern's arguments in favor of inclusion (pp. 152–5) persuasive, although I am not sure that he has solved the problem of placement.

24. James Duban also draws a firm distinction between the author and the narrator of *Billy Budd*, but his purpose is to absolve Melville of responsibility for a narrative viewpoint which to him (and me) seems only a shade less conservative than that of Vere. (*Melville's Major Fiction: Politics, Theology, and Imagination* (DeKalb: Northern Illinois Univ. Press, 1983), pp. 221–48.) Other critics who reject the idea that Melville's sympathies are with Vere and England in its struggle with revolutionary France manage to do so without positing a subversive relationship between author and narrator. The most forceful statement of this position with which I am familiar is Bruce Franklin's in "From Empire to Empire: *Billy Budd, Sailor*," *Herman Melville: Reassessments*, ed. A. Robert Lee (London: Vision Press, 1984), pp. 199–216. Joyce Adler, who is very good on the connections between war and atheism in *Billy Budd*, contends in *War in Melville's Imagination* (pp. 160–83) that Melville implicitly condemns Vere for denying God. This is pretty much the view of the critic whose approach is closest to my own, Rowland A. Sherrill, in *The Prophetic Melville: Experience, Transcendence, and Tragedy* (Athens, Ga.: Univ. of Georgia Press, 1979), pp. 200–21. Sherrill argues that Vere rejects the supernatural, or "wonder-world," of which Billy is an emissary in a fallen world. Some critics, with whom I differ much more than I do with Sherrill, still agree with the view urged long ago by Yvor Winters that, on Melville's showing, Vere's motives were prudential and his actions, in the circumstances, necessary and right. (*In Defense of Reason*, pp. 230–1.) For a thoughtful development of this view, see Thomas Scorza, *In the Time before Steamships: Billy Budd, the Limits of Politics, and Modernity* (DeKalb: Northern Illinois Univ. Press, 1979), pp. 115–45.

25. See *Lycidas*, 58–60, and especially *Paradise Lost*, VII, 32–8. Milton's references are to the end of the Orpheus story. Orpheus is torn to pieces by a group of intoxicated Bacchantes – an event for which parallels are not far to seek in the politics of any period and especially of the late eighteenth century.

26. Melville appears not to have been perfectly conversant with legal practices in the British Navy in 1797. (See Hayford and Sealts, pp. 175–6 and 178–9.) But there is no way to be sure, finally, whether he did or did not know that he was investing Vere with greater latitude, hence greater responsibility, than a British ship's commander would have been burdened with at that time. Perhaps Melville's attitudes in such matters was rather like Vere's. Vere, we are told, "was glad it would not be at variance with usage to turn the matter over to a summary court of his own officers, reserving to himself . . . the right of maintaining a supervision of it, or formally or informally interposing at need" (pp. 99–100). But Vere was also prepared to depart from usage when occasion required. So, we may surmise, was Melville prepared to depart from the historical record in obedience to a – in literature – higher law than that which prescribes factual correctness. In any case, as all advanced students of *Billy Budd* know, Melville was concerned not just with practices in the British Navy in the

later eighteenth century but also with practices in the American Navy in 1842 when Alexander Slidell Mackenzie, Captain of the brig *Somers*, persuaded his fellow officers (among them Melville's cousin Guert Gansevoort) to join him in hanging a midshipman and two sailors for allegedly plotting mutiny. As Melville must have known, Cooper was sufficiently interested in the case to publish a pamphlet attacking Mackenzie – another Cooper–Melville link, but one that cannot have pleased the latter. Certainly the parallels between the *Somers* case and the *Bellipotent* case are fascinating and almost infinitely suggestive, but Melville is quite correct to say that "the circumstances" aboard the one ship were "different" from those on the other (p. 110). Recent studies of these parallels which single out the *Somers* case as the major "source" of *Billy Budd* are James Duban's in *Melville's Major Fiction*, pp. 221–48, and Michael Paul Rogin's in *Subversive Genealogy: The Politics and Art of Herman Melville* (New York: Alfred A. Knopf, 1983), pp. 294–316. For useful background information, see Harrison Hayford, ed., *The Somers Mutiny Affair* (Englewood Cliffs, N.J.: Prentice-Hall, 1959).

27. Quotations from "Timoleon" are from *Collected Poems of Herman Melville*, ed. Howard P. Vincent (Chicago: Packard, 1947), pp. 209–15. See Robert Shulman, "Melville's 'Timoleon': From Plutarch to the Early Stages of *Billy Budd*," *Comparative Literature*, 19 (1967), 351–61. Also see William H. Shurr, *The Mystery of Iniquity: Melville as Poet, 1857–1891* (Lexington, Ky.: Univ. Press of Kentucky, 1972), 152–5. Melville may well have recalled the lines which, at the end of Book Eleven of *The Prelude*, Wordsworth addressed to Coleridge, then in Sicily, in 1805:

> The city of Timoleon! Righteous Heaven!
> How are the mighty prostrated! They first,
> They first of all that breathe should have awaked
> When the great voice was heard from out the tombs
> Of ancient heroes. If I suffered grief
> For Ill-requited France . . .
> Have been distressed to think of what she once
> Promised, now is; a far more sober cause
> Thine eyes must see of sorrow in a land,
> To the reanimating influence lost
> Of memory, to virtue lost and hope,
> Though with the wreck of loftier years bestrewn . . .
> To me the grief confined, that thou are gone
> From this last spot of earth, where Freedom now
> Stands single in her only sanctuary.

Quoted from *The Poetical Works of Wordsworth*, ed. Thos. Hutchinson and revised by Ernest de Selincourt (London: Oxford Univ. Press, 1936), p. 574. I quote from the 1850 version of the poem, which would have been the one Melville knew. The passage referring to Timoleon in the 1805 version of *The Prelude* differs very little from the later one. Melville, or Melville's narrator anyway, sounds very like the Wordsworth whom Keats and Shelley considered an apostate. By 1805 Wordsworth was aligning the tyrannicide Timoleon with England in words which anticipate the judgment of "the narrator" of *Billy Budd* that that nation was "then all but the sole free conservative one of the Old World" (p. 22).

28. Matthew Arnold, "Dover Beach," *Matthew Arnold: Selected Poetry and Prose*, intro. by Frederick L. Mulhauser (New York: Rinehart, 1953), p. 90.

7 THE HERO AND HEROINE OF HISTORICAL ROMANCE

1. Nina Baym, *Women's Fiction: A Guide to Novels by and about Women in America, 1820–1870* (Cornell Univ. Press: Ithaca, 1978), pp. 29–30. The fiction which Professor Baym discusses is just as concerned with questions of dependence and independence in relations between men and women, and just as sceptical of the sanctity of traditional gender roles, as the historical romances which I examine in this chapter. Some of these nineteenth-century novels written by and for women, e.g., Susan Warner's best-selling *The Wide, Wide World* (1850), achieve a remarkable "Dutch" fidelity and shrewdness in their pictures of domestic manners which give them literary as well as social-historical interest. But the best historical romances, whether written by men or women, tend to treat the same or similar themes with more historical and philosophical depth as well as considerably richer and more refined literary art. The most powerful American woman fictionalist of the period, Harriet Beecher Stowe, belonged to neither of these "schools," although *The Minister's Wooing* (1859), set in eighteenth-century New England, is a kind of historical saint's legend, and although her more famous treatments of racial relations in the old South had a bearing (for those who cared to see it) on gender relations. In *The Feminization of American Culture* (Alfred A. Knopf: New York, 1977), chapter 5, especially pp. 184–7, Ann Douglas points to the pacifist, hence essentially antiheroic, and ultimately anti-historical nature of early and mid-nineteenth-century American women's fiction. For a vigorous defense of writers like Susan Warner, see Jane Tompkins, *Sensational Designs: the Cultural Work of American Fiction, 1790–1860* (New York: Oxford Univ. Press, 1985). In her important general "essay" *Toward a Recognition of Androgyny* (Alfred A. Knopf: New York, 1973), pp. 47–55, Carolyn Heilbrun argues for a distinction between Richardsonian novels of character, predominantly feminine in orientation, and Fieldingesque novels of incident, predominantly masculine and reminiscent of (essentially militaristic) epic forms. Obviously it would be unwise to press this distinction too hard, but it seems generally right and in line with what I have said about Fielding, epic, and historical romance in chapter 2.

   As I show later in this chapter, it is entirely possible to argue against the view that Scott "'remasculinized' a genre in danger of becoming female." See Judith Wilt, *Secret Leaves: The Novels of Walter Scott* (Chicago: Univ. of Chicago Press, 1985), pp. 116, 218, and 146–52. Scott supplies the grounds for both views of his fiction, and both are correct.

2. George Eliot, *The Mill on the Floss*, ed. Gordon S. Haight (Oxford: Clarendon Press, 1980), p. 282. There are many discussions of the light/dark dichotomy. Among the most famous, or notorious, are D. H. Lawrence, *Studies in Classic American Literature* (T. Seltzer: New York, 1923) and Leslie Fiedler, *Love and Death in the American Novel* (Criterion Books: New York, 1960).

3. Cf. Michael Davitt Bell's discussion of the resemblance between the plot of Greek New Comedy (as summarized by Northrop Frye in *Anatomy of Criticism*) and that of many historical romances. *Hawthorne and the Historical Romance of New England*, pp. 149–50.

4. Harriet Martineau, "The Achievements of the Genius of Scott," *Tait's Edinburgh Magazine* (January 1833), 11, 456.

5. Edith Wharton, *A Backward Glance* (D. Appleton Co.: New York, 1934), pp. 14–15.

6. Friedrich Schiller, *Essays Aesthetical and Philosophical* (London, 1879), pp. 275–6.

7. One of the most illuminating examinations of Scott's male protagonists and

particularly of their quixotic forebears is Alexander Welsh's *The Hero of the Waverley Novels* (1963; rpt. Atheneum: New York, 1968).

8. Incestuous and even necrophiliac overtones can no doubt be detected in Flora's last reported words about Fergus: "Do you remember . . . you once found me making Fergus's bride-favour, and now I am sewing his bridal-garment. Our friends here . . . are to give hallowed earth in their chapel to the bloody reliques of the last Vich Ian Vohr. But they will not all rest together; no – his head – I shall not have the last miserable satisfaction of kissing the cold lips of my dear, dear Fergus!" (p. 323). Isolated from its context, this passage seems sufficiently lurid; but a reader seeking Romantic Agony in *Waverley* would be bored and frustrated. Scott's account of attitudes to marriage in the eighteenth century is in close agreement with Lawrence Stone's in *The Family, Sex and Marriage in England 1500–1800* (London: Weidenfeld & Nicolson, 1977).

9. While many critics simply condemned *The Sorrows of Young Werther* and its literary progeny as licentious and inflammatory, others claimed that Goethe's novel provided a highly moral warning of the dangers of Wertherism. For an example of anti-Wertherian satire which Scott is likely to have known and found suggestive, see Charles Lloyd's *Edmund Oliver* (1798), a novel based fairly closely on the personalities and actions of two very Sensible authors – Coleridge (who feared, and caused his friends to fear, a suicidal tendency in himself) and Mary Wollstonecraft (who attempted suicide on a couple of well-publicized occasions).

10. *The Heart of Mid-Lothian*, ed. Andrew Lang (London, 1898), pp. 777–8.

11. The phrase comes from Scott's *Life of Napoleon Buonaparte*, II, 63.

12. Adam Smith observes that women warriors are found among herding peoples. Of course Jeanie is neither a warrior nor a formidable she-bear like Helen MacGregor or Esther Bush, but the basic stadialist contention is not that women in pastoral societies are all amazons but rather that among herding folk duties and activities are not rigidly segregated along gender lines. Fundamentally anti-racist, stadialist thinking is, for the same reasons, anti-sexist. See chapter 3 for further information and discussions concerning the social and literary implications of stadialist thought. Innumerable are the recent contributions to the nature *vs.* nurture debate as it relates to gender. One highly recommendable paper on the subject by an anthropologist is Sherry B. Ortner's "Is Female to Male as Nature Is to Culture?," *Woman, Culture, and Society*, ed. Michelle Zimbalist Rosaldo and Louise Lamphere (Stanford: Stanford Univ. Press, 1974), pp. 67–87.

13. "Endicott and the Red Cross," *Twice-Told Tales*, p. 435.

14. Although Frederick Crews has surprisingly little to say about his subject's immediate family – father, mother, sisters, wife, children – his *The Sins of the Fathers: Hawthorne's Psychological Themes* (Oxford Univ. Press: New York, 1966) offers the most illuminating Freudian reading of American fiction with which I am acquainted. An able recent study of Hawthorne's treatment of family relationships is Gloria Erlich's *Family Themes in Hawthorne's Fiction: the Tenacious Web* (New Brunswick, N.J.: Rutgers Univ. Press, 1984). For a fresh exhumation of the Hawthorne family skeletons and further discussion of dark heroines, see Philip Young, *Hawthorne's Secret: An Untold Tale* (Boston: David R. Godine, 1984).

15. Cooper's attitudes to women were distinctly more conventional and prudish than Scott's. When, near the end of his life, he at last recognized the growing strength of the movement for women's rights, he created a "liberated lady," Mildred Millington, in *The Ways of the Hour* (1859) who denounces the "bondage" of marriage and turns out to be insane. There are intriguing parallels between this

radical feminist and the aged revolutionary patriot, Lionel's father, in *Lionel Lincoln* who also turns out to be mad. See Nina Baym, "The Women of Cooper's Leatherstocking Tales" (1971), rpt. *Images of Women in Fiction: Feminist Perspectives*, ed. Susan Koppelman Cornillon (Bowling Green University Popular Press: Bowling Green, Ohio, 1972), pp. 135–54.

16. Hawthorne to Horatio Bridge, 19 January 1855, quoted by James R. Mellow, *Nathaniel Hawthorne in His Times* (Houghton Mifflin: Boston, 1980), p. 456. At the time that Hawthorne thus exposed himself to future generations of scholars, *Uncle Tom's Cabin* and Susan Warner's *The Wide, Wide World* were the best-selling American novels.

17. For studies of Elizabeth Peabody, see Louise Hall Tharpe, *The Peabody Sisters of Boston* (Little Brown & Co.: Boston, 1951) and Gladys Brooks, *Three Wise Virgins* (E.P. Dutton: New York, 1957). Most serious critical discussions of the character of Hester take note of Hawthorne's anti-feminism.

18. Harry Shaw borders on paradox but is essentially correct, I believe, when he states that, "Jeanie is not intended to be complex in the manner of a heroine of Flaubert. Far from being moral but limited, Jeanie is moral because she is limited. She is also interesting because she is limited." *The Forms of Historical Fiction*, p. 230.

19. Ernest Hemingway, *A Moveable Feast* (Jonathan Cape: London, 1964) develops a theory of fictional composition and representation which appeals to the ideas and authority of Post-Impressionist painters. Cather does likewise in her essay "The Novel Démeublé" (1922), *Willa Cather on Writing: Critical Studies on Writing as an Art*, ed. Stephen Tennant (Alfred A. Knopf: New York, 1953). See note 26 below.

20. For Cather's praise of *The Scarlet Letter*, see *Willa Cather on Writing*, pp. 41 and 58. R.W.B. Lewis discusses Wharton's opinions of and attitudes to *The Scarlet Letter* in *Edith Wharton: A Biography* (Harper & Row: New York, 1975), pp. 237 and 521.

21. Margaret B. McDowell, *Edith Wharton* (Boston: Twayne Publishers, 1976), pp. 40–1.

22. Most extended discussions of Cather's fiction take some note of her strong heroines and ineffectual males. A recent discussion is Deborah G. Lambert, "The defeat of a Hero: Autonomy and Sexuality in *My Ántonia*," *American Literature*, Vol 53, No. 4 (1982), 676–90. Only quite recently have biographers ventured to comment on the possible relationship between Cather's lesbianism and her portrayal of gender roles. My own feeling is that it is evident, in *My Ántonia* anyway, chiefly in the implicit but powerful and pervasive case Cather makes for tolerance and enjoyment of human variety.

23. *The Country of the Pointed Firs* (Houghton Mifflin: Boston, 1896), pp. 163–4.

24. "My First Novels [There Were Two]" (1931), *Willa Cather on Writing*, p. 93.

25. "The Best Stories of Sara Orne Jewett" (1925), *Willa Cather on Writing*, p. 58.

26. In the essays collected in *Willa Cather on Writing*, she refers approvingly to Stevenson by name on three occasions (pp. 16, 39, 88) and alludes to the doctrine of significant simplicity twice (pp. 40, 102) without attributing it to him. The point is not that the doctrine originated with him but rather that he gave it an authoritative formulation in the amicable debate which Henry James began in "The Art of Fiction" (1884), and that Cather's most important essays on the art of fiction demonstrate her thorough familiarity and basic agreement with Stevenson's position. Her own most cogent formulation, in an essay significantly titled "On the Art of Fiction" (1920), weds Stevenson's significant simplicity to James's Impressionism:

> Art, it seems to me, should simplify. That, indeed, is very nearly the whole of the artistic process; finding what conventions of form and what detail one can do without and yet preserve the spirit of the whole – so that all that one has

suppressed and cut away is there to the reader's consciousness as much as if it
were in type on the page. (p. 102)

27. *The Age of Innocence*, intro. by R. W. B. Lewis (1920; Charles Scribner's Sons: New
York, 1968), p. 84.

28. From the publication of *The House of Mirth* onwards, critics of both sexes have found
Wharton's chief male protagonists spineless wonders. Not untypical is Josephine
Lurie Jessup's comment that Newland Archer is "too patently of straw" and that his
"complete pliability in the hands of women, on earth and in the grave, forms too
weak a contrast for the daring of the Countess Olenska." *The Faith of Our Feminists:
A Study in the Novels of Edith Wharton, Ellen Glasgow, Willa Cather* (Richard R.
Smith: New York, 1950), p. 18. More recent studies have a tendency, which I
endorse, to view Wharton's males as not altogether unworthy of the ministrations of
an Ellen Olenska, a Lily Bart, or a Mattie Silver. See, for example, Carol
Wershoven's thoughtful *The Female Intruder in the Novels of Edith Wharton*
(Associated University Presses: East Brunswick, N.J., 1982).

8 THE HISTORICAL ROMANCE OF THE SOUTH

1. *Life on the Mississippi* (1883; rpt. New American Library: New York, 1961), pp.
266.

2. Rollin G. Osterweis documents the pervasive presence of Scott in antebellum
Southern culture; that presence is not at issue. My contention is that Mark Twain and
Osterweis mistake what is largely, although not wholly, an effect for a cause. See his
Romanticism and Nationalism in the Old South (New Haven: Yale Univ. Press, 1949). A
good brief critique of the Mark Twain–Osterweis thesis is Jay Hubbell's discussion of
Scott's Southern vogue in *The South in American Literature* (Durham: Duke Univ.
Press, 1954), pp. 188–93. Hugh Holman makes the shrewd observation that it was the
"unusual intensity" of the South's concern with history that kept it "reading Scott
and naming its towns, its homesteads, and its children for Scott's places and
characters long after the rest of the nation had turned to other kinds of fiction." *The
Immoderate Past*, p. 9.

3. *The Messages and Papers of Jefferson Davis and the Confederacy, Including Diplomatic
Correspondence 1861–1865*, ed. James D. Richardson (new edition; Chelsea House-
Robert Hector Publishers: New York, 1966), p. 37.

4. William R. Taylor, *Cavalier and Yankee: The Old South and American National
Character* (George Braziller: New York, 1961).

5. *The Papers of Thomas Jefferson*, ed. Julian P. Boyd *et al.* (Princeton Univ. Press:
Princeton, 1953), VIII, 468.

6. Jefferson's Southerners, agriculturalists but also slave-owners, have traits both of the
second (pastoral) and third (agrarian) stages of society; his Northerners, traders and
manufacturers, belong to the fourth stage. Of course climate and religious
background also contribute to the making of these characters; or, to view the process
somewhat differently, climate and religious background help to determine the
modes of subsistence, hence the traits, characteristic of the two regions. See my
discussion of stadialist theory as reinterpreted by Jefferson in chapter 3.

7. W. H. Gardiner, review of *The Spy*, rpt. in *Fenimore Cooper: the Critical Heritage*, pp.
56–7.

8. Reflecting on the first encounters between the Founding Fathers, Hawthorne asked:
"Could the Virginia descendant of the Cavaliers, and the New-Englander with his
hereditary Puritanism – the aristocratic Southern planter, and the self-made man

from Massachusetts or Connecticut – at once feel that they were countrymen and brothers?" ("A Book of Autographs" [1844], *The Snow-Image and Uncollected Tales*, p. 362.)

9. *Battle-Pieces and Aspects of the War*, pp. 261–2.

10. In *The Brazen Face of History: Studies in the Literary Consciousness in America* (Baton Rouge: Louisiana State Univ. Press, 1980), p. 238, Lewis P. Simpson comments that it is more accurate to speak of "a flowering of modern literature in the South" than of "a modern flowering of southern literature" and goes on to speak of a "common core of masters" who influenced writers like Tate, Warren, and Faulkner: Flaubert, Turgenev, Proust, Mann, Joyce, Yeats, and Eliot. Tate himself makes a similar point in a passage quoted later.

11. W.J. Cash outlines a typical rags-to-riches Southern life story in chapter I of *The Mind of the South* (Alfred A. Knopf: New York, 1941).

12. Drew Gilpin Faust, *James Henry Hammond and the Old South: A Design for Mastery* (Louisiana State Univ. Press: Baton Rouge, 1982), pp. 3, 201, 226–8.

13. *Notes on the State of Virginia* (1781), ed. Thomas Perkins Abernethy (New York: Harper and Row, 1964), pp. 155–6. (Query XVIII).

14. For the development of the Boone legend and its relationship to Leatherstocking, see Henry Nash Smith, *Virgin Land*, pp. 54–76.

15. Elizabeth Madox Roberts, *The Great Meadow* (1930; rpt. New York: New American Library, 1961), p. 110.

16. Perhaps *Roots* has replaced *Gone with the Wind* as the Southern historical romance, but whether it will have the astonishing staying power of Mitchell's book remains to be seen.

17. Tate was actually born in Kentucky but was led by his mother, a Virginia gentlewoman, to believe that he was born in Fairfax County, Virginia. See "A Lost Traveler's Dream" (1972), *Memoirs and Opinions 1926–1974* (Chicago: Swallow Press, 1975), pp. 5–14.

18. "The Profession of Letters in the South" (1935), *Essays of Four Decades* (Chicago: the Swallow Press, 1968), p. 532.

19. *The Battle-Ground* (New York: Doubleday, Page & Co., 1902), p. 512.

20. Lee's farewell message reads: "After four years of arduous service, marked by unsurpassed courage and fortitude, the Army of Northern Virginia has been compelled to yield to overwhelming numbers and resources. I need not tell the survivors of so many hard-fought battles, who have remained steadfast to the last, that I have consented to this result from no distrust of them; but, feeling valor and devotion could accomplish nothing that would compensate for the loss that would have attended the continuation of the contest, I have determined to avoid the useless sacrifice of those whose past services have endeared them to their countrymen . . . With an increasing admiration of your constancy and devotion to your country, and a grateful remembrance of your kind and generous consideration of myself, I bid you an affectionate farewell." *Recollections and Letters of General Robert E. Lee*, by His Son Captain Robert E. Lee (Garden City: Doubleday, Page & Co., 1921), pp. 153–54.

21. For a perceptive discussion of Glasgow's "social philosophy," see Richard Gray, *The Literature of Memory: Modern Writers of the American South* (Baltimore: Johns Hopkins Univ. Press, 1977), pp. 27–34. For a discussion of *The Battle-Ground* as a historical novel of manners, see Holman, *The Immoderate Past*, pp. 46–54.

22. "Old Orders Changing (Tate and Lampedusa)" (1960), rpt. in *Allen Tate and His Work: Critical Evaluations*, ed. Radcliffe Squires (Minneapolis: Univ. of Minnesota Press, 1972), pp. 140–8.

23. "The End of the Old Dominion" (1960), rpt. in *Allen Tate and His Work*, p. 130. Smith's and Kermode's admiration for *The Fathers* is not shared by everybody. For a thoughtful, though I believe mistaken, critique of Tate's supposed racism and failure to make the Posey family historically credible, see Alan Holder, *The Imagined Past: Portrayals of Our History in Modern American Literature* (London & Toronto: Associated Univ. Presses, 1980), pp. 92–113.

24. "A Southern Mode of the Imagination" (1959), *Essays of Four Decades*, p. 592.

25. *The Fathers*, intro. by Thomas Daniel Young (Baton Rouge: Louisiana State Univ. Press, 1977), p. xxi. Young's introduction offers the best critical discussion of the novel that I have come across.

26. The verse quoted is from Yeats's "A Prayer for My Daughter."

27. "What Is a Traditional Society?" (1936), *Essays of Four Decades*, pp. 549–51.

28. Richard H. King, *A Southern Renaissance: The Cultural Awakening of the American South, 1930–1955* (New York: Oxford Univ. Press, 1980), p. 79.

29. Albert J. Guerard, *The Triumph of the Novel: Dickens, Dostoievsky, Faulkner* (New York: Oxford Univ. Press, 1976), p. 306.

30. Cleanth Brooks, *William Faulkner: Toward Yoknapatawpha and Beyond* (New Haven: Yale Univ. Press, 1978), pp. 283–300. Brooks buttresses his case with evidence and arguments drawn from two of our greatest historical studies of the South: Eugene Genovese, *The World the Slaveholders Made* (1971) and C. Vann Woodward, *American Counterpoint* (1971).

31. Eric J. Sunquist, *Faulkner: the House Divided* (Baltimore: Johns Hopkins Univ. Press, 1983), pp. 101–3.

32. David Levin, "*Absalom, Absalom!*: The Problem of Re-creating History," *In Defense of Historical Literature*, p. 130.

33. In *The Great Meadow*, Roberts implies that the marriage of these two strains yielded a pioneer stock which combined the strengths of both, making them courageous to transplant and determined to build well. More pessimistic and conservative, and perhaps more deeply Southern, Tate seems to have suspected that the blend was more likely to lead to confusion. Such, at any rate, was the notion behind his unfinished family chronicle novel, "Ancestors of Exile," as described in a letter to Ellen Glasgow dated 31 May 1933, quoted in Radcliffe Squires's *Allen Tate: A Literary Biography* (New York: Pegasus/Bobbs Merrill, 1971), pp. 128–9. Faulkner's Sutpen never really amalgamates with the Mississippian descendants or facsimiles of the F.F.V.'s.

34. *Absalom, Absalom!* (1936; New York: Modern Library, n.d.), p. 261.

35. *Speak, Memory: An Autobiography Revisited* (1967; New York: Pyramid Books, 1968), p. 168.

36. Letter to Harrison Smith dated February 1934, *Selected Letters of William Faulkner*, ed. Joseph Blotner (New York: Random House, 1977), pp. 78–9.

37. To speak to the living, Tiresias must be supplied with living blood. In Canto 1 Ezra Pound uses this episode of the *Odyssey* as a kind of epic simile for translation and, more generally, for the historian's imaginative recovery of the secrets and wisdom of the dead. Hawthorne and Tate imply an analogy between the historian's achievement and the resurrection of the dead and disclosure of their secrets at the Last Judgment.

38. Letter to Robert K. Haas received 15 December 1938, *Selected Letters of William Faulkner*, pp. 107–9.

39. *I'll Take My Stand* (1930), the manifesto of the Agrarians, was authored by "Twelve Southerners."

40. *The Pioneers, or the Sources of the Susquehanna: A Descriptive Tale*, p. 456.
41. *Go Down, Moses* (1942; New York: Vintage, 1973), p. 182.
42. Letter to Robert K. Haas dated 26 January 1949, *Selected Letters of William Faulkner*, pp. 285–6.
43. *Pudd'nhead Wilson, A Tale*, ed. Malcolm Bradbury (1894; Harmondsworth: Penguin Books, 1969), pp. 157–8.
44. Letter to John Taylor dated 1 June 1798, *Papers of Thomas Jefferson*, x, 46.
45. Holman documents Faulkner's interest in detective fiction and makes the apt comment: "that a novel based on concepts from Greek tragedy should be cast in the structural form of a detective novel also should not be surprising; as W.H. Auden pointed out many years ago, the detective story is the Greek recognition scene played as an end in itself." "*Absalom, Absalom!*: The Historian as Detective," *The Roots of Southern Writing*, pp. 169–70. Henry Nash Smith documents Mark Twain's interest in detective fiction in *Mark Twain: The Development of a Writer* (Cambridge, Mass.: Harvard Univ. Press, 1962), pp. 180–1.
46. My awareness of the importance of this international "mystery" fiction of the 1830–80 era I owe primarily to the learned and perceptive dissertations of three Stanford graduate students: Jenny Franchot, Wyn Kelley, and Robert Levine.
47. "Dreamland," *The Works of Edgar Allan Poe*, ed. John H. Ingram (London: A.C. Black, 1899), III, 29. The relationship between *The Mystery of Marie Roget* and its sources in a widely reported murder in New York (not Paris) has itself been the subject of much fascinating historical detective work. See John Walsh, *Poe the Detective: The Curious Circumstances Behind "The Mystery of Marie Roget"* (New Brunswick, N.J., 1967).
48. Charles Swann discusses *Benito Cereno* as a detective novel in "Whodunnit? Or, Who Did What? *Benito Cereno* and the Politics of Narrative Structure," in *American Studies in Transition*, ed. David E. Nye and Christian Kold Thomson (Odense; Odense Univ. Press, 1985), pp. 199–234.
49. For fuller accounts of Mark Twain's ideas of history, see Roger B. Salomon, *Mark Twain and the Image of History* (New Haven: Yale Univ. Press, 1961) and Henry Nash Smith, *Mark Twain's Fable of Progress: Political and Economic Ideas in "A Connecticut Yankee"* (New Brunswick, N.J.: Rutgers Univ. Press, 1964).
50. Carl Becker, "Everyman His Own Historian," *The American Historical Review* XXXVII (January 1932), 222.
51. In a note appended to *The Fathers* in 1975, Tate explains that spontaneous fraternal feeling pulled the trigger that killed Semmes Buchan (p. 313). Now what an author consciously or unconsciously reveals about his intentions past or present in writing or rewriting a book is part of the contextual information available to us in interpreting it. However, I believe that Tate's elucidation of what he meant nearly forty years earlier can have little if any special authority and should influence our reading of *The Fathers* much less than the letters, essays, and poems he wrote during the late 1930s. An eruption of fraternal feeling is doubtless the most likely explanation of George's action if a single explanation is sought; but I think that Tate at the age of 39 wanted his characters' motivation to be more complex and ambiguous than did Tate at the age of 76.
52. Preface to *Lyrical Ballads, The Poetical Works of Wordsworth*, p. 738.

9 RETROSPECT: DEPARTURES AND RETURNS

1. Cather, *O Pioneers!* (Boston: Houghton Mifflin, 1913), p. 113.
2. Scott, *The Bride of Lammermoor* (London: Dent, 1906), p. 183.
3. Hawthorne, *The House of the Seven Gables*, ed. William Charvat *et al.* (Columbus: Ohio State Univ. Press, 1965), p. 8.

Index